THE BERBER IDENTITY
MOVEMENT AND THE CHALLENGE
TO NORTH AFRICAN STATES

The Berber Identity Movement and the Challenge to North African States

Bruce Maddy-Weitzman

UNIVERSITY OF TEXAS PRESS
Austin

Requests for permission to reproduce material from
this work should be sent to:
 Permissions
 University of Texas Press
 P.O. Box 7819
 Austin, TX 78713-7819
 www.utexas.edu/utpress/about/bpermission.html

⊗ The paper used in this book meets the minimum requirements
of ANSI/NISO Z39.48-1992 (R1997) (Permanence of Paper).

LIBRARY OF CONGRESS CATALOGING-IN-PUBLICATION DATA
Maddy-Weitzman, Bruce.
The Berber identity movement and the challenge to North African
states / Bruce Maddy-Weitzman. — 1st ed.
     p.   cm.
Includes bibliographical references and index.
ISBN 978-0-292-74401-1

  1. Berbers—Ethnic identity.   2. Berbers—Politics and
government.   3. Morocco—Politics and government.
4. Algeria—Politics and government.   5. Nationalism—
Morocco.   6. Nationalism—Algeria.   I. Title.
DT193.5.B45M327   2011
964′.004933—dc22
                                                2010051823

First Paperback Printing, 2012

For Edie, Shira, and Daniel

CONTENTS

NOTE ON TRANSCRIPTION
AND TERMINOLOGY

For the purposes of clarity and simplicity, I employ the Arabic letters *ayn* (ʿ) and *hamza* (ʾ) in the middle and at the end of a word, but not at the beginning, and, for the most part, the common French spelling of Arabic names and places (e.g., Kabylie, not Kabylia; Mohamed, not Muhammad). With some reluctance, I also employ the commonly written "Hassan" for what are two distinct names in Arabic, "Hasan" and "Hassan." As for the use of "Berber" and "Amazigh," the reader will see that there are times when it was appropriate to use one, as opposed to the other, and that at other times, I use them interchangeably, without prejudice.

ACKNOWLEDGMENTS

This book could never have been completed without the assistance of numerous individuals and institutions, to which I am delighted to pay tribute. More than a decade ago, Ofra Bengio pushed me to research the question of state-Berber relations in Algeria, placing me on the path that eventually led to this study. All along the way, she provided invaluable counsel and perspective. My ongoing discussions with Meir Litvak on matters related to ethnicity, nationalism, and collective memory were of much benefit. Mordechai Tamarkin saw my inquiries into the subject of modern Berber identity as material for a book before I did. Over the course of our ongoing conversation on the subject, Paul Silverstein has generously shared his own research with me and tendered innumerable helpful suggestions, enriching my understanding substantially. Both he and Robert Mortimer closely read the entire manuscript, offering numerous constructive comments, as did an additional anonymous reader, resulting in its substantial improvement. Naturally, I am responsible for whatever remaining shortcomings there are.

Nabil Boudraa was kind enough to invite me to participate in a large-scale international conference, "The Berbers and Other Minorities in North Africa: A Cultural Reappraisal," at Portland State University in 2005, which proved to be an extremely fruitful conclave. In 2007, I organized a double panel called "Tribe, Ethnicity and State: The Multiple Aspects of the Berber World," sponsored by the American Institute for Maghrib Studies, at the annual Middle East Studies Association conference, in Montreal. Like the Portland conference, this was important for shaping my thinking, and I thank the participants—Paul Silverstein, Jane Goodman, Hugh Roberts, Katherine Hoffman, David Crawford, Azzedine Layachi, Hamoud Salhi, and Lisa Anderson—for their contributions and goodwill.

As my research assistant during the formative stage of this study, and colleague and friend since then, Samir Benlayashi not only helped me make sense of my material, but contributed numerous enlightening insights into Moroccan society. Conrad Rein expertly translated important German-language sources for me. Thanks are also due to Tal Grebel and Matt Oppenheimer for their work as research assistants.

I am grateful to former directors Asher Susser and Eyal Zisser, and current director Uzi Rabi, of the Moshe Dayan Center for Middle Eastern and African Studies at Tel Aviv University, my professional home throughout my career, for their ongoing support for this project. Special thanks are also due to Jane Goodman and Ken Stein for their encouragement, to Robin Stoller and Ayelet Levey for providing me with a number of publications each, and to Claude Brenier-Estrine of the Institut de Recherches et d'Études sur le Monde Arabe et Musulman (IREMAM) for enabling me to peruse her large collection of material on the Amazigh movement and for sharing her own insights on the subject.

Research for the book was funded by a grant from the Israel Science Foundation. Support was also received from Tel Aviv University's Research Authority and the Amira Margalith Summer Internship program at the Moshe Dayan Center. I am grateful to all three bodies, to Paul Spragens for his expert copyediting of the manuscript, and to Jim Burr, Wendy Moore, and Lynne F. Chapman of the University of Texas Press. Special thanks are also due to Ms. Chapman for preparing the index, and to Elena Lesnick for assisting in the preparation of the maps.

My e-mail exchanges with Rabah Seffal more than a decade ago marked the beginning of my interaction with members of the Amazigh identity movement. Since then, I have interviewed and/or exchanged views with Amazigh scholars and activists on three continents and in cyberspace, including: Hassan Aaouid, Mustapha Akebdan, Brahim Ahiat, Yiddir Achouri, Maxime Ait Kaki, Azzedine Ait Khalifa, Abdellah Benhssi, Ahmed Boukous, Mokhtar Bouba, Driss Bouljaoun, Ahcene Bozentine, Mohamed Chafik, Salem Chaker, Izza Lahyan, Mohamed Chtatou, Maryam Demnati, Karina Direche-Slimani, Mohamed Elmedlaoui, Moha Ennaji, Yassin Errahmouni, Mohammed Errihani, Zohra El Fikhi, Khalid Hajjioui, Smail Hakim, Hassan Idbelkassem, Kahcen Idrissi, Mohamed El Ouazguiti, Lahcen Oulhaj, Abdelmalik Oussaden, Boubker Outaadit, Hassan Ouzzate, Rachid Raha, Moises Santana, and last but not least, the peripatetic Mounir Kejji, formerly of the Tariq Ibn Zyad Center in Rabat, whose goodwill in facilitating many of my meetings in Morocco was always present. I am grateful to each of them for their willingness to share their thoughts, experiences, and publications with me. I hope that I have not forgotten anyone, but if I have, I apologize for doing so.

INTRODUCTION

The Maghrib—i.e., the Islamic "West," roughly encompassing the present territories of Morocco, Algeria, Tunisia, Libya, and Mauritania in Northwest Africa—has, as L. Carl Brown reminds us, long been recognized by historians and social scientists as a useful unit of analysis. It was there that an "imprint of geography with history, terrain with theology," produced a distinct mix of political, social, cultural, and linguistic attributes that marked it off from the Mashriq (the Arab-Islamic "East"), Africa south of the Sahara, and the northern Mediterranean littoral.[1] Central to this mix since the beginning of recorded history have been its native Berber-speaking peoples. To Muslims from the East, as Fatima Mernissi points out, the Islamic West has always had the image as being "strange" (*gharb*) or "foreign" (*gharib*), which she attributes in part to its Berber heritage.[2] Even today, following decolonization, decades of state centralization, and concerted Arabization policies, North Africa's *berberité* is not just about heritage and folklore: Berber speakers are commonly said to constitute approximately 40–45 percent of the population in Morocco, 20–25 percent in Algeria, and 8–9 percent in Libya, albeit only 1 percent in Tunisia.[3] In recent years, other scholars have also reminded us of what perhaps should have been obvious. The Maghrib's Berber element, declared anthropologist David M. Hart, in a pithily titled article, "Scratch a Moroccan, Find a Berber," formed the basis of "the whole North African edifice," and was not merely a residue and thus neatly consignable to state-sponsored folklore festivals,[4] as both Western modernization theorists and an earlier generation of Maghribi nationalists, inspired by the notions of Islamic reform and Arabism, had surmised.[5] In contrast with the bulk of Arab and Islamic writers, the Algerian liberal Islamic philosopher Mohamed Arkoun acknowledged, as Hart did, the underlying Berber ethnicity and culture of North African societies.[6]

The point about Berber centrality to North African history and society seems so obvious that one may wonder why it needs stating: after all, what is the history of a region if not the history of the people who lived there? But in the case of the Berbers, the matter is not so simple. Based on scanty prehistoric evidence, their collective, tribe-centered existence as speakers of varieties of a common language can be no more than a reasonable presumption. The varieties of their language have been transmitted, until recently, almost exclusively orally, and their history was traditionally written from the perspective of others, who usually depicted them as semisavages requiring a civilizing hand. They appear in the Greek and Roman annals under a variety of names, including "Africans," "Numidians," and "Moors," as well as a number of tribal designations, and as, along with others outside the Empire, "barbarians" (*barbaroi*). As a "Berber" collective, they were first written into the historical record by the chroniclers of the conquering Arab Muslim armies in the seventh century. The Arabic word *barbar* ("babble noisily," "jabber"), related to *barbaroi,* was applied to the people whose language seemed so odd, hence the name "Berber."[7] By the medieval period, six centuries hence, the great North African Arab writer Ibn Khaldun had elevated the "Berbers" into a "race" (nation), granting them equal status with the other great nations of the world. Nineteenth-century French colonial administrators and scholars would revive this construct, which had fallen into disuse, in order to distinguish "Berbers" from "Arabs" and thus better entrench their rule. Today, the term is viewed by many Berbers as pejorative and, as their modern ethnonational consciousness deepens, is increasingly being supplanted by "Amazigh" (lit. "free man"; pl. "Imazighen"; f. singular "Tamazight"). "Tamazight" also refers to the Berber language, both specifically to the variant spoken by Middle Atlas Berbers and, nowadays, covering all Berberophones. There are three primary Berber dialects in Morocco, rooted in three distinct regions—from south-southeast to north: Tashelhit, spoken by roughly 8 million persons, and Tamazight and Tarrifit, each spoken by approximately 3 million persons. Algeria has two primary versions and four smaller ones: Taqbaylit, from the Kabylie region, spoken by 5 million persons; Chaoui, from the Aures region southeast of Kabylie, the language of 2 million persons; Tamzabit, of the 200,000 Ibadi Muslims of the Mzab valley in the south around Ghardaia; Znati, the dialect group of 150,000 persons in the Touat-Gourara area in the country's southwest, in the Sud Oranis oasis straddling the Moroccan border, and in the Ouargla region east of Mzab; Tachenouit, in the Chenoua and Zaccar Mountains west of Algiers, spoken by 100,000; and Tamesheq, the dialect of Algeria's approximately 100,000 traditionally

Amazigh-Speaking Regions

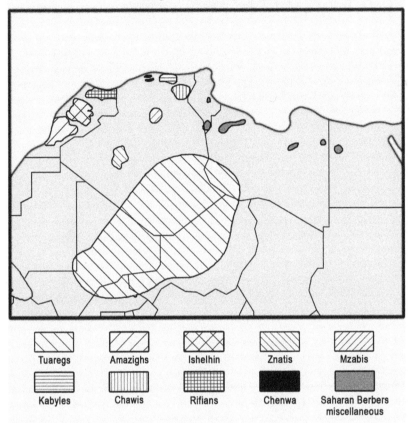

Tuaregs	Amazighs	Ishelhin	Znatis	Mzabis
Kabyles	Chawis	Rifians	Chenwa	Saharan Berbers miscellaneous

nomadic Touaregs of the far south (more than a million Touaregs live in adjacent Mali and Niger).[8] These numerous dialects, as well as those spoken in Libya, Tunisia, and Egypt's Siwa oasis, are generally understood to be variants of a single language, which belongs to the family of Afro-Asiatic (previously classified as Hamito-Semitic) languages.[9]

Some modern-day Amazigh militants take great umbrage not only with the term "Berber," but with "Maghrib" as well, viewing them, not wholly unreasonably, as one more indication that their status is politically, socially, culturally, and historically subordinate. Their reaction is even more forceful when "Maghrib" is joined together with "Arab," a term given institutional expression in 1989 with the establishment of the five-member "Arab Maghrib Union" (*ittihad al-maghrib al-ʿarabi*), encompassing Morocco, Alge-

TAMAZGHA – ⵜⴰⵎⴰⵣⵖⴰ

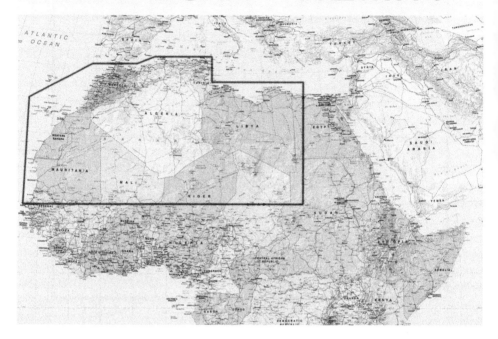

ria, Tunisia, Libya, and Mauritania.[10] The Amazigh Culture Movement's own term of choice is "Tamazgha," defined as the landmass which stretches westward across North Africa from the Siwa oasis in Egypt's Western Desert to the Atlantic Ocean, extending to include the Canary Islands, and encompassing much of the Sahel lands as well.

However special they considered the Berbers, Ibn Khaldun and the French colonialist administrators, and historians who would follow in Ibn Khaldun's footsteps half a millennium later, were especially exercised by the failure of the Maghrib region to develop as a durable social and political center over the *longue durée*. The reason for this, Robert Montagne, Charles-André Julien, and others believed, was the Berbers' innate rebellious and anarchical tendencies, which repeatedly threatened settled society. But these tendencies, rooted in the particularism of tribe and village,[11] also were believed to give the Berbers their inner essence in the face of more powerful conquering civilizations. This type of analysis, emphasizing overarching metahistorical themes and such problematic notions as "national character," or even the somewhat less problematic concept of *mentalité,* is largely passé today, as it appears reductionist and tends also to etch in stone the differences between groups. The considerable merits of French ethnographic and historical work notwithstanding, the marriage of scholarship to the colonialist agenda, particularly the reification of the Berber "essence" in order to distinguish "good" Berbers from "recalcitrant" Arabs, was clearly a distortion of a much more complex reality. Moreover, it not only failed as a policy but also delegitimized any possibility of Berber specificity within the budding nationalist discourse and praxis.

Modern Arab identity, as propagated first by intellectuals and subsequently, beginning in the interwar period, by nationalist movements throughout the Arabic-speaking world, placed the Arabic language at the center of the project. In Algeria and Morocco, too, beginning in the 1930s, "Arabness" and accompanying links to the Arab-Islamic East developed into a central definitional component of their respective national movements, although not at the expense of the legitimacy of the territorial state as such (as was frequently the case in the Mashriq lands).

In Algeria, the subordination and delegitimation of Berber specificity and agency had first sprouted during the "Berberist crisis" in 1949. The episode, however marginal to the overall evolution of the Algerian nationalist movement, starkly illustrated the way in which Berber-Arab ethnic differences could be instrumentalized by rival political currents. Members of the Algerian *ulama* were especially vehement, harshly condemning the Berber language as inferior, vulgar, and degenerate in comparison to Arabic, the language of God, embodied in the Qur'an (notwithstanding the yawning gap between classical Arabic and spoken Algerian Arabic). This attitude was similar to trends in Europe among the promoters of nationally accepted, "high" written languages, which themselves had to be standardized before claiming their allegedly "natural" authority prescribed by the language ideology most commonly associated with Johann Gottfried Herder.[12] It existed as an undercurrent in Algeria's bitter war for independence between 1954 and 1962, continued to be prevalent after independence, and was part of a wider postcolonial phenomenon in Africa in which marginalized ethnic groups were further subordinated to the visions and policies of newly ruling groups.[13] Notwithstanding the profound differences between the Maghrib and sub-Saharan Africa, Maghribi dynamics did run parallel, to some extent, to those farther south. Within the Maghrib, such marginalization occurred not only in Algeria, but also rival Morocco. Ruling groups in both promoted their particular versions of the "state" and the "nation" at the expense of important societal forces. In spite of the polar-opposite nature of the Moroccan and Algerian regimes,[14] central aspects of their respective legitimacy formulas employed during the last fifty years were identical: emphasis on their heroic struggle against colonialism and a broader affinity with Arab nationalism. Thus, throughout the first decades of independence, governments adopted educational and cultural policies designed to make Arabic a fully functioning tool in every aspect of life, which went hand in hand with efforts to attain mass literacy. To that end, the promotion of Arabic as a modern print language was crucial. The prime target of these efforts was the French language, which had struck roots during the colonial era as the language of government and public life. But Tamazight, particularly its Kabyle variety, Taqbaylit, was no less a target, for it had no place in the Algerian leadership's vision for the future. Like its republican counterparts elsewhere, newly independent Algeria placed great emphasis on social engineering, in order to forge an individual and collective persona. The Istiqlal Party aspired to act in a similar fashion in Morocco, but never achieved the requisite hegemony over the political system to do so. Like its fellow monarchies elsewhere in the Middle East, the Moroccan palace acted more as a supreme arbiter over society than as a disruptive, transforming force.[15] But regardless of the differences between the Moroccan and Algerian political systems, Berber aspects of their societies, cultures, and histories were given short shrift, even as the process of state consolidation and economic integration into a single market went forward, inexorably drawing the Berbers themselves into their national orbits.

For a long time, this didn't seem to matter, as the Moroccan sharifian Alaoui monarchy and Algeria's Front de Libération Nationale (FLN)–led single party–army regime battled successfully to attain hegemony at the expense of rival political forces. Morocco's King Hassan II survived (albeit barely) two attempted military coups in the early 1970s and was succeeded after his death in 1999 by his eldest son Mohamed, in a peaceful and orderly manner. Algeria's state-building model appeared to be more successful than Morocco's during the early decades of independence. However, its eventual brutal trial by fire ended up being much worse. Beginning at the end of the 1980s, acute economic distress and social malaise led a portion of the ruling military-bureaucratic elites to attempt a radical and ill-prepared democratic experiment, one that imploded in the early 1990s and resulted in a prolonged and bloody conflict between the authorities and a militant Islamist insurgency, costing an estimated 150,000 deaths and all the attendant damage to the social fabric. But just as the Moroccan monarchy had managed to survive and maintain its hegemony over Moroccan political life, Algeria's ruling military-bureaucratic elites were able to survive the Islamist challenge and renew their authority over Algerian society.

Nonetheless, the saliency of the regimes' legitimacy formula has been eroded with the passage of time and the broader fragmentation of the Arab state system.[16] More specifically, Morocco and Algeria are both characterized by entrenched authoritarian regimes lacking genuine democratic legitimacy, strong Islamist opposition movements and smaller groups that engage in *jihadi* terrorism, economic systems that have lagged far behind other regions in the increasingly globalized economy, and large youthful populations clamoring for jobs or visas to the West, with resulting migration and social pressures on European countries. Taken together, these challenges pose serious questions regarding the future of their societies, political systems, and even the very nature of their collective identities.

Where do the Berbers fit into the picture? Writing in the early 1970s, Ernest Gellner, who among his myriad pursuits carried out important fieldwork among Moroccan Berber tribes, declared that "in his heart, the Berber knows that God speaks Arabic and modernity speaks French," and dismissed the likelihood that the Berbers might ever develop a more encompassing ethnic identity beyond their particular tribal loyalties within an Islamic milieu.[17] One can infer that for Gellner, the process of modernization would eventually, but inexorably, lead the Berbers to assimilate into those larger frameworks of modern national states colored with an Islamic hue that emerged throughout the Arabic-speaking lands during the twentieth century. From a different angle, while granting them ethnic status, Lawrence Rosen argued quite cogently that ethnicity constituted only part of a Moroccan Berber's social identity, and not necessarily the most important one.[18] Ch. Pellat stated in the authoritative *Encyclopaedia of Islam* that the Berbers are heterogeneous and historically lacking in all sense of community, thus failing to constitute a truly distinct nation.[19] An American political scientist writing at the end of the 1970s declared unequivocally that the Berbers were well on the way to assimilation within Arab-Muslim nation-states.[20] Two subsequent and important edited collections on the modern Moroccan state barely refer to the Berber populations, let alone present them as significant actors in the wider political and social realms.[21]

However, almost under the radar, new ways of Berber imagining, in the sense used by Benedict Anderson,[22] among segments of their diverse community, and new forms of political, and proto-political action have emerged in recent decades. The result is the Berber/Amazigh Culture Movement, a transnational phenomenon of ethnocultural assertion that cuts across national boundaries. Berber speakers across North Africa, led by Algerian Kabyles, have taken on many of the attributes of a modern *ethnie:* "a named unit of population with common ancestry myths and historical memories, elements of shared culture, some links with a historic territory and some measure of solidarity at least among [its] elites."[23]

This should not have been surprising: as we know from Clifford Geertz, Joel Migdal, and others, the process of societal modernization, the move from a segmented to an integrated society, is neither unilinear nor unidirectional, and often reinforces and refashions primordial affiliations even as they lose some of their original functions. Indeed, we can see in both Algeria and Morocco that the assertion of "traditional" Berber identity among portions of the Berber populations actually contains elements of a more modern ethnic-type identity. From another angle, and notwithstanding the radically different contexts, a number of attributes of the nation-forming process in Europe among nondominant ethnic groups analyzed by Miroslav Hroch[24] are also recognizable among modern-day Berbers, even while many of the traditional economic, legal, and political functions of the tribe have all but disappeared.

The Berber Culture Movement in North Africa and the Diaspora is an amorphous, many-headed phenomenon with a clear core demand: the recognition by state authorities of the existence of the Amazigh people as a collective, and of the historical and cultural Amazighité of North Africa. The most immediate and concrete manifestations of that recognition would be to make Tamazight an official language equal to Arabic, and to begin redressing the multitude of injustices that have been inflicted on the Berbers over the last half-century, through corrective educational, social, and economic policies. In Algeria, Berber movement demands are more overtly political, the result of decades of tension, punctuated by bouts of overt confrontation between the regime and the territorial and cultural core of resurgent Berberism, Kabylie. In Morocco, the scene has been less confrontational, and less overtly political, but has significantly evolved in that direction in recent years. The socioeconomic component of the new Berberism varies from place to place as well, but clearly cannot be divorced from the other factors driving the movement.

Regardless of the specifics in each country, the Berber Culture Movement is engaged in contentious politics: it wants nothing less than to refashion the identity of North African states, rewrite their history, and fundamentally change the basis of collective life there. As with other minority movements worldwide, the Amazigh Culture Movement trumpets the importance of genuine political democracy and cultural pluralism. In the Amazigh case, the existing bogeyman, i.e., the prevailing order that needs to be combated, is based on a combination of what they view as Arab-

Islamic and Jacobin-style authoritarianism, manifested in both Islamist and more secular nationalist varieties.

To be sure, Berberism, in both its specific territorial-state context and its broader pan-Berber one, poses no current threat to the territorial integrity of any of the Maghrib states. Nor does it pose any serious threat to ruling elites, which themselves contain important Berber components. Its ability as a social movement to engage in the important task of resource mobilization has begun to jell, but its capacity to sustain and transform remains an open question. In 1980 and 2001, Kabylie experienced two important "episodes of contention," a notion that, according to social movement theorists, contains some combination of mobilization, identity shift, and polarization. One may ask whether the result of these episodes was what is known in the literature as a "threshold crossing," namely a cognitive conversion into a more self-conscious and determined political community by the public being targeted by the particular movement, in this case, the Kabyles. Moroccan Berbers are operating in a different context, but the signs of activism, particularly among students, are manifest, and have been unintentionally reinforced by the state's recognition of the movement's potentially subversive capacity.[25]

Berberists may identify viscerally with the Kurds, especially those of Iraq, who after a long trail of tears and tribulations have attained many of the attributes of collective national revival, culturally and politically. They also gaze with great interest toward Spain's Catalonia region, their exemplar of an ethnonational community's successful, peaceful attainment of linguistic, cultural, and administrative autonomy. Achievements of Basque nationalists in introducing the Basque language, Euskara, into the public sphere in Spain's Basque region have also been noted as worthy of emulation. In comparison to these three cases, Berberists lag far behind. Nonetheless, an explicitly Amazigh identity movement, backed by and intertwined with elements of the Berber Diaspora, has become part of the larger political and social spectrums in North Africa's two leading countries. Berberism has also begun to reverberate in Libya. The Touareg of the Sahel countries, particularly Niger and Mali, have been in open, often violent conflict with their central governments for years. They are outside the scope of this study, but they too have not been entirely untouched by the modern Berberist current.

Modern Berber identity has multiple strands, from the illiterate female keeper of the household in the southeast of Morocco, to the rugged Kabylian villager in Algeria, to the Touareg camel-driving nomad, to the

Paris-based intellectual. These strands are so diverse that one may even ask if there is anything at all that unites them. This study will seek to analyze the underpinnings and the dynamics, both within particular Berber communities and between them and state authorities, that resulted in the emergence of a modern Berber identity movement in the decades after independence, just when many thought that Berber culture and specificity could be consigned to the museum. An underlying assumption of this analysis is that modern Berber identity as an idea and, increasingly, as a movement serves as a tangible counterpoint to both state-dominated political and social life and opposition Islamist currents. The interaction of this evolving, ethnic-type identity with other forms of collective affiliation—tribal, national, and religious—will be an important component of state-society relations in Morocco and Algeria for years to come, as governments, ruling elites, and the populace at large struggle to come to grips with myriad economic, political, and sociocultural pressures a half-century after achieving independence.

PART I   *Entering History*

One

ORIGINS AND CONQUESTS

Africa, the Mediterranean Basin, Arabia

T he purpose of this chapter and the following one is to give a succinct overview of the history of North Africa from antiquity to independence, with an emphasis on its Berber components, particularly in the territories that constitute modern-day Algeria and Morocco. This is not a Berberist reading, per se, although such a reading can hardly be ignored either. In any case, the intent is to dispassionately present the main developments of Maghribi history from the mists of time to the end of modern colonialism—political, social, cultural, religious, and legal—from the angle of the Berber-speaking populations, and their interactions with other social and political groupings and forces. Guiding this brief overview is the notion that the numerous manifestations of being Berber, including the existence of various forms of a single language, social organization, territorial cores, and daily praxis, were durable enough to enable the inclusion of Berbers within the broad category of premodern *ethnies* expounded by Anthony Smith.[1] This Berber-centered account confirms Miroslav Hroch's stipulation that the nation-formation process "is a distinctively older phenomenon than the modern nation and nationalism." From this perspective, Hroch's insistence that any interpretation of modern national identity cannot ignore the peculiarities of premodern national development, or degrade it to the level of a mere myth, resonates loudly.[2] Ironically, the Berbers rate nary a mention by Smith himself, apart from a map of the Mediterranean world between 200 BC and AD 400 in one of his books, which denotes the territory of Numidia (encompassing portions of modern-day Algeria and Tunisia).[3] In any event, most ethnic identities are like that of the Berbers: "nuanced, mutable, their boundaries and characteristics changing with time."[4]

HISTORICAL BEGINNINGS:
A POTPOURRI OF NAMES AND NOTIONS

Even with regard to proper names, one is immediately confronted by a bewildering potpourri: Garamantes, Gaetulians, and Maures
in the early Greek and Roman chronicles; Baranis and Butr, two overarching categories mentioned by Arab chroniclers supposedly differentiating
those who wore the *burnus* (a one-piece hooded cloak) and those who wore
the *abtar* (a brief tunic, cut short), and which were said to provide most of
the recruits to the conquering Arab forces, while some of the Baranis were
said to be Christians, and thus liable to the poll tax;[5] and the subsequent
division of Berber tribes into the Sanhaja and Zenata, supposedly according to linguistic criteria, notwithstanding each group's lack of geographic
contiguity and other apparent common attributes. Within this division are
other familiar, albeit long-since-vanished names of various groups—the
Kutama of what today is northeastern Algeria, which provided the initial backbone for the Fatimid revolution that swept into Egypt from the
west in the latter part of the tenth century, founding their new capital,
al-Qahira (Cairo), in 969; the Lamtuna (*al-mulaththamun;* "veiled ones"),
one of the great Sanhaja Berber nomadic tribes dominating trans-Sahara
trade that underpinned the Almoravid (*al-murabitun*) empire (1053–1147);
and the Masmuda Berbers of the Middle Atlas Mountains, from whose
ranks came the founders of the Almohad (*al-muwahiddun*) Dynasty (1121–
1269), which at its peak dominated all of North Africa and Andalusia, the
western Islamic world.

Both Muslim chroniclers and French colonial-era scholars were keen
on determining the origins of the Berbers: the Muslims so as to legitimize
and ensure the Berbers' Islamization and Arabization and thus integrate
them into the larger Islamic *umma,* and the French, in order to best serve
the colonial project (each of these efforts is discussed below). In fact, contrary to these neat and politically driven versions of Berber origins, the
Berbers' geographical and anthropological origins are themselves veiled:
as far as can be determined, they are multiple, emanating from the Mediterranean, Nile Valley, and the Sahara, resulting in a composite population
during Neolithic times.[6]

The gradual emergence in the Sahara during the second millennium BC
of a lighter-skinned warrior aristocracy ascendant over black cultivators,
a pattern that would repeat itself in more modern times in the Sahel region, is testified to by numerous Saharan sites of prehistoric cave art, the
most famous being the Tassili n'Ajjer National Park in southeastern Alge-

ria, a UNESCO World Heritage site. The northern, Libyan equivalent of the Tassili groups ("Libu," in ancient Egyptian) came into increasing contact with Egypt through trade, migration, and conflict: invaders of the Nile Delta from the west, in 1220 BC and again in 1180 BC, reportedly suffered thousands of casualties.[7] Two hundred thirty-seven years later, in 943 BC, the Libyan-Egyptian interaction reached a peak, with the founding of the Pharaonic "Libyan Dynasties" by Sheshonk I, from the Libico-Berber Meshwesh tribe, who had wrested control of the state from the previous dynasts. They would rule Egypt for more than two hundred years, a point of considerable symbolic significance for modern-day Berber "memory workers" in line with Smith's stipulation that "the secret of identity is memory," requiring the salvaging and reappropriation of the ethnic past.[8] Like their counterparts in ethnonational movements elsewhere, Berber memory workers engage in a dialogue between the present and the past, as they seek to recover, fashion, and promote a collective memory that will help consolidate modern Berber identity.[9]

In this instance, the symbolic importance of the ascent of Sheshonk I cannot be overstated, for according to the Berberist understanding, it marked the moment of entry of the Amazigh people into recorded history. To that end, in 1968, the Paris-based Académie Berbère (see Chapter 3) chose to propagate a Berber calendar with the approximate year of Sheshonk's ascent as its starting point (950 BC). Accordingly, the dates of both the Gregorian and Berber calendars (but not the Muslim one!) are used on the masthead of the Rabat-based monthly *Le Monde Amazigh (al-Alam al-Amazighi/Amadal Amazigh)*.

Fast-forwarding five hundred years, we find Herodotus referring to another of the Saharan Berber warrior groups, the Garamantes of the Fezzan region in the Libyan desert, who constitute "the first proto-historic peoples of the Maghrib whose settlement sites are known archaeologically."[10] Herodotus's interest in North Africa, however questionable his accuracy,[11] indicates the growing intertwining of the Mediterranean region, and the arrival of new forces on its southern littoral. Carthage was founded by Phoenicians from the city of Tyre, traditionally in 814 BC. By the fifth century BC, it had become the dominant commercial power of the central Mediterranean and would remain so until its destruction by Rome in the Punic wars, between 261 and 146 BC. Apart from the approximately one-hundred-year Vandal interlude, ending in AD 530, Roman/Byzantine rule of the North African littoral and points south lasted, albeit in an ever-shrinking area, until the Arab conquests in the late seventh century AD.

For the Berber populations, the political impact of these developments was extremely significant. They emulated Carthage's territorial
consolidation by establishing larger entities of their own, in the territory west and south of that controlled by Carthage. Originally, the third-
century-BC Greek historian Polybius dubbed all Africans not subject to
Carthage as "Numidians"; the name acquired a specific geographical sense
after the Roman occupation.[12] The Numidian kingdoms, known initially
by the names of three main tribal groups, the Massyli, the Masaesyli, and
the Mauri (from which derives the Roman region of "Mauretania," roughly
corresponding to much of today's Morocco), became bound up with the
Roman-Carthaginians wars, while emulating the pomp and accompanying
modes of rule of the other Hellenized monarchies throughout the Mediterranean. These kingdoms were led by figures such as Syphax, Massinissa,
Jugurtha, Juba I, and Juba II. Eventually, they fell by the wayside, incorporated in one form or another into Roman Africa, thus bringing an end
to North Africa's, and the Berbers', first experience of internally generated
social and political organization.[13] Much more than the Libyan Pharaoh
Sheshonk, the stories of these kingdoms, and particularly the struggle of
Jugurtha against Rome, have resonance for contemporary Berberists. Like
other modern ethno-national/cultural movements, the Amazigh Culture
Movement has been engaged in a "search for a usable past."[14] The Helle-
nistic kingdoms of North Africa provide sufficient "proof" that Berbers
had agency in ancient history and were capable of large-scale organization and development. They also have resonance for some North African
nationalist historians seeking to "decolonize" history, like Abdallah Laroui,
who sought to combat colonialist historians' presentation of North African
history as one that proved the inherent inability of "natives" to overcome
their internal divisions and operate on a large scale. In that vein, Laroui
posits the Jugurthine war against the Romans (112–105 BC) as "having the
character of a national struggle."[15]

Such a classification is anachronistic. But there is certainly room to deconstruct the notion of the undifferentiated tribesman. Brett and Fentress
stand together with Laroui's devastating critique of the "timeless Berber"
thesis, which focuses on an allegedly inherently disunited and unstable
Berber social structure. The Berber Numidian and Mauretanian kingdoms
in the last three centuries before Christ, they declare, "were states in every
sense of the word."[16] The last five centuries before Roman rule, they emphasize, demonstrated "the ability of the African populations to adapt to
and exploit new situations," testified to by the development of states, urban

structures, and a written language. But they also note that it is unclear how these affected "the basic nuclei of society: the family, and the clan, or their beliefs." This cultural duality is very much central to Berber society throughout history and up till the present day.[17]

Language, of course, is almost always a central component of larger-scale group identities, whether one speaks of premodern *ethnies* or modern ones, creating "a density of . . . ties enabling a higher degree of social communication within the group than beyond it."[18] Sociolinguistics view language as a social phenomenon: it is "not merely a means of interpersonal communication and influence . . . a carrier of content," but actually is itself content, "a referent for loyalties and animosities, an indicator of social statuses and personal relationships, a marker . . . of societal goals and large-scale value-laden arenas of interaction that typify every speech community."[19] More recent scholarship emphasizes the need to understand how speech communities are constructed through processes of conflict, competition, exclusion, boundary-making, differentiation, and transgression. Sociolinguists are now increasingly interested in what Gal and Woolard term "the relationship between the process of the public construction of languages and the linguistic construction of publics . . . how different images of linguistic phenomena gain social credibility and political influence, both within the academic disciplines of language and in larger social fields; and the role of linguistic ideologies and practices in the making of political authority."[20] They differ in emphasis with Benedict Anderson's influential study of nationalism, which postulated that "the convergence of capitalism and print technology on the fatal diversity of human language created the possibility of a new form of imagined community, which in its basic morphology set the stage for the modern nation."[21] Drawing on Jürgen Habermas's work on the public sphere, Gal and Woolard stress that "a public is not simply a collection of social structural features that result from a circumstance such as the introduction of print. Rather, it is in part an idea, a framing of such structures and practices that, while moveable, malleable, and borrowable, is hardly inevitable."[22] As shall be subsequently seen, these insights are useful for understanding the dynamics of the modern Amazigh identity movement, which places supreme value on the Berber language as the repository of Berber culture and history, and as an object that requires rescue, development, and elevated status.

Indeed, the very matter of Berber linguistic origins, as well as continuity, remains somewhat controversial.[23] Brett and Fentress suggest that the advent of the Neolithic in the lower Nile Valley and Delta area, beginning around 4000 BC, led to a major rise in population density and consequent movement of peoples both northwest and east, carrying new techniques and a related language, known to us only as "Libyan." Given the "remarkable similarity" of Berber languages, Brett and Fentress suggest that their spread across North Africa was relatively uniform and over a relatively short period of time, with the decisive break between them and old Egyptian coming prior to the definitive drying out of the Sahara between 2500 and 2000 BC.[24] Interestingly, a recent study suggests that the break was not so definitive after all, pointing to Amazigh etymological roots of the language of Pharaonic Egypt.[25] In any event, according to Laroui, the Maghrib had achieved a linguistic and cultural unity prior to the arrival of the Phoenicians and Romans, accompanied by an economic duality—agriculturalists and pastoralists. Subsequent research postulates a more sympathetic vision of pastoralists in North Africa, pointing to increased social stratification and a more developed material culture.[26]

But the relationship between ancient Libyan and modern Berber is clearer to some scholars than others.[27] David Cherry, in his 1998 book *Frontier and Society in Roman North Africa,* leans decisively toward Fergus Millar's earlier study, which seriously doubted the existence of a "coherent linguistic and social continuum" from the pre-Roman "Libyan" population to modern-day Berbers.[28] The local language outside of the towns and the upper classes in Roman Africa, according to Millar, was "a mere peasant *patois,*" based in large part on Punic, which was, according to Saint Augustine and newer documentary evidence (e.g., public inscriptions and private monuments, written in "neo-Punic"), "a common spoken language throughout the lifetime of Roman Africa."[29] Why Cherry leans to this view, even if it apparently fails to jibe with his statement that there is "no real evidence for the Punicization of Algerian society" apart from one area,[30] is not clear. And if the language of everyday discourse in the non-urbanized areas of Roman rule was "indigenous," and "mostly untouched by Roman practice,"[31] why would this not also have been the case during the early centuries of Punic rule?

A more satisfying explanation is that there was a continuum involving a mixing of Punic and Berber in certain areas and among certain societal groups, as part of larger social, political, and cultural dynamics then at work. "Tyrians" were said to be transformed into "Africans" during the final century and a half of Carthage's existence, thanks to the influence of native Libyans. In turn, the latter became, in Susan Raven's words, "the upholders of neo-Punic language and traditions during subsequent centuries."[32] According to Laroui's formulation, foreign pressure led to tripartism, first socio-political, then, after a process of consolidation, extending itself to every aspect of life: economic, cultural, linguistic, geographic. The first division was social: assimilated subject, nonassimilated subject, and free natives; later it became geographical (cities, country, desert), economic (commerce, agriculture, nomadism) and possibly linguistic (Latin, Punico-Berber, Berber).[33]

Clearly, then, Berbers were neither merely passive victims of imperial conquest by the ancient world's bearers of "modernity" and "globalization" nor staunch resisters of it. This depiction, employed by colonialist, Eurocentric, and anticolonialist historians alike, represents a crude stereotype of Punic and Roman North Africa. In particular, North Africa's urban areas, beginning with Carthage, appear to have been social, economic, and cultural entrepôts, bringing about partial fusions or syntheses among its population, along with varying degrees of military and cultural resistance.[34] Whether we call North Africa's native inhabitants Berbers, Punics, Numidians, or Africans, it is clear that under Rome, there were various degrees of co-optation and interaction, and that the vast bulk of the Roman population there, both civil and in the army, was of African origin.[35] The second century AD produced one peak: an "African" domination, in Latin, of the empire's intellectual life. Politically, too, the African impact was far-reaching: nearly one-third of the Roman Senate in the 180s was of African origin, and shortly after that, Septimius Severus, born in Leptis Magna, a Roman *colonia* in what subsequently came to be known as Tripolitania, became the first African-born emperor (AD 193–211). Septimius was a full member by birth of the Romanized North African elite, as his father, "a Punic," had been granted citizenship. Upon becoming emperor, he made Punic an official language of Leptis Magna.[36] In contrast, the famous orator, philosopher, and playwright Lucius Apuleius (c. AD 123/5–c. AD 180), who was born in Madaurus, a Roman colony in Numidia on the border with Gaetulia, now the town of Mdaourouch, Algeria, defined himself as "half-Numidian, half-Gaetulian."[37] For his part, the playwright Terence initially reached Rome in the second century as a slave, i.e., from the lower less-assimilated portions of the Berber population.[38] As with the Hellenized kings of earlier centuries, so too do the luminaries of Roman Africa serve as iconic figures for modern Amazigh memory workers, providing further tangible evidence of both Berber deep-rootedness and the Berbers' contribution to advanced civilization. This is crucial not only for the collective self-image of modern-day Berbers but also as a rebuttal to Arab-

Islamic views of the Berbers as having lived in a North African version of *jahiliyya* (the pre-Islamic "age of ignorance" in Arabia), whose redemption would be achieved by an enlightened "opening" (*fath*), i.e., the arrival of Islam.

Christianity arrived in Roman North Africa during the second and third centuries AD, brought by sailors and merchants from the east, and perhaps from Rome itself. By the mid-third century, it had become the dominant religion of the urban poor; by the end of the century, it had spread to the countryside as well, indicating a widespread discontent with the authorities. But just prior to Christianity being officially established as the state religion by the Edict of Milan in 313, the Catholic Church was itself challenged in North Africa by the Donatist schism, a challenge that lasted almost a century and became frequently intertwined with outbreaks of tribal unrest and rebellion. The Donatists are sometimes linked to the so-called rebellious Berber spirit, but this essentialist view should be discredited by now. As has always been the case throughout North African history, Berbers/Libyans/Punics/Africans could be found in all camps—martyrs, saints, bishops, leaders, rebels, etc. Indeed, on the "orthodox" flank one finds Saint Augustine, one of the Four Doctors of the Church, whose teachings have resonated throughout the ages among Christians. Saint Augustine's mother, Saint Monica, was Berber/Punic, giving birth to him in the provincial Roman city of Tagaste, now Souk Ahras in Algeria's northeast highlands, sixty miles from present-day Annaba. As Bishop of Hippo, he played a decisive role in the final suppression of the Donatist heresy. Overall, Laroui's caution regarding the Donatist schism is well taken: the long conflict "indicates the social importance religious problems had assumed, even if the causes of the conflict were elsewhere." As is so often the case, resistance to the established order was being expressed through the use of religious idioms and tools. The rural wing of the Donatist rebellion was clearly made up of Berbers, but there is not enough evidence to suggest that it was really Donatist. Moreover, "the chronology of Christianization, the socio-racial structure and finally the numerical evaluation of African Christianity remain beyond our reach."[39]

From its height in the second century, the reach of Roman rule began to contract. The Vandal interregnum (429–533) and subsequent reconquest, this time by Byzantium, did nothing to inhibit the weakening of central authority in the areas beyond the North African coast. North Africa during these years has commonly been understood as slipping back toward the pre-Roman pattern of fragmentation into tribal groupings, with an increasing degree of pastoral nomadism, and a decline in urban society, although followers of Fernand Braudel have challenged this with their "anti-chaos theory," pointing to uninterrupted urban settlement and a permanent division of labor between the second and thirteenth centuries.[40] Colonial historians rediscovering this period looked askance upon North Africa's decline, attributed it at least in part to the Berbers' uncivilized recalcitrance, and defined France's role as to complete the task started by Rome. In response, Laroui accounted for the decline of civilization (i.e., of social, political, and cultural life under larger frameworks) in North Africa as being due to "blocked historical development," in which Maghribi society was characterized by "increasing social dispersion," stemming not from a stagnating tribal system but from "a dialectic response." Freedom from Rome's, and later the Church's, universality, he says, "became the name for a return to protohistory" (i.e., social dispersion, anchored in the tribal system).[41] One consequence is that the Berber language recovered substantially during the post-Vandal, Byzantine period.[42]

THE ARRIVAL OF ISLAM

The conquest of Byzantine North Africa by Arab armies bearing the banner of Islam resulted, over time, in the religio-cultural unification of the entire region, including the areas that had remained beyond the old Roman *limes*.[43] To a far lesser extent, it also resulted in the region's linguistic Arabization: classical Arabic gradually become the language of law and bureaucracy, while urban communities and some rural and pastoral groups eventually fashioned and adopted Maghribi dialects of Arabic that were influenced heavily by Berber. For North Africa's far-flung, variegated Berber tribal groupings, the impact of Islam's arrival in North Africa via Arab conquest can hardly be overstated. Over time, Islam would come to profoundly influence nearly every facet of their lives. If there was a semblance of collective memory of the pre-Islamic epochs among the Berber populations, it disappeared. Their myriad experiences over the next millennium would include: fierce resistance to, and subsequent oppression by, the victorious and sometimes scornful Arab conquerors; participation in the ranks of the conquerors as they swept across North Africa and into the Iberian peninsula; religio-political revolts and religious heresies; the creation of Berber Islamic states and empires ruling over vast swaths of territory; and finally, a renewed loss of centrality and eventual marginalization in the centuries preceding the imposition of European colonialism. The historian Ira Lapidus sums up the six-century-long formative period of

Islamic state formation in North Africa, the "Caliphal phase," as a period in which Islam served as the basis of political solidarity among factious Berber tribes. Religious authority, he says, was joined to revenues from commerce and the support of a segmented tribal society. Hence, the conquering Arab-Muslim elites supplied both the authority and the ideology for the first wave of Berber Muslim state formation.[44] Still, one must be careful not to allow the prioritizing of religious appeal to unduly diminish the tribal *asabiyya* of the core groups of political and religious contestation movements. Moreover, it seems fair to assume that there was at least an implicit ethnic appeal among wider strata of these various groups.

The term "Berber Islamic empires," while often employed in surveys of North African history,[45] still may seem strange to the uninitiated. Such a reaction derives from the cumulative impact of long-accepted readings of North African history following the rapid Arab conquest and the area's almost complete Islamization over the centuries. In this view, the Berbers were usually seen as having merged with their Arab-Islamic conquerors, and after a bit of initial unpleasantness, creating a cultural and social synthesis—a particular Maghribi-ness, so to speak. Subsequently, intensive interest in the Berbers by French colonial rulers produced a backlash against anything that smacked of Berber particularity, a reaction employed with considerable effect by the Algerian and Moroccan nationalist movements, respectively. Maghribi nationalists certainly had an interest in emphasizing what was common among their populations, in order to forge modern political communities to combat colonialism and attain independence. In the independence era, as Rosen wrote in the early 1970s, Berber-Arab differences at the everyday level in Moroccan towns and villages, while certainly present, were contingent upon a host of intermediating factors.[46] Thus, the anthropologist Abdallah Hammoudi, even while expressing understanding of the demands for cultural recognition by the modern Berber elite, could say that no one spoke of a Berber-Arab cleavage prior to the colonial era.[47]

However, the actual history of the Islamization of the Maghrib is far more complex than the traditionally accepted Arab-Islamic narrative would have it, and cannot be reduced to a few pat formulas. At the center of this complexity are the varied reactions by the Berber populations to the Arab invaders and subsequent processes of Islamization, a story that combines "circumstance, dialectic and tribal society."[48]

One important fact to be kept in mind is that, unlike previous conquests of North Africa, the Islamic one was made by a society that was itself tribally organized,[49] thus helping shape the nature of the encounter between invader and native. In addition, Arab conquerors came imbued with a universalist message and worldview that left no room for autonomous existence of the mostly nonmonotheistic Berber tribes, as they did not belong to *ahl al-kitab* (People of the Book) and thus could not receive protected *dhimmi* status. Their choices were stark: accept Islam, be enslaved, or submit to the sword. At the same time, religious praxis in North Africa from the beginning of the Common Era appears to have been highly syncretist, combining elements of Judaism, Christianity, and paganism, and marked by active proselytizing by both of the monotheistic faiths. Jewish and Christian communities existed in the coastal towns of what was Roman and Byzantine North Africa, and apparently in smaller numbers in the interior as well. The existence of "Judaized" (as distinct from "Jewish") tribes is considered to be a historical fact; similarly, one can't rule out Christianity's presence among the more pastoral populations. In this atmosphere, the message of Islam may have found a fertile soil in North Africa (as it did, in fact, in Arabia, in a not dissimilar atmosphere).

All of these factors appear to have been in operation during the first half-century of Arab expansion westward from Egypt, beginning in 647, with the launch of the first expedition by Caliph Uthman bin Affan, and the founding in 670 of the military garrison town of Qayrawan in what is today the interior of Tunisia, about 160 km south of Tunis. By 710, Muslim forces had reached Tangier (Tanja), adjacent to the Straits of Gibraltar, and in 711, the first expedition crossed over to Iberia, inaugurating a nearly eight-century epoch of Muslim Spain (al-Andalus/Andalusia). The historical accuracy of the details of the initial conquest of North Africa is clearly suspect, coming to us with a time lag of over a century, and from the perspective of the victor only, with didactic and literary purposes uppermost in the chroniclers' minds. At the center of the accepted narrative is the story of the mythical Kahina (lit., "female seer," or "priestess"), of the possibly Judaized Jrawa tribe in the Aures Mountains, who is said to have taken over the leadership of Berber tribal resistance to the Arab forces. It includes an account of the Kahina's initial successes and eventual defeat by Hassan bin al-Nuʿman al-Ghassani, sometime between 693 and 702, preceded by a scorched-earth policy that allegedly caused the Berber tribes to turn against her; her adoption of a captured Arab officer, Khalid, as her son; and her dispatch of him and her two other sons to the Arab side once she realized that all hope was lost. From initial presentations of the Kahina as the prototypical antihero, representing everything counter to Islamic values, subsequent accounts were rendered in a manner indicating a desire to reconcile Berber Muslims with their Arab conquerors. The absence of any verifiable knowledge of her personal life, and even her real name (Dihya?), increased her mythological status, so much so that she is sometimes presented as the mother of another semimythological figure from this period, Tariq Ibn Ziyad, the commander of the mostly Berber Muslim forces who led the crossing of the Straits of Gibraltar and then disappeared from history, leaving only the rock that bears his (corrupted) name, Jabel Tariq. In the modern era, too, the Kahina has been adopted, in turn, by French colonialists, Arab nationalists, Jews and Zionists, feminists and Berberists.[50]

Regardless of the historical accuracy of the Kahina story, the dual response of fierce resistance and switching sides to join the winning camp appears to have been a not uncommon Berber reaction to the initial Arab conquest. The remnants of Byzantine rule in the coastal areas could not stand up to the tribal-religious energies unleashed by the conquerors and thus quickly succumbed. Latin-speak Christian communities would survive in North Africa in ever-decreasing urban pockets and in agricultural oases for a few hundred years, mostly in Tunisia, until disappearing entirely under the pressure of the Almohad conquests.

Nonetheless, the process of cultural symbiosis between Arab conqueror and Berber native had only just begun and was fraught with difficulties. Berber tribal units in Arab armies could only have client (*mawali*) status, linked to Arab tribes or prominent personalities, while the onerous *jizya* (head tax) and *kharaj* (land tax) were imposed on Berber populations, in contradiction to Islamic law, which dictates that these taxes are supposed to be imposed only on infidels. Moreover, the initial resistance and the circulation among the conquerors of alleged sayings of the Prophet characterizing the Berbers as a perfidious people served to justify even more extortionate demands by Arab governors, including levies of female slaves and unborn lambskins to Damascus, and slave recruits for the Muslim army. Isma'il bin Ubayd Allah, the enlightened governor of Ifriqiya between 718 and 720, briefly reversed this policy. However, after the death of the Caliph Umar bin Abdul Aziz, Isma'il was replaced by Yazid ibn Abi Musli, who among other acts of oppression had his name branded onto the forearms of his Berber guards. Yazid's act enraged his guardsmen, who rose and killed him. Twenty years later, Damascus revived its original demand for female slaves and lambskins, while the regional governor attempted to implement caliphal policy mandating the confiscation of one-fifth of conquered lands (*khums*). Hence, the stage was set for the first great Berber self-assertion in the Islamic milieu, the Kharijite revolt (739–742), which broke out in Tangier, led by Maysar al-Mathaghri. Concurrently, the newly established Muslim administration in al-Andalus was threatened by an uprising of Berbers in sympathy with their brothers across the straits, a clear expression of tribal and ethnic solidarity.[51]

The Kharijite revolt, the first of countless reform movements in Muslim history, had originated in Iraq in opposition to Umayyad material excess and lack of piety, preaching equality among the believers, and branding the Umayyads as apostates. Its appeal to newly Islamicized Berbers chafing under the Umayyads was natural, and the parallels with the Christian Donatist movement's actions hundreds of years earlier are considerable.

Given the fact that none of the various manifestations of Kharijism ultimately managed to triumph over what we now recognize as mainstream Sunni Islam, there has long been a tendency to consign the Kharijites to the category of a heretical movement. However, as Michael Brett reminds us, they did not stand in opposition to an established orthodox majority. Rather, "in the middle of the eighth century they were in competition for the right to represent the entire community."[52] Moreover, the various strands of the Kharijite movement in North Africa were further manifestations of the syncretist character of religious belief and praxis that predominated throughout the millennium.

As it happened, it was the Abbasids who overthrew the Umayyad caliphate and replaced it with their own, in Baghdad. Islamic North Africa, for its part, splintered into a number of more local dynasties. Many of the tribal groupings commonly classified as Zenata Berbers initially adopted the dogma and practices of the Ibadiyya, an offshoot of the Kharijites. The Banu Midrar Berbers, having fled south from Tangier following the failed revolt of 739–742, established the city-state of Sijilmassa in what is today southeastern Morocco. The Rustamid Ibadites, led by an imam of Persian origin, did the same in Tahart, 225 km southwest of today's Algiers. Together, these towns controlled the northern trans-Saharan trade routes. Neither of the communities survived in those locations past the tenth century, and Ibadi Berber Muslims are today relegated to small isolated communities in Mzab in Algeria (see Chapter 7), Jerba in Tunisia, and Jabal Nafusa and Zuwarrah in Libya (see Chapter 5).[53] From a very different angle, the founding sharifian Moroccan dynasty in Fez at the end of the eighth century, the Idrissids, owed its success to the embrace of the powerful Awraba tribal group, which one hundred years earlier had opposed the Arab conquests but had since adopted Sunni Islam.[54]

By contrast, Ifriqiya came under the control of the Aghlabids, a local Arab dynasty that had originated as military governors of the region, thus befitting the area of North Africa first conquered and settled by Arab Muslims. But in the beginning of the tenth century, the Kutama Berbers of the western reach of Ifriqiya, in what is now northeastern Algeria, formed the backbone of a revolt against their rule. As had been true with the Zenata Berbers more than a century earlier, they expressed their opposition in Islamic terms, acknowledging a militant Isma'ili Shi'a as the divinely guided Mahdi ("Redeemer," presaging the End of Days according to widespread Muslim belief) and caliph. The resulting Fatimid dynasty ruled Ifriqiya throughout most of the century, beating back challenges of the Umayyads of al-Andalus and their allies, the local Fez-based Maghrawa Berber dynasty, and then moved into Egypt, where it went on to play a major role in Islamic history. The vacated area, encompassing parts of present-day Algeria, Tunisia, and Libya, was left to the local Zirid dynasty, which belonged to the Talkata tribe, a sedentary part of the Sanhaja confederation. The Zirids cultivated the Sunni Maliki school of Islamic law (*madhhab*) and practices, unlike the Fatimids, and ultimately split with their former overlords, recognizing the spiritual leadership of the Abbasid caliphate.

As this cursory account shows, initial Berber reactions to the arrival of Islam, however varied, passed fairly rapidly from the stage of resistance among some of the tribal groupings to an overall adoption/adaptation mode. Subsequently, Berber dynasties great and small, underpinned by different combinations of tribal confederations, would arise within an overall Islamic milieu. But one, in particular, constituted a fundamentally different response to the general religious and political ferment of the time—the establishment of a counter-Islam, if you will, by an amalgamation known as the Barghwata,[55] whose various elements belonged to the Masmuda tribal confederation, and who came together under the banner of Salih Ibn Tarif (749–795) in Tamesna, the central coastal plain of today's Morocco.

The origins of the Barghwata kingdom were in the Kharijite revolt. Taking refuge from the caliph's troops in Tamesna, Ibn Tarif, one of the revolt leader's closest associates, is said to have proclaimed himself, around the year 744, the Prophet of God. Armed with a Berber Qur'an, composed of eighty sections (Suras), he attracted the Berber tribes of the region to his banner. Some people believe that his grandson, Yunis Ibn Ilias, may actually have been the driving force behind the proclamation of Ibn Tarif as the Mahdi of the Berbers and the composer of the new Qur'an, whose actual text has not survived. Doctrinally, the new religion contained a number of variations on Islamic praxis, and was strictly enforced, befitting its Kharijite origins. Ironically, this response, however heretical it may have been for orthodox Muslims, confirmed the power of the new faith that had arrived from the East over the previous decades, even as it was appropriated and refashioned for local usage.

The Barghwata kingdom survived for more than three hundred years before disappearing at the hands of the Almoravids in the middle of the eleventh century. However, Morocco's official history of the period has studiously ignored it, owing to its heresy, and knowledge of its actual workings has always been considered scarce. But in recent years, scholars and Amazigh movement activists have taken a special interest in the Barghwata, encouraging the publication of a variety of studies and tracts. In their eyes, the Barghwata represent an authentic assertion of Berber identity like no other during the millennium of Islamic rule, a cultural reaction emanating from the desire for self-preservation.[56] Also mentioned in this vein is a similar, albeit even less-known, development among a portion of the Ghomara, a Masmuda Berber grouping, in the area of Tetouan in the north of today's Morocco, where in 925 Hamim al-Ghomari al-Motanabbi claimed to have received a revelation from God in the Berber language, portions of which were quoted by Ibn Khaldun some four hundred years later.[57] Conversely, modern-day voices from Morocco's Islamist current, the chief competitor with the Amazigh movement insofar as they each offer a political-historical-cultural discourse countering that of the Moroccan state (see Chapter 6), have not hesitated to brand the Amazigh movement's activities and demands as "Barghwatism."[58]

Meanwhile, in al-Andalus, the myriad "Berber" aspects of developments—social, political, and cultural—both fascinate and raise questions. The vast majority of the Muslim conquerors in the eighth century were Berber tribesmen, a fact that usually gets lost when mentioning the high Islamic culture that subsequently emerged there. For example, a recent glowing account of the multicultural flourishing of Islamic Spain, in referring to the Berbers, focused only on the violence and destruction wrought on Madinat al-Zahra and Cordoba by newly arrived Berber tribesmen in 1009 and 1013 and the repressive and religiously intolerant Berber Islamic dynasties that followed from North Africa.[59] Neville Barbour essentially presents the same picture: for two centuries, he writes, Umayyad rulers were engaged in trying to fuse together the territory's myriad ethnic and religiously monotheist "races" into an Arabic-speaking state with a common sense of nationality. The process reached its peak under Caliph Abdurrahman III (d. 961), but was subsequently undermined by factionalism and the importation of new Berber troops who didn't belong to *ahl al-Andalus*. Some Arab sources characterized these cumulative processes resulting in the destruction of the caliphate as largely due to the period of political and ethnic tensions known as *al-fitna al-barbariyya* (the word *fitna*—"sedition," "dissension"—has an extremely negative connotation in the political lexicon of Islam).[60]

Scholars generally agree that al-Andalus during the eighth and ninth centuries was characterized by a considerable degree of ethnic tension, involving the large number of Berber tribal units who conquered and then were settled on the land, mainly in the southern regions, followed by periodic fresh waves of troops brought in to bolster the rulers; a much smaller number of ethnic Arabs; the steadily growing number of converts from among the Hispano-Roman "native" population; and so-called Slavs, Christians imported from other parts of Europe who were then converted to Islam and also held a variety of functions.[61] But the nature and the underpinnings of this ethnic tension are less clear. Otto Zwartjes states that the discord between Berbers and Arabs that had accompanied the conquest of North Africa by Muslim forces had never disappeared, and the conflict between them was continued in al-Andalus, while he acknowledges that mutual migrations and political unity led to the exchange of many cultural phenomena between the two sides of the Straits.[62] David Wasserstein, by contrast, is firm in his belief that the "old" Berbers quickly abandoned their language and ethnic affiliation in favor of Arabic, finding no evidence for their survival in the administrative and religious institutions and cultural expressions of the new Islamic entity in the West.[63] Similarly, Peter C. Scales stresses the altered social-political reality in al-Andalus, which differed fundamentally from the nomadic, tribal way of life underpinned by Ibn Khaldunian *asabiyya,* suggesting that Berber ethnicity was being attenuated over time—i.e., "no *asabiyya,* no Berber." At bottom, says Wasserstein, these "old" Berbers assimilated into a larger Arab-Andalusian ethnic identity that by the eleventh century was fully formed.[64]

Nonetheless, even as they shed the components of their original identity and assimilated into a larger sociocultural entity over time, would it not be logical to assume that the Berbers themselves impacted substantially the development of Andalusi society and contributed to its makeup in one form or another? Moreover, if the language component of an ethnic Berber identity quickly disappeared, as Wasserstein insists, while ethnic tensions persisted, even among the "old" Berbers, then one must acknowledge the strength of other components of ethnicity—familial, economic, political, and perhaps even in the realm of collective memory.

Pierre Guichard is unhappy with the very notion of a rapid fusion of Arab and Berber elements within the indigenous Hispanic population, pointing to clear evidence of the continuing strength of tribalism after the original invasions.[65] Scales, while acknowledging the strength of some of his arguments, emphasizes that the polarization that did exist was not tribal or racial in nature, but "party" (i.e., factional) and personal. The Berbers, he says, had ceased to exist in the eyes of the tenth-century Andalusi writers, who were focused on the urban components of society, leaving open the question of continued Berber tribal resilience in the rural areas.[66] Thomas Glick, for his part, uses archaeological tools to make points similar to what he calls Guichard's "toponym sleuthing."[67] Moreover, he expresses skepticism regarding the generally accepted notion that there were no purely Berber-speaking centers in al-Andalus by the tenth century.[68] Perhaps part of the answer to the conundrum lies in the probability that Berber language, being unwritten, survived at the lower levels of society, within the home and its immediate environs and among the lower classes in general, while upwardly mobile Berbers joined in more fully with the fusion process. Such a pattern is familiar to students of Berber history and culture from ancient times until the present. Indeed, Helena De Felipe makes this very point regarding the durability of Berber identity in frontier regions, noting the persistence of Berber personal names in genealogical charts. Our knowledge of al-Andalus's urban life from Arabic sources, she emphasizes, is far greater than what we know of the frontier, requiring further research.[69]

In any case, the survival of some type of collective identification among portions of Andalusian Berbers, for the better part of two hundred years, may have laid a fertile base for renewed ethnic tensions occasioned by the increasing import of "new" Zenata Berber cavalry contingents by the Cordoba caliphate to bolster its rule. Berber units would be brought from North Africa again in 1263 in order to defend Granada. The images of Berbers held by the Arab and Arabized military and administrative elite, as well as by mostly native converts of the lower socioeconomic strata, were overwhelmingly negative. The importing of "new" Berbers to bolster the caliphate created highly conflictual situations, particularly among the lower classes of Cordoba. But I would suggest that the heightened degree of anti-Berber expression was also drawing on older, durable themes (for the relationship between origin myths and ethnic tensions in Andalusia, see below).

Whereas the Barghwata and Ghomara provided localized spiritual-communal alternatives for their Berber populations, the rise of the Almoravids in the mid-eleventh century, followed by the Almohads, less than one hundred years later, had a profound impact throughout North Africa and Andalusia. Their political achievements, the unification of North Africa and portions of Andalusia, were unprecedented. Architecturally, culturally, and intellectually, the mixing of North Africa and Andalusia produced great works. For our purposes, it should be noted that it was the first time in recorded history that the unifier of North Africa came not from the North or the East but from within the indigenous population—the Almoravids, a Sanhaja Berber dynasty from the Sahara Desert, and the Almohads, from the Middle Atlas Masmuda Berbers. Abd al-Mu'min, the successor to Ibn Tumart, the founder of the Almohad Dynasty, was the first non-Arab to appropriate the Qur'anic title of *amir al-mu'minin*.[70]

The third great Berber Islamic state, which arose on a portion of their ruins, was the Banu Marin (Marinid) Berber dynasty, a heterogeneous confederation of Zenata Berber tribes, which ruled from Fez and projected considerable power throughout the Maghrib and Andalusia between the thirteenth and fifteenth centuries. Concurrently, the Hafsid dynasts would establish themselves in Ifriqiya, also proclaiming themselves as heirs to the Almohads. Moreover, for a brief moment amidst the cataclysmic conquest of Baghdad by the Mongols in 1258, the scion of a Berber family from the High Atlas, Mohamed al-Mustansir, Hafsid sultan from 1250 to 1277, was the leading Muslim monarch, recognized as Caliph by the sharif governor of Mecca and Egyptian Mamlukes.[71]

It was especially thanks to these dynasties that Ibn Khaldun classified the Berbers as a "great nation." To be sure, none of the Berber Islamic states acted in the name of an overarching "Berber" identity, or even in the name of their own lineage. The Almohads' winning formula, says Lapidus, consisted of "a combination of a royal household, a hierarchical religious organization, a tribal military elite with Berber and Arab tribal allies, and a Spanish-type administration."[72]

It was from this point onward that the Berbers became more fully Islamized, which in turn gave impetus to the process of linguistic Arabization, particularly in sacred matters. But, as Maya Shatzmiller shows, this was no simple matter, involving, instead, complex dynamics of resistance, assertion, and acculturation. Correctly, in my view, she sees the Berbers in ethnic terms, notwithstanding all of their variations and nuances, both in terms of self-definition and the perception of others. Her emphasis is on the acceleration of the dynamics of Berber acculturation to and alienation from the Islamic state, in which Berber "resistance was expressed from within the mainstream of Maghrebi Islam." Yusuf ibn Tashfin, the founder of the Almoravid dynasty that inaugurated this new wave of Islamic piety and militancy, did not have a proper command of Arabic, according to

Arabic sources. The Friday *khutba* (mosque sermon) given by the Almohad Caliph Abd al-Mu'min was delivered in the Berber language, which was used in other public ceremonies as well. The Berber language was accordingly permitted for use in religious books, and imams and *khatibs* who could recite the *tawhid* (profession of faith in the Oneness of God) in Berber replaced existing Arabic-speaking functionaries in Fez.[73] Over time, however, the Fez religious establishment, being distant from the center of Almohad power in Marrakesh, resumed its role of making appointments from among its own members. But upon assuming power, the Marinid government reverted to the Almohad practice of "staffing Islamic institutions with Berber speakers, defending the legitimacy of the Berber language and legitimizing the Berber speaking population in a religious context."[74]

Nonetheless, this pattern would not last. As Islam became institutionalized and great centers of learning were established in Fez and other urban centers, accompanied by the continuous influx of Arab tribesmen from the East, Arabic was confirmed as North Africa's preeminent language for faith, commerce, and politics, although, as Brett says, the context in which Arabic evolved as a vernacular in these lands remains obscure.[75] Berber dialects, on the other hand, remained largely oral, and the preserve of local tribal and familial settings. As recounted by Brett and Fentress, Berber speakers in the lowlands and level uplands of the Maghrib were either absorbed into an Arab tribal structure speaking an Arabic dialect or almost entirely identified with the tribal peasant population and concentrated in more rugged and inaccessible regions, such as the Djurdjura to the east of Algiers.[76]

By the fifteenth century, the age of Berber Islamic dynasties was coming to an end. The political unity attained by the Almoravids and Almohads, and the achievements of the Marinids, who had aspired to re-create the empires of their predecessors, had faded away. They were replaced by more localized dynasties: the Nasrids in Granada, the Wattasids in Morocco, the Zayyanids (also known as Banu Abdul Wad) of Tlemcen, and the Hafsids in Ifriqiya,[77] accompanied by an increasing emphasis on sharifian origins by seekers of power in order to legitimize their claims. This trend, occurring in the context of institutional disintegration and decadence, Iberian pressure and intervention, and Sufist development and dissemination,[78] penetrated down to the local tribal level, as Berber tribes concocted fictitious genealogies to link themselves with the Prophet. Of course, these efforts were done for practical purposes, as establishing a sharifian connection was likely to have a tangible impact on the tribe's social, political, and material well-being. But these genealogies also constituted the latest in a centuries-old intellectual effort to place Berber origins within an eastern Semitic-Arab/Islamic context.

Origin Myths

Central to Ibn Khaldun's classification of the Berbers was the provision of an eastern Arab origin myth. It was the outcome of hundreds of years of discussion regarding the subject. Shatzmiller lays out two chronological periods in the development of the myth of the Berbers' Arab origin, the first covering the ninth to the twelfth centuries AD, and the second the twelfth to the fifteenth. Within the first period, she says, there were several schools, "Eastern," "Andalusian," and "Ifriqiyan," which succeeded one after the other. Following the Islamic conquest of North Africa, Arab writers quite naturally sought to determine the Berbers' origins. One commonly expressed view was that they descended from Jalut (Goliath), whose followers had fled Canaan after being defeated by David. Another version traced the Berbers to the aftermath of the Biblical Flood story. Accordingly, their ancestor was Ham, the son of Noah, who was said to have been born in, or chased to, the Maghrib. In both cases, they were most likely drawing on older Roman, Greek, and Jewish traditions, which most likely were influenced by the immediately preceding and lengthy Punic period of North African history. Ibn Khaldun also repeated the legend of the Yemeni conqueror Ifriqish, who had left behind the ancestors of major Berber tribes such as the Kutama and Sanhaja, thus making them truly Arab in origin.[79]

Not surprisingly, as Shatzmiller shows, the polemics over Berber origins were bound up from the beginning with extant political issues. The numerous Berber revolts against ruling authorities prompted a wealth of forged *hadiths* lambasting them as perfidious enemies of the faithful. In response, others extolled them as the most pure and devoted of Muslims, even claiming that the Berbers sent a delegation to the Prophet Mohamed asking to be among the first to join the new community of believers.

Shatzmiller links the expansion and elaboration of these origin polemics to "*al-fitna al-barbariyya,*" the ethnic tensions in Andalusia in the tenth and eleventh centuries between Berbers, both "old" and "new," and Arabs.[80] The denial by Arab Andalusian genealogists during this period of the Berbers' (particularly Zenatas') Arab Eastern origin in favor of a Western, Iberian origin, she says, indicates the degree of animosity that existed, and their desire to block the sharing of political, economic, and social power by Berber groups, whom they accused of the sin of *shu'ubiyya*.[81] There is no little irony here: a local Iberian-origin narrative was tendered by a rival ethnic group in order to prevent the Berber community from sharing power in that very place, the opposite of modern-day anticolonial norms. Such was the power of Islam.

The Berber response, which was steadily elaborated over time, was an effort to "deconstruct and reconstruct the official history of their conversion,"[82] in an act of simultaneous resistance to their social status and accommodation to overarching Islamic norms. The resulting "Boasts of the Berbers" (Mafakhir al-Barbar) literature provided Ibn Khaldun with a source for his writings.[83] Ascribing Semitic and Arab origins to the Berbers served an important purpose: allowing the learned Muslim class to airbrush out of their collective memory the less benign aspects of the Arab-Muslim conquest of North Africa, and even promote a reconciliation based on the return of long-lost cousins to the fold. To be sure, these competing origin myths never percolated down to the masses of Berbers, as far as can be ascertained. But over time, their thoroughgoing Islamization left most Berbers with no awareness of their actual past. All that they were left with were tribal genealogies, which increasingly included fabricated sharifian lineages.

THE OTTOMAN PERIOD — RETREAT TO THE MARGINS

The Ottoman conquest of Cairo in 1517 from its Mamluke rulers inaugurated a four-hundred-year presence on the African continent and southern portion of the Mediterranean littoral. Two years later, without prior planning, Ottoman rule was formally extended westward along the North African littoral, the consequence of rising Spanish and Habsburg power in the Central Maghrib and their struggle with the Ottoman fleet for control of the western Mediterranean, and the concurrent weakening of the Tunis-based Hafsid sultanate and Tlemcen-based Abd al-Wadid dynasty. Central figures to the story were the brothers Barbarossa, Khayr al-Din and Aruj, Aegean Muslim privateers who had established a presence in the eastern Maghrib as early as 1504 and answered the pleas of the population of Algiers in 1516 to defend them against the looming Spanish threat. In need of backing, Khayr al-Din offered his services to the Ottoman sultan in 1519, who appointed him *beylerbey* (governor-general) of North Africa and dispatched contingents of janissary forces to the country.

To be sure, he would in 1520 temporarily be defeated by the religio-tribal leader of the Kuku tribe in Kabylie, acting in conjunction with the local Hafsid ruler. However, he would reconquer Algiers in 1525, and achieve the submission of the Kuku to Ottoman authority.[84] Over time, the Ottoman janissary units, known as the *ojaq,* would become the central ruling institution of a new administrative-territorial entity, Ottoman Algeria, whose greatest influence and independence would be achieved in the seventeenth century, thanks to agricultural wealth, a strong manufacturing sector, and corsairs that roved the Mediterranean and Atlantic waters. At its peak, as Phillip Naylor reminds us, Algiers would have over 100,000 inhabitants, and the regency would be sovereign in all but name, leading a nationalist Algerian historian writing in the 1960s to label it as an "Algerian Ottoman Republic."[85]

Moreover, the entry of Ottoman rule into the Central Maghrib laid important groundwork for the future modern-day territorial states of Algeria, Tunisia, and Libya. The Ibn Khaldunian cycle of tribal-religious conquest and subsequent decline was broken, as Khayr al-Din's original *beylerbeylik* was divided into three provinces, or regencies, based in Algiers, Tunis, and Tripoli, respectively. By the eighteenth century, Tunis and Tripoli would be ruled by independent hereditary dynasties, still loyal to the sultan but increasingly intertwined with native elites. By contrast, the Algeria *ojaq,* headed by a *dey,* largely remained a caste apart, dependent on the continuous influx of new recruits from the Ottoman east, and ideologically committed to their Turkish identity and ties to Constantinople, even as the importance of the Algerian province to the Sublime Porte would decline over time.[86] For their part, Berberophones largely remained in their more peripheral mountainous villages or served as mercenaries or auxiliary troops for the *dey* or often powerful provincial *beys.*

Alone among North African entities, the Moroccan sultanate managed to remain outside of Ottoman suzerainty. Sharifian descent became the legitimating formula for dynastic rule, first under the Saʿadians, in the late sixteenth century, and then, beginning one hundred years later, under the Alaouis.[87] Like the Ottoman regencies to the east, Moroccan rulers ultimately established a durable, if sometimes tenuous, preeminence over the country's disparate and geographically fragmented social groupings.

Whether in the Ottoman domains or the Moroccan sultanate, Berber populations were increasingly consigned to the periphery of society, and the Berbers as a named group gradually faded from view. Ironically, their marginalization came as the notoriety of the "Barbary states," a name apparently derived from the Arabic word for Berber,[88] spread throughout Europe, thanks to large-scale privateering by corsairs ("pirates," in the European discourse) against "infidel" shipping in the Mediterranean, carried out for both economic and religious reasons, and to the benefit of local rulers.

This does not mean, of course, that on the cultural level, Berbers ceased to contribute to the shaping of North African societies. As noted earlier, Hart pointed to the enduring, bedrock strata of Moroccan culture, particularly those themes connected to tribal forms of social organization, and identifies them as Berber. In the religious field, the Moroccan historian Mohamed el-Mansour suggests that we should see the importance of the Berber factor in the Maliki rites' adoption in and adaptation to the North African setting. The unchallenged supremacy in North Africa of the Maliki *madhhab,* unlike in other areas of the Muslim world, he postulates, derives directly from the fact that it best met the needs of Berber tribesmen. It was, he said, "formulated in a manner very similar to that of tribal customary law tables (*alwah*) found in every Berber village."[89] Moreover, given the fact that Maliki rites and jurisprudence are considered to be the most straightforward and least philosophical of the four Islamic schools of law, they could easily be transmitted in a simplified fashion, making them appropriate for illiterate Berber tribesmen who had difficulty mastering Arabic.[90] Paradoxically, a stress on the Berbers' lack of mastery of Arabic (with exceptions, of course) reinforces the notion of a deep-rooted Amazigh-speaking society up until modern times.[91]

The preeminent intellectual of the contemporary Moroccan Amazigh movement, Mohamed Chafik, rhetorically asks the same question that Mansour sought to answer, as he seeks to emphasize the Amazighité of North African Islam. Interested in the totality of Amazigh intellectual production as a tributary of Islamic culture, Chafik enumerates the numerous Amazigh Maliki scholars, while not forgetting to mention the Ibadi Kharijites as well. He also refers to a number of Imazighen who "left their indelible mark" on Islamic Sufi thought.[92] On the popular level, what is known as the *murabit* revolution in Morocco during the fifteenth century, the rise to prominence of religious orders centering on a purported holy man or miracle worker (*murabit*/shaykh/saint) and the resilience and continued deep-rootedness of Moroccan religious heteropraxis,[93] must also be understood in the context of enduring Berber culture synthesized with Islamic notions that provided more spiritual sustenance than Maliki legalism could offer.[94] Of course, memory is always selective, as much about forgetting as about remembering.[95] In this case, modern Amazigh memory workers interested in forging a usable past, and having a general preference for a post-Islamic identity, refrain from referring to episodes and aspects of the Berber Islamic experience that cast it in a negative light—the religious fanaticism of the Almohads, for example, which resulted in massacres and forced conversions of Jews, Christians, heretics, and other purported enemies.

Politically, as well, Berber tribes were a permanent part of the landscape and could be found on both sides of the mythical and overly rigid *makhzen/siba* dichotomy (see Chapter 2), ranging, in fact, across the spectrum from unswerving support and alliance with the central authorities to isolation and autonomy from it. Of course, their own fractious intertribal conflicts, later enshrined by colonial administrators and scholars as part of an allegedly ineffable Berber character, were also very much part of the story, and affected tribal-regime dynamics as well. In any case, over the course of the seventeenth and eighteenth centuries, the gradual weakening of Ottoman power vis-à-vis Christian European states, and the declining economic importance of the Mediterranean sea-lanes in the face of the growing transatlantic trade, left the Ottoman North African regencies and the Moroccan Sharifian Empire alike increasingly stagnant, weak, and ripe for foreign domination. To be sure, the challenges posed by Christian European states had been felt as early as the fifteenth century, and the Ottoman arrival in North Africa was part of a larger maneuvering for power and influence throughout the Mediterranean region. But now, the balance of power that had been established in earlier centuries began to irreversibly fray. European power projection was increasingly felt, beginning with economic penetration, which would eventually culminate in full-blown occupation. The effect throughout North Africa, and on its Berber communities in particular, would be profound and transformative.

France's conquest of Algiers in 1830 and initial years of rule constituted an "old-school" kind of imperial policy.[1] However, just as the Ottomans extended their rule of Algiers in an improvised, unplanned way and ended up maintaining a presence for three hundred years, the initial absence of French intention to permanently rule Algeria was soon superseded. The dynamics of France's conflict with the various tribal, ethnic, and regional groupings that together constituted the Muslim Algerian community, combined with the dialectical processes shaping the emergence of modern French identity, resulted in a venture unique to nineteenth-century colonialism: the destruction of precolonial elites, institutions, and ways of life and the incorporation of the territory into sovereign French territory. These actions were underpinned by large-scale European settlement and takeover of the country's most productive lands and a triumphalist ideology based on the concept of *mission civilisatrice*. France's imperial adventure in North Africa, the crown jewel of which was Algeria, would eventually lead it westward into Morocco, eastward to Tunisia, and southward into the Sahel. Ironically, Algeria and Morocco both owe much of their existence as independent states exercising sovereignty over their entire territories to the colonial experience, notwithstanding the bloody resistance to French conquest and, generations later, following World War II, the struggle by national movements to rid themselves of the French yoke. In Algeria's case, just as the French conquest and transformation of the country was extraordinarily violent, so too was the struggle for independence. The brutal eight-year war (1954–1962) was, for a long time, painted by Algerian nationalists in exclusively heroic terms; only now are the darker sides of those years beginning to be acknowledged.[2]

What of the Berber populations? Even as they sometimes offered the fiercest resistance to French penetration and conquest, the Berbers would come to occupy a special place in French thinking, a population whom ideologues and policy-makers would deem as potential partners in the colonial project. The results, in both practical and ideological terms, would vary in both time and place. But, like all other elements of Moroccan and Algerian societies, the Berber populations would be profoundly shaped by the experience, within their own communities, regarding relations with non-Berber elements in society, and with the French.

ALGERIA

On June 14, 1830, a French expeditionary force numbering 34,184 combatants landed on the shores of Ottoman Algeria, 27 kilometers west of Algiers. Its ostensible justification was punitive: three years earlier, Hussein Dey of Algiers had struck the French consul Pierre Deval three times on the arm with a flyswatter, in anger over a perceived insult. By July 5, it had conquered the city and its surroundings, expelled the Dey, and brought to an end nearly 300 years of Ottoman sway over the region and 1,100 years of Islamic rule.[3] Prior to French colonization, and notwithstanding its heyday in the seventeenth century, Algeria rarely, if ever, developed any significant power/civilizational centers of its own, sandwiched, as it were, between Tunis-centered Ifriqiya and al-Maghrib al-Aqsa (Fez, Marrakesh, etc.), and the degree of integration between state and society, if one can use these terms to describe premodern entities, was much less than in Tunis and less than in Morocco as well. Society was highly segmented, markets were fragile, and competition and rivalries among the different segments, and between them and the central government, were perpetual and often violent. Still, John Ruedy suggests, the widespread rebellions of coalitions of tribal and religious elites during the initial decades of the nineteenth century occasioned responses from the central authorities that may have set Algeria on a new course, had they been allowed to play themselves out. There were, he says, some indications that the office of the *dey* may have been on the way, between 1817 and 1830, toward becoming a proper monarchy, which would have rallied wider sectors of the population and formed the basis, eventually, for a more modern type of state-building project.[4] However, the French conquest put an end to that.

Algeria would not be just another overseas European colony, or even a nearby protectorate, as Morocco and Tunisia would become. Rather, the colonial project would claim Algeria as an integral part of metropolitan France, Algérie Française, and massively settle it with French citizens and a variety of groups from southern Europe, e.g., Spain, Corsica, and Malta, who over time were awarded French citizenship.[5] They and their descendants would number one million persons on the eve of Algerian independence in 1962, constituting approximately 11 percent of the country's total population. The impact of France's Algerian experience, on both Algeria's Muslim population and on France, would be profound and its consequences far-reaching and ongoing, right up until the present day.

Nowhere was this truer than in Kabylie, the Berber-speaking, mostly mountainous region east-southeast of Algiers. Constituting approximately two-thirds of all of Algeria's Berberophones,[6] Kabyles have been at the heart of the myriad aspects of French Algeria: violent subjugation, a complex and often contradictory "civilizing mission," the emergence of a modern Algerian Muslim identity project, and a brutal, no-holds-barred war for independence. One eventual outcome was the gradual fashioning of a modern Kabyle identity, within the larger Algerian Muslim population. As a group, the Kabyles eventually acquired some of the tools of "modernity," particularly the French language and a modicum of modern education, earlier than the rest of Algerian Muslim society, which ironically helped thrust them into the elite of the independence movement. However, from the moment of Algerian independence, Kabyle specificity would be situated uneasily within the body politic, often opposed to Algeria's new ruling forces. Over time, Kabyles would become the most politicized of all Berber groups and heavily shape Berberist discourse and practice throughout North Africa and the Diaspora.

The very name "Kabylie" ("land of the Kabyles," "Tamurt Leqvayel") suggests the indeterminate nature of the population's collective identity in precolonial times. Derived from the Arabic *qaba'il* ("tribes"), the term was reportedly in usage, sometimes interchangeably with *jiba'il* ("mountaineers"), during the sixteenth to eighteenth centuries with reference to the Berber-speaking highlanders of the Ottoman Algerian Regency.[7] It was formally applied by French colonial administrators, who subdivided the region into Grande Kabylie and Petite Kabylie. The population was organized into tribal groupings, numbering 126, 70 of which constituted political units organized into approximately 12 tribal confederations living in approximately 1,700 villages,[8] with some kind of larger, albeit loose, collective solidarity expressed through their identification with Sufi brotherhoods and affiliated marabouts. More broadly, it is fair to say that the centuries-old processes of linguistic Arabization across North Africa had touched the Kabyle heartland far more slowly than in the lowlands. At the same time, the region was hardly a closed space. The harshness of temperatures, rocky terrain, dense forests, and poor soil quality stimulated emigration to more hospitable climes among the Arabs of the plains and coastal areas, and the development of a Kabyle trade network involving the manufacture and sale to the Arabs of commercial crafts, spearhead by members of the Rahmaniyya religious brotherhood.[9] Both aspects of Kabyle duality—strong manifestations of tribal and language-based particularism anchored by a religious order, along with a network of social, economic, and political interactions with the wider world—would be heavily influenced by French colonialism.

France's conquest of Algeria was piecemeal, owing in part to the difficulties involved, and even more so to differences within the French leadership over goals and means. Owing to its forbidding topography, Kabylie was initially avoided as France struggled to extend its control across the northern portion of the country, from west to east. Most Kabyles themselves had viewed the Emir Abd al-Qadir, the charismatic sharifian son of the head of the Qadriyya order based in the western Oran region and leader of an anti-French coalition between 1832 and 1847, as another seeker of power, and thus remained largely aloof, a point that did not escape French attention. But by the end of the 1840s, the logic of France's conquest, now being increasingly wedded to the settler-colonial project, dictated the conquest of Kabylie's Djurdjura massif as well. The strategic garrison town of Fort National was established in 1857 as a "throne in the eye of Kabylie," and formal resistance ceased for a time.

By this point, already, French military and civilian officials were hard at work gathering basic data regarding this new subject population for the purpose of more efficient control. This enterprise took many forms and included a keen interest in the cultural underpinnings of the society. For example, Colonel Adolphe Hanoteau (1814–1897) collected over fifty Kabyle poems and songs, which he believed would reveal the essence of the Kabyle personality and level of intellectual and moral development.[10] The story of the Kahina's resistance to Muslim invaders captured the imagination of French writers, who drew parallels to the martyrdom of Jeanne d'Arc and retold and elaborated on the story in ways that suited the colonial project.[11] Out of these efforts was born the Kabyle Myth, or "Vulgate," a series of beliefs and ideological constructs that would heavily shape French perceptions and policies toward North Africa in subsequent decades. At the core of this worldview, which was in line with nineteenth-century racialist and social Darwinist theories, was the belief that the Berbers were higher on the pecking order of human civilization than Arabs. French ideologues built up an elaborate image of the Kabyles as a people whose origins were European, who had once been mainly Christian and had been Islamized only superficially, as demonstrated by what was seen as their essentially primitive, naturalistic folk religion. These clannish, brutish mountain men appeared to Europeans as being similar to medieval Scotsmen or Provençals, and thus appropriate raw material for the guiding hand of civilization to be provided by enlightened French administration.[12] Moreover, this leading civilization itself was the self-designated inheritor of Rome, whose historic role was to complete Rome's civilizing mission by regaining the lost territories of Latin North Africa.[13] A series of dichotomies supposedly depicting the main contours of the population of the newly conquered areas was thus laid out: sedentary versus nomad, mountain versus plain, Berber versus Arab, Occident versus Orient, folk religion and Christianity versus Islam.

Colonial policies would profoundly affect Kabyle society. But, as Mohammed Harbi has written, there is no need to look for explanations of Kabyle specificity in colonial ethnological clichés regarding Berber irredentism, theories of anti-oriental Berberism, or sociological naïveté regarding the primitive communism of "free republics" of Kabylie. Rather, the explanation for its particularity can be found in the convergence of several factors, including its partial and delayed Arabization, and consequently the survival of Berber culture; the contribution of colonial policies to the eventual formation of the Kabyle elite; its role as human reservoir for immigration, external and internal; and the underlying social cohesion of Kabyle society. As a result, Kabylie and its inhabitants would find themselves at the heart of Algeria's sociopolitical and cultural problems, both past and present.[14]

The complex realities in Algeria and France quickly muddied colonial concepts. Following his visit to Algiers in 1860, Emperor Napoleon III sought to create circumstances for meaningful coexistence of Muslims and Algerians within the framework of French sovereignty, proclaiming his desire to establish an "Arab kingdom" (*royaume arabe*) under French tutelage, and rejecting the notion of state ownership of all of Algeria's lands. French settlers were keenly worried about these developments, while drawing strength from the appointment in 1867, to the position of archbishop of Algiers, of Charles Martial Allemand Lavigerie, who militantly advocated assimilation and conversion to Christianity of Algeria's Muslims. France's resounding military defeat by Prussia in 1870 brought an end to the Second Empire and the assumption of civilian rule in Paris and Algiers, putting paid to Napoleon III's pipe dream of comity between Algeria's Muslims and European settlers and interests. Meanwhile, the late 1860s were terrible times for Algeria's Muslim population. Three hundred thousand died of a cholera epidemic in 1868, as did half of the cattle, and famine was wide-spread. In Kabylie, the ruling *khalifa,* Mohamed al-Moqrani, found himself backed into a corner. His father had cooperated with the French in their struggle against Abd al-Qadir and been rewarded with the appointment as *khalifa* of Grande Kabylie in 1838, with Moqrani inheriting the post in 1853. However, as the French expanded their direct control and extended their land confiscations, his resources were diminished, including the loss of the right of corvée labor. The breaking point came when his guarantee of debts of tribesmen during the famine could not be made good, at a time when his backers among the French military authorities lost power to the incoming civilians. Seeking a way out, Moqrani launched what was intended to be a limited rebellion. However, it quickly ballooned into a wider uprising, encompassing a 300 km long swath of territory and one-third of the entire Muslim Algerian population. Moqrani himself tried to cut a deal with the French authorities but was killed in action.[15]

The war was ruinous for Algerian Muslims, and particularly for the Kabyles: not only did many thousands die in the fierce fighting, a war indemnity of 36.5 million francs, ten times the annual tribute, was imposed; all lands of tribes that had participated in the rebellion were sequestered; and 70 percent of the capital of those involved was levied, in either land or indemnity. One-third of the indemnity was allocated to French victims of the rebellion, and the rest was devoted to expanding colonization. From that point on, up until World War I, Algeria's Muslims would have no alternative to surviving as best they could under a system geared entirely to the needs of an ever-expanding settler colonial society and systematically seeking to undermine and control existing Islamic institutions, particularly the *habous*—the pious endowments that underpinned Islamic charitable, educational, and legal functions.[16] Accommodation and even cooperation with the authorities were now a matter of survival and in some cases actually enabled the continued preservation of elements of precolonial culture and institutions.[17]

The fact that Kabylie had been the center of the anti-French uprising must have given pause to the advocates of the Kabyle Vulgate. Nonetheless, whether for security reasons, an unshakable faith that Kabyles could be transformed into junior partners in the colonial enterprise, or both, Kabylie received a disproportionate share of French attention in the coming decades. To be sure, the lion's share of governmental expenditures on education was directed to the steadily increasing European population. For example, in the year 1912, 82 percent of educational spending was directed toward the children of Europeans, and less than 18 percent toward Muslim children, even though there were six times as many Muslim schoolchildren as there were Europeans. But within this miserly allocation, the proportion allocated to the Kabyles stood out: As of 1882, half of the seventy-five schools established for Muslim children were located in Kabylie. Taxes were lighter than in other areas, the functioning of the village councils (*tajmaʿat*) as a judicial forum at the expense of the *qadi* was encouraged, efforts were made to codify Kabyle customary law (*izerf*) for the purpose of supplanting Shariʿa law, numerous *qadis* (judges) of Islamic law had their positions abolished or reduced to the status of notaries and were encouraged to deliver their judgments in French, and French names were given to towns. French interest was also manifested in the academy: in 1885, a chair in Berber studies was established in the Faculty of Letters of what would eventually become the University of Algiers.[18] Inevitably, France's fierce debates at that time over its own national identity, particularly the role of religion and state, ensured that Kabylie would be an additional arena of contestation. As part of the Catholic Church's efforts, Cardinal Lavigerie established the Pères Blancs (White Fathers) order, whose goal was to convert Kabyles to Christianity.[19] Although the number of Kabyles who actually did so was minuscule, it was probably higher than among any other Muslim community in the Middle East.[20]

The results of France's special attention would be manifold, at once strengthening and transforming Kabyle particularity. Kabyles were drawn more closely into the French cultural orbit, with French becoming their second language to an even greater extent than among the rest of Algeria's Muslims. They thus eventually acquired the tools by which they would attain disproportionate influence within Algerian Muslim society, which was being led by French rule, willy-nilly, along the path of greater national integration. As with much of the rest of Algeria's rural population, the combination of land confiscation for colonial purposes and increasing population growth, beginning in the 1880s, made it ever more difficult to eke out an existence, resulting in the increased movement of Kabyles down from the mountains to Algerian cities in the plains and along the coast in search of a livelihood. This would eventually lead to the emergence of an important stratum of merchants, capitalist farmers, and white collar professionals such as doctors, lawyers, administrators, and teachers. Decades later, this would be translated into an overrepresentation of Kabyles in the Algerian state apparatus. Indeed, between 1891 and 1950, nearly all of the state-recruited teachers for Algiers were Kabyles.[21] Ironically for France, Kabyles would also come to have considerable influence in the independence movement, as the colonial enterprise would inexorably promote political and economic integration not just of the country's territory, but also of its population. This would include the spread of spoken Algerian Arabic among the Kabyles and the weakening of the Kabyle language, much to the dismay of colonial officials.

Another important outcome of France's Kabyle orientation was that Kabyle emigration patterns were also reoriented toward France, beginning at the end of the nineteenth century, and became numerically significant in the years after World War I. By the mid-1920s, the number of North African workers in France totaled about 100,000. Of these, the vast majority were Algerians, most of whom, in turn, were Kabyles. Their politicization soon followed: in 1926, the Étoile Nord Africaine (North African Star; ENA), the first permanent Maghribi political organization in France, headed by Messali al-Hajj (who himself was an Arabophone, not a Kabyle), was founded with the support of the French Communist Party. By the mid-1930s, it had largely divested itself of the Communists' internationalist agenda in favor of an explicitly nationalist one. Messali began to attract followers inside Algeria as well, and the seeds for Algeria's war of independence were planted. As the most Westernized group in Algerian Muslim society, Kabyles disproportionately joined political parties, unions, and student associations, further contributing to their preeminence during the fight for independence.

An essential component of the nationalists' rejection of French domination was the articulation of a modern Algerian identity, based on territory, Islam, and affiliation with the Arab world. This formula, articulated by *salafi*-minded reformist *ulama,* led by Shaykh Abdul Hamid Bin Badis, rejected the path advocated by the *evolués,* the narrow stratum of French-educated Algerian white collar professionals, epitomized by Ferhat Abbas. It was Abbas who declared in 1936 that "the Algerian *patrie* is a myth. I have not found it. I have questioned history, I have questioned the living and the dead, I have visited the cemeteries—no one has spoken to me of it." The fate of Algerian Muslims, he insisted, was bound up with France, which should be true to itself and confer equal rights upon its Muslim citizens.[22] The *evolués* probably never had a chance of developing a "third way" that would somehow bridge the political, social, and cultural divide between Algeria's Muslims and Europeans. But the power of the French settler community, within Algeria and in the halls of power in Paris, rendered stillborn any substantive attempts at ameliorating the Algerian Muslims' status and avoiding the descent into unspeakable violence and bloodshed that would tear Algeria apart and eventually bring about what had long been deemed unimaginable—France's disengagement and withdrawal from its prized possession across the Mediterranean Sea.

As James McDougall has shown, the question of Berber identity was very much on the mind of the Algerian *salafi* reformers. Concurrent with France's 1930 centenary celebration of its conquest of Algeria, three works were published tying Algeria to the Mashriq. The historian Tawfiq al-Madani presented the Arab-Muslim conquest of North Africa in a way which sought to demonstrate that Arabs and Berbers were not irreconcilable, adopting and elaborating on long-standing Muslim narratives that placed the Berbers within the realm of the Semitic East. Initial Berber resistance, he said, was due to the Berbers' misinterpretation of the Arabs' intentions, assuming that they were like previous conquerors who simply sought to exploit them. He presented their commanders, Kusayla and the Kahina, as honorable, repeating the old story that the Kahina entrusted the Muslim general Hassan bin al-Nu'man with her two sons. Eventually, he said, the Berbers came to understand that the Arab conquerors were the harbingers of civilization and that Islam offered them equality. Another *salafi* writer, Mubarak Milli, accused the French historian Henri Garrot of defaming the Kahina, "a great Berber queen," by claiming that she had run away and hidden in a tunnel. In a direct reversal of the French grand narrative, which depicted the post-Roman North Africa as an unadulterated story of decline, obscurantism, decay, and exploitation, the *salafi* historians insisted that it was Islam which brought civilization and enlightenment to the region, with the implication being that the process would repeat itself in the modern era.[23]

Arab-Islamic identity remained the foundation of Algerian nationalism throughout the anticolonial movement. Still, it was not bereft of controversy. In 1948–1949, an episode known as the "Berberist crisis" pitted young Communist-leaning Kabyle intellectuals and activists drawn from secondary schools and universities against Messali's domination of the nationalist movement and the dominant formula of Arab-Islamic Algeria. Algerian identity, they declared, was intimately linked with the population's employment of Berber dialects and Algerian colloquial Arabic, as opposed to the modern standard Arabic being developed in Egypt and the Fertile Crescent, with which most Algerians were not familiar. Not surprisingly, the advocates of this view were secular, and distant from religion. They were also more militant than the nationalist movement's leadership, favoring immediate armed insurrection, and were unhappy with what they viewed as the undemocratic nature of the movement.[24]

The political and cultural seeds of this dissident current in the national-ist movement had been sown in previous decades. The assertion of Kabyle Berber specificity within the Algerian national movement was an out-growth of what can only be termed a budding cultural nationalism. Al-ready, back in 1925, Si Amar Ou Saïd Boulifa had authored *Djurdjura dans l'histoire*. Even earlier, in 1904, he published the first collection of poems (*Isefra*) of the venerated Kabylian writer and poet Si Mohand U M'hand. As Jane Goodman points out, Boulifa partially perpetuated the terms of the Kabyle Myth in his framing essay and notes, but also sought to counter Hanoteau's effort to authoritatively determine the nature of Kabyle culture by "return[ing] the interpretation of poetry to indigenous hands."[25] Within the ENA, a first generation of Kabyle nationalists emerged, all educated in the French system and with a middle-class background. For them, there was no contradiction between nationalism and Kabyle-Berber tradition: for example, in a speech attacking the Italian occupation of Ethiopia in 1935, Amar Imache, the ENA's secretary-general and Messali's rival, picked up the slogan "l'Afrique aux Africains," and emphasized the historical con-tinuity of the Berbers in their resistance to foreign rule and assimilation.[26] For Imache, as for Berber culturalists ever since, opposing assimilation did not preclude being steeped in the ways of the French language and culture, while also emphasizing fidelity to the Berber language and communal vil-lage traditions, which could and should underpin the political culture of an independent Algeria. Since 1945, supporters of Kabyle Berber specificity within an emerging Algerian national identity were recruited from among Francophile intellectuals, including Christians. Thus began the amalgama-tion of modern Berberism and supporters of the French language, adding a further complication to Algeria's subsequent language wars. These were also years in which Kabyle youth, organized under the banner of "Scouts musulmans en Kabyle," were mobilized around the national idea with a Berber component, composing nationalist hymns in the Kabyle language.[27]

The response to the Kabyle activists' challenge in 1948–1949 was fierce. Messali felt threatened enough to condemn their ideas as "Berberism," which Algerian *ulama* decried as a "reactionary doctrine of imperialism" designed to divide the Algerian people. Kabyle media outlets were de-nounced for such alleged sins as broadcasting the poem "La message de Yougourtha" by Mohammed Cherif Sahli and a play called *La Kahena* by A. Nekli.[28] Kabyles would not be real Algerians, it was said, so long as they continued to speak the "jargon" that "burns our ears." Sheikh Bashir al-Ibrahimi, the head of the Algerian *ulama,* declared that the Islamization of North Africa had brought the Berbers out of the "dark ages," liberating them from an imposed misfortune. The submission of the Berbers to the Arabs was, he said, brotherly and respectful, and not a criminal or violent one.[29] The crisis was resolved bureaucratically by exclusion of spokesmen of the Berberist approach from the ranks of the Parti du peuple algérien-Mouvement pour le triomphe des libertés démocratiques (PPA-MTLD), the main Algerian nationalist party, the most militant anti-Arab of them being Rachid Ali Yahia, who had a leading role in the party's activities in France. The "Berbero-materialists" were eliminated from power by fellow Kabyles Abane Ramdane, Belkacem Krim, and the future Colonel (Ait Hamouda) Amrouche. Ironically, they would all later be charged by their adversaries within the FLN as being "Berberists" themselves.[30]

How should the "Berberist crisis" be viewed, historically? Clearly, the failure of the so-called "Berberists" to gain any traction, politically speaking, demonstrates the marginal nature of their efforts vis-à-vis the Kabyle public. Nonetheless, it serves as a reminder that the Algerian nationalist project was not a one-size-fits-all affair, and was in fact superimposed uneasily over Algeria's ethnic, tribal, and geographical divisions. This, of course, is hardly unique in the experience of nationalist movements. In Algeria's case, though, the shortcomings and limitations of state-building and nation-building in the pre-independence years would contribute to the high level of violence within the Muslim community during the war of independence. These shortcomings would take on new forms after independence. One eventual manifestation would be the intensification and expansion of the Berberist current in opposition to the state authorities and the official version of Algerian national identity. This does not mean that the 1949 "Berberist crisis" was an inevitable precursor of what was to come, but it certainly did demonstrate that Algerian Muslims hardly spoke in one voice, and that the Berber-Arab ethnic cleavage could, under certain circumstances, pose challenges to national unity.

Juxtaposed with the Berberist militants in 1949 was another Kabyle, Hocine Ait Ahmed, who subsequently attained the status of one of the historic leaders (*chefs historiques*) of the revolution. Ait Ahmed had impeccable familial credentials: the house in which he was born, in 1919, was a pilgrimage site, owing to his late grandfather, Cheikh Mohand el Hocine, one of the spiritual leaders of the Rahmaniyya brotherhood and known for his resistance to French rule. His mother's family contained a similar anticolonial background. Of course, as was commonly the case in Algeria, the dichotomy of resistance to, versus acceptance of, colonial rule was not the whole story for his family: Ait Ahmed's father was a *caid* (*qa'id;* local government official) and rich farmer, i.e., prospering under French rule, and sending his son for schooling in a French *lycée.*[31]

Ait Ahmed challenged Messali on the grounds of the latter's excessive monopolization of power and unwillingness to adopt more militant action against the French, not on the basis of an explicitly Berber or Kabyle agenda. He subsequently wrote that conservatives and legalists used Berberist tendencies of more radical elements of the nationalist movement as a pretext to remove them from power.[32] Nonetheless, Ait Ahmed's power base would remain overwhelmingly Kabyle. During the years of struggle against France and the subsequent decades, Ait Ahmed's activities, guided by the notion that Kabyles were the avant-garde of Algerian patriotism, would reflect much of the complexity and ambiguity of the Berbers' place in Algerian society.[33]

Ait Ahmed was hardly the only prominent Kabyle. In fact, Kabyles played an essential role in the struggle for independence, at both the elite and mass levels. From 1947 onward, a small group of Kabyles under the leadership of Belkacem Krim clandestinely organized anti-French activities.[34] Ait Ahmed joined them in 1949. They became the core group of the FLN-led 1954 revolt, whose first shots were fired on November 1 in Kabylie. Thanks to the insistence of Krim, Kabylie was defined as one of the six autonomous zones of battle, and not divided up administratively into two, as the (Kabyle!) spokesman of the revolutionary leadership, Mourad Didouche, advocated. It would seem that Kabylie's importance as a center for resistance to French rule reinforced the prominent place that its population already had in all strands of the Algerian independence movement. By late 1956, Kabyles held commanding positions or were disproportionately represented in nearly every political and military grouping involved in the struggle against French rule, both in Algeria and in France. Two of the five members of the leading Comité de Coordination et d'Exécution (CCE) were Kabyles, and six of the seventeen members of an expanded council were Berbers (five Kabyles and one Chaoui). After reorganization, three of the nine members of the inner circle, the Comité Révolutionnaire d'Unité et d'Action (CRUA), were Kabyles.[35]

However, the 1949 episode left its imprint on the suspicious and often contentious leadership of the national movement, adding another layer of stress to an already extremely difficult situation. For example, the fear of regionalism, underpinned by the awareness of Kabyle particularity, was apparent during the FLN's constitutional discussions of 1954.[36] Alistair Horne states that one of the reasons that the nine leading figures of the movement opted for the principle of collective leadership through the CRUA was that picking either an Arab or a Kabyle to head it "might have run the grave risk of alienating one or other race" [*sic*].[37] The prominence of the Kabyles among the leadership was used against them by their adversaries in the movement, who played on the undercurrent of ethnic tensions referred to guardedly in the war diary of one of the leading Kabyle intellectuals of those years, Mouloud Feraoun.[38] Tensions between the inside and outside movement leaderships during the eight years of war reached a peak following the FLN's first Congress, convened by the inside leadership in the Soummam valley in the heart of Kabylie during August–September 1956. The gathering, and the platform that emerged, tendered a guiding vision of the Algerian revolution striving for "the rebirth of an Algerian state as a democratic and social republic and not for the restoration of a monarchy or a theocracy of a bygone age."[39] The conference was deemed by the external leadership as a direct challenge to their authority; the ensuing tensions also had a Berberist component. As part of the nationalists' bitter internal power struggle in 1956–1957, Ben Bella and Boudiaf circles accused the Kabyles of wanting to take over the revolution. Debates over the unification of the army found Krim demanding equal representation between Berberophones and Arabophones. He eventually lost out, as did the officers in Kabylie who had followed him, thanks primarily to the shift in power to the external leadership following the harsh defeat inflicted by the French on the internal forces in 1956–1957. The Kabyles thus lost much of their preeminence in the movement's leadership. To be sure, the motives for the eventual murders of Krim and Ramdane were not sectarian per se; nor was the post-1962 crackdown on Hocine Ait Ahmed's followers in Kabylie purely, or even primarily, an ethnic matter (see Chapter 3). Nonetheless, one cannot dismiss the Kabyle dimension of either the Algerian nationalist movement or of post-independence politics. Hugh Roberts even goes so far as to say that the defeat of the internal leadership greatly damaged the process of Kabyle political integration into the Algerian Muslim nation.[40] Ethnicity, then, may be a generally weak and largely dependent variable, but one ignores it at one's peril.

MOROCCO

In some respects, Morocco Berber realities and the experience under colonialism resemble those of Algeria: the division into distinct geographical areas; the tribal nature of traditional society; the importance of Islamic Sufi-centered brotherhoods in social and religious life; strong resistance, but also accommodation at times, to the French colonial power, which sought to play the Berber card against the urban Arabophone elites to strengthen its rule; and active participation in the nationalist struggle for independence. At the same time, the Moroccan experience differed in significant ways, historically, demographically, and socially.

In terms of self-definition, including its institutional and cultural underpinnings, Morocco possesses many of the attributes that one usually associates with states considered to have a relatively high level of cohesion. The modern Moroccan state traces its origins to the establishment of the Idrissid dynasty at the end of the eighth century by a descendant of the Prophet Mohamed, in the early phase of the Islamization of North Africa. Since that time, ruling dynasties have come and gone, and the extent of their rule has expanded and contracted, but a political and societal center has existed in Morocco's core area pretty much ever since.[41] By way of comparison, among the other Arab countries, only Egypt can be said to have a greater, and historically more enduring, degree of "stateness" than Morocco.[42] A symbolic aspect of Morocco's "stateness" over the *longue durée* is the mausoleum of Mawlay Idriss II, in the heart of Fez's thousand-year-old medina. Idriss's father had founded the town, and the nucleus of what would be the first Moroccan Islamic dynasty, in 789. His son made it his capital in 810. The shrine, built around his tomb, which was "discovered" in 1437,[43] is frequented by a steady stream of supplicants asking for divine intercession. No other Arab-Muslim state venerates its founder in such a fashion, combining political and religious attributes in a daily rite of affirmation.

Geography and topography both had much to do with the fact that Morocco was the only portion of North Africa that didn't fall under Ottoman suzerainty. Up until the end of the nineteenth century, Morocco's geographical remoteness from the East and relative unimportance for Europe allowed it to maintain a degree of social and political distinctiveness and continuity, and avoid some of the worst, most traumatic aspects of European imperialism. That said, Morocco was hardly a peaceful oasis. Its political system has been pointedly described as "a stable system of violence," in which the raison d'être of a rudimentary military and administrative apparatus (*makhzen*: lit., storehouse, strongbox, or treasury), headed by the sultan, the commander and defender of the faithful, was the collection of taxes to pay the army to crush the tribes to collect still more taxes.[44] Moreover, European economic penetration had begun much earlier, in the coastal regions. Political and military domination would follow.

As France strove to consolidate and extend its control over Algeria in the decades after the 1871 uprising, it would be driven inexorably toward greater involvement in Moroccan affairs. These were years in which the whole of North Africa, from the Atlantic to the eastern Mediterranean coast, became increasingly the object of rival European machinations. France would establish its protectorate over Tunisia in 1881, Great Britain would seize full control of Egypt in 1882, and Tripolitania and Cyrenaica would fall under Italian sway in 1911. Morocco, the only remaining independent entity in North Africa, was the subject of fierce competition for influence among Great Britain, Spain, and Germany, as well as France, a competition that on some level allowed it to maintain at least formal independence as European powers shied away from anything that might stimulate a chain reaction of steps by others. Following the ignominious military defeats at the hands of France in 1844 at Isly, and of Spain in 1860 at Tetouan, the *makhzen* sought to adopt reform measures in both the military and financial spheres in order to better cope with the expanding challenges from across the Mediterranean. However, these were only desultory efforts, a pale shadow of the Ottoman Empire's policies of defensive modernization. By the end of the century, if the Ottoman Empire was the "sick man of Europe," the Sharifian Moroccan Empire was essentially catatonic, having lost control of its finances to European commercial and governmental interests, and being riven by internal divisions and challenges and thus ripe for complete subordination.[45] Calculated to avoid a repeat of the difficulties faced in subduing Algeria, France's official policy toward the Sharifian Kingdom at the beginning of the twentieth century was, in its own words, one of "peaceful penetration," which would later evolve into "pacification." One cannot help but be cynical of the term, let alone avoid the sexual connotations of rape first contained in de Tocqueville's much earlier advocacy of the "unveiling" of Algerian Muslim society by the conquering "enlightened" French civilization. Indeed, by the time that France completed its "pacification" of Morocco in 1934, an estimated twenty-seven thousand French soldiers (the majority of them local Berber tribesmen recruited into the French military as auxiliary forces, who became known as *goumiers*) had been killed in the process, along with untold numbers of those resisting France's overtures.

In fact, France never had one single method for gaining control and ruling Morocco, as could hardly be expected, given the country's geographical and social diversity. Military penetration into the tribal lands of the Moroccan periphery, beginning with those bordering French Algeria, was guided by the "oil stain" (*tache d'huile*) theory, namely, the establishment of French outposts of power and civilian services on the edge of specific tribal regions, to entice the local population into cooperative relationships. French influence, so the thinking went, would thus spread like an oil stain, and the strategy was then to be repeated in the next area. Of course, in the face of resistance, other, less benign means were to be used.

More than anyone else, the author of this approach, and of France's grand strategy toward Morocco in the first decades of the century, was Marshal Hubert Lyautey. Having served in Algeria, Lyautey was determined to demonstrate respect for Morocco's indigenous traditions and social structures, while ensuring the extension and consolidation of French control and the remaking of the country in ways that were commensurate with French interests. This approach was enshrined in the 1912 Treaty of Fez, which formally established the French protectorate. The treaty took great care to preserve the shell of existing Moroccan institutions, and particularly the sultanate, and the personal standing of the sultan, while essentially removing the Sharifian Empire from the family of nations, as it lost its independence, both internally and in the field of foreign relations.[46] This paternalism was full of contradictions, to be sure, but did result in a lesser degree of societal upheaval and destruction than had occurred in Algeria.

A special variant of French paternalism would be developed regarding Morocco's Berber speakers, who on the eve of the French takeover still constituted a decisive majority of all Moroccan Muslims. France's image of the Berbers would help guide its policies and be integrated into an overall worldview regarding the nature of Moroccan society and political life.

French officials and scholars initially knew very little about the complexities of Morocco's diverse and far-flung Berber communities, and were quite guarded in their evaluations. However, it wasn't long before the weight of *la mythe Kabyle* made itself felt and was adapted to fit Moroccan circumstances.[47] Hence, the obvious political, social, and economic differences between urban settled life and the rural-tribal world formed the basis of a comprehensive, albeit flawed, understanding of Moroccan history and the country's political and social structures. This can be summed up via the *blad al-makhzen-blad as-siba* dichotomy, the first connoting the areas ruled by the sultan, and the second, the "lands of dissidence," beyond the sultan's authority. This dichotomy exerted a powerful hold on generations of Western scholars, and has only recently been supplanted by more nuanced explanations underscoring the continuum of relations that always existed between the sultan and his subjects in the *siba,* even when they were in conflict, or when the sultan's weakness prevented him from being able to assert his authority and collect the expected tributes.[48] Once fashioned, the *makhzen-siba* conceptual dichotomy was then mechanically applied to the population: The *makhzen* was characterized as a strictly hierarchical authority, from the sultan, the *amir al-mu'minin* (Commander of the Faithful),[49] on down, composed of primarily urban city dwellers who were ethnically Arab or had been Arabized, and who adhered to orthodox Islam of the Maliki school, with their lives regulated by the Shari'a. The *siba,* by contrast, was understood to be composed of primarily acephalous rural-tribal groupings living in uneasy balance with one another, while practicing an internal self-government via *tajmaʿat,* which constituted a form of rudimentary democracy. Although Moroccan Berber society and "tribalism" are in fact by no means coterminous,[50] the Berberité of so much of the Moroccan countryside inexorably led the French authorities to reify the *makhzen-siba*/Arab–Berber dichotomy, and incorporate it into diverse policies for different regions, all under the classic imperial dictum of *divide et impera.*

For France, divide and rule also meant permitting Spain to have control over its traditional sphere of interest in the north of Morocco, as well as over remote enclaves in the far south. However, Spain's capabilities of imposing order were not those of France. Hence, before further examination of the French protectorate years, one must refer to the most significant rebellion in the twentieth century involving Berber communities—the 1921–1926 war in the Rif region against Spanish rule, led by Mohamed bin Abdelkrim al-Khattabi, whose Rifian Republic would temporarily unite the Berber tribes of the region and whose ultimate suppression required French intervention.

Who was Abdelkrim, and what was the nature of the rebellion that, at its peak, inflicted the most catastrophic defeat on any colonial army in the twentieth century, at the battle of Annual from July 22 to August 9, 1921, where more than ten thousand Spanish soldiers died, including their commanding general Manuel Fernández Silvestre, who may or may not have committed suicide, and thousands more were captured?[51] What was the meaning of the Rifian Republic that he established? Should Abdelkrim be best understood as a traditional tribal chieftain who sought to maximize the power of his tribe, the Ait Waryaghar, over other tribes through conquest and domination? Along these same lines, does the Rifian rebellion fall into the category of "primary resistance" to colonialism, i.e., one not imbued with modern nationalist ideologies and organizational structures, but rather motivated by a tribal-*jihadi* ethos in opposition to the West?[52] Alternatively, is Abdelkrim best situated in the stream of Islamic reformism that was washing over North Africa and the Middle East in those years?[53] If so, how can this be reconciled with his admiration for Turkey's Kemal Attatürk as a modernizer and nation-builder? Was Abdelkrim a Moroccan nationalist? Did he see himself as an alternative to the sultan? And how is his legacy contested today between Amazigh activists, for whom he is an iconic figure, and the official national narrative? All of these questions remain relevant, and not just for the disinterested historian.

In a comparative examination of the religious influences on the thoughts and actions of Abdelkrim and Algeria's Abd al-Qadir, the leader of the first organized resistance to French conquest in Algeria a century earlier, Pessah Shinar emphasizes Abdelkrim's purely Berber, non-Arab, and non-sharifian origins, as a member of a leading clan in the Banu Wuriaghal (Waryaghar) tribe. Abdelkrim's relatively short term of studies at Fez's venerable Qarawiyyin University, he says, was unlikely to have given him a solid grounding in Arabic and Islamic culture. However, it was sufficient to confer upon him status and prestige among his illiterate fellow tribesmen.[54] He would eventually become chief *qadi* in the Spanish presidio of Mellila, as well as holding a variety of functions in the Spanish zone of influence. Thus, for almost two decades prior to the rebellion, Abdelkrim acquired knowledge of and familiarity with European ways, and even had a number of Spanish friends.

The combination of tribal standing, religious knowledge, and understanding of European power politics put him in good stead. Shinar sees Abdelkrim as creating an embryonic state that combined a mixture of traditional and modern features—a national assembly (a modern form), but composed of the chiefs of Berber tribal councils, and a republic, a modern term, but denoting in this case a confederation of autonomous tribes. Abdelkrim's actions, he says, were "the first manifestation of modern militant Arabo-Berber[!] nationalism and Islamic modernism in a purely Berber environment."[55] In that vein, Abdelkrim had no sympathy for maraboutism or Sufism, and sought to limit the influence of the *turuq* (religious orders), in line with *salafi* thinking. Overall, says Shinar, Abdelkrim's experience with Rifi maraboutism was a bitter one, which he himself subsequently acknowledged.[56]

Strangely, Shinar concludes his insightful analysis by emphasizing the irony of how "a dissident Berber movement was able to fire the enthusiasm and imagination and speed the growth of nationalism among sophisticated urban young men of the bourgeois class that had little in common with the rude and rapacious mountain tribes, whom it was traditionally taught to fear and despise."[57] But in fact, the Moroccan Arab urban class essentially shared the views of the colonial press, which painted Abdelkrim as a *rogui,* a rebellious, fanatical, and ignorant tribal pretender to the throne of the Sharifian Empire. At the moment of truth, the urbanites of Fez did not rise up on Abdelkrim's behalf, when his forces were camped only 40 km from the city. Rather, they sat on their hands while French forces overwhelmed him, ensuring the continuation of the protectorate, and the preeminence of the sultan and the urban Arab elites. Abdelkrim was exiled, and would never return to Morocco, even after independence was achieved, dying in Cairo in 1963.

The Moroccan political class during the protectorate years would continue to hold relatively dim views of Abdelkrim. While eventually recognizing him as a *mujahid* battling for freedom against the imperialist powers, they could hardly be happy with the exiled Abdelkrim's rejection of all political activities, as opposed to military ones, as being a "waste of time."[58] Their ambivalence toward him apparently derived from concern over doing anything that would diminish the status of the sultan and the urban Arabic-speaking classes. It was, after all, the latter who formed the political backbone of the subsequent nationalist movement, and who had been largely passive, and even supportive of the protectorate, during the Rif rebellion.

By the end of the 1920s, French officials viewed their standing in North Africa with satisfaction. In Algeria, this would be expressed in gala (and to Algerian Muslims insulting) celebrations in 1930 observing the one hundredth anniversary of France's conquest of Algiers, which included a reenactment of the events in full period costumes.[59] That same year, in Tunisia, a Eucharistic Conference was organized by the archbishop of Carthage, an event that Habib Bourguiba, the first president of independent Tunisia, later said had marked the beginning of his nationalist commitment.[60] In Morocco, the French seemed to have complete control over the area they defined as *le Maroc utile* ("Useful Morocco," areas with economic worth), plus the areas necessary to protect them (*le Maroc necessaire*),[61] while the Abdelkrim episode was receding into the past without complications. Definitive subjugation of the last vestiges of Berber tribal resistance in the Middle and High Atlas Mountains was clearly just a matter of time and would be completed within four years. However, at precisely this moment the French authorities inadvertently sparked the beginning of organized opposition among the urban educated classes, particularly the younger generation,[62] activity that is universally considered to mark the birth of the Moroccan national movement. What was France's mistake? It pushed the "Berber button," in a way that could not be ignored, by highlighting the Berber-Arab dichotomy in religious terms. On May 16, 1930, it issued what quickly became known as the "Berber *dahir*" (an administrative edict, signed by the sultan, i.e., with the force of law), which explicitly formalized the status of Berber councils in tribal areas, enabling them to adjudicate certain cases according to customary law and introducing French law into the region in the event of more serious criminal cases. In other words, it explicitly removed the tribal regions from Shariʿa jurisdiction. To be sure, the *dahir* was not dissimilar to an earlier one issued in 1914. This updated one also allowed specific tribes to opt out in favor of Shariʿa jurisdiction if they chose to do so. But this was unsatisfactory for Morocco's urban elites, particularly the younger elements who were the products of the new competing educational systems, the French one and the *salafi*-minded alternative "Free Schools." Moreover, the heavy-handed French response to the initial petitioners against the *dahir* immediately backfired. Mosques were used as the focal point for organized protests in which the *dahir* was widely depicted as the first step toward the conversion of the Berbers to Christianity. For months, the traditional *latifa* prayer of supplication in times of distress was heard in Moroccan mosques, as the pious beseeched Allah "not to be separated from our brothers, the Berbers." The sharp reaction to the *dahir* was not confined to Morocco, but reverberated throughout North Africa and the Near East.

At bottom, according to Lawrence Rosen, France's error in promulgating the Berber *dahir* and its policies regarding the Middle Atlas and High Atlas Berber communities (see below) was one of "misplaced concreteness"—that is, France gave "reified and primary status to a distinction (Berber/Arab) which, in actual operation, is one of more ambiguous and subsidiary importance."[63] The application of anthropological insights to analyses of matters of political history surely enriches the discourse. Still, one must be careful not to go overboard in the other direction. Generalizing from Berber-Arab interactions at a particular time and place may be appropriate in certain instances and less appropriate in others. Contemporary Berber-Arab realities may be even more different from those examined by Rosen thirty years ago than the realities of 1930 were.

In any case, the newly energized nationalists had found an ideal cause against which to mobilize. As for the Berbers themselves, although some tribes did opt out in favor of Shariʿa, for the most part, their voices were not heard during the entire controversy. As in Algeria, the Berber was used as the "national signifier,"[64] while also being implicitly stigmatized by the association with France. Latter-day Amazigh movement activists would revisit the 1930 *dahir* in an effort to remove this stigma and present an alternative to the long-accepted narrative of the event.[65] Ironically, as C. R. Pennell has noted, while some Arabic speakers rioted in the cities against the *dahir* that split Berbers away, some Berbers continued to resist being united to the rest of Morocco by the French army.[66] Meanwhile, as pacification proceeded, the use of customary law expanded as well. David Hart concluded from this in a 1997 article that the Berber continued to prefer "the shrine over the book," and that his terminal loyalty was and remains tribal, not national,[67] even though most tribal functions eventually disappeared in post-independence Morocco.

Notwithstanding the tumult engendered by the 1930 *dahir,* and perhaps even reinforced by it, France sought to deepen its links with Morocco's disparate Berber communities in order to counterbalance the weight of the urban Arab sectors and limit the likelihood of a broad-based national movement crystallizing. Ironically, the integrative aspects of French rule—the complete pacification of the country, the progressive integration of the national economy and its linking to the world economic system, the steady flow of people from rural to urban areas, and the introduction of a modern educational system—would eventually outweigh these efforts, helping to undermine France's goal of separating Arabs from Berbers. Indeed, as in Algeria, French officials would be horrified to learn that the number of Berber speakers had actually declined during the first two decades of the protectorate, a result of these integrative trends, which dragged the Berbers more fully into the Arabic-speaking milieu. Middle Atlas Berbers, in particular, were exposed to the wider world and to Moroccan nationalism, beginning with Moroccan Arabic, through military service. The experience, which included the placing of Berber troops from different tribes together and thus creating additional bases of social solidarity, contributed to their eventual incorporation into the independent Moroccan state, even though they did not shed their Berber identity. So did the sending of the sons of mainly Middle Atlas Berber notables to the military academy located at the Dar al-Bayda palace in Meknes.[68]

Meanwhile, however, French policies proceeded apace in the Middle and High Atlas regions, albeit in two very different fashions. In the former, the absence of preponderant power among a particular tribe had made the pacification of the region a very lengthy affair, and its administration, accordingly, promised to be problematic. Part of France's response was to establish a school that initially was for the children of local notables, in order to impart the skills needed for junior bureaucrats serving the colonial order. The Collège d'Azrou, located in the mountain village of Azrou 90 km from Fez, opened its doors in 1927. Studies were predominantly in

French, with additional classes in both Berber and Arabic. Over time, the school would prove to be an avenue for upward mobility, as the number of students who were from precolonial notable families would eventually constitute less than 10 percent of the student body, and less than 15 percent were from relatively wealthy ones.[69] For illiterate tribesmen, the value of coming into contact with graduation certificates, according to anecdotal evidence, was talisman-like. One graduate's uncle reportedly told him that in his day, a man spoke via his weapon, but now that the authorities had imposed themselves on the tribal world, the "new gunpowder" of their society was education.[70] Many of the Collège's graduates would eventually fulfill the roles envisaged for them, not only under the French, but in independent Morocco: according to Mohamed Benhlal's calculations, of the 320 *caids* serving in the Berber regions in 1960, 250 of them were graduates of the school.[71] In other words, a new Francophone rural Berber elite had been created. In 1942, its graduates founded the Association des Anciens Elèves du Collège d'Azrou (AAECA), led by Abdelhamid ben Moulay Ahmed Zemmouri, who two years later would be a signatory to the Manifesto for Independence, a seminal event in the history of the Moroccan nationalist movement. The Association was the first structured organization in the Berberophone regions that had no tribal reference framework. The network it provided for this new elite would prove to be durable, and its members were eventually integrated into various segments of the postcolonial national structure: AAECA graduates included General Mohamed Oufkir, who would become the regime's strongman under King Hassan II until his downfall in 1972; Mahjoubi Aherdane, one of the leaders of the Liberation Army, which fought the French in the last stage of the independence struggle, and subsequent founder and longtime leader of the promonarchy Mouvement Populaire; and Hassan Zemmouri, who, like his cousin Abdelhamid, would hold a number of cabinet posts in subsequent years. A portion of this elite would eventually go on to play the Hrochian role of working to fashion a modern Berber ethnolinguistic identity in response to the twin processes of urbanization and state centralization. Together, these processes weakened traditional rural-tribal bonds and the place of Tamazight in Moroccan society, and ideologically subsumed the Berbers under the banner of an Arab-Islamic national state.

Of course, this is not what the French had intended. But inevitably, Berber students were affected in ways that contradicted France's desire to isolate the rural Berber world from the predominantly urban one: the educational experience both affirmed the value of the individual and gradually socialized the students toward nationalism.[72] As part of that trend, Algerian and Moroccan Arabic-language teachers were brought in to teach the Berber students Arabic.

For this newly emerging elite, there was no contradiction between their Berber identity and Moroccan nationalism. Nonetheless, urban nationalists were inevitably suspicious of the goings-on in Azrou. No less a person than Allal al-Fasi, one of the leading figures of the nationalist movement during the decades leading up to independence, inveighed against the alleged evangelization of Berbers by Christian missionaries taking place there. Others would do so as well. These stories were subsequently denied by leading Collège graduates such as Mohamed Chafik,[73] but they were accusations that were easy to make and easy to repeat, fitting into the anti-*dahir* sentiment that had been awakened in 1930. Just having studied at the school would be a stigma. After independence, its graduates were viewed by both the elite urban bourgeoisie and lower urban sectors as products of French colonialism. After the failed military coup of 1971, whose leaders were overwhelmingly Berbers, Collège graduates were considered even more suspect, and its alumni association hastened to destroy its archives (a copy was preserved elsewhere). No wonder that the members of the first generation of graduates, such as Chafik and Dr. Abdelmalik Oussaden, would eventually take their place among the venerable members of the modern-day Moroccan Amazigh movement.

The High Atlas and Anti-Atlas mountain ranges, the Souss Valley, and southeast regions presented the French protectorate authorities with a very different set of circumstances than the politically fragmented often-warring tribes of the Middle Atlas. During the middle and latter part of the nineteenth century, a number of Berber tribal leaders consolidated and extended their hold over broad swaths of territory that included key mountain passes through which the caravans carrying goods and people flowed from across the Sahara. They became known as the *grand caids,* belonging to the Goundafi, Glaoua, and Mtouggi tribes. At times, they would accumulate more power than the sultan himself, who prudently appointed them to high positions. By the middle of the 1920s, the second decade of the protectorate, the Goundafi and Mtouggi power bases had been gradually undercut by French administrators. But Si Thami El Glaoui would become the single "super" *caid,* a close ally and client of the French until the very eve of independence. His brother Madani had served as grand *wazīr* under the last pre-protectorate sultan, Abdelhafiz, during 1907–1912. Over time, Thami would accumulate an extraordinary amount of wealth, in effect becoming a big capitalist: acquiring cobalt and manganese mines, olive-oil and fiber factories, huge tracts of irrigated lands in the Haouz, near Marrakesh, and real estate in Casablanca, Marrakesh, and elsewhere. He came from a "winner take all culture" and ruled accordingly: taking percentages of just about every commercial activity in his region, including prostitution; presiding over lavish feasts for distinguished guests, particularly in the family mountain heartland redoubt of Telouet; and showing no mercy to those who crossed him. Though he was utterly corrupt, the French found him an important ally from the beginning of their imposition of the protectorate in the south and their various pacification efforts. Giving Glaoui free rein to maintain feudal-style rule may have been a very different tactic than that used in the Middle Atlas, but it was intended to serve the same end, namely, the distancing of large parts of the Berber areas from the influence of the nationalists. French colonial administrator–turned–scholar Jacques Berque scornfully characterized French policy as an attempt to create a "Parque Berbère." "These tribes would be France's sequoias," he said. Ostensibly the beneficiaries of measures undertaken in the name of preserving "authentic" native culture, France's Berbers "would remain good savages, worthy of love and respect, but whose ultimate promotion would consist of an NCO's stripes."[74]

The *grand caids* had always taken care to maintain their formal allegiance to the sultan, even when it was obvious to all that their power sometimes exceeded his. Thami El Glaoui had been no exception to the rule, but this changed in the early 1950s, as Paris tried to stanch the budding sentiment for independence, led by the Fassi-based Istiqlal Party, which now drew on the support of an increasingly discontented urban proletariat. Clearly the French sought to manipulate the situation, instigating Glaoui against the sultan, and vice versa. But Glaoui was also a cunning player and viewed his own interests as contrary to the direction in which Istiqlal wanted to take the country. After purportedly confronting the sultan at one point by declaring that he was no longer the Sultan of Morocco, but only "Sultan of the Istiqlal,"[75] Glaoui sent a contingent of his followers to camp outside the walls of Fez in February 1951 to pressure the sultan to sign a number of decrees tendered by the approving resident-general, Alphonse-Pierre Juin. In 1953, Juin's replacement August-Leon Guillaume, Glaoui, and the head of the powerful Kittani brotherhood, Adelhay El Kittani, mobilized many of the other older members of the notable class in order to depose the sultan and replace him with an elderly, obscure member of the Alaoui family, Moulay Ben Arafa. Glaoui himself may have dreamed about being sultan, but that would have required a quick reordering of his family tree to find Alaoui-sharifian origins. Such genealogical sleights of hand had often been engineered by wannabe sharifians in the past, but in this context, it was hardly possible. Nor was the overthrow of the Alaoui house and establishment of an entirely new dynasty. The default option of finding another, more compliant Alaoui to assume the throne turned out to be a nonstarter as well. Ben Arafa proved to be just about the worst choice possible, someone both unknown to the public and unsuitable to sit on the throne at such a tumultuous moment, while the exiled Mohamed V immediately became a symbol for Moroccans to rally around. By the time he returned in triumph, after a fifteen-month absence, Glaoui, now ill with cancer, could only prostrate himself before Mohamed in a gesture of obeisance and reconciliation. Glaoui would pass away on January 31, 1956; his palace in Marrakesh would be thoroughly looted, his economic empire destroyed, and his kasbah in Telouet abandoned, falling into ruins. Interestingly, although it may have lost much of its patrimony, the Glaoui family did not entirely become persona non grata in the new state. One of Glaoui's sons, Abdessadeq, served for years in a number of official capacities, both in the legal system and as a Moroccan diplomat. More recently, he has written a book that constitutes an effort to rehabilitate his father's name by presenting his father's actions in what he calls a "more objective and complex light."[76] Latter-day Berberists would choose to completely ignore the legacy of the most powerful Berber of the twentieth century, in contrast to their embrace of Abdelkrim.

However, before Glaoui's unhappy denouement could play itself out, the anti-French agitation and violence that had emerged in Morocco's urban concentrations in 1953–1954 needed to spread to the countryside. On October 2, 1955, three French outposts in the north-central Taza region were attacked by ragtag half-traditional, half-modern units known as the Army of Liberation. Overwhelmingly Berber in composition, while commanded by both Berbers and Arabs, its operations would be decisive in the closing stage of Morocco's struggle for independence. It would also mark the latest manifestation of supratribal Berber identity, this time for the purpose of ridding the country of foreign rule and restoring the sultan, the clearest symbol of collective identity among Morocco's populace, to the throne. Its was an affective, implicit nationalism, lacking both the ideological constructs of the *salafi*-inspired national movement of the urban centers and a specific Berberist agenda.[77] Although the bulk of its fighting was in Berber areas, Arabs were incorporated at all levels of command, a number of its leaders came from outside the area, and the Istiqlal actively recruited followers among the Berbers from different regions. To be sure, and as has generally been the case with independence movement struggles, internal bloodletting was not absent, although it did not remotely approach the level of Algeria. For modern-day Berberists, the killing of Liberation Army commander Abbas Messaʿadi in 1956, apparently on the order of Mehdi Ben Barka of the Istiqlal, was one of the great crimes of the liberation struggle, and the opening shot of the Istiqlal's bid to marginalize the Berbers in an independent, Arab-Islamic Moroccan national state.

PART II *Independence, Marginalization, and Berber Reimagining*

Three

MOROCCO AND ALGERIA

State Consolidation and Berber "Otherness"

From the outset, the newly independent states of Morocco and Algeria were intimate rivals, offering competing geopolitical, ideological, and sociocultural visions and orientations.[1] Within just over a year of Algeria's achieving independence, the two countries would find themselves in a sharp, albeit brief, armed conflict against one another, the "War of the Sands."[2] Twelve years later, their rivalry would manifest itself in the struggle to determine the future of Spain's Saharan territory adjacent to both countries: Algeria (and Libya) supported the Polisario independence movement, in line with prevailing international norms pertaining to decolonization, while Morocco insisted on the "reunification" of the territory with its Moroccan motherland, based on precolonial fealty of local tribes to the sultan.[3] More than thirty years hence, the still-unresolved issue acts as the primary barrier to achieving a lasting Moroccan-Algerian rapprochement that would, in turn, enable the moribund five-nation Arab Maghrib Union to resume functioning.[4]

Given their vastly different historical experiences and social makeup, one could hardly expect the post-independence dynamics of each country's "Berber question" to follow similar paths. Still, the vision of their respective ruling elites was basically the same: incorporating and subsuming the heterogeneous, tribe-oriented speakers of primarily unwritten Berber dialects under the rubric of a homogeneous national identity, based on a common Sunni Islamic faith and praxis according to the Maliki school; giving primacy to the Arabic language, thanks to both its status as the sacred written language of the Qur'an and the need for a unifying, standardized idiom for building a modern society and political community; and fashioning an official legacy of the struggle for independence. The primary linguistic fault line, as far as state elites were concerned, was not between Arabic and Berber, but between Arabic, the official national language of both Morocco and Algeria, and French, which was widely employed in government, commerce, and education. Nor were ethnic differences deemed insurmountable to state-building. In both countries, French colonial attempts to "divide and rule" through emphasis on Berber distinctiveness vis-à-vis the Arabic-speaking populations had been discredited and rendered a failure. Thus, victorious nationalist elites were confident that upon achieving independence, they would successfully complete the task of national integration and state-building, and relegate the Berbers to folklore status.

Indeed, the relative number of Berber speakers declined in the decades after independence. But ironically, both countries also witnessed a gradual increase in the self-conscious manifestations of Berber culture and the demands of Berber groups. This could be explained, in part, by the threat factor: the concern with preserving cultural and linguistic traditions perceived as being under siege. No less important was the poor performance of the state in satisfying both material and social-psychological needs, resulting in widespread alienation and an ideological vacuum, particularly among both countries' expanding youthful populations, creating the impetus for new social movements. Thus, eighteen years after achieving independence, Algeria would be shaken by the "Berber Spring," a significant outburst of particularist Kabyle ethnic identity, in the face of official opposition, posing a challenge to the accepted political-cultural order. As with all significant developments in Algeria, the rise of a Berberist current, and the state's heavy-handed response, were watched closely next door, as the Moroccan authorities sought to derive the appropriate lessons from the confrontation and Moroccan Berberist elements closely calibrated their next moves.

ALGERIA

The state that was established by the victorious Front de Libération Nationale in 1962 was the first true "Algerian" state in history, as foreign rulers (Turkish, French) had previously imposed their rule there on the local population.[5] The FLN had succeeded in uniting various segments of Algerian Muslim society around the banner of national struggle and attempted during the first post-independence decades to employ its hard-won legitimacy in the service of building a united modern state. However, notwithstanding the new state's prevailing ideological guideposts of socialism, populist nationalism, and Third World leadership, the Algerian elite remained highly factionalized. Hence, the process of transferring the new regime's revolutionary legitimacy to a more institution-based legitimacy would prove to be daunting.

As far as Algerian Berber communities were concerned, they would, as in Morocco, face the pressures of state policies promoting modernization and homogenization, including large-scale Arabization campaigns. However, the relationship between the post-independence Algerian state and significant portions of its Berber community would from the very outset prove to be far more adversarial and overtly politicized than in its neighbor to the west.

As William Quandt has written, a Kabyle leadership group with close ties to the Kabyle population at large had never developed during the 1950s, and other sources of intraelite cleavage, such as personal relations, were more important than Berber-Arab distinctions. This continued to be true during the early days of independence. Nonetheless, as Quandt takes care to point out, there was a Kabyle dimension to the power struggles that engulfed the Algerian elite in the aftermath of independence. What came to be known as the Tizi-Ouzou group, established in July–August 1962 and led by Belkacem Krim and Mohand Ou el Hadj, the military commander of the Kabyle *wilaya* during the war of independence, was initially the largest armed group opposing Ahmed Ben Bella's and Houari Boumediene's efforts to consolidate power in newly independent Algeria. (Tizi-Ouzou is the largest town in Greater Kabylie, although neither the group's leaders nor its followers were exclusively Kabyle.) That Kabylie was a problematic area for Algeria's new power bosses was demonstrated by the fact that it registered the lowest percentage of voter participation in the September 1962 referendum confirming Algeria's independence and new political system. This pattern repeated itself in the September 1964 legislative elections. Interestingly, and notwithstanding the radically different context, this continued to be the case after the restoration of competitive national elections beginning in 1996.

Hocine Ait Ahmed had initially refused to take sides in the factional struggles besetting the leadership of the infant state. However, his developing opposition to the ruling Ben Bella–Boumediene faction led him to establish a party, the Front des Forces Socialistes (FFS), in 1963 and to mobilize his supporters in armed revolt, not, to be sure, in the name of Kabylie or Kabyle rights, but in the name of opposing the emerging hegemony of the FLN. The situation was, to an extent, reminiscent of the early post-independence Rifian revolts against the Istiqlal in Morocco (see below). According to Charles Micaud,

> the revolt had . . . no separatist objective; Kabyle peasants
> were used by some Kabyle leaders in Algiers as a power base
> to increase their authority in the central government. There
> was no attempt at opting out of the political system, but
> rather at demanding greater participation and integration in
> the new nation-state.[6]

Indeed, the FFS did not speak for all Kabyles: half of the Kabyle deputies in Algeria's national assembly condemned its actions.[7] Nonetheless, at
least some of the new ruling hierarchy were ready to brand the Kabyles as
secessionists and favored a policy of isolation and containment of the region through the employment of military force. Once again, ethnicity was
instrumentalized by the parties to a dispute over concrete matters, thus
giving preexisting ethnic affinities more tangible qualities. The episode was
certainly traumatic for many young Kabyles. The iconic activist and singer
Matoub Lounès, whose murder in 1998 would be a seminal moment in the
history of the Algerian Amazigh Culture Movement, later wrote that it
triggered rejection for everything Arab. Likewise, his sister Malika Matoub
noted that the youth of that generation had just experienced the curfews,
killings, deportations, and imprisonment of their parents carried out by the
French during the war of liberation. With their tears having barely dried,
she said, they now had to confront the unacceptable fact that the Algerian
army, the army of their own country, was now "invading our mountains
and encircling our villages."[8]

    Ait Ahmed's efforts were a failure. His arrest, October 1964 death sen-
tence, which was commuted to life imprisonment in April 1965 by President Ahmed Ben Bella, and escape from prison and flight to Switzerland
on May 1, 1966, seemed to mark the end of the Berber question in Algerian
political life.

    Indeed, writing in the late 1960s, Quandt suggested that Algerian politi-
cal life during the next decade would not be seriously colored by Berber-
Arab rivalries. Moreover, he hypothesized that the combination of existing
government policies promoting economic development in rural Berber regions and the avoidance of overt discrimination against Berbers in political
and administrative life was likely to lead to the integration of Berbers into
the Algerian nation without major conflicts, and the probable decline, over
time, of Berber identity among the public at large. At the same time, he
held open the possibility of Berber ethnic particularism and the creation of
a Berber leadership with links to the broader segments of the population

emerging as a consequence of modernization. This could especially happen, he suggested, if the government pursued policies of rapid Arabization, economic neglect, and discrimination in hiring practices for administrative posts. Overall, however, the regime's apparent sensitivity to the potential for Kabyle discontent, combined with the state's increasing capacity, seemed to preclude any serious Berber problem in the foreseeable future.[9]

State and Community: The Sharpening of Kabyle Identity

Instead matters took a different course. Upon returning from exile in 1962 to assume the presidency of newly independent Algeria, Ben Bella had declared, "nous sommes des Arabes" (we are Arabs). "Socialisme Arabo-Islamique" was adopted without serious debate as the regime's guiding ideological formula: the state sought to solve the problem of mass illiteracy and build a uniform national identity by insisting on the hegemony of the Arabic language and a revolutionary, anti-imperialist, and anticolonialist single-party regime aligned with so-called progressive forces in the Arab world. These principles were clearly and repeatedly articulated in foundational texts, including the Charters of 1964 and 1976 and the 1976 Constitution.[10] Spearheaded by Minister of Culture Ahmed Taleb Ibrahimi (the son of Bashir al-Ibrahimi, the head of the Algerian *ulama* during the 1948–1949 "Berberist crisis"), the translation of this vision into reality produced a more strident policy of Arabization directed against the predominance of French in Algerian life, while also opposing any notion of equality between Arabic and the Berber dialects.[11] Algeria developed "a kind of bicephalous economy based on two different standards, [which] resulted in incalculable social, cultural, and ideological contradictions." Poorer Algerians of rural origin made up a high percentage of a post-independence generation educated exclusively in Arabic, whose opportunity for economic advancement was limited.[12] State Arabizing policies in the 1970s included efforts to Arabize (*ta'aroub;* lit. "becoming Arab") the Algerian media and educational system through the high school level, with university-level education officially projected to be entirely Arabized as of December 1980. Given the shortage of teachers trained in literary Arabic, thousands of teachers had to be imported, mainly from Egypt. As the Abd al-Nasir regime was cracking down hard on its Islamist opposition, it was all too eager to find an outlet abroad for the energies of its adherents. Hence, many of the teachers brought an orthodox, Muslim Brotherhood–oriented Islamic sensibility with them,[13] which included an ingrained belief in the superiority of the Arabic language over all others—French, dialectal Arabic, and of course the Berber dialects. Their views clashed with those of a sizeable portion of the Kabyle community, many of whom were French-educated and even secular, and were disproportionately represented in public administration and the educational system. Viewed more broadly, "the old colonial fissures which split the country [were] revived with even more bitterness," as a "cultural civil war" was unceasingly waged, reproducing "a manufactured split between Arabophones and Francophones," resulting in cultural fragmentation and a denial of otherness whose cumulative effect on society, and particularly Algerian youth, has been staggering.[14]

The inevitable ethnic, social, and political differences of postcolonial Algeria surely would have been attenuated had the government been more attuned to Kabyle sensibilities in the cultural sphere. But it was not to be. Modern-day Kabyle Amazigh activists paint a dark picture of the period:

> It was strictly forbidden to speak [the] Kabylian language
> in the army, the administration and courts, obliging there-
> fore the Kabylians to learn Arabic and to use it in those places
> even when they had to talk to members of their families. . . .
> It is also during this period that the Algerian State sent in[to]
> the Kabylia schools flocks of Arab teachers brought from
> Egypt, Syria, Iraq, and Palestine to force our schoolchildren
> to express themselves in class only in Arabic. And to reinforce
> the presence of the Arabic language in Kabylia, [Houari]
> Boumediene's regime [1965–1978] started its program of
> "one thousand socialist villages." Villages which were built
> smack in the middle of Kabylia and which served as settle-
> ments to the nomadic Arabs brought as agriculturists to work
> in agrarian cooperatives set especially in plains, such as those
> situated at the outskirts of Imcheddalen, Tazmalt, and Ak-
> bou, in the departments of Bouira and Bejaia. As for the ad-
> ministration, acting in favour of the Arabic language, it took
> great pleasure in falsifying the Kabylian toponyms, which
> (fortunately not all) underwent both structural and seman-
> tic changes. Thus, "Ilmaten" became "El-Maten," "Imchedda-
> len" became "Mchedellah," "Tala-G'udi" became "Ain Zebda,"
> "Iazzugen" became "Azazga"; in brief, the visitor would imag-
> ine himself in any other Arabic-speaking region of Algeria.[15]

Ironically, the state's efforts to promote socioeconomic development also helped to sharpen Kabyle collective consciousness. A boom of sorts occurred in Tizi-Ouzou, whose population almost doubled between 1966 and 1977 (from just under twenty-seven thousand to forty-five thousand), and the region witnessed a greater degree of economic and social integration. Hugh Roberts makes the case that a major outcome of this process was that the Kabyle population as a whole, and the Kabyle bourgeoisie in particular, had now acquired a substantial material interest in the status of their mother tongue, all the more so in light of the authorities' accelerated socialist and Arabization policies.[16] Kabyles could in fact be found throughout the political and state-sponsored economic hierarchies. Salem Chaker, on the other hand, emphasizes that the Kabyle "technical elite" was more concerned with preserving and developing further its privileged position within the state hierarchy.[17] In any case, the regime's efforts to centralize its authority and promote national integration also had the contrary effect among a portion of Kabylie's cultural producers and transmitters and a considerable number of Kabyle youth. A more modern, collective Kabyle-Amazigh consciousness was being fashioned, involving what Anthony Smith calls the processes of historical reappropriation and vernacularization of political and cultural symbolism.[18] One area where this came to be demonstrated on a regular basis was the football stadium of Tizi-Ouzou. Around the world, football (soccer) has become intertwined with identity politics and ethnonational conflicts;[19] in this case, the locus of Kabyle adoration and assertion was Jeunesse Sportive de Kabylie (JSK). Each match was a festive assertion of Kabyle identity, replete with banners and headgear sporting Berber emblems and inscriptions in Tifinagh characters (an ancient script found in rock and tombstone engravings in North Africa, still employed by the Touaregs, and now a symbol of modern Amazigh identity). Indeed, for its supporters, the club's initials stood for "Je suis Kabyle." The team's president even took to exhorting the players during the halftime of games while wearing a white woolen burnous, a symbol of traditional Kabyle village life, and then presenting it to them with a call to fight for it.[20]

One need not accept uncritically the militant Kabyle critique of Algerian state policies to recognize that the vigorous negation and repression of linguistic-cultural expressions of Berber particularity created a backlash among portions of the community. Initial stirrings of Berber militancy among secondary school and university students crystallized in a number of places, including the *lycée* in Tizi-Ouzou, a number of *lycées* in

Algiers, the Faculty of Letters at the University of Algiers, and the university dormitories of Ben-Aknoun.[21] The first organized manifestation of this backlash had come already in 1968, emerging from anti-Boumediene student unrest, as activists of the newly formed Mouvement Culturel Berbère (MCB) clandestinely distributed tracts supporting cultural pluralism and the recognition of Berber cultural and linguistic rights.[22] It would expand in the 1970s and reach a peak in 1980.

Given the efforts of the new Algerian state to impose a hegemonic cultural and historical narrative on what had always been a fractured and highly contested society, and given the importance of poetry, storytelling, and music in oral cultures in general and Kabyle culture in particular, developments in these spheres were especially significant in the first decades after achieving independence. Jane Goodman has written a rich, and even at times moving, analysis of the "New Kabyle Song" phenomenon, which emerged in the 1970s, foregrounding the rise of a young Kabyle singer, Idir (lit. "to live"; his real name is Hamid Cheriet). Though he was unknown at the time, Idir's 1973 song "A Vava Inouva" ("Oh My Father") was swiftly adopted by Kabyles, and other Berbers as well, as an important modern marker of their identity. The text, written by the poet Ben Mohamed, referred to a traditional Kabyle story told by elderly women, with the song depicting a grandmother "seated at the hearth, spinning tales far into the night as the snow falls outside," while adding new verses which made it clear that the act of storytelling was being evoked as cultural memory. The outcome was a simultaneous engendering among its listeners, both in Algeria and the Kabyle Diaspora, of "a sense of deep recognition and a feeling of novelty." Although the singer and poet certainly could not have imagined that their song would become an iconic element of a modern vernacularized Kabyle Berber culture, their efforts were consciously directed toward both recovering and revitalizing Kabyle cultural expressions, precisely at the moment that the new Algerian national state sought every means possible to build a homogeneous, Arab-centered national culture. As Goodman explains, "the music itself and the circuits through which it moved [radio stations in both Algeria and France, cassette tape recorders, the budding world music scene] helped to produce Berber heritage as an object of desire."[23] Other luminaries of the genre came to include Lounis Ait-Menguellet, Ferhat Mehenni, and Matoub Lounès, who drew on earlier musical texts of Taos Amrouche and Slimane Azem.[24] Mehenni's activism would eventually lead him to promote the idea of autonomy for Kabylie within a federal democratic Algeria (see Chapter 7).

The Kabyle French Diaspora:
Strategic Depth and Cultural Articulation

Throughout the modern era, Diaspora communities have frequently played crucial roles in the shaping of modern ethnic identities, both cultural and political, among their compatriots "back home." Their inputs have been as varied as the circumstances surrounding each particular case. The motivations underpinning this involvement have been just as varied, but almost universally connected to the identity-building needs of emigrants whose ties with their home communities had inevitably been altered but not entirely broken, and for whom complete and total assimilation into their new environments was generally not an option. The result, as Paul Silverstein says, is that "diasporas and transnational social movements have become constitutive features of the contemporary political landscape."[25]

"A Vava Inouva" was the first Algerian song ever to be played on French national radio. While appealing to a broader swath of listeners, the station managers were also acutely aware of the existence of a large Kabyle audience. In 1954, more than half of the 212,000 Algerians in France were Kabyles. By 1975, after the imposition of serious restrictions by both the French and Algerian governments on emigration from Algeria to France, the proportion had declined, even as the total number of Algerians in France had increased more than fourfold, to approximately 900,000. Best current estimates hold that persons of Kabyle origin make up between 30 and 40 percent (approximately 800,000) of the total number of individuals of Algerian origin in France.[26] A rough extrapolation backwards to the mid-1970s, based on a similar proportion, renders the number of Kabyles in France as approximately 400,000. Indeed, by that time, France had become a crucial intellectual and broader cultural arena for the complex process of retrieval, reinterpretation, production, and dissemination of Kabyle culture.

The establishment of the Académie Berbère in 1967 and the Groupe d'Études Berbères (GEB) at the University of Paris–VIII–Vicennes in 1973 marked the first organizational developments in this regard.[27] Founded in March 1967 as Académie Berbère d'Echanges et de Recherche Culturels, and renamed in May 1969 as Académie Berbère Agraw [lit., "gathering," "reunion"] Imazighène, the first group was the work of a small collection of Kabyle luminaries from the worlds of scholarship, arts, and politics, including the novelist, anthropologist, and linguist Mouloud Mammeri, the singer Taos Amrouche, the former French army officer Abdelkader Rah-

mani, and ex-FFS militant Bessaoud Mohand Arav. At the outset, it declared its intent to promote greater awareness and knowledge of the Berber question within universalist terms. The Berbers, in the view of the
association's members, served as a prototypical example of a marginalized
people whose culture had been severely devalued; the group's overall objective, they declared, was to safeguard ethnic minorities and "oppressed
peoples . . . dominated . . . by institutions and disciplines not compatible
with their real needs and aspirations" and to struggle against the homogenizing effects of contemporary technocratic civilization. The alteration of
the association's name in 1969 marked a shift toward a more particularist,
Berber-centered agenda. Its primary objective was to make the general
public aware of the history and civilization of the Berbers and to promote
their language and culture.[28]

Berberist discourse during those years was polemical and passionate,
openly trumpeting the superiority of Berbers over Arabs and replete with
personal attacks, reflecting the powerful personality of the Académie's
founder and leader, Mohand Arav. This style, says Karina Direche-Slimani,
was often to the detriment of its objectives. Mohand Arav, notwithstanding his education, was in temperament a man of the *maquis* (lit. "bush," i.e.,
in Algeria, those who had taken to the hills to resist the French). A former
FLN member during the war of independence, he had fiercely denounced
the FLN's bloody internal settling of scores, and particularly the killing of
Colonel Amrouche and Abane Ramdane,[29] earning him a death sentence
from Algerian president Ben Bella in 1963. He participated in Ait Ahmed's
losing post-independence insurrection against the new regime, and then
went into exile in France, where he quickly published a book, *Le FFS, espoir
et trahison,* dedicated to "all of the Kabyle women raped by Boumediene's
soldiers and all of my companions/countrymen who refused to join them."
In it, he held Ait Ahmed responsible for the insurrection's defeat, because
of his "political instrumentalization" of the battles in Kabylie.[30]

Financial problems made it difficult for Agraw Imazighène to maintain
ongoing activities, and it would finally cease functioning in 1976. Responding to Algerian government pressures, and following Mohand Arav's arrest
and conviction on a charge of racketeering (manipulated by the authorities, according to one of his followers at the time, Ould Slimane Salem),
the French authorities expelled him to Spain in 1978. From there, he took
up residence on Britain's Isle of Wight (receiving official status as a political refugee), where he lived the rest of his life. For thirty-seven years, then,
this combative, take-no-prisoners Kabyle Berber figure lived outside of
his home country, making just a single emotional visit in November 1997

after finally receiving travel documents from the Algerian authorities.[31] Just prior to his death in 2002 and interment in Kabylie, Mohand Arav published his personal account detailing the history of the Académie, in which he spoke of the special pain caused by "vassalized Kabyles" who were "more royalist than the king" in disavowing the language and roots of their ancestors.[32] Nonetheless, the Académie did establish a presence among the Kabyle immigrant community, often giving unemployed immigrants shelter for the evening, teaching all those who knocked on its doors a modified Tifinagh script for writing in Taqbaylit, and publishing pamphlets (*Imazighen* and *Itij* ["Sun"]), whose readers were overwhelmingly between the ages of eighteen and thirty. Activists made the rounds of two thousand Kabyle-run coffeehouses in Paris alone to distribute the Académie's leaflets and monthly bulletin. While Paris-based, its publications circulated informally and clandestinely within Algeria, often being brought into the country by returning travelers.[33] Overall, Agraw activities helped to lay the groundwork for the development and dissemination of a historical consciousness and modern cultural identity among Kabyles, which radiated out to other North African Berber communities as well.[34]

The Groupe d'Études Berbères was made up of university students and scholars, who split from the ranks of the Académie Agraw Imazighène in 1972 over the latter's overly politicized approach. The GEB had a not dissimilar agenda, but expressed it in a more dispassionate manner. It regularly published the *Bulletin d'études Berbères,* until 1978; Kabyles in Algeria regularly contributed to it, and the journal was circulated in Algeria in the same way that the publications of Agraw were. In 1978, some of its members then initiated the publication of the more scholarly *Tisaruf* ("Small Steps"). Indeed, one of the GEB's chief successes was in achieving intellectual and scientific legitimacy for Berber language and culture studies, as it forged links with various scholars and institutions, and not just from the Berber community. In fact, its academic sympathizers and participants in its scholarly work would come to include such leading intellectual luminaries as Ernest Gellner, Pierre Bourdieu, Germaine Tillion, and Lucette Valensi.[35] Other GEB participants disseminated Berber cultural products to broader audiences via publications and events, through a collective named Imadyazen ("The Poets"). Their activities produced an additional group, Les Ateliers Imazighen ("The Imazighen Workshop"), which sought to animate cultural and social life through publications, theater, music, and poetry. In turn, its organizational framework would provide important political support during the Berber Spring events in 1980 (see below), and its members took an active part in the Kabyle-based political parties, Ait Ahmed's FFS

and the Rassemblement pour la Culture et la Démocratie (RCD), following its creation in 1989. The association published the reactivated FFS's 1979
platform, which was the first official political text by any Algerian party
that called for political and institutional measures by the state that would
give equal treatment to the Berber language as a national language in order
to make up for the time lost since independence. Its use, the FFS platform
declared, was an "inalienable right" that neither "interior colonialism" nor
"foreign colonialism" could proscribe.[36] The explicit foregrounding of
Berber identity as part of its demands for a transformation of the Algerian
political system indicates that Ait Ahmed was cognizant of the changes that
Kabyle society had undergone and determined to remain firmly ensconced
in his core constituency.

No discussion of this period of Kabyle Berber intellectual and cultural gestation, in both Algeria and France, would be complete without
mention of the numerous studies on North African prehistory by Gabriel
Camps, who eventually initiated the authoritative *Encyclopédie Berbère*.[37]
Camps himself was born in French Algeria and did all of his studies there.
After completing his doctorate at the University of Algiers in the last years
of French rule, Camps became head of the Centre de recherches anthro-
pologiques, préhistoriques et ethnologiques (CRAPE), which even after
independence continued to be supported by France's Centre national de
la recherche scientifique (CNRS). In 1969, he moved to Aïx-en-Provence
University, and was replaced as head of CRAPE by a person of unusual stat-
ure, Mouloud Mammeri.

Novelist, playwright, linguist, anthropologist, ethnographer, and educator, Mammeri was a towering figure, perhaps the single most important
contributor to the rise of the modern Berber Culture Movement, even
while detesting any formal status and avoiding the role of organizer.[38] His
intellectual oeuvre encompassed a broad range of topics covering a wide
spectrum of Berber communities in Algeria and Morocco, including the
Touareg. His two mammoth books of Kabyle poetry—*Les Isefra, Poèmes
de Si Mohand ou Mhand* (1969) and *Poèmes kabyles anciens* (1980)—have been
characterized as the "quintessential essence of *taqbaylit, la kabylité*," em-
bodying the whole of Kabylian society, history, values, aspirations, and
daily life, inspiring the modern generation of Kabylian youth.[39] During
1965–1973, Mammeri taught a seminal course on Berber language and culture at the University of Algiers. The university's Chair in Berber Studies
had been established nearly one hundred years earlier, as an integral part
of France's attempt to reify Berber-Arab differences and deepen its rule.
Not surprisingly, the Chair was abolished at the outset of independence,

following the departure of its occupant, A. Picard. When Mammeri suggested its revival in September 1962 to Minister of Education Saʿid Mohammedi, the response was utterly dismissive: "tout le monde sait que ce sont les Pères Blancs qui l'ont inventé la berbère" ("the whole world knows that 'the Berber' was invented by the White Fathers").[40]

But just over three years later, it was the minister's replacement, Ahmed Taleb Ibrahimi, the leading advocate of an Arabized national culture, who asked Mammeri to teach a course in the ethnology section of the Faculty of Letters. The outcome was hardly what the minister could have been hoping for. These were "heroic years," according to Rachid Bellil and Salem Chaker, in which the number of students in the course gradually grew from a handful to dozens, and even one hundred. It served not only as a beacon of knowledge about their roots for young Kabyle students, but also had a significant impact socially, becoming a site for networking, planning, and identity-building projects.[41] As director of CRAPE during 1969–1978, Mammeri oversaw the emergence of a new generation of researchers documenting and analyzing the fabric of marginal social groups living in the pastoral and rural communal milieus—their oral literature, religious practices, and juridical structures, all of which were being severely impacted by the development policies of the new revolutionary state. In doing so, he had to tread delicately, and often uncomfortably, for this agenda was hardly in sync with that of the state authorities overseeing all educational and scientific institutions, including CRAPE. Thanks to his efforts, ethnologists and anthropologists, Berber-centered and non–Berber-centered alike, found in CRAPE an institutional refuge from an increasingly Arabized climate that was hostile to their research.[42]

In retrospect, one can see that tensions between the state authorities and the Kabyle Berber identity current were on the rise during the 1970s. Certain cafés, hotels, and restaurants, and even administrative offices, were transformed into non-Arabic-speaking zones, exclusively utilizing Tamazight and French.[43] In 1974, when Arab singers replaced Berber ones at the annual Cherry Festival in Larba N At Iraten (formerly Fort National), they received a hostile reception from a Kabyle audience that turned into a riot (perhaps premeditated), which had to be suppressed by troops and police, reportedly resulting in three fatalities.[44] On July 5, 1977, at the championship football match for the Algerian Cup, pitting Kabylie's beloved JSK against Nasr Athlétique de Hussein Dey from an Algiers suburb, before a raucous, mostly Kabyle crowd in Algiers, the Algerian national anthem was drowned out by the shouting of Kabyle nationalist slogans such as "A Bas les Arabes" ("Down with the Arabs"), "Imazighen, Imazighen," and

"Vive la Kabylie" ("Long live Kabylie"). The scene was repeated at the end of the game during President Boumediene's presentation of the Cup to the victorious JSK squad.

The authorities were sufficiently disturbed by the incident to compel the thirty-year-old club to be shorn of its Kabylie affiliation: initially, the name was changed to Jamiʿat Sariʿ al-Kawakib (the Swift Stars Club), and in 1978, the team name was again changed to Jeunesse Électronique de Tizi-Ouzou (JET), and integrated into the state-owned utility Sonelec (Société Nationale d'eau et d'électricité), in line with a new sport law requiring all teams to be affiliated with state economic or administrative units (the original name would only be restored in 1990).[45] Another such "debaptism" was the relocation to Algiers of *Fichier de documentation berbère,* a publication founded in Kabylie in 1946 by the Pères Blancs, and its concurrent renaming as *Le Fichier périodique,* with its eventual shutdown four years later, in 1977. This heavy-handed response was part of a larger pattern during these years, marked by the barring of Kabyle singers from public performances, the censorship of numerous songs, a ban on the circulation of tapes, the cessation of Kabyle-language broadcasts of JSK games, the gradual dismantling and ultimate closure of Radio Algiers' Kabyle channels, the shutdown of Mammeri's Cercle Berbère and course at the University of Algiers, and the eventual reorganization and subordination of CRAPE, driven by an official view that condemned the entire field of ethnology as a "colonial science."[46] In 1974–1975, the state also issued new regulations forbidding the registration of children with non-Muslim names, and providing officials with an exhaustive list of examples, while in the spring of 1976, two hundred mainly Kabyle youth were arrested and interrogated for a number of weeks over their possession of the bulletin of the Académie Berbère, with some sentenced to between eighteen and twenty-four months in prison. In May 1979, a Kabyle-language performance of the Algerian writer Kateb Yacine's play *La guerre de 2000 ans* was barred from production at the newly established university in Tizi-Ouzou.[47] At critical junctures, the authorities would also invoke, in so many words, "the Berberist danger" to national unity. One such telling incident came in December 1978: with Boumediene on his deathbed, a shipment of arms was allegedly dropped by a Moroccan plane to a group of Kabylian regime opponents along the coast near the city of Bougie (Béjaïa), led by a former Liberation Army officer. The regime's daily mouthpiece, *El Moudjahid,* issued ringing patriotic declarations against the "criminal operation," which was designed to undermine national security. The true facts of the incident remain a mystery.[48]

As explained by one author sympathetic to the Berberist agenda, the repressive nature of the Boumediene regime necessitated confining Berber demands to the cultural sphere and avoiding overt political challenges to the regime's authority. Doing so also "had the added advantage of being attractive to Berbers across the political, ideological and social class spectrum."[49] At bottom, however, the Berberists saw the transformation of the Algerian political system into a genuinely democratic framework as the only way to guarantee their cultural and ethnic rights. This synthesis was articulated in the FFS's 1979 platform, which advocated a "democratic revolutionary alternative" to the existing repressive and fake socialist regime,[50] the central theme of modern Berberist discourse until today.

The Berber Spring

In March 1980, eighteen years after the attainment of Algerian independence, the simmering tension between the state authorities and self-conscious Kabyle Berbers burst forth in open confrontation, in what came to be known as Le Printemps Berbère ("the Berber Spring"; Tafsut Imazighen). The immediate background to the unrest was an official commission's decision in December 1979 to entirely Arabize primary education and the social sciences and humanities in the universities, increase the process of Arabization in the secondary schools, and place greater emphasis on religious education in primary schools. Implementation remained another matter. Nonetheless, the Berber/Arab-Islamic cultural and linguistic battle lines were now being drawn more sharply. Concurrently, the demise of the last tolerated symbol of Berber culture, a Kabyle-language radio program, was rumored to be imminent. The spark to the confrontation came with the authorities' last-minute banning of a scheduled March 10, 1980, lecture on the role of poetry in traditional Kabyle society by Mouloud Mammeri at Hasnaoua Tizi-Ouzou University, following the recent publication of his book on the subject, in Tamazight and French. More than one thousand students waited for him in vain, as he was stopped at a police roadblock, taken to the governor (*wali*) of the region (who had apparently ordered the ban), and told that the lecture carried the "risk of disturbing the public order."[51] Why the ban was imposed was never clear, particularly since Mammeri had recently been allowed to deliver a similar lecture in Constantine.[52]

In any case, its cancellation produced precisely the result that the ban had been designed to prevent. The students went on strike and demonstrated in protest against cultural repression. Sympathy protests were organized in Algiers and other areas, as well as strikes in schools and businesses in the Kabylie region. The actions had a trans-class character, involving factory workers and villagers, as well as students, businessmen, and professionals.

In the early hours of April 20, the police cracked down, storming dormitories, a factory, and a hospital, and the strike was brought to a crashing halt. Common knowledge long held that between thirty and fifty persons were killed and hundreds wounded in five subsequent days of clashes between activists and participants in sympathy demonstrations, on the one hand, and the police, on the other. In fact, apparently not a single fatality was incurred.[53] Nonetheless, the clashes resonated beyond Algeria, grabbing the attention of the French media, in particular, as well as international human rights organizations. To be sure, the Algerian authorities restored order fairly quickly. But the implications of the events turned out to be extremely significant: for Kabyles, for Berber culturalists everywhere, for Kabyle-state relations, and for the Algerian polity as a whole.

The very name quickly given to the events, "Berber Spring," evoked the cultural flowering in Prague in 1968 before the Soviet crackdown, and became a "memory site" (*lieu de mémoire*).[54] They would be commemorated annually by myriad Berber culture groups and associations that would eventually blossom, and serve as a crucial marker in the emerging collective narrative of repression, alienation, the reawakening of the self, resistance to oppression, and ultimate explosion in a renewal of long-standing demands. Mammeri's already exemplary status reached new heights, and he would become an iconic figure in the movement, even before his death in a road accident in 1989.[55]

To be sure, as Roberts notes, the movement was more united in what it opposed, state repression, than in what it demanded (cultural pluralism? Amazigh revivalism? laissez-faire economics?). In his view, the regionwide and trans-class response to state repression was primarily an expression of a traditional code of honor, namely, "the imperative defence of *nif*, self-respect," particularly as people's own younger brothers, sisters, and cousins were on the receiving end of the state's blows.[56] And as Jane Goodman has shown, the Fanon-type narrative of Berber struggle and liberation, which mirrors the Algerian state's own official self-definition of its struggle for freedom, tends to obscure the complex institutional and conjunctural factors that enabled Berber activists to mobilize their energies at that moment. From this angle, the spark lit by the cancellation of Mammeri's lecture was not one of spontaneous combustion, but rather resulted from an act of extraordinarily bad timing by the authorities, given what Goodman calls "the Kabyles' very mastery of state-based systems of governance and communication that enabled them to pull off a relatively organized and politically productive two-month insurgency." Institutional and ideological processes—the state's Arabization policies and resulting feelings of marginalization among Kabyle youth, the opening of the university in Tizi-Ouzou just two years earlier, the development of Berber associations in France and circulation of both individuals and materials between France and Algeria, and the temporary appropriation by Berber students of the student governance system—had intertwined. Hence, she says, the date of the crackdown, April 20th, could itself "become available for both political mobilization and individual self-constitution."[57]

The uncertainty of the official response, both before and after the crackdown, spoke to the confusion over how best to handle what was at that point an extraordinary and unprecedented challenge to the state's authority. Regime spokesmen talked darkly of imperialist and neocolonialist plots against national unity and the revolution, and of agitation by the exiled Ait Ahmed and others who frequented "Parisian salons."[58] At the same time, the authorities sought to mollify the Kabyles: the twenty-four activists being held in detention were released in June without trial, and promises were made to accommodate the Berber cultural agenda, including increased Berber-language courses (to be taught in Arabic, however), the creation of a university chair in Berber studies at Hasnaoua Tizi-Ouzou University, and the allowance of popular culture programs. In general, however, their implementation was short-lived, and the new Cultural Charter discussed at the FLN central committee meeting that summer made no explicit reference to the Berber aspect of Algeria's national culture, which was "a synthesis of the collective experience, our Muslim religion, our Arabic language, our membership in the Arab-Islamic civilization, and our popular culture patrimony."[59] The official discourse surrounding the meeting and afterwards emphasized the Arab origins of the Berbers, and the subsequent ethnic and cultural intermixing that took place under Islam, which in essence returned the Berbers to their origins.[60] Casual observers might have easily concluded that the Berber Spring was merely a spasm or hiccup, part of the inevitable growing pains of the new Algerian state.

However, this was far from the case. Kabyle activist and researcher Salem Mezhoud argues that what happened in Kabylie in the spring of 1980 was "by far the most important, perhaps most revolutionary event" in the history of independent Algeria up to that time. As such, it inaugurated "a new era of opposition to the Algerian regime," and thus prepared the ground for the October 1988 riots and ensuing events that shook the

Algerian state to its core.[61] One may perhaps take issue with his categorical linkage between the two episodes, but the Berber Spring was nevertheless a seminal development in the history of Kabyle-state relations. According to Benjamin Stora:

> The effect of the "Berber spring" was to produce, for the first time since independence and from within Algeria, a public counter-discourse of real import, in a country operating on the principle of unanimism. In that compact universe, where society and state, private and public mingled together in a single bloc, the blossoming of autonomous popular associations and organizations gave texture to Algerian society.[62]

From that point on, the regime's Jacobin-like efforts to forcibly mold society under a single state socialist, Arab-Islamic banner appeared increasingly bankrupt, and the regime's tough line brought about results opposite of the ones intended, catalyzing both "civil-national" and "ethnocultural" kinds of actions among the Kabyles. An estimated three hundred persons, at the very least, were sentenced to prison terms between 1980 and 1988 for various "Berberist" offenses, such as participating in demonstrations, distributing pamphlets, recruiting, etc.[63]

Indeed, a number of factors combined to politicize growing numbers of Kabyles during the 1980s: the legacy of Kabyle self-assertion embodied in the Berber Spring resonated with increasing vigor; the regime failed to draw the proper conclusions from the 1980 events and remained inattentive toward Kabyle grievances; and Algerian society as a whole, under President Chedli Benjedid and his policies of economic liberalization, became increasingly polarized along a number of fault lines (e.g., rich/poor, regime/opposition, and religious/secular). One especially important factor for Berber activists was the increasing Islamization of Algerian public life, in which the regime sought to relegitimize its rule by competing with newly assertive Islamist trends for the possession of Islamic virtues. "Islam in Algeria," wrote one scholar, "[had] been nationalized exactly like the land and the industry."[64] Official efforts in this vein included the building of thousands of new mosques, tacit encouragement of Islamist toughs to intimidate communists and Berberists and treating their excesses with a light hand, the adoption in 1984 of a Shariʿa-inspired Family Code, a redoubling of Arabization efforts by state institutions, and passivity in the face of the expansion of nonofficial Islamist political and social action. Street mosques headed by young Saudi Wahhabi-trained clerics proliferated, attracting disaffected urban youth and the poor. The authorities did pursue and ultimately destroy the small Algerian Armed Islamic Movement of former Algerian army officer Moustapha Bouyali, which called for a holy war against the regime. But the growing strength of Islamist currents and increasing dissatisfaction with the regime, against the background of a severe economic downturn at mid-decade following the collapse of oil prices, portended trouble.[65] For Berberists, it was a case of picking one's poison. Their response, against the background of the Berber Spring, was an enhanced ethnic and cultural militancy and self-consciousness, coupled with emphasis on the priority of democratizing Algerian life. In turn, this response left them open to charges that they were "enemies of Islam."

How to organize in a system where all civil groups had to be approved by the authorities was no simple matter for Kabyle Berber activists. The solution, for some at least, was to frame their struggle in both national and universal terms: in early 1985, they established the Association des Enfants de Chouhada ("Association of the Children of Martyrs," children of those who had died in the war of independence, and thus had certain privileges not available to the general public) and the Ligue Algérienne des Droits de Defense de l'Homme ("Algerian League for Human Rights"; LADDH). A leading spokesman of the Association was the son of the late legendary guerilla commander Colonel Amrouche; the effective head of LADDH was from the same family as Rachid Ali Yahia, of the 1948–1949 "Berberist crisis."[66] Roberts refers to the existence of competing trends within the activist community during the 1980s: a more specific Berberist tendency, organized under the still-clandestine MCB, which was preoccupied with particularist identity questions, and a liberal-democratic statist tendency, expressed in particular by the Ligue.[67] At this point, however, the two tendencies complemented one another. Fairly quickly, the themes of the Association and the Ligue, which focused on the promotion of democracy and the rule of law, sparked the ire of the authorities, who arrested twenty-three activists (all but two of them Kabyles), charging them with an "attack on the authority of the state by calling for a regime change; making and distributing tracts; un-armed gathering; and creating illegal associations." In mid-December 1985, they were brought to trial. Unusually, they were given a wide space to express their views and in the presence of the foreign press, no less. The reason, perhaps, was because international human rights organizations had already been mobilized on their behalf, thus compelling the Algerian authorities, concerned with burnishing the country's image, to be more lenient in the trial procedure than they normally were. In that, they miscalculated badly. The defendants' court statements, which draped their demands for recognition of Berber identity in the mantle of universal human rights, turned the proceedings into an indictment against the state. Although all but one of the defendants was convicted, large cracks had been exposed in the façade of Algerian oneness.[68]

Writing at the time of the Berber Spring, Roberts wrote that there was "not the slightest basis for separatism in Kabylia," and that what was at issue was "the participation of the Kabyles in Algerian cultural, economic and political life at the national level. . . . The essential objectives of the Berberist movement can be seen to be entirely assimilationist in nature."[69] This remained true a decade later, if by "assimilationist" one avoids the connotation of losing one's individual and collective identity in the larger whole, and limits the term to encompass political and cultural pluralism within a unified entity. But the struggle for Algeria's soul, which would be inaugurated by the democratic explosion in the wake of large-scale street violence in October 1988, followed by the implosion of both state and society beginning in mid-1991, placed the Berber/Kabyle question in a very different context.

MOROCCO

The forty-four-year protectorate era had laid down many of the institutional foundations for a territorially unified and centrally governed independent Moroccan state, with a monarchical form of government. However, the task of state-building had only just begun. Consolidating control over Morocco's geographically, economically, and socially diverse regions; achieving a consensus among the political classes regarding the modus operandi of the political system, i.e., how power was to be exercised and by whom; and confirming an overarching national narrative that would serve to legitimize the system and help bind society together constituted daunting tasks. Moreover, ensuring national unity and regime stability required the propagation and implementation of an effective strategy of modernization and development, in the face of the country's widespread poverty and illiteracy: of the country's eleven million persons at the moment of independence,[70] nearly 90 percent were illiterate, with only 2 percent of women knowing how to read and write and less than 35 percent of school-age children actually in school.[71] The socioeconomic challenges were acute, in the rural and urban sectors alike. More than two-thirds of the population was rural-peripheral, outside of major urban areas, and often utterly bereft of even the most rudimentary connections to the state authorities, without a connecting road, water and electricity lines, or a school.[72] Urban areas, too, were highly problematic: steady increases in rural-to-urban migration during the protectorate era had already produced massive shantytowns (*bidonvilles*) on the edge of major cities, bereft of essential services, whose residents had traded one type of hard-scrabble mode of living for another. Independent Morocco's decades-long high rates of unemployment and underemployment and the country's stubbornly slow decline in the rate of illiteracy would testify to the state's ongoing shortcomings.

Where did the Berber populations fit into the picture at the onset of independence? As mentioned in Chapter 2, the 1955 armed uprising in the mostly Berber rural regions, embodied by the actions of the ragtag Liberation Army, along with the widespread visceral support for the exiled Sultan Mohamed, had marked the death knell for the protectorate. The Berber population acted neither as a large cohesive unit, nor in the name of a specific Berber-Moroccan identity. As one scholar has noted, the Berbers readily accepted Arab commanders in the Liberation Army, surely a sign of their willingness to affiliate with the Moroccan national project, and the sultan who headed it, as a whole.[73] At the same time, the process hadn't been tension-free, with the most serious incident coming with the murder of Liberation Army commander Abbas Messaʿadi, as ordered by the Istiqlal's Mehdi Ben Barka. The episode left deep scars, helped contribute to the subsequent formation of the Mouvement Populaire,[74] and would be revisited by Berber militants a generation later. The Istiqlal-Berber fault line would prove enduring: a 2002 cover story on the affair in the Amazigh movement monthly *Le Monde Amazigh* included a facsimile "Wanted" poster, with Ben Barka's image.[75]

The first years of the new state witnessed a number of episodes of dissidence in Berber regions: in the Tafilalt, in the southeast part of the country in 1957; in the Rif in 1958–1959, involving the large Tgzinnya and Ait Waryaghar tribes; in the far south, involving Liberation Army elements; and in the Middle Atlas highlands in 1960, led by the *grand caid* of Beni Mellal, Bashir ben Thami. For the most part, they constituted not so much a blanket rejection of the new state as an assertion of Berber tribal prerogatives and local patronage systems against the domineering, patronizing ways of a "modern," Istiqlal Party-dominated administration.[76] In the north, these included Istiqlal efforts to impose its own, mostly French-speaking administrators on Rifian Berbers, who spoke Berber and Moroccan Arabic, and whose contact with government administrators had largely been in Spanish during previous decades. In other words, and particularly between spring and November 1958, it was not so much that the opposition stemmed from rejection of the central government as from the appointing of outsiders to official posts, at the expense of local Rifians. The fact that the Istiqlal, as the self-styled bearers of high Andalusian Arab culture (notwithstanding the irony that its appointees conducted official business in French), held an unabashed attitude of cultural superiority toward the tribal roughnecks of the Rif was not lost on them either. In addition, the closure of the land border with Algeria had brought hardship to the region, depriving many of seasonal employment in the agricultural sector, while the withdrawal of the Spanish army from northern Morocco left its Rifian soldiers without gainful employment or viable alternatives. Their slogans included "Down with the government, Long Live the King," and "Ben Youssef [Mohamed V] is our King and Abdelkrim is our leader[!]."[77] However, a second round of unrest in December 1958–January 1959 constituted a more substantive attempt to regain tribal autonomy. Hart notes that it was in fact the first corporate action by the Ait Waryaghar since the Abdelkrim revolt more than three decades earlier.[78] It would also prove to be the last. Given its underlying antistate thrust, it was, not surprisingly, dealt with harshly by the central government. In early 1959, Crown Prince Moulay Hassan, commanding units of the Forces Armées Royales (FAR), put down the revolt, assisted by future regime strongman Colonel Mohamed Oufkir, a Tamazight-speaking Berber from the Tafilalt.[79] Among the Rifians, there are those who still remember the brutality employed to repress the uprising. Fatalities most likely numbered in the thousands, many incurred through wholesale indiscriminate bombings of villages, the rape of Rifian women by the FAR was said to have been "semi-systematic," and Oufkir's interrogation methods were notoriously chilling.[80] Throughout Hassan's long reign as king (1961–1999), he avoided visiting the Rif region, which remained one of the country's poorest and most problematic areas, even while making no effort to downplay what had happened.[81] Indeed, in response to widespread violence in 1984 in protest against food price increases, Hassan issued a stern warning that the Rifians would experience his forceful hand again if they did not desist from their protests.[82]

To be sure, Hassan's exercise of royal power against Rifian rebels hardly constituted an endorsement of the Istiqlal's agenda, either for the region or the country. In fact, the troubles in the Rif helped spark a process by which the earlier partnership between the Palace and the nationalist parties against the French, forged on the basis of overlapping interests, began to dissolve. The majority of the leaders of the nationalist movement had sought to limit the power of the king, with the hope that Morocco could be fashioned as a constitutional monarchy in which the king would be primarily a symbol of national unity, but without substantial powers. Some even hoped to abolish the monarchy entirely, and have it replaced by a republican regime, as had occurred in Tunisia. Ideas of this sort may have also infiltrated the ranks of the military people who were close to King Hassan II, spawning two failed coups in the early 1970s (see below). However, King Mohamed V, and his son and successor Hassan II, had no intention of subordinating themselves to the civilian politicians. Indeed, the post-independence monarchy was fashioned into the country's central ruling institution, both symbolic and substantive, drawing on the increasing powers of a modernizing and centralizing state to dominate society, while anchoring itself in a particular version of Morocco's long-standing political, social, and cultural traditions.[83] Over time, Hassan II progressively emasculated all opposition through an adept mix of brutal repression, co-optation, arbitration between different social groups and power centers, the calibrated distribution of royal benevolence and largesse, and the tireless promulgation of religious and national symbols around the royal personage. Hassan also made apt use of Algeria's emergence in 1962 as a geopolitical rival with a competing sociopolitical model to nurture patriotic sentiments among the Moroccan populace. These were expertly tapped during the October 1963 "War of the Sands," and again in 1975–1976, as Morocco moved to extend its control over the Western Sahara in order to prevent the establishment of an independent, pro-Algerian entity on Morocco's southern border. With great skill, Hassan turned the issue into one of supreme national importance, making it the central glue of his regime, using it to achieve political quiescence for more than fifteen years. Overall, then—with a bit of luck and a good deal of skill, reinforced by an effective bureaucratic and repressive machinery and support from the West and Arab oil monarchies—Hassan ruled with an iron hand, and not just reigned, over his subjects for thirty-eight years. In Weberian terms, his authority and legitimacy derived from a combination of charismatic and institutional factors.

Hassan's way of addressing the whole matter of the relationship between the Berber communities and the state's authority was far more subtle than the approach taken in neighboring Algeria. Whereas Algeria's national project was dominated by a single, revolutionary ideology and party, the Moroccan monarchy's slogan of "Allah, al-Watan, al-Malik" ("God, Homeland, and King") was based on a more inclusive, and conservative, notion of Moroccan national identity under the rubric of the monarch's persona, the *amir al-mu'minin,* a position of both religious and temporal significance that carried great resonance in rural, less educated areas in particular. The Berbers could, at least in theory, be comfortably included within this large "tent." To reinforce the message of inclusion and in line with a long-standing Moroccan tradition of political marriages to cement alliances with key social actors, Hassan married two Berber women originating from the powerful Zaiane tribe of the Middle Atlas region, Lalla Latifa Hamou and Lalla Fatima. Doing so further reinforced Morocco's fragmented political system in which the king would stand at the apex as the supreme, infallible authority and arbiter of conflict.[84]

Mohamed Hassan al-Ouazzani's Parti Democratie d'Independence (PDI) helped organize the Berbers for this supportive role in the first years of independence.[85] Even more important was the emergence in 1959 of a predominantly Berber political party, the Mouvement Populaire (MP), representing the rural sector, which was encouraged to share in the patronage/spoils of power. As a result, rural Berbers constituted an important component of promonarchy political forces that acted to prevent the Istiqlal and its leftist breakaway party, the Union Nationale des Forces Populaires (UNFP), from achieving hegemony over the political system. The Istiqlal's pronounced anti-Berberism, which welcomed Berbers only to the extent that they had put aside their particularist identity as a relic of the colonial past, also benefited the MP,[86] whose founding congress in 1959 was marked by an unabashed defense of the *blad* (countryside) and Berberism.[87] The MP supported Hassan II unreservedly and was rewarded accordingly in his confrontation with the Istiqlal and other opposition parties during the political crisis of 1962–1965, a crisis that resulted in a decisive victory by the Palace and the imposition of a decade-long state of emergency and suspension of normal political life.[88]

Another crucial pillar of his rule with a Berber aspect was the military: the newly formed FAR was commanded by Berbers who had achieved officer rank in the French military. Without them, it is doubtful that Hassan would have survived the politically turbulent 1960s.[89] But the 1970s would be a different story (see below).

Notwithstanding the Palace's success in attaining hegemony over political life with the help of important Berber elements, its formula for incorporating its Berber populations into the Moroccan national state hardly constituted an endorsement of the Berber component of Moroccan identity, as such. Some contemporary Amazigh analysts argue that the monarchy's legitimacy claim, based on its sharifian origin, is essentially an endorsement of an Arab-Islamic version of Moroccan identity, at the expense of the Berbers. This is an oversimplified view, for it ignores the historical centrality of sharifian descent in Moroccan political culture, even for Berbers themselves. Nonetheless, Amazigh movement activists had some justification for their complaints. As part of its permanent strategy of balancing off the various forces in Moroccan society, the monarchy took both symbolic and concrete steps in line with the Istiqlal vision of what Moroccan society should look like. Hence, Morocco joined the League of Arab States in 1958; in speaking at the eleven hundredth anniversary of the founding of the Qarawiyyin school of higher Islamic studies in 1960, Hassan praised the school as having tied Morocco's destiny to Islam and Arab culture; in 1961, a fundamental law was passed defining Morocco as an Arab and Muslim state, in which the national and official language was Arabic; that same year, an Arab League–backed institution to promote the Arabization of the educational system was opened in Rabat.[90]

As was true in Algeria and elsewhere, nation-building in Morocco assigned a key role to the educational system, and a crucial aspect of forging their education systems was the defining of an appropriate linguistic ideology and its translation into appropriate policies.[91] On the declarative level, Arabization was a near-universally-held value, deemed crucial for forging a modern national identity and cohesive society. However, policy-makers and elites in both countries faced a special dilemma, owing to the deep penetration of French as the lingua franca during the colonial period, as well as the prevalence of unwritten Berber dialects and colloquial Maghribi Arabic (*darija*). (The wide gap between the latter and Modern Standard Arabic, a modern, middle form of the language between dialectal and classical Arabic, is even wider than a similar gap in Egypt.)

Regarding Berber identity and the Berber language, there was hardly any difference, at least on the declarative level, between the monarchy's orientation and that of the Istiqlal and most of the more secular left-wing parties. Primary school textbooks in newly independent Morocco stressed that Moroccan history began with the arrival of Islam and the Idrissi sharifian dynasty. Berbers, the "sons of Mazigh," were ethnicized into Arabs: the Berber language was a sister to Arabic, the Berbers' origins were said to be in Yemen, and they lived primitively in caves until Islam showed them the light. These themes were familiar ones, going back a thousand years. For the Moroccan urban elites now engaged in state-building and nation-building, they were quite convenient, confirming their privileged position in the new national hierarchy. To an extent, they were endorsed by the Palace as well, certainly implicitly, and even at times explicitly. Writing in 1968, the kingdom's official historian, Abd al-Wahab Ben Mansour, succinctly laid out his preferred vision for the future of Berber dialects in

Morocco. Bringing an Arabized education system to the country, coupled with a parallel expansion of the transportation system, would result, he said, in the disappearance of Berber within fifty years, to be replaced by standard and colloquial Arabic.[92] Mohamed Abd al-Jabri, one of the leading scholars of Arab-Islamic thought of his generation, an active figure in the UNFP, and a fervent advocate of Arabization, expressed a similar view. He explicitly consigned the Berber language, as well as colloquial Moroccan Arabic, to the status of local dialects, and therefore unworthy and incapable of serving as a national unifier and providing the means of achieving radical social and cultural transformation. Moreover, Jabri was of the view that the Berber dialects, in particular, should be destroyed entirely, and to that end, he advocated their banning from schools, radio, and television.[93] Ironically, Jabri himself originated from a Berber family from the Tafilalt region. While disagreeing on much else, the Istiqlal and the majority of the UNFP were of similar mind regarding the need to submerge the Berbers into a larger Arabized milieu. This was pithily expressed by UNFP leader and subsequent murdered icon, Mehdi Ben Barka, who once told an interviewer that the "alleged Berber problem" was simply a residue of the cultural politics pursued by the protectorate regime: "Le Berbère est simplement un homme qui n'est pas allé a l'école" ("The Berber is simply someone who hasn't gone to school").[94] This approach, emphasizing the need to fashion a "new man" on the ruins of "feudal, reactionary" mentalities and social structures, has been a common one among left-wing revolutionary ideologies throughout the history of national and social movements.

If the advocates of Arabism, whether of the more traditional Arab-Islamic or more secular leftist–Arab nationalist variety, had any complaints, it was that matters were proceeding at too slow a pace. The issue at this point was not the status of Berber but of French, in which the bulk of the Moroccan elite had been educated. The doctrine issued in 1966 by Minister of Education Mohamed Benhima, a nonparty politician who would subsequently serve as prime minister during 1967–1969, emphasized the importance of bilingualism (Arabic and French). Benhima's tepid approach to Arabization was hotly contested by the Istiqlal, in line with its emphasis on the Arab-Islamic components of Moroccan identity.[95] The less strident pace of Arabization, in comparison to Algeria, may be understood as another indication of the Palace's adroit balancing act among competing social forces. It also points to a recognition of the impossibility of achieving swift implementation of such a far-reaching vision, given the limited resources possessed by the new Moroccan state.

Of course, Moroccan Berbers themselves were hardly of one mind regarding the new state's vision and policies of national integration. While the MP and the army constituted two crucial frameworks for incorporating Berber sectors of Moroccan society into the newly independent national state, they were not the only ones. Left-wing parties, particularly the UNFP, attracted some interest, both from Berber intellectuals, most of whom had graduated from the Collège d'Azrou, and from the large-scale network of Soussi traders and grocers that competed with the Fassi elite over the divvying up of the economic pie.[96] Some of the intellectuals would eventually become disillusioned with the absence of any recognition of the Berber component in the Left's thinking, and act accordingly.

The Traumas of the Failed Military Coups

Meanwhile, no sooner had the Palace succeeded in achieving hegemony over the political system than it faced a threat from another, more dangerous source, the military. Almost miraculously, King Hassan escaped death in successive attempted coups, in 1971 and 1972. But the episodes were extremely traumatic for the country and their impact far-reaching, on the state as a whole, and on the Berber communities in particular, for most of the senior and junior officers involved in the two *coups manqués* were Berbers from the Rif and Middle Atlas Mountains.[97]

There is a broad consensus among scholars that the motivations behind the coups were not explicitly "Berber" in nature. Still, it is also generally agreed that there was a "Berber coloring": a certain level of solidarity to the plotters' activities characterized by common backgrounds, professional and social links, and concern for both their personal and the country's future, particularly in light of increasing manifestations of corruption and the material and political assets being rapidly accumulated by the predominantly Fassi civilian elite.[98] In both cases, the coups were led by King Hassan's closest collaborators, General Mohamed Medbouh and General Mohamed Oufkir, respectively. John Waterbury also speculates that the rebel officers may have sensed the rising frustration in the junior ranks of officers regarding their lack of promotion, and acted to preempt them before being removed themselves. This possibility also contained a "Berber" dimension, as the process of recruitment into officers candidate schools since independence had overwhelmingly favored the urban, literate Arab middle classes.[99]

If the coups were not explicitly "Berber," the ramifications for many Berbers, let alone those families, clans, and regions from which the plotters originated, surely must have made them feel like they were being targeted as Berbers. The mostly Arabophone urban bourgeoisie, namely, the merchant families of Fez and their offshoots in Casablanca, were quick to conclude that the coup constituted a Berber challenge to their privileged position in society; the Istiqlal Party, which largely represented their interests and worldview, sharply condemned the coup attempt as "a manifestation of retrograde Berber nationalism."[100] Heavily stigmatized by the coups, large numbers of Berbers were purged from the security services, and Berbers would be excluded from sensitive positions in the government and Palace dealing with security, foreign affairs, and finance. One year later, an additional, if amateurish, challenge to the regime arose, this time emanating from the Middle Atlas region and inspired by radical leftists ("pan-Arabists," in the language of modern-day Amazigh activism) with the support of Algeria and Libya. Ironically, this too would stigmatize the Berbers. Hence, they could now be accused of being antistate for being both "anti-Arab" and "pan-Arab."

As part of his reassertion of control over the military after the second coup attempt, King Hassan announced on February 22, 1973, his decision to dispatch motorized infantry units to Syria to help defend it against Israel.[101] The move allowed him to both bolster his Arab nationalist credentials and distance the commanders and their units from home. Denying the "colonialist accusations" of racism and that Morocco was "divided between Arabs and non-Arabs," he foregrounded Morocco's Arab identity, emphasizing that "Morocco is a Muslim state, whose language is Arabic, and it is a member of the Arab League." He also proclaimed his faith in the army's loyalty, which had been unfairly called into question by those who besmirched its image and stigmatized its reputation.[102] Following the October 1973 Arab-Israeli war, however, Hassan acknowledged the heavily Berber cast of the army, declaring that in participating in the fighting, the army had redeemed the Berbers' honor.[103] Nonetheless, the very harsh individual and collective punishments meted out to the perpetrators of the coups, as well as to those involved in the abortive 1973 revolt, sent a more lasting message. Waterbury characterized the failed coups as bringing an end to the clientele relationship that had been constructed by King Hassan since ascending to the throne in 1961.[104] André Coram, for his part, concluded his analysis of the failed 1971 coup by pointing to a parallel between the French protectorate's cultivation of the rural Berber milieu and its military elite as a counterweight to the urban Arabic-speaking elites, and a similar policy pursued by the Moroccan monarchy after independence: in both cases, he noted, it turned against them.[105] In the latter case, however, the consequences were far more severe.

Discussion regarding the role of General Oufkir, who continues to this day to be a controversial figure in Morocco, and within the Amazigh movement, remains circumspect. Oufkir was born in 1920 in the Tamazight-Berber-speaking village of Boudnib, in the Tafilalt oasis east of the Atlas Mountains, near the Algerian border. In addition to his native Tamazight, he would become fluent in French, as well as speaking Tashelhit and Moroccan Arabic (unlike King Hassan II, Oufkir had a less than perfect command of literary Arabic). Oufkir's father had been a French-appointed local *caid*. He himself had studied at the Collège d'Azrou and then the military academy in Meknes. As a career soldier, he served in the French army in Italy and Indochina. After rising to the rank of major and serving as aide-de-camp to General Raymond Duval, the commander of France's forces in Morocco, and then to France's various resident-generals, he became Sultan Mohamed V's chief aide-de-camp in 1955, having played a role in bringing about the latter's return from exile.[106] Under King Hassan, Oufkir rapidly assumed the role of regime strongman, willing and able to employ all means necessary to repress dissent and ensure the stability and supremacy of the regime. These measures included personally machine-gunning rioters in Casablanca from his hovering helicopter in March 1965 and apparently supervising the kidnapping and murder of the exiled Ben Barka in Paris.[107] Following the traumatic, failed first coup attempt at the king's Skhirat palace in July 1971, Oufkir was named defense minister and placed in charge of securing the army's loyalty. However, even at the time there were suspicions, never entirely refuted or proven, that Oufkir may have had connections to the plotters. In any case, he was deeply distressed by the harsh punishment meted out to so many of his friends and colleagues, highlighted by the swift, and televised, execution of ten of the leading plotters, and his relationship with the king deteriorated sharply. One year later, he almost certainly made a bid to remove Hassan from power, commanding an attempt by Moroccan fighter jets to shoot down the king's plane as he returned from France.[108] Hassan's improbable survival cost Oufkir his life, officially by suicide, more likely by execution at the hands of Ahmed Dlimi, his deputy and successor. To take further revenge, and to send a clear message to future would-be plotters, Hassan caused Oufkir's wife and four children to "disappear" for eighteen years, consigning them to a living hell in remote prisons that they barely survived, though upon attaining freedom they managed to tell their stories to the world.[109]

Oufkir, like Glaoui before him, has understandably gone almost completely unmentioned by contemporary Amazigh activists who seek to "remember, recover and reinvent" the history of a marginalized and ignored
community.[110] For most of them, Oufkir was the prototypical *Berbère de
service,* doing the bidding of the king in order to advance his own interests,
without reference to the Berber community's needs. In private, though,
some Amazigh activists speak more favorably of Oufkir, justifying his
attempted coup as the outcome of Hassan's failure to heed his warnings
against the rampant high-level corruption that had infested the *makhzen,*
right up to the level of the king's brother.[111] In this context, it must be
noted that Oufkir's overall worldview was not dissimilar to theirs, and
was perhaps even more radical than that of many of the Rabat-based intellectuals who would come to spearhead the Amazigh Culture Movement.
Oufkir was utterly disdainful of the urban Arab political and cultural elites
and would have preferred that Morocco not be a member of the Arab
League.[112] For what it is worth, Oufkir's daughter Malika reports in her
best-selling book that when she and her brother were finally captured after
having escaped from prison and signaled to the outside world that they
were alive and had done so, junior policemen who encountered them in
the police station where they were brought burst into tears, telling them
that "you have restored the Berbers' pride. You have brought your father
back to life."[113] If this is in fact true, then it serves as additional indication
that Oufkir's popular image among the next generation of Berbers serving
in the security forces was a favorable one.

Politics and Culture: First Stirrings of Berberism

In his analysis of nineteenth-century national movements
in Central Europe, Miroslav Hroch notes that the reactions of nondominant ethnolinguistic groups to the centralizing policies of both "absolut-
ist" and "revolutionary" national states were extremely diverse. Such was
the case as well among the Moroccan and Algerian Berber communities.
In Morocco, the predominant pan-Arab, revolutionary, Third World orientation of Ben Barka and the bulk of the Moroccan Left during the 1960s
and 1970s, along with the authorities' declared policy of Arabization and
the general low esteem in which urban Arabs held recent Berber migrants
from the rural regions, reinforced the Berbers' marginalization in the post-
colonial order, both individually and in terms of the specific markers of
Berber collective identity. In response, some Berber students, teachers, and
university staff, originating mainly in the South, especially the Souss re-

gion, and now living in Rabat, felt compelled to engage in their own Berber identity-building project. The centrality of intellectuals in this beginning phase of the Berber movement's history in Morocco was congruent with the role of intellectuals in similar movements elsewhere.[114] Ironically, they were largely the product of the newly Arabized educational system, although some were entirely fluent in French as well.[115]

Initial efforts by Berber intellectuals and students included the establishment of small discussion groups and literacy courses in Tashelhit for newly arrived rural migrants. On November 19, 1967, they formalized their activities, founding the Association Marocaine de Recherche et d'Echange Culturel (AMREC), the first Berberist cultural association in Morocco. AMREC was headed by Brahim Akhiat, a thirty-six-year-old high school math teacher who was born in the Agadir area (Ait Swab) but had lived most of his life in Rabat. Its members, and activists in other, subsequent Berber associations as well, constituted, in the main, intellectuals who had been affiliated with secular left-wing political organizations and became disillusioned with their mainly pan-Arabist and Third World homogenizing "modernist" orientation, which left no room for Berber alterity. Some came to this conclusion during years of imprisonment following their involvement in the 1973 UNFP-led attempted uprising or affiliations with other radical left-wing organizations. The decisive moment for one prominent Berberist was when prison guards refused to allow inmates to speak Berber with their visiting families.[116] Hassan Idbelkassem, who helped found the Rabat-based Nouvelle Association de la Culture et des Arts Amazighs (subsequently known simply as Tamaynut; "New") in 1978, had been involved with the UNEM (National Union of Moroccan Students) and arrested in 1974 on the grounds that writings from the illegal Marxist-Leninist *23 Mars* publication were found in his possession.[117] Mohamed Chafik, for his part, who would eventually became the dean of Morocco's Mouvement Culturel Amazigh, had also been a sympathizer of the UNFP, but had not engaged in political militancy against the regime. Rather, he assumed various roles within the power structure, while continuing his intellectual pursuits on behalf of Berber culture.

To be sure, the climate for Berberist activity was not propitious: what the contemporary Amazigh movement calls the two variants of pan-Arab discourse, the secularist and the *salafi,* would leave very little space for Amazigh-centered cultural and political activity. Indeed, the absence of any reference to "Amazigh/Berber" identity in AMREC's name demonstrated the reticence in going public with a defense of Berber language and culture. Similarly, the organization's founding statute referred only guardedly and euphemistically to its mission, stressing the importance of "cultural heritage" and the "proper culture of our country." Confined mainly to academic forums during its first years, AMREC would subsequently seek to attract a wider audience for its message through the sponsoring of the music group Ousman ("Lightning Flashes") and other broader-themed cultural activities, beginning in the mid-1970s. Other musical groups would follow in their footsteps, placing the Berber culturalist agenda on stage, literally and figuratively, to the delight of some Moroccans, and to the dismay of others.[118] As the trauma of the military coups gradually receded, additional groups would be founded during the 1970s.

Berber political groupings in those years, while supporting school programs to teach Berber dialects, rarely displayed militancy in encouraging Berber cultural projects. Indeed, the MP, and Mahjoubi Aherdane in particular, are often criticized by movement activists as having been, like Oufkir, *Berbères de service,* and for not advancing the Amazigh agenda. The criticism is at least partially justified, for the MP's loyalty to the monarchy was unswerving and constantly prioritized over specific Amazigh issues. The MP, one activist told me, was the party of "destruction of identity," as Aherdane had agreed with Hassan II not to discuss identity issues for twenty years.[119] In Aherdane's own view, there was "no regionalism and no separatism" in Morocco, for Berbers and Arabs could not be disassociated from one another. At the same time, he told an interviewer, being a Berber and defending the language were not a matter of protecting a vague folklore but "wanting to preserve a culture . . . a human and spiritual richness that flows through our veins."[120] In fact, part of the MP's actions in counterbalancing the Istiqlal did contain an explicitly Berber component, continually demanding the teaching of Berber dialects in the education system.[121] In 1977, the MP, shedding some of its historical timidity on the subject, formed a parliamentary group on behalf of the preservation and dissemination of Berber culture. Aherdane's opposition to the Istiqlal was colorfully demonstrated in his exchange with fellow government minister and Istiqlal deputy secretary-general, Mohamed al-Douiri, in a parliamentary debate in 1977. During a discussion of the Istiqlal's program to Arabize the educational system and public life, Douiri criticized Aherdane for not employing the "national language," as Aherdane was speaking at the time in French. In response, he demonstratively switched to Tamazight![122] Seeking to preserve government harmony on the issue, the Interior Ministry turned to Mohamed Chafik, former Minister of State for Higher Education, and at the time director of the Collège Royal. Chafik's report on the subject, which was presented to the government on April 26, 1978, stated that familiarity with the Amazigh language among all portions of Moroccan society was a national necessity, for it was central to the heritage of all Moroccans. It should therefore be taught in all levels of education, from primary schools upwards, along with Arabic and French. Concurrently, the MP held a conference entitled "Towards a New Society," calling for recognition of the Berber language as the country's mother tongue and for the creation of a language and civilization institute to preserve and promote Berber culture. Indeed, government plans to that effect had already first been mentioned in 1975, and in 1979, an "obscure committee" in the Chamber of Deputies approved the establishment of an Institut National d'Études et de Recherches Amazigh.[123] It would take more than two decades before the notion would be translated into reality, with Chafik's positioning between the state and the movement activists proving to be crucial (see Chapter 6). In the meantime, the subject had now at least been explicitly brought into the political realm.[124]

The years 1980–1982 were marked by a number of small gestures by the Moroccan authorities toward the Amazigh Culture Movement. In 1981, the bimonthly journal *Amazigh,* whose purpose was to provide a public forum for discussion of issues related to Berber language and culture, and sensitize a larger cross-section of society to the subject, began appearing, initially in French. Its initiators were Chafik, Dr. Abdelmalik Oussaden, Chafik's classmate at the Collège d'Azrou and longtime activist, and Mahjoubi Aherdane. The latter's son, Ouzzin, was its publisher. In order to expand beyond the confines of restrictive academic and intellectual settings, both French and Arabic-language editions were planned, and the journal was to be sold in book kiosks all over the country. To that end, seven thousand copies of the first issue, in French, were printed. The title of the journal, as well as the use of Tifinagh graphics on the cover, served to announce that the Berber movement was moving into a more assertive phase, one that rejected the state's policy of confining Berber cultural manifestations to the realm of folklore.

At the same time, its publication could not have occurred without the approval of the Palace. Indeed, Aherdane's centrality to *Amazigh* indicates that the king's interest at that point was to modestly expand the space for public expression of Moroccan Amazigh identity. It is probably no coincidence that the go-ahead for publication was concurrent with the tumultuous events of the Algerian "Berber Spring." As has been true in many cases, developments in Algeria provided a template for Moroccan leaders on how *not* to act, and how instead to fashion alternative policies that would help Morocco avoid Algerian-style social and political unrest. The fact that

Hassan II was busy shoring up a national consensus behind his efforts to incorporate the Western Sahara into Morocco and concerned with heightened levels of socioeconomic distress also contributed to his willingness to allow for a greater measure of Amazigh collective expression. Additional demonstrations of this newly liberal attitude were his assent to the creation of a Commission Nationale pour la Sauvegarde des Arts Populaires, headed by the elder Aherdane, and Chafik's naming to Morocco's most prestigious intellectual body, Le Académie Royal, on November 25, 1980.

Further public assertiveness by cultural activists came August 18–31, 1980, with the holding of what was intended to be an annual colloquium on "popular culture," held in Agadir, by the Berber association, L'Association de l'Université d'Été d'Agadir (AUEA).[125] The university in Agadir would itself become an important arena of Berberist cultural expression, among both its largely Amazigh student body, hailing from the surrounding southern regions, and faculty. The purpose of the colloquium was the promotion of systematized research on Berber topics, including language, literature, and the arts. The broad participation of Amazigh intellectuals from across Morocco in a conference held in the "deep south," the traditional home region of the Ishelhin, symbolized and validated the more inclusive, ethnocultural nature of the emerging Moroccan Amazigh identity, at least for the participants.[126]

However, even during this brief period of relatively liberal expressions and assent to Amazigh activities, there were important limitations on Hassan's strategy of inclusiveness, and more generally on the Moroccan *makhzen*'s willingness to countenance any meaningful alteration of the political and cultural status quo. Even as the authorities found it necessary and useful to cultivate Berber notables and politicians and acknowledge some aspects of traditional Berber culture, they remained keen on preventing overt manifestations of Berber particularity of the modern, ethnopolitical type. Ahmed Boukous, a linguistics professor and one of AMREC's founders (who is now the head of the Royal Institute of Amazigh Culture; see Chapter 6), was not allowed to hold a passport for many years; Hassan Idbelkassem, Tamaynut founder and subsequent movement representative in numerous international forums, was incarcerated for one week during 1982 for putting up a sign written in the Tifinagh script denoting his law office.

The latter incident was only a small part of the authorities' shift away from relative benevolence at that point. Much stronger measures were taken against Ali Sidqi Azaykou, Amazigh poet and educator, lecturer in history at Mohamed V University in Rabat, and president of the Association des Anciens Elèves du Collège d'Azrou. Azaykou had been one of the original members of AMREC, but left the organization in the mid-1970s to found another group, whose membership included the son of the legendary Abdelkrim al-Khattabi. More bluntly political than other activists during these years, Azaykou even evoked the option of political autonomy for Moroccan Amazigh, a demand, he said, that paralleled those of the Basques in Spain and the IRA in Northern Ireland.[127] On July 14, 1982, Azaykou was sentenced to one year in prison, after having refused to ask the king for clemency,[128] for causing affront against the religious foundations of the Moroccan state and therefore offending the public order. His crime was the publication in April of his Arabic-language article "Fi Sabil Mafhum Haqiqi Li-Thaqafatna al-Wataniyya" ("Towards a Real Understanding of Our National Culture") in the first Arabic-language issue of *Amazigh*. Written under a pseudonym, Ait Zulait (referring to the Zulait tribe of southwestern Morocco), the article constituted a frontal attack against the advocates of Arabization, who falsely linked the primacy of Arabic to Islam and preached incessantly the need to replace foreign languages with Arabic in order to promote a national culture while acting in an entirely contrary manner in their own lives. In fact, he said, their real agenda was to wipe out the country's "third language," i.e., Tamazight, spoken by the masses of Amazigh speakers languishing in poverty, while ensuring that foreign languages would be accessible only to the lucky few.[129]

The trial, conviction, and sentencing of Azaykou were the first undertaken by the Moroccan state against a Moroccan intellectual. Why was he dealt with so harshly, receiving a prison sentence that would adversely affect his health from then on? Part of the answer, apparently, was that the article was written and published in Arabic, and would thus be potentially available to a wider, non-French reading audience. The authorities may have desired to make an example of him in order to warn others not to follow his path. Using French, the language of the colonial past, in order to get ahead was one thing. But using Arabic to advocate the raising of Tamazight to equal status with the language of the Holy Qur'an, i.e., to use Arabic to desacralize itself and end its status as the sole official language in Morocco, was quite another. In addition, the Azaykou episode may have been triggered by something quite personal to the king: the appearance of a *New York Times* article on June 6, 1982, during his visit to the United States, that referred approvingly to the Berber struggle for recognition in Morocco and specifically to the journal *Amazigh,* and included quotes from Chafik and journal editor Ahmed Bouskoul. The latter, along with Ouzzin Aherdane, would be interrogated for eleven hours by the police, and the journal would be completely shut down shortly afterwards by Prime Minister Maati Bouabid (of the pro-Palace Union Constitutionnel Party) after publishing only two more French-language issues. As part of the closure, Ouzzin Aherdane and Bouskoul were arrested and Chafik was dispatched to early retirement from his position as director of the Collège Royal.[130] The second session of the summer colloquium at Agadir, in summer 1982, could be held only unofficially, and the third would convene only six years later.

Azaykou died on September 10, 2004, at the age of sixty-two. His passing was entirely ignored by the Moroccan national media, and even the brief daily television news bulletin in Tamazight mentioned it only at the end of the broadcast. This fact was noted bitterly by one Amazigh writer, who compared it to the widespread coverage given to the deaths of other Moroccan writers and artists.[131] Amazigh movement activists have since given Azaykou a prominent place in the pantheon of those who have struggled to rescue and promote Amazigh culture.

Hostility toward Berber self-assertion was expressed in 1984 from a different, albeit traditional, direction, the Moroccan Left. Allal al-Azhar, of a small, radical left party, the Organisation de l'Action Démocratique et populaire (OADP), published a book attacking the Berber Culture Movement as a relic of colonialism whose goals ran counter to Moroccan national interests. To be sure, he wrote, learning the Berber language was a necessary part of absorbing Morocco's national cultural heritage, calling it a "democratic solution." Nonetheless, he depicted the Berbers as a subordinate group within Morocco's Arab-Islamic milieu, highlighting the absence of a written language and high culture of the kind that enable the Persians to resist Arabization. Ironically, the book repeated the long-established view of French colonial-era writers that the Berbers were inherently incapable of forming a coherent large-scale and durable entity because of their tribal nature and social organization. Morocco, the author wrote, could be a successful modernizing national state only if its national identity was based on the Arabic language, which bound it to the rest of the Arab countries. This, too, echoed earlier themes: it was, essentially, a modernized view of traditional Arab-Islamic orthodoxy that viewed the Berbers as being in need of a civilizing hand. While the *makhzen* could only be pleased with the book, many of the OADP's members, being Berbers themselves, were not, and Berber movement intellectuals attacked it in a number of forums.[132]

Overall, the combination of a partly inclusive, corporatist-pluralist model of state-society relations, the ever-present hand of repression, and

Berber geographic diversity resulted in public quietude throughout the 1980s on Berber-related matters, as opposed to the convulsions of the 1980 Algerian "Berber Spring." Based on the results, the Moroccan authorities' treatment of the Amazigh issue during the 1980s was undoubtedly viewed by them as having achieved its aim. When compared with the highly charged atmosphere in Algeria surrounding *le question kabyle,* the Moroccan Amazigh project during the 1980s, and the challenge posed to the state, appeared to the untrained eye to be essentially nonexistent, or at best, an esoteric curiosity.

Four

ALGERIAN STRIFE,

MOROCCAN HOMEOPATHY,

AND THE EMERGENCE OF THE

AMAZIGH MOVEMENT

A̲t its outset, the decade of the 1980s had been envisaged by Arab leaders as the "decade of development."[1] However, matters turned out differently. These years were marked by a steep decline in the price of oil at mid-decade, the eight-year Iran-Iraq war, which bled the two countries white (causing an estimated one million casualties and costing hundreds of billions of dollars, at the very least), renewed violence in the Arab-Israeli sphere (the 1982 Lebanon war and the outbreak of the first Palestinian intifada), and further internecine sectarian violence in Lebanon. By its end, most Arab states appeared to be suffering from a broad commonality of ailments: unproductive and uncompetitive economies, expanding, youthful populations that placed great stress on state capabilities, and stunted political systems, in which ruling elites were overwhelmingly concerned with maintaining their privileged positions.

Over the preceding decades, state capacity, reflected in both the military-security and bureaucratic-civilian spheres, had expanded exponentially. As a result, the balance between state and society had tilted decisively toward the authorities, who had managed to dominate society in the name of the state. Gone were the days when regimes could be swiftly overthrown by a small coterie of army officers. Indeed, between Colonel Mu'ammar al-Qaddafi's overthrow of the Libyan monarchy in 1969 and the military coup in Sudan in 1989, not a single one of the fifteen core member states of the Arab League had experienced regime change.[2] However, it was clear that preserving a regime's hold on power was a simpler matter than genuinely coping with underlying social, economic, and political problems, which threatened to eat away at the legitimacy of the ruling elites, even if they still possessed the aura of having led their countries to independence. Some analysts spoke of "stalled" states unable to mobilize their societies for concerted and lasting development;[3] others, such as Nazih Ayubi, spoke of the emergence of "fierce" states, which dominated their populaces through all-pervasive and heavy-handed *mukhabarat* (intelligence and security services). For Ayubi, the Arab state was now "overstated": it had become too strong, in one sense, enabling it to dominate society in unhealthy ways, while lacking the capacity to provide the answers to society's problems.[4] By the end of the decade, these problems appeared all the more intractable in light of concurrent far-reaching changes that were underway in other parts of the world: the collapse of Communist regimes and the end of the Cold War, and the so-called "third wave" of democratization being experienced in Latin America and elsewhere.[5] From another angle, Moroccan sociologist Mohammed Guessous spoke of the phenomenon of "azmatology" (*azma* is the Arabic word for "crisis"), namely, the continuous preoccupation among Arab writers and thinkers with understanding the nature of the crisis confronting Arab states and finding ways to ameliorate the situation. While being unable to tender game-changing solutions, Arab states, oil producers and non–oil producers alike, were forced to adjust their policies to a more difficult reality.

Emmanuel Sivan has written about the phenomenon of the Arab state in crisis mainly in the context of the expanded reach of Islamist movements.[6] This would certainly be the case in Algeria, and eventually be so, albeit in a more attenuated fashion, in Morocco as well. But the necessity of state retrenchment and adjustment would also widen the civic space available for renewed Berberist assertiveness in both countries. In fact, the expanded reach of Islamist movements in both Algeria and Morocco posed challenges to the Berberists and provided new impetus for their activities, albeit in radically different contexts: Morocco's was one of evolving, controlled expansion of civic space and political pluralism; Algeria's was one of a sudden and large-scale political opening, followed by a violent implosion. In both countries, Berber cultural and political activism would substantially interact with, and impact upon, the larger political playing field.

ALGERIA

By the late 1980s, the bloom had long since been off the rose of the Algerian republic, as twenty-five years of independent existence had proven to be less prosperous and harmonious than nationalist ideology had promised. The precipitous fall in the price of oil and natural gas, beginning in 1985, left the Algerian authorities with far less largesse with which to pacify their restless and youthful population. Economic liberalization measures caused price rises and increased unemployment, imposing additional hardship on much of the population, which had doubled in size in just over two decades' time. Alienation from and contempt for state authorities were widespread, especially among the so-called "wall-leaners" (*hittistes*), the large number of male youth in urban areas idling away the days. Violent youth riots in Constantine in November 1986, demonstrations demanding the improvement of housing conditions in Algiers, the Bouyali band's attacks on the armed forces, and the increasing weight of Islamic norms and strictures, highlighted by the adoption in 1984 of an extremely conservative Family Code,[7] in what had long been trumpeted as a revolutionary socialist country, all indicated that something was amiss. Intraelite fighting pitted the old guard of the FLN, which opposed the post-Boumediene era's economic liberalization measures, against the Benjedid-led group of reformers, which advocated more far-reaching ones. As matters came to a head, Benjedid may have sought to discredit the old guard by provoking a confrontation between the security forces and the populace, a widely held view in Algeria.[8] In any case, the resulting violence in October 1988, popularly dubbed an "intifada" in an evocation of the concurrent Palestinian intifada ("uprising"; lit. "shaking off"), was considerable, and not easily controllable. As had happened during the Berber Spring disturbances in 1980, rioters attacked the symbols of the state, including national and local governmental and FLN offices. But this particular wave of unrest was far more violent, and the security forces' response was far harsher as well. The events began on the evening of October 4th as protesters, mainly children and young people, took to the streets to complain of widespread price increases and growing scarcity of basic necessities. Cars and store windows in one working-class neighborhood of Algiers drew the wrath of some. The next day, the riots turned violent in the city's commercial center, with numerous public buildings being targeted. The army then began to intervene, and so did Islamist militants, giving the rioting a more explicitly political cast. The outcome was brutal: between four and five hundred persons were killed by the security forces, two to three hundred in Algiers alone, and many more were presumably wounded. Thousands were arrested.[9]

No less surprising than the sudden violence was the response of Algeria's president, Benjedid: almost overnight, Algeria was transformed from a populist authoritarian single party–army state to a wide-open playing field for political groupings, civic and cultural associations, and print media, in which the FLN's monopoly on power was broken. As Roberts explains, the struggles within the Algerian elite, which had already lost much of its legitimacy, led Benjedid to suddenly open up the gates of democratization and political liberalization, resulting in the creation of no less than forty-four political parties in 1989–1990, and the publication of numerous independent daily and weekly newspapers and magazines.[10] Of course, the most significant, by far, of these parties would be the Islamist Front Islamique du Salut (FIS).

The first organized Berberist reaction would actually be a nonreaction: while the violence raged across Algerian cities in October 1988, Kabylie was utterly quiet. Some suggested that Kabyles were simply apathetic, uninterested in the events taking place elsewhere. This explanation, perhaps more of an accusation than anything else, is unsatisfactory. A more plausible one is that Berber activists were keen on avoiding giving an excuse to the security services to implement a contingency plan for cracking down harshly against any manifestations of antiregime activity.[11] A third explanation, one which doesn't necessarily contradict the second, is that the MCB activists, caught off guard by the outbreak of unrest, were promised a reward for good behavior, namely, permission to Dr. Saïd Saadi, a veteran MCB figure going back to 1980, to form a more explicitly Berberist political party, which he did on February 9, 1989, the Rassemblement pour la Culture et la Démocratie (RCD; the party would be formally recognized by the authorities in mid-September). For the authorities, this could have been a case of killing two birds with one stone—keeping Kabylie quiet while encouraging another pole for Kabylian sympathy that would compete with both Ait Ahmed's FFS and, no less importantly, the Islamists, as part of Benjedid's overall strategy of manipulation.[12] The problem with such a neat package explanation is the timing: can we assume that Benjedid's plans for wholesale political liberalization were already formulated during the days of the riots themselves, thus allowing for the promise of a quid pro quo? What we do know, as Hugh Roberts has pointed out, is that the ex-chief of police and ex–interior minister, El Hadi Khediri, has acknowledged that he enlisted Saadi's help in ensuring quietude in Kabylie, and that his successor as minister Aboubakr Belkaïd subsequently liased with Saadi regarding the recognition of the RCD.[13] Indeed, the RCD's behavior toward the state during the 1990s was two-faced, unlike that of the FFS, which would remain staunchly oppositionist, to the point where the RCD may well have been irretrievably co-opted by at least a portion of the authorities.

In any case, from the moment of Benjedid's bold but ill-starred leap into the political unknown, Berber cultural and political groups mushroomed, taking advantage of the unprecedented opening of civil space and the political marketplace. As we have seen, up until that point, all legal associative life was governed by the state, and Berber culturalists had had

to operate either informally, clandestinely, or under the rubric of existing state-sanctioned bodies, in some cases even the FLN's youth organization. However, in February 1989, that all changed, as the state withdrew its
monopoly on organized public life. By July 1989, 154 cultural associations
had been established in Kabylie alone, including in just about every large
village. Associations were established in other Berberophone regions as
well (the Aures, Mzab, Jebel Chenoua, and among the Touareg in Ahaggar-
Ajjer), and among Berber communities in Algeria's major cities (Algiers,
Constantine, and Oran). Their agendas varied widely. Many were local in
character, promoting the cultural and historical patrimony of their specific
areas, while others had more of an educational/scientific bent. Common
to just about all were the promotion and diffusion of a written Berber language.[14] Still, the Kabyles remained the epicenter of Berberism in Algeria,
and ties with Berber associations from other regions were minimal at best.

Politically, the party that retained the largest amount of political loyalty
in Kabylie was the FFS, led by the aging but still formidable Ait Ahmed,
who returned from exile on December 15, 1989, just weeks after the party
had officially been legalized. Ait Ahmed's continued appeal was based on
what one Berber activist called "his pristine record of honesty and historical prestige."[15] In contrast, Saadi's newly established RCD lacked the broad
social base of the FFS, constituting a much narrower strand of intellectuals, artists, white collar professionals, and activists. Their political programs
were not identical either. The FFS continued to promote a national agenda
from its Kabyle base, and Ait Ahmed refrained from explicitly advocating
the formal separation of religion and state. Instead, he evoked a religion
that promoted "de culte et de méditation, de tolérance et de fraternité"
("veneration and meditation, tolerance and brotherhood").[16] The RCD's
platform, by contrast, was more explicitly modernist-secular Berber. To
the RCD, Ait Ahmed was sadly out of touch with Algerian contemporary
life. A journalist sympathetic to the RCD said that it represented "a break
with the past and openness toward a new future," while characterizing Ait
Ahmed as a man "with no political future; he is 70 years old and a constant
loser, who misread history."[17] But the RCD's French-derived explicit message of *laïcité,* along with its narrower social base, virtually ensured that the
RCD would never achieve mass appeal.[18] Hugh Roberts actually goes so far
as to say that the combination of the RCD's obsession with French conceptions of secularism and the state and with the language/identity issue, its
ignoring of other potent features of Kabyle political culture, and its openly
declared alienation from the Algerian national legacy was disastrous for the
Berberist movement. The RCD, he concluded, was "not so much a con-

tinuation of the Berberist movement but its gravedigger."[19] While having the virtues of clarity and originality, this conclusion seems overly harsh, and one that underestimates the staying power of the Berberist worldview.

In general, according to Paul Silverstein, the FFS and the RCD were widely perceived by Kabylians as the equivalent of rival village clans (*lessuf*), "embodiments of the ritualized antagonism that is written into Kabyle village social relations and spatial arrangements." They drew their symbolic capital from different historical events, the FFS from the war of liberation and the RCD from the Berber Spring. This deeply rooted bifurcation, says Silverstein, seriously encumbered the MCB.[20] However, one may also view matters from a different perspective more favorable to the admittedly amorphous movement. Despite the FFS-RCD competition, or perhaps even owing to it, the Kabyle-Berber cause was significantly advanced at this juncture, as festivals, colloquiums, journals and newspapers, and university activities proliferated in the newly liberalized atmosphere of Algerian public life. As the Islamist movement gained traction elsewhere, the Berberists sharpened their own message. Algerian society was becoming increasingly polarized, and the historic ruling FLN and its nationalist-populist ideology were adrift.

Countrywide municipal and provincial elections on June 12, 1990, provided the first test of strength for competing political forces in the new Algeria. The two Kabylie-based parties took diametrically opposed positions regarding participation: the FFS boycotted the process, calling it a farce, because the elections, it said, were to be conducted according to the ruling FLN's interests. In Ait Ahmed's view, the proper method of exercising popular sovereignty would be to dissolve Parliament and elect a new constituent assembly that would define the power of all institutions.[21] Democracy, he said, had not yet been properly ingrained into Algerian life. Without fundamental changes such as the ending of the "virtual slavery" of women, massive investments in education, and the guaranteeing of free trade, Algeria's democratic experiment, he feared, could prove to be a false dawn.[22] In a show of strength, up to 200,000 persons marched in Algiers on May 31 in support of the FFS's boycott, condemning acts of violence against women and bars serving alcohol, which had been perpetrated by FIS's shock troops, and demanding the abrogation of the regressive 1984 Family Code. Ait Ahmed's diagnosis was trenchant, but his preoccupation with the regime's manipulation of events caused him to underestimate the strength of the FIS, which he called "completely artificial."[23] The boycott of the municipal elections was partially observed but constituted a tactical error, for it left the field open to the RCD, which opposed the boycott, and, more importantly, to the FIS. The possibility of the FFS becoming a true third force on the Algerian political scene, however limited to begin with, was thus further weakened.

The real story of the elections was the sweeping victory of the FIS candidates, who won approximately 55 percent of the just under 8 million valid votes cast (61 percent of the more than 13 million eligible), giving them 853 of 1,539 municipalities and 32 of 48 provinces. Candidates of the formerly hegemonic FLN finished a distant second. The RCD's candidates received 5.65 percent of the votes in municipal elections and 2.08 percent of the provincial election votes. The RCD's support was, as expected, concentrated in Kabylie, where it won a majority in 87 municipalities and 1 provincial assembly, that of Tizi-Ouzou. Saadi was quick to call the FFS boycott a mistake. His opposition to the FLN, which still dominated Parliament, was no less vehement than Ait Ahmed's. But his concern with the FIS's success led him to again differ with Ait Ahmed on the proper course to pursue during the subsequent months. Postponing the upcoming parliamentary elections, even if it meant maintaining the current FLN-dominant Parliament, and establishing a government of national transition were, in Saadi's view, the only way to forestall the FIS from attaining power. Ait Ahmed, however, favored a continuation of the electoral process, in which he was now prepared to participate, having recognized the error of his ways in boycotting the municipal balloting.

The confrontation between the emboldened Islamists and the hard-pressed Benjedid regime steadily escalated during the remainder of 1990 and throughout 1991, and tore further at the already tattered fabric of Algerian society. The state did take some steps to allow increased expression of Berber identity, permitting, for example, the opening of departments of Berber language and culture at the universities in Tizi-Ouzou and Béjaïa. However, these and subsequent measures failed to fundamentally affect linguistic and cultural politics.[24] The regime's main priority, as it had been throughout the 1980s, was to compete with the Islamist opposition on the playing field of Islamic values and principles, leaving alienated Berberists on the sidelines. Once again, this alienation was vividly expressed through the vehicle of JSK football. Three weeks after the municipal elections, the championship match of the Algerian Cup brought out thousands of JSK supporters, who booed during the playing of the Algerian national anthem and held up huge banners declaring "Nous ne sommes pas des Arabes," "Tamazigh di likoul" ("Tamazight to the Schools"), and "Grand Maghreb berbère." The match was, in fact, a reflection of the overall tense atmosphere in the country, being characterized by clashes between JSK supporters and those of the rival Médéa club, a large police presence, and FIS supporters who chanted "Allahu Akbar" throughout.[25]

The revised Algerian Constitution, approved in a national referendum on November 3, 1989, had reaffirmed the status of Arabic as the country's sole official language. In a move clearly designed to counter the FIS's appeal, the FLN-dominated Parliament passed a measure in late 1990 insisting that official institutions be fully Arabized by July 1992, and all institutions of higher learning by 1997. For good measure, it forbade the importation of computers, typewriters, and any other office equipment that did not have Arabic-language capabilities, and threatened the closing of businesses that employed French in advertising or labeling of merchandise.

The regime's accelerated measures of Arabization occasioned a massive, 500,000-strong protest demonstration in Algiers in December 1990, organized by the FFS.[26] But even as Algeria lurched toward the political and social abyss, Ait Ahmed refused to take sides between the FIS and the authorities. Thus, he sharply condemned the regime's postponement of the June 1991 parliamentary elections, the crackdown on the FIS leadership, and reportedly large-scale human rights violations against detained Islamist activists. At the same time, he insisted that the FIS should not be allowed to gain a monopoly on public life. "Nous refusons," he told an interviewer, "le faux choix entre la république intégriste et l'état policier. Nous voulons casser ce dilemme en redonnant la parole à la population" (We refuse the false choice between the fundamentalist republic and the police state. We want to rescind this dilemma and restore the voice of the population).[27] He approved of the appointment in the summer of 1991 of a government of technocrats, headed by Ahmad Sid Ghozali, for it took power out of the hands of the FLN's old guard and included at least one overt FFS supporter: the new economy minister, Professor Hocine Benissad, one of Algeria's better-known economists, who would have been an FFS candidate for Parliament. By contrast, Saadi supported the crackdown on the FIS and postponement of the June elections. The FIS, he told an interviewer, should be dissolved, for it "uses democracy to organize civil disobedience . . . [and] believes that violence is a strategy to take power."[28]

Ait Ahmed's vision of a pluralist, tolerant democratic Algeria was swiftly overtaken by events. Nationwide parliamentary elections, finally held in late December 1991, produced an overwhelming triumph for the FIS, which won 188 out of the 231 seats decided in the first round of elections, with a total popular vote of 3.2 million out of 6.9 million valid ballots.[29] One hundred ninety-nine seats remained to be contested in runoff elections in mid-January. With the FIS only 28 seats short of an absolute majority after the first round, its domination of the new Parliament was assured. FLN candidates garnered 1.6 million votes, but only 15 seats. The FFS received 510,000 votes. However, owing to the heavy concentration of its supporters in the Kabylie districts, it won 25 seats, making it the second-largest grouping in Parliament, with the prospect for a few additional gains in Algiers in the second round. The RCD fared poorly, garnering only 160,000 votes (2.9 percent) and winning no seats. Saadi was himself defeated in Tizi-Ouzou by an FFS candidate.

The crucial question for Algeria at this juncture was whether the FIS would be allowed to gain control of Parliament through the completion of the electoral process. True to form, the two Kabyle parties differed on the next step. Saadi was openly in league with those sections of the Algerian political, military, economic, and cultural elites who favored a nullification of the process that, if carried forward, would "bury" Algeria and condemn it to chaos. Ait Ahmed, by contrast, declared that the cancellation of the second round of elections would make Algeria look like a banana republic and insisted that one could not destroy a democracy in order to save it.[30] On January 2, 1992, an FFS-sponsored demonstration, attended by over 300,000 persons, called for the strengthening of democratic institutions, including the presidency and the Constitutional Council, which would oversee the numerous challenges to results in specific election districts. Only thus could the threats posed by both the hard-liners in the regime and the Islamists be rebuffed.

Yet as has so often been the case in modern Algerian history, events took a different course than that advocated by Ait Ahmed. On January 10, the military deposed Benjedid, nullified the electoral process, and banned the FIS. A new, more violent epoch in Algerian politics was thus inaugurated: a no-holds-barred struggle between armed Islamist movements and the security forces, which cost up to 150,000 lives, tore Algerian society asunder, and left the populace terrorized and terrified. Against the background of a brutal conflict between the state authorities and an armed Islamist insurgency bent on capturing power, Algeria's well-rooted authoritarian political-cultural patterns would reassert themselves in a big way. The Algerian scholar Abdelkader Yafseh describes Algeria as "l'Etát-clan," in which "clans" (not in the strictly literal sense of kinship ties) inserted loyal followers into state institutions, thus protecting their interests under the wings of ostensibly legitimate institutions.[31] This strategy would help to successfully defeat the Islamist insurgency, avoid regime collapse, and enable the authorities to reintroduce a degree of pluralism in public life, beginning in 1995, including political parties, elections, and competitive, and sometimes utterly uninhibited, print media. But the country's military leaders, and Presidents Liamine Zeroual (1995–1999) and Abdelaziz Bouteflika (1999–), had difficulty persuading the public that they were acting in the general interest.[32]

Kabylie and the Civil War

As Algerian society as a whole became more polarized, the Berber aspects of the crisis were brought into sharper relief as well. Kabyle Berber artists were physically attacked during the years of civil war by the Islamists, not as Berbers as such, but as symbols of a decadent, evil culture that they promised to eradicate. The fact that some of the artists were militantly opposed to the Islamists made them even more inviting targets. Still, ascribing a Kabyle dimension to these attacks is unavoidable. Two prominent examples were the murder of Tahar Djaout, a Kabyle writer and polemicist (he was attacked on May 26, 1993, and died a week later, on June 2), and the kidnapping of the singer Matoub Lounès, in September 1994, by the Group Islamique Armé (GIA) faction of the Islamist insurgency. The latter incident brought 100,000 Kabylians into the streets in Tizi-Ouzou demanding his safety and threatening *la guerre totale* if he was to be harmed.[33] Notwithstanding the death sentence proclaimed against him by the GIA, Lounès was released two weeks later.

One enduring fear among Algerian Berberists has been that the authorities would strike a deal with the Islamists at their expense, notwithstanding the bitter strife between the regime and the Islamists during the 1990s. One attempted dialogue with the Islamists initiated by Zeroual in 1993–1994 occasioned harsh words from Saïd Saadi: the move, he said, "was merely a relentless pursuit of the same old policy. If it is to enable the [political] clans to survive by plunder, we know where that will lead us." What was needed, he insisted, was for the government to step down and "free the state from the clans," and for all forces in Algerian society opposed to both the government and the fundamentalists to mount a comprehensive resistance. Strikes, boycotts of schools, and armed self-defense were all means to be employed.[34] However, as is so often the case in Algerian politics, there was more to this call than met the eye. Saadi's concern with a possible government-Islamist deal dovetailed with his support for the *eradicateur* faction in the Algerian military. This faction, in turn, was sympathetic to assisting Kabyle villages in organizing their own self-defense militias against the Islamists.

Fall 1994 marked a milestone in the contentious history of Kabylie-state relations. Three widely observed general strikes were conducted in support of the long-standing demand for official recognition of Tamazight and Berber culture, the last in protest against Zeroual's failure to refer to Berber grievances in a nationwide television address. Even more impressive was the extended school strike throughout Kabylie, involving 700,000 students, between September 1994 and March 1995. One of the strike's central demands was the official recognition of Tamazight; the state insisted that this could only be done through a national referendum. Knowing that it was likely to fail, movement leaders rejected the notion on the grounds that official recognition was a fundamental human right according to the United Nations charter. According to one analyst, the climate in Kabylie was one of "latent insurrection," which the state would not be able to ignore.[35]

Broad recognition of the Berber aspect of Algeria's existential crisis now came from two opposing forces within the Algerian firmament. In January 1995, a joint declaration of eight opposition parties gathered together in Rome under the auspices of the Sant'Egidio Roman Catholic public lay association, including the FFS (but not the RCD), recommended the restoration of the rule of law and the democratic process in Algeria and the relegalization of FIS in return for the cessation of violence.[36] It also stated that "the components of the Algerian character are Islam, Arabism, Tamazight, and the two cultures and languages contributing to the development of that character. They should have their place and should be strengthened in the institutions, without any exclusion or marginalization."[37]

The FFS's presence in Rome, and the RCD's absence, highlighted their opposing positions. Throughout the years of strife, the FFS doggedly stuck to its established principles. The only alternative to the regime's "scorched earth logic," declared Ait Ahmed (who had returned to dividing his time between Switzerland and France), was a "dialogue for historic reconciliation." Direct dialogue with the Algerian army, the only possible guarantor of a democratic solution, was absolutely essential. FFS demands from the regime included lifting the state of emergency, the release of political prisoners, the abrogation of special courts and laws, and guaranteeing freedom of political activity. It favored parliamentary elections under a system of proportional representation—following a transitional process to be monitored by a national parliamentary committee—underpinned by a democratic constitution.[38] It was only within such a national framework that Kabyle specificity could be properly cultivated. In contrast, and reflecting the RCD's opposition to the Rome declaration, Matoub Lounès characterized Ait Ahmed's participation in the Rome conference as tantamount to supporting terrorist operations in Kabylie against the Berbers.[39]

Three months after the Rome meeting, and just days after massive demonstrations in Kabylie commemorating the fifteenth anniversary of the Berber Spring, the Algerian authorities acknowledged the legitimacy of Tamazight as well, through the establishment of a Haut Commissariat à l'Amazighité (HCA) attached to the president's office and headed by the venerable and venerated Mohand Ait idir u Amrane.[40] The HCA, said the official announcement, would be "charged with the rehabilitation of Tamazight [culture] . . . one of the foundations of the national identity, and the introduction of the Tamazight language in the systems of education and communication."[41] As in the case of King Hassan's statement in Morocco the previous year (see below), Berber culture had now been legitimized by the authorities, though the announcement fell short of enshrining Berberist movement demands in law. As in Morocco as well, the Algerian authorities, although reluctant to go too far in embracing the Amazigh movement, now viewed the country's Berberist current as being potentially useful in helping to counteract Islamist forces.

The declaration establishing the HCA was a milestone in the Berberists' long struggle for recognition. Nonetheless, satisfaction with the declaration was not universal. Saadi's wing of the MCB (MCB–Coordination Nationale) supported the statement and its accompanying call for an end to the school boycott. Yet the FFS wing of the MCB (MCB–Commission Nationale) and the autonomous Union of Education and Training Workers withdrew from the concurrent negotiations to end the strike with the president's representatives before they were concluded. Ironically, it was the FFS that was now the more militant proponent of Berber rights, declaring that the government had not gone far enough in giving official recognition to the national character of Tamazight. The opposing stands of the RCD and the FFS stemmed from their contrary orientations vis-à-vis the regime: the RCD continued to maintain common cause with the authorities in the struggle against the Islamists, whereas the FFS remained part of the political opposition to the regime. This split was reflected in the November 1995 presidential elections: while the FFS boycotted it entirely, Saadi legitimized the process by running as a candidate himself, winning 1,115,796 votes (9.3 percent).

In any case, the authorities adopted additional incremental measures in the direction of the Berberists. Tamazight was introduced during 1995 in a number of governates, beginning with the fourth year of elementary school. The following year brought movement in the constitutional sphere as well. The Algerian Constitution was altered to recognize the Amazigh component of Algerian identity alongside the Islamic and Arab ones, none of which, it emphasized, could be employed for party propagandizing and politicking. The move was a step forward, but because it fell well short of official constitutional recognition of the Amazigh language, it was not received favorably in Kabylie. In a referendum to approve the amendments on November 28, 1996, voter turnout in Tizi-Ouzou was only 25 percent, and of these voters, 63 percent rejected the amendments.[42] (By contrast, the amendments were approved overwhelmingly in the country as a whole.) Indeed, even as President Zeroual adopted incremental measures to try and placate militant Berberists, other actions were far less to the liking of movement activists. The passage of a law in 1996 compelling the sole use of Arabic by Algerian governmental and civil institutions and in all commercial contracts drew strong protests in Kabylie, and among Francophone speakers in general.[43] So did Zeroual's attempts to institutionalize and legitimize his rule through presidential, parliamentary, and municipal elections. Although he had participated in the 1995 presidential elections, Saadi refused Zeroual's subsequent entreaties to join the regime and renewed the RCD's strident opposition to what it called a "presidential dictatorship." Algerian political life was clearly perceived in Kabylie as falling far short of what was desired, namely, the recognition of Kabyle Berber specificity within a more genuine pluralist and democratic order.

Eighteen months later, in mid-1998, Kabyle anger burst forth in a way not seen since 1980. The background was twofold: the 1996 Arabization law was scheduled to go into effect on July 5; and Matoub Lounès was murdered on June 25, just a few weeks after having returned from France, where he had lived for most of the time since his kidnapping in 1994. The law, declared the RCD, was racist, and tantamount to bringing the FIS to power; in response, the law's proponents accused its opponents of raising the issue to conceal their allegiance to the French language. Against this background, Lounès's assassination lit the spark. Lounès had long been a thorn in the side of both radical Islamist groups and the authorities, militantly proclaiming his Kabyle Berber identity and rejecting the Arab-Islamic basis of the state. He had only just finished preparing his fourth CD since the start of Algeria's civil strife. Its title song, "Open Letter To . . . ," constituted a brazen challenge to official conceptions of Algerian identity, with its utter rejection of Algeria's post-independence order and defiant assertion of Amazigh identity in the context of struggle. Amazigh lyrics were set to the tune of the Algerian national anthem, whose altered refrain was "And betrayal, and betrayal, and betrayal":

> The resurrected forces of injustice have brought tragedy.
> They have dyed our roots, which are now crumbling.
> They have used religion to paint Algeria Arabic . . .
> Hungry but peaceful, we will never submit
> As strong men and women, we will never wear the yoke
> No tragedy can impede our journey
> Just as floods do not unroll ancestry
> With our identity and wisdom, we will free Algeria.[44]

The authorities blamed the GIA for Lounès's murder, but his adoring and angry Kabyle public thought that the blame should be spread further. Lounès's funeral procession on June 28 turned into an antigovernment demonstration of 100,000 persons that erupted into weeks-long outbursts of protest and violence in Kabylie, including attacks against government property and the tearing down of Arabic-language signs. Banners and slogans at the funeral procession included "no peace without the Berber language," "we are not Arabs," and "pouvoir assassin, Zeroual assassin." The demonstrations subsided after several weeks, and the continued rivalry between the FFS and RCD weakened Kabyle leverage on the authorities.[45]

Writing in *Le Monde,* Kabylie-born Professor Salem Chaker, of the Institut National des Langues et Civilisations Orientales (INALCO) in Paris, whose numerous scholarly works on Berber language and culture allow one to call him the "dean" of modern Berber studies, declared that since 1980 the simple question for Berbers was "to be or not to be." The youth of Kabylie, in particular, had responded to the post-colonial era by asserting their Berber identity within the Algerian state. However, he said, the regime's responses were not only insufficient, but in light of its relentless Arabization policies, a threat to Kabyle collective existence. What was needed, Chaker declared, was to break the taboo: the Algerian state as constituted in 1962 was not "ours" and must change. Linguistic and cultural autonomy for Berber-speaking regions, especially Kabylie, within a democratic Algeria, was the need of the hour.

Chaker had already raised the possibility of a federalist model for the country. Other voices now also spoke explicitly of Kabylie "borders" and "areas" and called for the federalization of the country. Indeed, the Canada-based Kabyle scholar Amar Ouerdane had published a text advocating federalism as a solution to Algeria's crisis, pointing out that the most advanced states in the world were federal states.[46]

For the Algerian authorities, heavy-handed and uncompromising repression of Amazighité in Kabylie, where the Berberist agenda had attained predominance, was no longer possible. But to the chagrin of activists, the state relentlessly opposed expressions of modern Berber identity elsewhere, prohibiting Tamazight signs, inscriptions on the mastheads of magazine covers, and cultural organizations, and forbidding the use of Tamazight first names outside of Kabylie.[47] With the Berberist parties holding less than 11 percent of the seats in Algeria's Parliament, their ability to serve as the vanguard for a transformation of the Algerian state was clearly limited. Moreover, they continued to work at cross-purposes. In a reversal of 1995, Ait Ahmed tendered his candidacy in the April 15, 1999, presidential elections, while Saadi did not, citing what he said was the government's open measures to rehabilitate the FIS. In that vein, also, MCB activists called for a boycott of the vote, citing the refusal of all candidates to advance the cause of Tamazight. The day before the vote, Ait Ahmed withdrew from the race, along with five other opposition candidates, citing vote-rigging and other indications that the elections would not be free and fair. As a result, former foreign minister Abdelaziz Bouteflika, the army's choice for president, was elected unopposed. Subsequently, he declared that Tamazight would never be consecrated in law as an official language in Algeria, and repeated what the authorities had stated during the 1994 school strike, that Tamazight could only be designated a "national language" through a referendum (in which non-Berber speakers, constituting the majority of the population, were unlikely to vote in favor of the idea).[48]

Interestingly, in light of his previous anti-Islamist and antiregime militancy, Saadi later expressed support for Bouteflika's national reconciliation referendum, held on September 16, 1999, while the MCB again called for a boycott of the vote and the FFS was lukewarm to it. The participation rate in the Kabylie region was less than half of the national average. Saadi also declared that Bouteflika's views on the recognition of Tamazight were more sympathetic than those of any other previous Algerian president. The outcome of Saadi's flirtation with the authorities came in December, when the RCD joined the cabinet of Prime Minister Ali Benflis (himself a Chaoui Berber), receiving two portfolios in a government that also included an Islamist party.[49]

By the late 1990s, the Algerian state authorities had succeeded in beating back the armed Islamist challenge, albeit at great cost. The Berberist movement's nightmare scenario of an Algerian Islamic Republic had not come to pass, and the territorial integrity and unity of the Algerian state were preserved. Ironically, had matters turned out otherwise, it is not inconceivable that Kabylie would have been placed on the road to separate existence, something along the lines of Iraqi Kurdistan. What remained was a sharpened Kabyle Berber collective consciousness, a continuing distrust of the authorities, notwithstanding the RCD's on-again, off-again relationship with them, and a need to take the Kabyle-Berber agenda into account if Algerian society was to be reconstructed and refashioned. Of course, neither the regime nor the small legalized Islamist groups had a genuine vision for a more inclusive and democratic Algeria. Nonetheless, if only for tactical and short-term reasons and however grudgingly, they too had finally begun to acknowledge the legitimacy of the Berberist current.

MOROCCO

The last decade of King Hassan's rule was marked by important incremental political, social, and economic changes from both "above" and "below" that significantly altered the Moroccan public landscape. In essence, Hassan sought to remake himself into a more benevolent, albeit still autocratic, reformer, controlling the pace of change and thus maintaining societal and regime stability—this at a time when, next door, Algeria had descended into horrendous civil strife. A central part of his strategy was a reaching out to the historic opposition political parties to entice them into a power-sharing arrangement. Over the course of the 1990s, Hassan gradually fashioned a consensus which ensured that the political game would still be dominated by the Palace while allowing for a greater degree of party competition and sharing of the spoils of power. This arrangement was grounded in constitutional reform that gave a bit more power to the Parliament and prime minister, as well as steps that encouraged the opening of Morocco to the global economy and allowed for the expansion of civil society. It culminated in the formation in February 1998 of a much-ballyhooed *gouvernement d'alternance,* headed by longtime opposition figure and former exile Abderrahman Yousoufi, of the Union Socialiste des Forces Populaires (USFP) party (whose core originated in Mehdi Ben Barka's earlier UNFP).[50]

To be sure, transforming Morocco into a "state of law," one of Hassan's proclaimed goals, was a Herculean task in which the real work still lay ahead. Nonetheless, a new atmosphere gradually evolved. Hassan's incremental approach, in which obstacles to change remained salient, was reflected in the Berber-state nexus during the 1990s. As with everything else that was occurring in Algeria, the increasing politicization of the Kabyle Berber community served as a warning light for the Moroccan regime. It also inspired Moroccan Berberists toward greater self-assertion.

The first significant indication that the Berber culturalists were intent on a more activist mode came in August 1991, with the issuance of the "Agadir Charter for Linguistic and Cultural Rights" by six different Berber culture associations, AMREC, Tamaynut, L'Association de l'Université d'Été d'Agadir (AUEA), L'Association culturelle Aghriss (founded in June 1990; later known as Tilelli ["freedom"]), L'Association Ilmas (founded in 1991, in the city of Nador, in the north of the country), and L'Association Culturelle de Sous. They were subsequently joined by five others. The Charter, the idea for which had first been suggested by Ahmed Boukous ten years earlier,[51] laid out succinctly the Moroccan Amazigh movement's worldview: Morocco's cultural identity was a plural one, whose oldest and most deep-rooted components were the Amazigh language, literature, and the arts. Amazigh culture, said the Charter, was a dynamic one, interacting with other cultures throughout history while not losing its foundations. However, it had been systematically marginalized in all spheres of Moroccan life. On the legislative front, the Charter said, there existed no texts affirming the Amazigh component of the national culture. Politically, notwithstanding "the massive participation of Amazighs in the armed struggle for the liberation of the homeland from the colonial yoke," the Moroccan political elites, along with the "*salafi* current," preferred to build a centralized national state based on an "exclusive ideology and linguistic and cultural uniformity" (*unitarisme*). On the sociocultural plane, declared the Charter, the state presented Amazigh language and culture as the "symbolic products of the disadvantaged rural world," which were to be excluded from the national realm and progressively jettisoned through Arabization policies. In the economic realm, the precariousness of Amazigh language and culture reflected the pauperization and marginalization of the population of the periphery, whose economic and social foundations were being destroyed. The Amazigh language and culture had fallen into a process of decay, said the Charter, accelerating their assimilation into an Arab-Muslim framework, reinforced by the massive dependence of the Moroccan countryside on the urban core. The Charter's Marxist-tinged analysis of this process—the corrosion of rural society's previous "collective ownership of the means of production, and mutual and collective management of the social contradictions by the group itself," by "concentration of capital and land ownership and the proletarianization and downgrading of the poor peasantry"—reflected the radical left-wing background of many of the document's framers.

Hence, both for the sake of the Amazigh people and Morocco as a whole, and "in the context of building the national democratic culture," the signatories of the Charter proclaimed the following objectives:

1. attaining a constitutional stipulation of the "national character" of Tamazight, alongside of Arabic;
2. reviving the moribund "National Institute for Tamazight Studies and Research," which would be charged with (a) developing a unified graphics system to adequately transcribe the Tamazight language, (b) standardizing its grammar, and (c) fashioning appropriate educational tools for its teaching;
3. integrating the Tamazight language and culture into the various areas of cultural and educational activities, particularly the public schools, as well as universities, where Tamazight language and culture departments should be established;
4. undertaking scientific research programs to benefit the Tamazight language at the university and academic levels;
5. according the Tamazight language and culture their rightful place in the mass media, both print and audiovisual;
6. encouraging production and creation in different fields of knowledge and culture in the Tamazight language;
7. creating, distributing, and utilizing the means of expression and learning of the Tamazight language.[52]

In 1993, Amazigh associations created an umbrella organization, the National Coordination Council; the 1990s would also witness the creation of a number of Amazigh-language journals: *Tamazight,* founded by Hassan Idbelkassem in December 1991; *Tamount,* the mouthpiece for AMREC, founded on Brahim Akhiat's initiative in 1994; and another *Tamazight,* founded in 1995 by Ahmed Adghirni. The trilingual monthly *Le Monde Amazigh,* the most important Amazigh periodical currently being published, was founded in 2001 by Rachid Raha, an independently wealthy activist and Rabat-based journalist hailing originally from the Rif.

Nineteen ninety-four proved to be a turning point in the history of Amazigh-Moroccan state dynamics. In March, a number of Amazigh activists addressed a letter to Morocco's prime minister asking for official recognition of Tamazight. On May 1, the Tilelli association used the occasion of traditional May Day demonstrations to organize a march on behalf of the Amazigh cause, in the town of Errachidia in southeast Morocco. Among its banners, written in French and Tamazight (but not in Arabic!), were the proclamations "No democracy without Tamazight" and "Hebrew is taught, but not Tamazight." Two days later, seven of the marchers were arrested and charged with agitation, disturbing public order, and spreading slogans that were in contradiction of the Constitution.[53] Four of the seven, teachers all, were released on May 17. The other three were sentenced to prison terms (two for two years, and the third for one) and fined ten thousand dirhams each. All seven were reportedly abused physically. The harshness of the authorities' action was quickly tempered, however. Following widespread publicity, with four hundred Moroccan attorneys volunteering to defend the teachers, their sentences and fines were reduced, allowing them to go free four days after their June 29th appeal.[54]

One could evaluate the episode in any number of ways. The authoritarian state apparatus had moved swiftly to punish the deviants, sending a clear message to all political and social forces that certain "red lines" were not to be crossed with impunity. It had then demonstrated its "benevolent mercy" in reducing the sentences. At the same time, Berber movement activists, keen on pressing the authorities to alter these previously inviolable red lines and thus willing to take risks for their cause, had won considerable publicity and sympathy. At a time when Morocco was keenly interested in improving its international image, particularly in the area of human rights, as well as promoting a greater measure of political pluralism at home, it was clear that the old rules of the country's political game were being modified. Sensitivity to the manifestations of Berberist self-consciousness was demonstrated at the very top of the regime, even before the original verdict's appeal, when Prime Minister Abdellatif Filali announced the government's intention to initiate television news broadcasts in the Moroccan Berber dialects. Soon afterwards, short daily news bulletins in each of the three main ones began airing on Moroccan state television. Regional radio broadcasts in the three dialects, which already existed, e.g., on Radio Agadir, would receive increased state funding as well. As Katherine Hoffman shows, these radio programs were central to the ongoing shift in Ashelhi identity (and among other Berber groups as well), a shift from being rooted in a specific place to a "decentralized practice of speaking." Speaking and hearing Berber in modern-day Morocco were becoming a marker of identity in ways not previously witnessed.[55]

The developments catalyzed by the Tilelli demonstration culminated that summer in King Hassan's annual August 20 speech on "Revolution of the King and the People Day," a commemoration of France's last-ditch, and

ultimately failed, efforts in 1953 to damp down the flames of Moroccan nationalism by exiling Sultan Mohamed V and his immediate family. As such,
it was the perfect moment for Hassan to both reach out to and contain the
Amazigh movement by initiating a major shift in the official Moroccan discourse regarding Amazigh identity. In preparing for the speech, Hassan had
actually requested from AMREC a document elaborating on the Amazigh
movement's precise demands.[56]

Wrapping the entire issue in the bonds of Moroccan patriotism, Hassan framed the subject in terms of Morocco's "historical deep-rootedness"
and national unity. The years of the French protectorate (1912–1956), he
said, were ones of almost unrelenting struggle, during which no one, and
no region, possessed a monopoly on heroism. To prove his point, he referred to the resistance displayed almost immediately, in 1914, at the battle
of El-Herri in the Khenifra region,[57] followed in 1921 by the battle of Annoual in the Rif region against Spanish forces (although Hassan made no
reference to Abdelkrim himself), and in 1934, at the climactic battle of
Jebel Bougafer, in Morocco's southeast, as France completed its long and
costly pacification campaign. By symbolically uniting the diverse regions
of Moroccan society in an overarching national narrative, Hassan gave the
Berber communities their due, however briefly, complementing the official and more conventional story line, which uses the urban-Arab sector's
response to the 1930 Berber *dahir* to mark the onset of the nationalist movement.

Of course, however much Hassan enjoyed expounding on his understanding of underlying historical dynamics, this was no mere history lesson.
Rather, his intentions were to justify the possibility of teaching Morocco's
"dialects" (*lahjat*) in the school system, at least in the primary grades, alongside of Arabic. In doing so, he partially embraced, and thus legitimized, the
Amazigh agenda, while indicating his determination to contain it within
acceptable parameters. Up until now, Hassan explained, the question of
the "dialects" had been a controversial one, engendering responses ranging
from "sincerity" (*sidq*) and "adulation" (*tamalluq*) to "demagogy" (*dimaghu-
jiyya*). In fact, Morocco's strength was in its diversity, he said, of which its
"dialects" were an integral part. To be sure, Morocco was an Arab-Islamic
country, holding fast to the Qur'an and the Arabic language in which it was
written. But Arabic civilization, which had come from the East, had not
canceled out Morocco's rich particularities, expressed in language, food,
dress, architecture, wedding celebrations, and songs. These particularities
were also biological: "We have to hold to the language of the Qur'an," Hassan stated, "but not at the expense of our authenticity and dialects, espe-

cially since there is not one of us who cannot be sure that there is in his dynasty, blood or body a small or large amount of cells which came from an origin which speaks one of Morocco's dialects."

Interestingly, Hassan framed his decision to legitimize the teaching of Amazigh as a defensive act designed to protect Morocco from Western intrusion and domination, a near-constant theme over the previous five hundred years of Moroccan history. The dialects were now necessary, he bemoaned, because "the West has invaded our homes." More than one of every three Moroccan houses was characterized by the mixing of Arabic with French or Spanish (and soon even English, he warned), creating a kind of "Esperanto" patois that could only be understood by those living there. The use of "Tarrifit, Tamazight or Tashelhit," together with Moroccan spoken Arabic and classical Arabic, was imminently preferable, he said, to the current "un-Moroccan" and "disfiguring" practice of mixing foreign and native languages together, and would provide "immunity for the future."

There was surely no small irony, and perhaps no small amount of cynicism, in the worldly, French-educated Hassan's call for Moroccans to "reject foreign languages in our homes and in the teaching of our sons and daughters." After all, throughout history, Morocco has always been a multilingual environment, and even after independence, its policies of Arabization had proceeded at a more measured pace and in a less confrontational atmosphere than in Algeria. But by framing the Tamazight-Arabic question in terms of a common Moroccan identity that needed bolstering against Western intrusion, Hassan had wrapped himself in the cloak of Moroccan nationalism in a way that he hoped would help manage and contain ethnic and sociolinguistic tensions. In doing so, he provided crucial legitimacy and encouragement for the Amazigh Culture Movement, even though key portions of the Moroccan elite remained ambivalent toward it, at best.[58] In 1995, Hassan followed up on his declaration by issuing a royal decree authorizing the necessary curriculum changes to permit the teaching of Berber dialects in schools.

For Amazigh activists, it was essential that Moroccan ethnic and cultural identity be framed in terms of an Amazigh-Arab personality. Abandoning or neglecting the Amazigh aspects of Moroccan identity, they declared, "would be a veritable outrage against ourselves, an intolerable mutilation of our personality, an amputation of our patrimony, and a denial of history."[59] Seeking to capitalize on Hassan's shift, movement leaders representing eighteen Amazigh associations presented a letter to the Royal Cabinet on June 22, 1996. Referring to their attachment to Moroccan "unity in its diversity," the letter advocated the constitutional redefinition of the kingdom as an Islamic state whose languages are Tamazight and Arabic, equally, with each being given the same chances to evolve. In addition, the letter stated, the Constitution should also specify Morocco's belonging to North Africa and "reinforce the unity of the region's peoples, who come from the same civilization and same history."[60]

Hassan's subsequent speeches over the next five years periodically reiterated that Berber was one of the three main components of the Moroccan identity, the others being Arab and Sahrawi (in line with Moroccan insistence that the contested Western Sahara was an integral part of its historical patrimony). Up until his death in 1999, however, the changes Hassan had heralded had still not been implemented, let alone the comprehensive measures advocated by the Amazigh associations. Particularly irksome was the intensification of the authorities' Arabization campaign. A new *dahir*, proclaimed in November 1996, attempted to block parents from giving their offspring names in Tamazight, or any other language. Accompanied by an official list of Arabic names, it stipulated that "the first name shall be an original Moroccan first name. It must not be of foreign origin . . . [it] shall not be based on the name of a city, a village, or a tribe. It shall not create a threat against the society's customs or national security." Moroccans living abroad were required to receive permission from the Moroccan authorities to use a foreign first name.[61] Moroccan Amazigh associations also complained about the acceleration of Arabization of names of towns, villages, and geographical landmarks, which in Morocco are overwhelmingly of Berber origin. Ironically, the acceleration of Arabization came at a time when space for autonomous political and cultural action in Morocco was increasing, pointing to the profound tensions and contradictions that continued to characterize Moroccan society.

Berberists and Islamists

The Berber Culture Movement's battle for national recognition was not merely against recalcitrant authorities oriented toward Arabism and Islamic identity. As in Algeria, the gradual loosening of the Moroccan *makhzen*'s control and increasing the degree of public space available for political, social, and cultural groups meant that the Amazigh movement would have to compete with an active, nongovernmental Islamist current.[62] Indeed, far more than the Berberists, Islamist movements were increasingly making their impact in the Moroccan public sphere, albeit in a largely nonviolent manner, in vivid contrast to the mayhem occurring next door in Algeria.

The Moroccan authorities' approach to the Islamist current was broadly similar to its strategy regarding all political groupings: combining the use of carrot and stick to entice, co-opt, repress, and/or suppress, depending on the particular circumstances and parties involved. Decades earlier, the authorities had employed Islamist militants to carry out violent acts against the Left. However, they eventually hunted down and broke up al-Shabiba al-Islamiyya, a small, radical Islamist group advocating the violent over-throw of the Moroccan monarchy, and condemned to death its leader, Abdelkrim Mouti'. Unrepentant, Mouti' has been in exile for more than thirty years. Although remnants of the group would continue to surface occasionally, as in a 1994 attack on a hotel in Marrakesh that killed two Spanish tourists, al-Shabiba al-Islamiyya faded into irrelevance.[63] Far more formidable was Abdeslam Yassine, a former Education Ministry school inspector and head of the officially banned al-Adl wal-Ihsan (Justice and Charity) movement. Yassine openly challenged Hassan's legitimacy—and that of any monarch in Islam—in a 1974 missive, "Islam or the Deluge." He later admitted to having prepared his burial shroud for the occasion. Instead, he was confined to a psychiatric hospital for three years and kept under various forms of detention for most of the next quarter-century. However, under Hassan's creeping liberalization in the 1990s, Yassine's movement was able to gather strength, particularly among secondary school students and on campuses. As a counterweight, the authorities actively promoted Sufi Islamic orders (*tariqat*) in order to diminish Wahhabi influences. They also encouraged the entry into the political system of other Islamist forces, ones that were willing to play by the state's rules, i.e., accepting the inviolability of the monarchy. Some of these were incorporated into an existing, albeit moribund, political party, the Mouvement Populaire Démocratique et Constitutionnel (MPDC), in time for the 1997 parliamentary elections. Eventually, this would produce the Parti de la Justice et du Développment (PJD [Hizb al-Adl wal-Tanmiyya]), which would join the front ranks of Moroccan parties in Parliament beginning in 2002.[64]

The gut instinct of the Moroccan Islamist current was that the Amazigh Culture Movement posed a threat to its own program for renewing and deepening the Islamization of Moroccan society. In 1997, Shaykh Yassine published a book entitled *Dialogue with an Amazigh Friend (Hiwar ma'a Sadiq Amazighi)*, in which he laid out his objections to the Berberist revival. To be sure, Yassine wrote, he did not reject the revival of Amazigh tradition or the discussion of its glorious history. Indeed, he emphasized, Amazigh history was filled with praise for the Islamic message, and it included active participation in waging jihad against tyranny and imperialism. As an *alim* and reformer, Rifian leader Abdelkrim was one such *mujahid,* he said, staking a counterclaim to Abdelkrim's legacy from that of the Amazigh movement (see Chapter 6). The problem, said Yassine, was that the Amazigh cultural revival had taken on a political dimension, and was being promoted as part of the Western efforts to foster a new world order aimed at debasing and fragmenting Islam and keeping it weak through the cultivation of ethnic differences and the promotion of a "godless secularism." As an example, he referred to the Paris-based World Amazigh Congress (see Chapter 5), which sought the "Amazighation of the Maghreb" (*tamzigh al-Maghrib*). The result, he warned, would be a disastrous fragmentation of society, in which its two peoples, Berbers and Arabs, would fight and kill one another, plunging the region back into the pre-Islamic *jahili* era of weakness and destruction.[65] Moreover, he claimed, the rejection of the primacy of Arabic, embodied in the demand for constitutional change to recognize Tamazight as an official language, and the efforts to revive the ancient Tifinagh script, was not only a service to Francophone imperialism but also tantamount to blasphemy against the Qur'an and Allah.[66]

The "friend" referred to in the title of Yassine's book was none other than Moroccan Amazigh movement doyen Mohamed Chafik, who had known Yassine for many years during their work in the Education Ministry and had engaged in exchanges with Yassine over a two-year period that were included in the book as well. While accepting the importance of the Arabic language and not denying Islam, Chafik rejected the notion that Berber identity should be repressed and subordinated, arguing with Yassine in Islamic terms, emphasizing that Islam is a religion of "reason, science and wisdom." In response to Yassine's frontal assault on the Amazigh movement's *laïque* affinity, Chafik tried to undermine him by claiming that the very notion of *la'ikiyya* (*laïcisme*) had been invented by Islam, albeit not by name. As proof, he cited Qur'anic verses declaring that there was no compulsion in religion, and emphasizing the rightness of dialogue and debate in religious matters, as opposed to compulsion and terror, according to the principle of *ijtihad* (see Chapter 6), upon which there were no limitations of place or time. In concluding one of his responses to Yassine, he cited the saying "the Arab is not better than the foreigner, nor the foreigner than the Arab, [one is distinguished] only by piety." As for accusations that the Amazigh movement was guilty of *shu'ubiyya,* he retorted that the original phenomenon in early Islam had been in response to Arab racism.[67] Chafik made his point regarding *laïcisme* and religion on many subsequent occasions, telling an interviewer, for example, that the Amazigh people, without having to renege on their Islamic faith, must distance themselves from "obscurantist fanaticism" through the employment of secularism, which was enshrined in the Qur'an.[68]

According to Chafik, Yassine and he had first met in 1955, Yassine was married to a former student of his, and, most importantly, Yassine's family, al-Hihi, originated in the Berberophone Haha region in southwestern Morocco and received its civil law name, Yassine, from the French in 1950–1951. Thus, although Yassine claimed a sharifian descent, he had Berber roots, the denial of which drew Chafik's criticism.[69]

Other Berberists responded to Yassine's treatise as well. Yassine had written that the modern Arabic used in the daily media was "weak" and "rotten," and could in no way be compared to the majesty of the Arabic of the Qur'an. The Amazigh scholar, poet, and activist Ahmed Asid responded by attacking the Islamists and the proponents of Arabization. Language in the modern age, Asid declared, needs both to be open to foreign influences and stem from one's own society in order to be able to deal with changing situations.[70] Moreover, Asid claimed, the insistence on Arabism and the nobility of the Arabic language as being the combined product of religious and national feeling had no basis either in religious texts or in the conduct of the Prophet's companions or the *ulama* in early Islamic times. Berberists, he emphasized, were not inherently hostile to the Arabic language, but rejected the notion that its protection required that Tamazight be sacrificed.[71] As for the traditional accusation that a "foreign hand" was behind the Amazigh movement, Berberists responded by pointing to the various forms of involvement on the part of Iran, Afghanistan, and Saudi Arabia on behalf of contemporary Islamist movements.[72]

Tensions between the two groups took a new turn in 1999, as plans went forward to publish a translation of the Qur'an into Tamazight, a project that had been ten years in the making. Amazigh intellectuals were said to believe that it would shake up Islam the way translations of the Bible into vernacular languages had helped to undermine the hegemony of the Catholic Church in medieval Europe. In this spirit, the translator, a scholar and high school history teacher in Casablanca, Johadi Lhoucine, was dubbed by some journalists a Muslim Martin Luther. Of course, the Qur'an had already been translated into more than forty languages. However, Moroccan Islamists viewed a Tamazight translation as posing a real threat to the primacy of Islam in Morocco as they understood it, and called Berberists the "new Barghwatists" (see Chapter 1). The publication by Berber activists of studies of the Barghwata and pre-Islamic Berber culture provided them with further ammunition in this regard.[73] In this particular instance, the authorities indefinitely blocked the publication of the translation, showing their ambivalence toward the promotion of Tamazight and their concern with maintaining social order. Eventually, though, they would relent.

At the same time, portions of Morocco's left-wing secular forces, including those within the *alternance* government, had become openly sympathetic with the Amazigh movement as part of their advocacy of greater democratization and promotion of civil society—and no less important, they valued it as a counterweight to the Islamist current. For example, in 1995, the ex-Communist Parti du Progrès et du Socialisme (PPS) declared at its national convention that Tamazight was a national language and part and parcel of Moroccan culture, and its French-language daily paper, *Al Bayane,* published a weekly page in Tamazight with Latin characters.[74] The USFP's *Liberation* daily and a few other papers did so on occasion as well. This trend within the government found favor among Berberists, for whom democracy was a basic prerequisite for the development of Amazigh culture.[75] Nor was this merely a matter of importance to intellectuals; as one activist noted, what really counted was how this affected matters of daily living—for example, whether, when a Berber went to a hospital and was unable to understand anyone, he was termed an "idiot."[76]

Even Istiqlal leader Mohammed Boucetta was quoted in the party's daily Arabic-language organ *al-Alam* as viewing the advancement of the Berber language as one of his priorities.[77] However, the party, which was also part of the *alternance* government established in 1998 and historically at odds with all forms of Berber specificity and particularism, remained wedded to its advocacy of Arabization, which was also commensurate with its Islamic modernist orientation. The more substantive embrace of the Amazigh movement by King Hassan's son and successor, Mohamed VI, would compel all Moroccan political forces, including the Istiqlal, to recalibrate their positions.

PART III *Reentering History in the New Millennium*

At the turn of the new century, scholars of the contemporary Maghrib were in general agreement that North African states, nearly a half-century after having achieved independence, were at a crossroads. Clement M. Henry characterized the regimes as "desperate," threatened by the burdens of economic adjustment programs and facing confrontations with Islamist oppositions. Benjamin Stora and I. William Zartman talked of the need for a redefining, or "re-contracting," of state-society relations. Abdallah Laroui, who was not only a preeminent historian of the region but also a committed Moroccan nationalist writing from an explicitly historicist/materialist perspective, quietly despaired over the failures of Maghrib governments and societies to become sufficiently "modern" and "scientific" in their mindsets to be able to interact meaningfully, and with agency, with the developed world.[1] More specifically, North African ruling elites faced many of the same challenges: reconciling the requirements for stability and the need for change, finding ways of giving their large, youthful, and increasingly urbanized populations a stake in the system, containing vigorous Islamist opposition movements, and managing the stresses while maximizing the opportunities produced by globalization processes.

Within this picture of general uncertainty, the presence of an ever more articulate Berber-Amazigh culture and identity movement making demands on the Moroccan and Algerian states was an increasingly relevant piece of the puzzle, even if the context in each was substantially different. The Berber question even gradually crept onto the public agenda in Mu'ammar al-Qaddafi's Libya, where Berberophones constituted only 8–9 percent of the population and were historically marginalized. The extension of the Amazigh movement to Libya was facilitated by another important development, namely, the systematic employment of various international platforms and organizations to advance the Berberist agenda. This was carried out by both individual Amazigh movement associations and a new actor with an ambitious name, the World Amazigh Congress (Congrès Mondial Amazigh; CMA).

Five

BERBER IDENTITY AND THE
            INTERNATIONAL ARENA

I n recent years, the expansion of an international discourse on human rights, which includes the recognition of the existence
and rights of subordinate, nondominant ethnolinguistic groups, has created new opportunities for the promotion of the Berberist agenda. Consequently, a number of Berber organizations, both in North Africa and the
Diaspora, have made the advocacy of the Berber cause in various international forums a central thread of their activities. In so doing, they sought
to bring pressure to bear not only on the Moroccan and Algerian states,
but also to highlight the repressive policies of Libya toward its largely marginalized Berber populace, and the dire straits of the Touareg in Mali and
Niger. In addition, they called European governments to task for their lack
of recognition of the Berber component of immigrant communities.

In particular, the phenomenon of accelerated globalization enabling
or prompting greater assertion of subnational identities—familiar from
the European Union (EU) experience—opened up new avenues through
which Amazigh activists could challenge the prevailing ethos of contemporary North African states. Given their marginalization during earlier waves
of "globalization," there is no small irony in the fact that the latest wave
helped stimulate and reinforce the fashioning of a specific Berber/Ama-
zigh ethnopolitical community. Most recently, the Internet, the symbol,
par excellence, of the contemporary global information revolution, has become an additional important tool in the construction of a "landscape of
group identity," i.e., the building of an "imagined" Amazigh community
worldwide. The number of Internet sites, listservs, and Facebook pages devoted to Amazigh matters has mushroomed, as has the uploading to You-
Tube of a full range of Amazigh-related events. These new technologies
have enabled the speedy dissemination of information and images, often
in real time, as well as stimulating discussion and contacts between activists worldwide,[1] thus taking Anderson's imagined community-building

to a whole new level. Ironically, Berber activists often characterize their fight as "part of the vast movement of resistance to globalization, which is a movement that is in essence against cultural identities."[2] One concrete outcome has been the forging of organizations whose agenda is explicitly pan-Berber. Naturally, these could only be based outside of North Africa. In essence, a two-way street was created, as the cultural, social, and political activities of Berbers living beyond North Africa's confines both helped strengthen and deepen the self-awareness and activities of the Berber communities back home, and reinforced their own hybrid identities. The outcome was a significant contribution to determining the multiple meanings of "being Berber" in the modern, increasingly globalized world.

International human rights organizations had first been mobilized in 1985 on behalf of twenty-three Kabyle activists being tried by the Algerian authorities for challenging the state's hegemonic discourse on national identity (see Chapter 3). Beginning in the 1990s, Berber organizations, both existing and new, expanded the scope of their activities into the international arena.

Among Moroccan associations, it was the Rabat-based Tamaynut that took the lead. Made up predominantly of lawyers and with approximately thirty branches nationwide, Tamaynut had signaled its desire to internationalize the Berber question in 1991 by translating the Universal Declaration of Human Rights into Tamazight.[3] Two years later, it was invited by the UN to participate in an international human rights conference in Vienna (June 14–25). Its leaders consulted with eight other associations in Rabat (five of which, along with Tamaynut, had been the original signatories of the 1991 Agadir Charter), and reached agreement on a document to be tendered to the UN meeting that foregrounded the juridical aspect of the Amazigh movement's demands, emphasizing that the Amazigh people fit the UN definition of "indigenous minority populations" whose legal rights were supposed to be protected under international law. The juridical angle had long been advocated by Tamaynut head Hassan Idbelkassem, who, together with his fellow lawyer and activist Ahmed Adghirni, attended the Vienna meeting. AMREC activists, by contrast, were not keen on emphasizing the Moroccan Amazigh's minority status and avoided using the vocabulary of "indigenous minority," for it clashed with the Amazigh movement's foundational notion that the large majority of the Moroccan population was in fact Amazigh in origin. Subsequent formative Amazigh movement texts would also reject the "minority" and "ethnic" labels. Nonetheless, AMREC did give the go-ahead to Tamaynut to present the document to the Vienna meeting.[4] It would be the first of many such interactions. In time, Idbelkassem would become a regular fixture at international gatherings advancing the rights of minority and indigenous peoples, including the Durban conference against racism in 2001, and as a member of the United Nations Permanent Forum on Indigenous Issues. He would also help found the Parti Démocrate Amazigh Marocaine (PDAM) in 2005 (the party would be banned by the authorities in 2007, and its legal status remained unresolved as of the end of 2009).

CONGRÈS MONDIAL AMAZIGH

Initial moves to institutionalize an international Berber movement came August 21–28, 1994, at the seventeenth Festival de Cinéma in Douarnenez, Brittany, which was devoted to the *peuples amazighs (berbères)*. The festival, whose Moroccan initiators included Idbelkassem, Adghirni, and Ouzzin Aherdane, included not only eighty-plus films and documentaries, but also exhibitions, debates, dramas, music, and distribution of information by twenty-five Berberist organizations based in France, Morocco, Spain, and Algeria (one only, IDLES, from Tizi-Ouzou). Clearly, the Bretons' own linguistic-cultural self-assertiveness in recent years had made Brittany an appropriate place for Berberist groups to convene. The very fact of the gathering, coming on the morrow of King Hassan's endorsement of the teaching of "dialects" in Moroccan schools and just a few months before the extended school strike in Kabylie over recognition of Tamazight, demonstrated that the Amazigh movement was expanding the arena of its activities. The participation of a Lyon-based Touareg association in the festival, and the declaration of support for the Touareg against governmental repression by Mali and Niger, gave further tangible expression to the "pan-Berber" imagining of "Tamazgha," and voice to the Berber community most distant from modern Amazigh stirrings. Moreover, it marked an expression of solidarity with the Touareg uprising in Mali and Niger, which had begun in 1990 against the background of political and ecological pressures that threatened the Touareg nomadic way of life and traditional autonomy from central authorities, a process that had begun during the era of French colonialism in West Africa and continued after independence.[5]

Indeed, one of the festival's two concluding declarations, signed by all of the participating organizations, was an explicit declaration of support for the Touareg people, in the face of the continuing "massacre" and "genocide" by the armies of Niger and Mali, supported by French arms, military advice, and economic aid, with an accompanying call to France to cease such support and for the United Nations to break its silence on the matter. The second declaration laid out the movement's demands for cultural and linguistic recognition for the Amazigh people in the territory of Tamazgha, "from the Canary Islands in the west to the Oasis of Siwa (in Egypt) in the east, from the Mediterranean in the north to Burkina Faso in the south." Tamazgha, it stated, was "both African and Mediterranean." While calling on governments to take practical measures to recognize Amazigh identity, constitutionally, culturally, and linguistically, the primary concern of the declaration was to apply pressure on them by internationalizing the issue, particularly through the United Nations framework, which itself had in recent years become more attuned to the problems and issues related to nonstate actors. To that end, it condemned North African governments' failure to implement a 1990 UN resolution proclaiming the "International Year of Indigenous Peoples" and demanded implementation of a follow-up UN resolution on February 8, 1994, proclaiming the "International Decade of Indigenous Peoples" (the resolution was renewed for a second decade in 2004). This would entail the establishment of monitoring committees to "protect and implement" the rights of the Imazighen. Moreover, the signatory associations proclaimed their intention to participate in the project of creating a World Amazigh Congress to "defend, develop and disseminate" Amazigh culture, language, and identity through democratic and peaceful means.[6]

The idea of a Congress had first been announced a month earlier, at the twelfth session of the UN's Working Group on Indigenous Populations, held July 25–29 in Geneva, where Idbelkassem was elected as president of the African group of indigenous peoples, and which included Moroccan and Algerian Amazigh, and Touareg Amazigh of Mali and Niger. The project then started to take shape during and after the Douarnenez festival. At Idbelkassem's suggestion, a committee of Diaspora activists was formed, which included Mabrouk Ferkal, the president of l'Association Tamazgha (Paris), Rachid Raha, the president of the Granada-based David Montgomery Hart Foundation, and Mouloud Lounaouci, head of l'Association Amazighe de Grenoble St-Martin. A second Paris-based committee representing Diaspora groups, the Comité de France pour la Préparation du Congrès Mondial Amazigh (CFPCMA), which focused specifically on preparing for the Congress, was established in accordance with a 1901 law governing associative life in France. Ferkal headed this committee, as well as being the coordinator of the other one, creating no little confusion and dissent among other participants.[7]

Nonetheless, the will to go forward was clearly present, enabling the holding of a "pre-congress" September 1–3, 1995, at Saint-Rome de Dolan, in southern France. One hundred delegates representing thirty-six Amazigh cultural associations in North Africa and the Amazigh Diaspora attended. Among them were representatives from nine Moroccan associations; as was the case with the gathering in Douarnenez, only a single delegate representing an Algeria-based association was present, owing to visa problems.[8] Ferkal was named head of a newly established body, the World Amazigh Congress (CMA), headquartered in Paris; the body's three vice presidents were Idbelkassem, Abdoulahi Attayoub, and Ouzzin Aherdane. As in Douarnenez, the conference issued a strong resolution in support of the Touareg people in the face of repeated "massacres" by the governments of Mali and Niger; the governments of Algeria and France were also held responsible for contributing to the gestation of the situation; and the international community as a whole was condemned for its silence.[9]

It would take nearly two more years before the Congress could be officially convened. Not only were there disagreements among various Berber associations regarding the purpose and makeup of the Congress, but the drafting of the founding statutes of the organization was kept under wraps, so as to avoid prematurely antagonizing North African governments. But the First World Amazigh Congress was finally convened August 27–30, 1997, in Tafira, a suburb of the city of Las Palmas, in the Canary Islands, the westernmost point of Tamazgha, the declared Berber homeland. The CMA was explicitly designed to be a nongovernmental international organization, independent of all governments and political parties, one that was peaceful, democratic, and dedicated to the defense of humane values, while rejecting totalitarian, sectarian, racist, and sexist ideologies. It was open to all functioning Amazigh associations. Nineteen cultural associations and political party representatives came from Morocco, which created a good deal of infighting among them both before and during the conference. Thirteen associations from Algeria were represented, although the Algerian authorities at the very last minute prevented most of the Algerian delegates from attending. Delegates from Libya, Burkina Faso, Mali, Mauritania, and the host Canary Islands attended as well, as did other representatives from nine European countries, the United States, and Canada. Representatives from regionalist movements in France, including the Cultural Council of Brittany, sympathizers from Ireland and Wales, and members of the European Bureau for Lesser-Used Languages attended as guests. The delegates, numbering more than 350, were mainly students, journalists and writers, artists, lawyers, and doctors. Ferkal, who had taken the lead in organizing the Congress during the previous two years, was replaced (temporarily, as it turned out) by Antonio Felix Martin Hormiga of the Canary Islands. The enthusiastic advocacy of Berber identity by the Canarian activists, none of whom spoke Berber, was a pleasant surprise for many of the other delegates. It turned out to be an unpleasant one for the Spanish authorities, who sensed a whiff of separatism emanating from the activists, with their newly discovered Berber identity serving as a convenient hook to distinguish themselves from the mainland. Indeed, resolutions by one of the committees at the Congress in support of self-determination for the Touaregs and Canarians were looked on with dismay not only by Spain, but by Algeria as well.[10]

In terms of institutions, two bodies were established: a thirty-nine-member Federal Council, the Congress's legislative arm, consisting of ten Moroccans, ten Algerians, ten persons from the Diaspora, mostly of Kabyle origin, four Canarians, three Touaregs, and two Libyans; and a ten-person World Bureau, the Congress's executive arm under the president's authority, composed of three Algerians, two Canarians, two persons from France, and one each from Libya, Nigeria, and Germany. The anomaly of there initially being no Moroccans among the latter group derived from a split among the Moroccan delegation, in which Idbelkassem and his supporters ceased their participation after having been excluded from places on the Federal Council by Aherdane's supporters, resulting in the suspension of the entire Moroccan delegation until their internal differences were worked out.[11] The CMA General Congress (CG) was to convene once every three years. Annual membership dues were fixed at $120 per organization. These dues, plus whatever might be received in donations and generated by CMA activities, would make up the budget of the organization. With the number of member organizations amounting to approximately one hundred in 2008, the CMA's financial resources were clearly minuscule.

Regarding the Congress's objectives and the means to achieve them, Article 4 of its governing statute laid out a twelve-point platform, designed at bottom to "defend and promote the cultural identity of the Amazigh nation," and to achieve official recognition of the Amazigh identity, culture, and language through constitutional and institutional steps. While stressing the need to ensure collective Amazigh rights, including the protection of Amazigh children from the "phenomenon of deculturation," the language of the platform was informed by the internationalist discourse on human rights, democracy, the rule of law, and the rights of women. In other words, the promotion of Amazigh identity and culture was an unabashedly and explicitly modernist project.

The very fact of the meeting was a feat in and of itself, policy and personal disagreements notwithstanding.[12] However, the organizational fortunes of the CMA would ebb and flow during its first decade of existence, as internal power struggles displayed at the founding conference, as well as the maneuvering for influence by North African governments, would continue to plague it: for example, in 1999–2000, the organization's legislative and executive arms temporarily split, resulting in rival gatherings and judicial proceedings to determine the legitimacy of CMA ownership in a French court.[13]

The fourth Congress (August 5–7, 2005) was a high point for the CMA, thanks to its location, the city of Nador, abutting Morocco's Rif region in northern Morocco, making it the first CMA Congress to be held within "Tamazgha." The willingness of the Moroccan authorities to allow such an event to take place underscored the regime's more accommodating approach toward the Amazigh movement. But a new ebb in the CMA's organizational fortunes would be reached in 2008. It was only natural for it to seek to hold its fifth Congress in Algeria, to give equal weight to the other primary community of North African Imazighen. Moreover, the site chosen was none other than Tizi-Ouzou, the epicenter of the events of the now-mythical Berber Spring. However, provincial government authorities refused to issue the permits necessary for convening the gathering, notwithstanding numerous legal efforts by the CMA, which eventually concluded that it had no choice but to postpone the gathering, scheduled to be held in late July, and seek an alternative venue. While four different Moroccan cities quickly bid for the right to host the conference, CMA head Belkacem Lounès, a Kabyle, attacked the Algerian authorities for discriminating against Imazighen in a press conference in Tizi-Ouzou, and called on UN and EU officials to apply pressure on the government to allow the conference to be held. The CMA also lodged a formal protest with the European Parliament. Writing in the Algiers daily *El Watan,* the journalist Omar Berbiche also attacked the Algerian government for its behavior, noting that while France was dedicating a street in the memory of Matoub Lounès, on the occasion of the tenth anniversary of his assassination, the Algerian authorities continued to censor history and deny identity, contradicting the Algerian Constitution's recent enshrinement of the Amazigh component of Algerian national identity[14] (see Chapter 7).

It was agreed in short order that the Congress would be held in Meknes, the second consecutive time that Morocco would provide the host venue. On October 5, Lounès held another press conference in Tizi-Ouzou, this time calling on the Moroccan and Algerian authorities to open their land border, closed since 1994, in order to make participation affordable for Algerian Amazigh delegates. He framed the request in universal terms, demanding "freedom of movement for Amazighs on their land, Tamazgha," citing Article 36 of the United Nations Declaration on the Rights of Indigenous Peoples.[15]

Meanwhile, the move of the conference to Meknes, implying renewed cooperation between the Amazigh movement and the Moroccan authorities, was apparently too much for two Moroccan Amazigh militants, Rachid Raha (who was serving as one of the CMA's vice presidents) and Ahmed Adghirni, the secretary-general of Morocco's first explicitly Amazigh political party (PADM), which had recently been banned by the authorities. The two flew to Algeria, only to be barred from entering. While being held in the airport terminal, they proclaimed the establishment of a new CMA Federal Council, creating a state of confusion. One Kabyle activist who served as a CMA vice president during 1999–2005 bemoaned the "Kafkaesque circus" that had overtaken the organization as internecine rivalries between "competing clans" damaged the image of the Congress.[16] Six months later, Raha and Adghirni demonstrated their militant opposition to the Moroccan authorities in another, more provocative fashion. In March 2009, Raha, claiming to be president of the CMA, appealed to the European Parliament to revoke the advanced status granted to Morocco the previous year, detailing a series of discriminatory, "anti-Amazigh apartheid" measures taken by the Moroccan authorities. Concurrently, Raha's CMA, together with Adghirni's banned PADM, issued a lengthy report challenging the Moroccan state's official report to the UN's Committee on Ending Racial Discrimination (CERD).[17]

Still, for all of its limitations and internal divisions, the CMA framework provided another vehicle by which to promote the Amazigh agenda, both in North Africa and in the Diaspora, vis-à-vis other international organizations. For example, its Federal Council, meeting in Paris in November 2000, recommended the application of pressure within Europe so that the European Charter for Regional or Minority Languages could be adopted and applied in all states.[18] Kabylie's "Black Spring" in 2001 (see Chapter 7) prompted a number of missives of protest from the CMA leadership to various international bodies and leaders, including UN Secretary-General Kofi Annan, UN High Commissioner for Human Rights Mary Robinson, the UN Working Group on Autonomous Peoples, the Durban international conference against racism, the UN Committee on Economic, Social and Cultural Rights, and European Union officials.[19]

By summer 2008, the CMA was clearly on the international organization map, seeking every opportunity to advocate the Amazigh cause and mobilize support from the international community. For example, just prior to the Meknes/Tizi-Ouzou episode, a pan-Amazigh delegation met in Brussels with officials from the European Commission and European Parliament. The participants included CMA President Lounès, Vice President Raha, Ferhat Mehenni (head of MAK, the movement for Kabylian autonomy; see Chapter 7), Adghirni, Alhader Ag Faki, representing the Touareg of Mali, Sidi Husseiny Ag, of the Touareg of Niger, and two Amazigh activists based in Belgium.[20] Detailing the problems faced by Amazigh groups throughout the Maghrib and Sahel countries, they emphasized the universal aspects of the issues at stake, employing the discourse of democracy and human rights, in calling on European parliamentarians to ensure that European commerce with these states be conditioned on their respect for these universal values. In this regard, the CMA was following a well-established pattern dating back at least to the trials of Kabyle activists in the mid-1980s for subversion and disloyalty to the Algerian state.[21]

The list of distinguished guests at the CMA's Meknes meeting was a veritable potpourri of representatives of ethnocultural minority movements around the globe, highlighting the ties being forged by the CMA. They included representatives from the Catalan and Biscay regional governments (Spain), a Catalan nationalist party, the Basque parliament, the Democratic Union of Bretonne, and the Maluku people of Indonesia. The Amazigh-Catalan relationship had been actively cultivated in recent years, with an exchange of delegations between Kabyle groups and Catalonian parliamentarians in 2007–2008. The Catalan presence at the Meknes conference was also financial, as the gathering was supported by both the Catalan General Government and the Catalan Agency for Development and Cooperation. Clearly, Catalonia relished its status as a model for the Amazigh movement and believed it useful to support CMA activities.

Libya, the CMA, and Amazigh Identity

Unlike Morocco and Algeria, Libya has mainly been an unremittingly hostile environment for the Amazigh movement. Numerically, Berberophones were estimated at no more than 8–9 percent of the total Libyan population of approximately six million persons, most of them Ibadi Muslims,[22] like their Algerian counterparts in Mzab. Traditionally they dwelled in the Jabal Nafusa highlands of Tripolitania or in desert localities such as the Cyrenaican town of Awjila. However, as has been the case in Algeria and Morocco, internal migration in recent years to Libya's main cities has resulted in a loosening of linguistic and cultural bonds among the younger generation. As is often the case in other nonurban Berberophone settings, Libyan Amazigh women tend to be monolingual in the local Berber dialect, while the men tend to be bilingual, in Arabic and Berber. The militantly pan-Arab revolutionary regime of Colonel Mu'ammar al-Qaddafi, which came to power in a military coup on September 1, 1969, was utterly opposed to any notion smacking of a specific Berber identity and harshly repressed whoever dared to suggest otherwise. Amazigh movement activists and associations thus could only function abroad. They routinely included Libya on a "black list" of regimes, characterizing Qaddafi as "practicing cultural and linguistic genocide" against the Amazigh people.[23] In 2000, the London-based Libyan Tamazight Congress (Agraw a'Libi n'Tamazight) was established, demanding constitutional recognition of Tamazight as an official language alongside of Arabic. The following year, an exiled Libyan Amazigh activist, Muhammad Umadi, established the Arabic-language Tawalt ("Word") website, which would play an important role in developing a resource base for Libyan Amazigh language and culture.[24]

Eventually, however, the existence and problematic status of Libyan Imazighen emerged out of obscurity, drawing Qaddafi's attention and resulting in a partial policy shift. Libya's unequivocal declaration to UN bodies that its population was entirely homogeneous (i.e., Arab) did not go unchallenged. With the help of Paris-based *Tamazgha*'s alternative report in 2004 to the Committee for the Elimination of Racial Discrimination (CERD), the body of experts that monitors the implementation of the UN's International Convention on the Elimination of All Forms of Racial Discrimination, CERD members pressed Libya for more information and acknowledgment of the status of Berbers (including Touaregs), as well as black Africans, in the country.[25]

On November 5, 2005, CMA President Lounès met with Qaddafi in Tripoli to discuss the Amazigh question, at the Libyan leader's invitation. The meeting caused more than a few raised eyebrows among Amazigh activists, who feared that Qaddafi was being legitimized without having changed his hostile attitudes and policies. But Lounès was encouraged by the meeting and subsequent developments. One month later, a follow-up delegation of Amazigh activists from North Africa and the Diaspora met with him for three hours, making Qaddafi the first North African leader to meet with an international delegation of Amazigh activists. They agreed to engage in an ongoing dialogue, which produced a joint committee and further meetings in 2006. Qaddafi's son, Sayf al-Islam, whose power and influence were clearly increasing, was supportive of the shift in favor of recognizing the Amazigh component of Libyan identity, resulting in the lifting of a quarter-century-old ban on the use of Berber names, which his foundation described as "an aggression which can no longer be ignored."[26] The thaw in the Libyan regime's attitude was clearly part of a broader policy to burnish Libya's international image.[27]

However, in early 2007, the budding thaw received an apparently sharp blow, as Qaddafi publicly rejected the idea of Berber specificity outside of an Arab identity. Providing his own somewhat idiosyncratic version of the classic Arab-Muslim narrative of Berber origins, Qaddafi declared that ancient Amazigh tribes[28] had died out from drought: "Where are the tribes of Mishwash [Meshwesh], Ribu, Libu, Samu, and Tihnu? We can't even pronounce their names. . . . We [Semitic Arabs] set out from Yemen until we came here [to Libya]. We went by land, by land [*barr barr*], so they called us 'Berbers.'" The Phoenicians, "who are Arabs like us," he said, came to North Africa by sea, settling on the coastal plains, while later waves of Arabs came with the advent of Islam. It was colonialism which came and said, "'you are Berbers, a different people. You are not Arabs.' They wanted to make us err concerning our history, our origin, and our civilization. . . . Libya," he declared, "is for the Libyans. We will not tolerate in Libya any ethnic zealotry [*shuʿubiyya*].[29] No one can say 'my origin is this, that, or the other.' Whoever says this is an agent of colonialism."[30]

The linking of modern Berber identity to colonialism was, of course, a long-standing approach by North African Arab nationalists. Why Qaddafi chose to speak about the subject at that particular moment is not known, but he clearly felt it useful or necessary to do so. For Amazigh movement activists, it was actually a golden opportunity to bring the Libyan Amazigh "file" into the wider public eye. They quickly organized an international campaign on behalf of Libya's Amazigh population, garnering hundreds of signatures on a petition titled "Qaddafi and the Amazigh: A Policy of Blatant Enmity." Signatories included a number of key figures in the newly formed International Organization for the Defense of the Rights of Minorities and Women in the Middle East and North Africa, whose founding conference in Zurich on March 24–26 gathered together leading liberal intellectuals and activists from across the MENA region.[31] CMA President Lounès, for his part, was especially offended. After all, he had endured criticism for promoting the dialogue with Qaddafi. In an open letter to the

Libyan leader, he painfully described their previous contacts, calling them "a moment of historical reconciliation which we hoped was going to make of Libya an example of dialogue between peoples and cultures." Hence, his bitter disappointment:

> What colonialism is capable of creating a people *ex nihilo,* with its language and traditions that go back several thousand years? How could colonialism have done this—given that when the first foreigner arrived on North African soil, he found that the Amazigh had already been there for a long time? . . . You even denied the evidence, when you assured us that the Amazigh problem did not exist in Libya. But . . . the Libyan Amazigh, like Amazigh elsewhere, face ostracism, exclusion, and discrimination of all kinds. . . . You say that "Libya is for the Libyans" and that you will not accept anyone's saying that they have this identity or that identity. So be it—but then [you] must immediately suppress any reference to Arab identity in all of the country's legislative texts, as well as in the names of political, economic, and cultural institutions, starting with the Arab Libyan Republic, Libyan Arab Airlines, the Union of the Arab Maghreb, etc. Then we will be entirely [favorably] disposed to speak of a "Libyan Libya," with its history, languages, and cultures. But if your conception of Libya is one of an exclusively Arab country, then for us, the fight for our identity continues. . . . We like to think that colonialism no longer exists. . . . But there is no worse colonialism than internal colonialism—that of the pan-Arabist clan that seeks to dominate our people. It is surely Arabism, in that it is an imperialist ideology that refuses any diversity in North Africa, that constitutes a betrayal and an offense to history, truth, and legality.[32]

As it happened, Qaddafi's regression to an earlier hostile discourse turned out not to be the last word on the subject, as the sharp response to his anti-Amazigh statement apparently made an impact. In the summer of 2007, the Libyan authorities renewed their charm offensive, allowing Amazigh activists to hold a conference in a Tripoli hotel, followed by high-profile visits by Sayf al-Islam and Prime Minister Baghdadi Mahmudi to the Jabal Nafusa area to inaugurate major development projects.[33] Libya now appeared to be tentatively following in the footsteps of Morocco and

Algeria, recognizing that the denial of Amazigh identity was counterproductive, while its acknowledgment and ameliorating policies, economic and cultural, could be politically useful. Of course, this did not mean that the road ahead would be a smooth one. The devil would be in the details regarding Libya's approach to the Amazigh issue, just as it has been with Morocco and Algeria. Indeed, one year later, the four Libyan members of the CMA's Federal Council and additional participants in the 2008 CMA Meknes conference were harshly attacked as being separatists and traitors working for the benefit of foreign interests. This came at a meeting of three hundred members of an organization calling itself "The Youth of Libya's Tomorrow," in the town of Yefren in the Jabal Nafusa region. The participants, many of whom were members of the regime's Revolutionary Committees, then marched to the house of one of the CMA Council members, who was a relative of exiled Tawalt founder Umadi, hurling stones at it and painting incendiary slogans such as "Death to Traitors" and "Physical Purification" on its walls in the presence of the police. They also warned of the consequences of participating in any future Amazigh-related meetings and promised to engage in additional punitive actions in other towns in the region. The CMA strongly condemned the incident, sought to mobilize the international community on the issue, called for an official Libyan government apology, and suggested that it might institute legal action against Libyan officials for their support of incitement to violence and racial hatred.[34] Lounès specifically mentioned it in his remarks to the plenary session of the UN's Durban II conference against racism and discrimination in Geneva on April 24, 2009, drawing a vocal protest from the Libyan representative, to which Lounès, in turn, rejoined that the day that North African states respect the rights and liberties of their citizens, he would be the first to congratulate them.[35]

The CMA, France, and Its Berber Community

Given the centrality of France's Berber community in the Amazigh movement, both numerically and organizationally, it was only natural that the CMA would address its particular issues as well. On February 22, 2005, it submitted a lengthy report to CERD, "France: Discriminations à l'égard des Amazighs." The document was an alternative report in opposition to an earlier French government one on the subject of discrimination in France. Noting that Berbers' immigration to France had begun at the end of the nineteenth century, and that they had played a crucial role in the industrialization of the country, particularly following the two devastating world wars during the first half of the twentieth century, the report claimed that today there are around two million Imazighen in France,[36] two-thirds of whom hold French citizenship, "contributing to the economic, scientific, artistic and athletic domains," mentioning such luminaries as singer Edith Piaf, singer-composer and actor Marcel Mouloudji, comedian Daniel Prevost, actress and singer Isabelle Adjani, and football superstar Zinedine Zidane. Moreover, the essential values of French society, it said, conformed closely to their own societal foundations: "democracy, liberty, secularism (*laïcité*) and equality." However, the report complained, Berber immigrants and their offspring continue to suffer from various forms of racism and intolerance, just as other immigrants do. Moreover, the failure of their own countries of origin to recognize their existence as a defined collective introduces an additional, sociocultural level of discrimination. The French government, said the report, repeatedly rejects Berber requests as being "political," and thus matters that should be taken up with their own countries. French policies of "censure, and persistent confusion of identity, constitute serious acts of symbolic violence and racism, which in the final analysis negate the very existence of a community of citizens, and therefore participate in the goal of erasing our identity." They also ran contrary to French law, as well as international conventions.

A particularly noteworthy aspect of the report was the blame placed on the French authorities for enabling radical Islamist groups to expand their penetration of their communities, at the expense of Berber identity and values. Government actions included urban housing policies of ghettoization, acquiescence to the intimidation of Berber girls regarding the donning of a head covering, and consigning social and educational responsibilities, in some cases, to individuals and groups linked to radical Islamists. "In France," the report declared, "it is not permitted for Mohamed not to be an Arab or a Moslem." "It is as if France categorizes all its North African population as being Islamic, denying a number of these North Africans the right to freedom of belief, and to benefit, in the same measure as all other French citizens, from freedom of thought and freedom of conscience. Such a practice is neither democratic nor just, nor conforms to republican values of liberty, equality, *laïcisme* and the respect of human rights."

Similarly, on the cultural and educational levels, the report lambasted France on a variety of matters. Especially disturbing was the state's agreement to let North African governments send teachers to teach Arabic to "French-born children" of immigrants, "based on foreign programs," while not recognizing Berber, the fourth- or fifth-largest language group in France, as one of the country's fifteen minority languages that could be studied in the country's high schools.[37] For those two thousand students who pursued the study of Tamazight for their baccalaureate exam, they could do so only through Berber associations, not their schools. Among the CMA demands was that France add to its list of officially sanctioned holidays the Amazigh holidays of Yennayer (Amazigh New Year, a traditional agricultural festival), occurring on January 12, and the "Amazigh Spring," occurring on April 20 (the day of the Algerian authorities' crackdown in 1980). In addition, it called for the establishment of Berber Civilization departments in universities, the allocation of an AM or FM radio frequency for a Berber-language station, "the creation of a Berber Cultural Center in Paris, to promote the Berber culture and undertake exchanges between it and other cultures of France, and the additional creation of French Berber cultural spaces in major cities of France where an important Berber population exists, to promote a multicultural message of peace, citizenship and tolerance."[38]

The CMA's critique of France's shortcomings was a succinct summary of the overall worldview of Franco-Berber associations, one which sought to fashion a hybrid Euro-Mediterranean identity rooted in France, modernity, democracy, and *laïcité,* while being proud of its Berber origins and desirous of cultivating and rejuvenating its Berber language and culture. To a large degree, as Paul Silverstein has astutely shown in the case of France and Algeria, both Berberists and Islamists were, by the 1990s, engaged in a kind of transpolitics, "the processes of collusion and contention, of appropriation and transformation, that link Algeria and France—Algerians and Franco-Algerians."[39] For Berberists, the search for a viable identity formula combined a vigorous privileging of Kabyle symbols of authenticity through which a nostalgic vision of their culture could be reproduced and transmitted, particularly the Kabyle house (*akham*), the adoption of new symbols of struggle, such as the Berber Spring and the "martyrdom" of Matoub Lounès, and a highly ambivalent view of the French state.[40]

But as one can discern from the CMA's critique itself, the deck was stacked against the Berberists. As one CMA official told me, it was difficult to "sell" this type of modern Kabyle identity to French-born youth who felt adrift, without roots in either country, suffering from an inferiority complex and in a generational conflict with their own parents, to boot, and who were thus especially vulnerable to religious fundamentalists who offered them easy solutions. Even in my interlocutor's particular case, the battle to transmit the Kabyle language and heritage was difficult, albeit for a different reason: his own son had acquired Polish, through his

Polish-born mother, but not Taqbaylit.[41] A recent massive study on how North African immigrants transmit languages to their French-born off-spring confirmed that such anecdotal evidence was not an isolated case: it showed that less than half of both Arabic- and Berber-speaking North African immigrants were transmitting their native languages to their children, and that three-fourths of those parents who had themselves been socialized at home in Arabic spoke Arabic with their children, while only approximately 50 percent of Berber speakers spoke Berber with their children.[42]

The response of the Berber associations to the massive car burnings and disturbances in Parisian suburban *banlieues* and other cities in October–November 2005 was also instructive: they completely disassociated themselves, and Berbers as a whole, from the events, blaming them entirely on Islamist and criminal elements. At that moment, it was simply not prudent to emphasize the Berber origins of a significant percentage of French Muslims.[43]

JEWS, BERBERS, ZIONISM, AND THE AMAZIGH MOVEMENT

One of the accusations by the Libyan anti-Amazigh demonstrators was that the Amazigh movement was acting in the service of "the CIA, Zionism, and Western imperialism." Of course, these have been common targets for demonstrators of various stripes in the Arab and Muslim worlds for decades, and tell much more about the demonstrators than the subject of their wrath. Still, the Amazigh movement is an easy, even natural target for these kinds of accusations, thanks to its rejection of the Arab-Islamic historical and civilizational narrative and its affinity with the universalist paradigm espoused in Western intellectual circles. Moreover, an additional aspect of the movement's overall orientation has been a quiet amenability toward Jews and Judaism, an unwillingness to line up reflexively alongside of the Arab world in its struggles against the State of Israel, and, among some militants, even a measure of admiration for the Zionist project, i.e., the revival of a national language and the successful assertion of ethnonational rights in the face of an antagonistic Arab and Muslim world.

History, myths, legends, and contemporary political agendas have combined to produce a fascinating picture of the relationships between Berbers and Jews throughout the ages. One of the results is a belief often voiced among Amazigh that they were once Jews, a view congruent with their larger historical narrative of being an ancient people situated in Tamazgha who interacted with successive waves of foreigners (of whom only the Jews are said to have come peacefully!).[44] This is not only heard in Morocco, but also in Algeria.[45]

To be sure, modern-day scholars tend to be skeptical regarding the depth and breadth of Jewish-Berber relationships in pre-Islamic and early Islamic times.[46] What is known is that Jewish communities existed in North Africa at least since the period of the Second Temple (destroyed in AD 70), and perhaps even earlier. (For example, tradition has it that a group of Temple priests [*kohanim*] brought a door and a stone from the destroyed First Temple [586 BC] and used them to establish the El Ghirba synagogue on the island of Jerba, in Tunisia. There is a similar tradition regarding the arrival of Jews in southern Morocco.) Even earlier, the ancient city of Carthage was founded in 813 BC by Phoenician seamen and traders who plied the North African coasts, and who may have included Hebrews. In any case, the Punic language was deeply rooted in the region well into the first centuries of the Christian era. This "Phoenician connection" to North Africa undoubtedly contributed to the popular belief of the Berbers' Semitic origins, making the Berbers cousins of the Jews (and Arabs) by virtue of race and language. Modern Amazigh activists also point to the story of the Kahina, the fabled Berber and possibly Jewish queen who led the resistance to the initial Arab conquest of Tamazgha, to "prove" their Jewish origins.

For the historian, the important point in this context is that collective and individual identities alike have always possessed a measure of fluidity, both in ancient and more modern times, even those that are commonly considered primordial. Indeed, religious belief and praxis in North Africa during the late Roman and early Christian eras were highly syncretist, often combining elements of Judaism, paganism, and Christianity. Jewish and Christian proselytization was common.

Among North Africa's resident Jews (*toshavim;* those who pre-dated the mass exodus from Spain and Portugal during the Reconquista), many lived amongst, and in proximity to, Berber communities, particularly in Morocco, up until the time of independence.[47] Did this mean that they were mainly Berbers who had converted to Judaism and had avoided Islamization, or were they primarily Jews who had originated elsewhere and become acculturated to the Berber milieu? The matter has been the subject of considerable discussion, but the answer cannot be definitively ascertained. Most likely, it is somewhere in-between. In any case, according to a 1936 census, three-quarters of Morocco's 161,000 Jews were bilingual in Berber and Arabic, and another 25,000 were exclusively Berber speakers.[48] As merchants, traders, and small artisans in the Atlas mountain villages, Jews often played an intermediary role between Arabs and Berbers, and between different Berber tribal groupings. As is true regarding overall Jewish-Muslim relations in North Africa, relations between Jews and Berbers are sometimes presented in overly idealized terms.

In earlier decades, Amazigh movement circles were extremely reticent to mention anything to do with the Arab-Israeli conflict or the belief in their Jewish roots. But in recent years, they have begun to be more open and blunt. A common complaint of theirs is that their governments spend an inordinate amount of energy on behalf of the Palestinian cause, at the expense of the real needs of their societies. One writer even suggested, presumably sarcastically, that Palestinian refugees could be resettled in the Saharan expanses.[49] In conversations with Israelis, Amazigh activists invariably inquire after the state of the Berber language in Israel, brought by Jews who had immigrated from Berberophone areas in Morocco, and are extremely disappointed to learn that it is not being passed down to subsequent generations. In Goulmima, a southeastern Moroccan Berber town formerly inhabited by Jews as well, an annual masquerade ritual has been transformed among the youth into an expression of Amazigh activism and militancy, including a rejection of Islamist discourse and identification with Judaeo-Berber culture and even Israel. The expressions of philo-Hebraism among the town's youth were so disturbing to some that the local Islamic imam issued a *fatwa* forbidding them, albeit to no avail.[50] More generally, the annual gathering draws many former Goulmima Muslims now living abroad, as well as Kabyle activists.[51]

This last example, an overt demonstration of contrariness, must be considered an isolated matter. For Arab nationalists and Islamists, though, it no doubt confirms the pernicious nature of the modern Berber identity movement. Inevitably, any sympathy expressed toward Jews and Zionism is seen as part of a new plot to divide and conquer Muslim lands. Indeed, in recent years, the entry of competing Amazigh and Islamist discourses into the public sphere, an outgrowth of the newly liberalizing policies of North African states seeking to better manage and relegitimize their rule, has produced a number of confrontations between the Amazigh movement and its Arab nationalist and Islamist opponents. Most, although not all, have remained in the verbal realm.

In the summer of 2007, a group of thirty-plus young Moroccan Amazigh, mainly from the Souss region, announced the establishment of an Amazigh-Jewish Friendship Association. Their platform, covering the promotion of cultural, political, and socioeconomic objectives, focused on three pillars: Amazigh, Judaeo-Amazigh, and Israel.[52] In essence, the "Judaeo-Amazigh" factor was serving as a bridge between the Amazigh movement and the State of Israel.

The news of the association's creation occasioned a heated debate on Iran's Arabic-language satellite television channel, al-Alam, between an Algerian writer, Yahya Abu Zakariya, and Ahmed Adghirni. Their sharp exchanges regarding the history and collective identity of North Africa presented starkly opposing views. Abu Zakariya emphasized the 1,400 years of Islam in North Africa, which decisively shaped its history and culture, including the Amazigh, who "were the epitome of steadfastness, resistance, and confrontation" against all colonialist attacks, while also doing "a great service to Islamic civilization . . . contributing to it to the greatest degree." Jews, on the other hand, he claimed, were utterly foreign to the region, only arriving from Andalusia following the Reconquista. Moreover, they "were the eyes of the French colonialist movement . . . : when the French army came to the Arab Maghreb, it was the Jews who led them to the *mujahideen*," and when the French left, the Jews quite naturally went with them. As for Moroccan Jews, and Jews in general, "I say that [they] have no conscience. They did not respect the sanctity of neighborly relations. The Muslims provided them with safety and protection. . . . When they joined the security services in Israel . . . did they remember the kindness the Moroccans showed them, or were they part of the conspiracy against the Arabs?"

In Adghirni's view, this type of talk was nothing less than anti-Semitism. "If only the Arabs had believed in friendship with the Jews all these years, we would not be seeing rivers of blood flowing, among the Arabs themselves, and between the Arabs and the Jews. The Amazigh have nearly 3,000 years of history behind us, throughout which the Jews lived together with us." Arab identity, on the other hand, "is specific to the Arabian Peninsula and to the countries concerned with this, but not to the Amazigh or the non-Arab residents of North Africa." As for the new Amazigh-Jewish association itself, Adghirni pulled no punches, declaring that "it has to do with friendship, which is a humanist value for the benefit of all peoples, including the Arabs. The Arabs replace friendship with enmity and war."[53] Six months later, another Amazigh-Jewish friendship association, Memoire Collective, was founded in the northern city of al-Hoceima. Its primary declared mission was to fight against manifestations of anti-Semitism. The group was harshly attacked by both Islamist and radical leftist pan-Arab circles, and its members subject to threats and intimidation.[54] Adghirni came to the group's defense, rejecting the notion that governments should have a monopoly on contacts with Israel, stating that the "blockade" to nongovernmental contacts had already been broken.[55] Adghirni's positions would be headlined in a Moroccan daily thus: "Amazigh-Jewish Rapprochement (*al-Taqarub*): The Time Bomb."[56]

Israel's January 2009 war with the Palestinian Hamas movement in Gaza stirred powerful emotions throughout the MENA region, as graphic scenes of death and destruction among Palestinian civilians were broadcast nonstop by Arab satellite television stations, led by al-Jazeera. Morocco witnessed widespread and repeated expressions of sympathy for the Palestinians and anger with Israel, which according to Abdallah Saaf, a Moroccan academic and former government minister, indicated the public's high degree of political consciousness and desire for involvement in public life. "The Amazighs," he said, "often depicted as hostile to Arab issues, asserted their visceral attachment to Palestine," along with massive numbers of Moroccans from across the political spectrum.[57] This "national" description of the reaction to the war, however, was not shared everywhere. In fact, the Israeli-Hamas war, and the responses to it, touched off a new round of accusations and responses between opponents and supporters of the Amazigh movement, making it another issue of contention between Islamists and Amazigh activists. On January 14, 2009, the Islamist PJD daily *Al-Tajdid* published a front-page article, entitled "Ya Amazigh al-Maghrib, Ayn Antum min Filastin?" (O Amazigh of Morocco, Where Do You Stand on Palestine?), criticizing the absence of Amazigh associations and activists from the solidarity demonstrations for Palestine:

> What is the justification for the silence of these dozens of groups, organizations, and individuals . . . ? What is the justification for the blackout of the Amazigh electronic and print media on the issue of Gaza? What has muted Amazigh human rights groups and kept them from denouncing [Israel], which was the least they could do? Or is this yet another sign that they are isolated, marginal, have nothing to do with the stand of the Amazigh masses, and represent only themselves?[58]

Similarly, a Moroccan Amazigh columnist warned Amazigh youth to be wary of plans whose secrets and meanings they may not understand, "[for] the Zionist entity has descended in force on the Amazigh ethnicity, in order to ignite civil strife in our countries."[59]

Ahmed Asid replied sharply to the *Al-Tajdid* attack, insisting on the Amazigh people's natural solidarity and identification with the Palestinians, in human and universal terms, which no one had a right to question. The problem in Morocco, he said, was that the Islamist and Arab nationalist trends had a complete monopoly on the organized demonstrations: the Amazigh movement categorically refused to be a part of anything of which they were in charge. Moreover, these protests had both blatant anti-Jewish and extremist Arab ethnic content (chants such as "khaybar khaybar ya-yahud," referring to the Prophet Mohamed's early battles with Arabian Jewish tribes, and "Arab blood is boiling in Rabat"). Asid was withering in his criticism of Hamas, especially its leadership in Damascus, which, like Hizballah's Hassan Nasrallah, issued empty slogans of struggle and victory while ordinary Palestinians suffered the consequences of their failed policies.[60] So was Moha Moukhlis, a journalist affiliated with Morocco's Royal Institute of Amazigh Culture (IRCAM), who attacked Hamas as "a gang of killers by proxy . . . fundamentalist criminals who conceive of their own people as cannon fodder," as well as the "genocidal Arab regimes" and the Arab-Islamic philosophy that he said underpinned "a culture of death . . . loyal to the Arab-Islamic tradition of conquests, invasions, killings and raids (*razzias/ghaziat*) . . . which cultivates hatred of the Other and misanthropy," particularly with regard to Jews. Yet the "Arab street," he continued, "has never dared to lift a finger against the crimes committed by the fundamentalists of Hamas and the Arab-Islamic regimes on non-Arab populations in Darfur, Kurdistan, Egypt, Syria, Libya, Algeria, [and] Niger." Instead, he declared, it insisted on sacrificing "the rights of the Amazigh people . . . on the altar of Arab fundamentalism, the danger that threatens the global civilization." Some Kabyle militants expressed themselves in a similar fashion.[61]

The year ended with an episode of a very different kind, which nonetheless demonstrated the extent to which some Amazigh activists were determined to situate themselves in opposition to prevailing norms and behavior in the Arab-Islamic Middle East. In November, an eighteen-person delegation of Moroccan Amazigh educators and activists representing a cross-section of the movement came to Israel to participate in a week-long educational seminar at Jerusalem's Yad Vashem Holocaust Memorial Museum. The visit was not only, or even primarily, a statement about the need for Moroccan educators to incorporate the study of the Holocaust and its lessons into their curriculum. It was also a statement of solidarity with Israel, and an effort to reach out to it, in opposition to the pan-Arab and Islamist currents in their own society. What's more, they had no compunction about publicity regarding the trip and did not hesitate afterward to respond to criticism voiced in the Moroccan and Arab media.[62] Some of the delegates participated in the founding of another Amazigh-Jewish friendship society, this one based in Rabat, in early 2010.

Six

MOHAMED VI'S MOROCCO AND THE AMAZIGH MOVEMENT

The ascension to the throne of King Hassan II's eldest son, Mohamed VI, following Hassan's death in July 1999, occurred smoothly and without incident, attesting to the degree of both stability and legitimacy that Hassan had attained in time to pass on to his eldest son. Notwithstanding Hassan's last years, the dominant image of his era was that of a supreme ruler who struck fear into his subjects' hearts. While not formally challenging the legacy of his father, Mohamed quickly sought to put his own stamp on Moroccan affairs as a kinder, gentler monarch attuned to the needs of his people, fashioning a new image as "king of the people" and "king of the poor." The return of prominent exiles, Mohamed's express commitment to do away with human rights abuses and promote the status of women, and the dismissal of the all-powerful interior minister, Driss Basri, were greeted enthusiastically in Morocco as the harbinger of a new era.

Nonetheless, the political classes and observers had two clashing sets of concerns, which were in tune with what Samuel Huntington famously classified as "the king's dilemma":[1] (1) The new and inexperienced king would not know how to reign in the Moroccan style—that is, with a strong hand, according to the traditional norms of Moroccan political culture—and thus would seriously destabilize the country; or (2) he would refrain from pursuing the necessary policies of reform, and thus keep a lid on Morocco's societal and political pressure cooker, until it eventually exploded. A decade into his reign, neither of these dire scenarios had come to pass. Morocco had significantly liberalized political and social life, if unevenly, while preserving political stability and retaining the essential features of a system characterized by "pluralism without democracy," dominated by the Palace. Given the periodic crackdowns on journalists who deigned to cross established red lines regarding the allowable amount of press freedom, and continued heavy-handed policies toward Islamists and Sahrawi nationalists, it was not unreasonable to speak of the Moroccan state under Mohamed VI as a modernized version of the traditional political system.[2]

The regime's political liberalization measures were supported by an official discourse centered on the promotion of democratization, human rights, and the rule of law, while seeking to anchor this discourse in a local context. To that end, the regime's guiding formula was "development and *ijtihad*." The first half of the equation stressed that the modernization of the economy, improvement of the welfare system, advancement of civil society, and controlled democratization of the political arena were the monarchy's supreme objectives, while the second half sought to confer legitimacy upon these far-reaching processes by linking them to the local culture. Hence, the regime undertook significant steps, the most important of which was the scrapping of the long-standing Personal Status Code, the *moudawwana,* which reflected religiously conservative and patriarchal habits and norms, in favor of a new Family Law that provided a far greater measure of equality to women.[3] Significantly, this reform, first announced in late 2003 and enacted into law in 2004, was carried out under the banner of *ijtihad*. As opposed to the Islamic juridical principle of *taqlid,* which demands strict adherence to tradition, *ijtihad* permits independent discussion and juridical rulings that are predicated on reason. The concern with Islamic norms was not marginal: coping with the growing weight of political Islam, both nonviolent and violent, has been one of the ongoing challenges of the regime during the last decade. Indeed, perhaps the single most important spur to the king's decision to scrap the old Personal Status Code after almost fifteen years of debate was the string of suicide-bombing attacks on May 16, 2003, by jihadist elements in Casablanca that killed thirty-three persons, shocking the Moroccan public and leading many Moroccans to call that day "our 9/11." They served as an alarm bell to the authorities, and to King Mohamed personally, regarding the serious danger posed by Islamist radicalism. The conclusions drawn from this traumatic episode were not only to crack down with an iron fist on bombing suspects and their supporters, but also to demonstrate even more firmly the king's determination to promote an alternative vision to that of radical Islam. His traditional speech on the opening of the Parliament's session in October 2003 constituted what one liberal Moroccan weekly publication called "the big bang." It was at this moment that Mohamed VI announced his decision to fundamentally change the country's personal status law in a way that would significantly improve the status of women, and even almost equalize it to that of men.[4] The subject had first appeared on the public agenda in the early 1990s, thanks to the efforts of women's groups and other liberal forces. Over time, it became perhaps *the* central issue in discussions on the future nature of Moroccan society. Up until Mohamed's "big bang" speech, the approach of the monarchy to the subject had been essentially dualist—in favor of advancing women's status and amending the existing personal status law, but in an exceedingly gradual way. Now, Mohamed chose to make his own "Great Leap Forward."

Less than two years later, the king took a further significant step away from Morocco's past in an effort to turn the page on the worst human rights abuses during Hassan II's reign, widely dubbed *les années de plomb* (years of lead), by means of well-publicized testimonies of people who survived the torture meted out in his father's prisons. Managed by the Equity and Reconciliation Commission (IER), the yearlong hearings (2004–2005) were not without serious flaws, placing substantial limitations on the reconciliation process: those responsible for the actual acts of torture were declared immune from possible prosecution, and even the mention of their names by their victims was forbidden. A number of them still hold official positions. It is thus impossible to speak about justice being fully served. Nonetheless, through the commission, unprecedented in the Arab-Muslim world, Mohamed VI sought to conciliate between various groups in Moroccan society and open a clean slate for the sake of a better future.[5]

The extraordinary IER process did not have an explicit Berber agenda. But Amazigh writers noted that the majority of the victims were, in fact, Amazigh,[6] including the head of the IER, Driss Benzekri, a signatory of the Berber Manifesto (see below) and subsequent minister for human rights.[7] Upon his death in 2007, Amazigh activists extolled him as a fighter for human rights and democracy, principles that they proclaimed proudly as being integral to the Amazigh movement. Overall, liberal forces, including Berber culture associations, were greatly encouraged by the king's actions on the issues of women's and human rights, for they corresponded to their own visions of a more pluralist and open society.

Perhaps the most visible initial aspect of the king's new style was his much-publicized marriage in 2002 to a young educated professional, Salma Bennani, which marked a break with a number of long-standing certitudes surrounding Morocco's rulers. Wives of Moroccan monarchs traditionally received no royal title, never appeared in public, or were even publicly mentioned by name. Princess Salma, on the other hand, took an active and public role in the life of the kingdom from the outset. She would give birth in subsequent years to two children, a boy and a girl, and photographs of the happy family were widely disseminated, providing an additional humanizing touch.

From the angle of Berber-Palace relations, Mohamed's decision to marry a woman from an urban, non-Berber background, instead of a daughter of one of the Berber tribal leaders, constituted a significant break from the tradition of the monarch's marrying the daughter of a rural Berber notable. However, while it indicated that the old post-independence formula of the monarchy's aligning with rural Berber notables was now less relevant, or at least less dependent on such Solomonic practices as sealing political alliances through marriage, it did not signify the end of the alliance. Rather, the Berber-Palace bond was revamped and expanded into the intellectual and cultural spheres. Interestingly, and notwithstanding the vastly different contexts of the late 1950s and the beginning years of the twenty-first century, Mohamed VI's modernizing of the bond, so to speak, served the same basic purpose as the one intended by his father and grandfather, namely, to provide an important counterweight to other political and social forces that threatened the monarchy's hegemony and ultimately, perhaps, its legitimacy.

THE RIF

The king's initial gesture toward his Berber subjects came just three months after his coronation, when he made a high-profile motorcade journey through the long-neglected northern Rif region and adjacent eastern province, visiting sixteen cities and towns accompanied by his brother, Crown Prince Moulay Rashid, and senior officials. Nor was the king's interest a onetime episode. Throughout the first decade of his reign, Mohamed VI maintained an abiding interest in the northern region, visiting frequently and pouring money into development projects, the centerpiece of which was the Tangier-Med port complex, scheduled to be completed in 2012. A central intended benefit of the new project was job creation and the weaning of the region from its dependence on drug smuggling: the region's proximity to Europe had made it a jumping-off point for clandestine immigration and a crucial source for smugglers who dominated the European drug market.[8] Needing EU political and economic support, Mohamed was eager to demonstrate that Morocco was serious about addressing common problems emanating from the region.

Mohamed's initial motorcade through the north in October 1999, and the outpouring of goodwill wherever he went, were especially poignant on a number of counts. Historically, the region was often outside the *makh-zen,* and its integration into independent Morocco remained only partial, socially and economically. As noted earlier, the forceful suppression of a Rifian revolt in January 1959 by the newly formed Forces Armées Royales (FAR), commanded by then–Crown Prince Hassan, had been forgotten neither by the population nor by Hassan. Thus, the tumultuous welcoming of Mohamed—in Tetouan, for example, the site of a particularly brutal massacre carried out by his father, he was greeted with rose petals—spoke volumes about the feelings of hope generated by his ascent to the throne.[9] In addition to promoting social and economic development and the alleviation of poverty, Mohamed also used his trip to explicitly promote Berber-Arab reconciliation in a highly symbolic fashion. The son of Rifian icon Abdelkrim journeyed from Cairo at the king's invitation to meet with him, and received a pledge to restore the neglected ruins of his father's headquarters in Ajdir.[10]

The episode pointed again to the multiple ways in which symbols and the legacies of individuals can be appropriated and reworked for specific purposes. For young Rifians, Abdelkrim had become a symbol of Berber pride, defiance, and independence, and the flag adopted by the Amazigh movement, sporting the letter "Z" [ⵣ] in Tifinagh script, was visible everywhere the king went, even being engraved into trees and telegraph posts.[11] More generally, Abdelkrim has become a preferred, even revered figure for modern-day Moroccan Berbers engaged in memory work, who point to his five-year "Rifian Republic," and particularly his decimation of Spanish forces at Annoual, to combat the accusations that Berbers too often collaborated with colonial rule, as well as the long-standing assertion that Berber identity is linked to older colonialist projects to divide Berbers from Arabs.

By acknowledging the legacy of Abdelkrim, a man who had been largely shunned by Moroccan urban Arab nationalist elites, Mohamed VI was obviously looking to emphasize that Rifian Berbers were an integral part of the Moroccan fabric, and thus expand the boundaries of collective Moroccan identity. However, important limits still remained. For example, detailed reports by the Maghreb Agence Presse on the state-sponsored commemoration of the 1921 Annoual victory, on July 21, 2008, made no mention of Abdelkrim himself while praising Sultan Mohamed V for leading the struggle for Morocco's liberation.[12] In addition, the Amazigh movement's plans to return Abdelkrim's remains from Cairo and have them interred in a mausoleum-cum-museum at the site of his Ajdir headquarters remain stalled.

Nor have Mohamed VI's gestures been extended to a painful epi-sode that highlights the *makhzen*'s historic indifference to the Rifian war, namely, the Spanish military's systematic use of poison gas against Rifian fighters and civilians, with the assistance of French and German manufac-turers. It is only in recent years that this matter has come to light, thanks in part to the work of a number of Spanish scholars and the British histo-rian Sebastian Balfour,[13] as well as two German journalists, who revealed German involvement in Spain's actions. *Le Monde Amazigh* has energeti-cally disseminated the Abdelkrim story, and particularly this shocking and sorry episode, giving detailed coverage of conferences treating the matter. The battle against marginalization and official indifference extends to the present: survivors of poison gas attacks and their offspring are said to suf-fer from numerous health problems, including inordinately high rates of cancer. But up until now, Moroccan authorities have ignored Amazigh demands and been unwilling to ask the Spanish government for acknowl-edgment and compensation for elderly survivors, fearing that it would ad-versely affect bilateral ties.[14] In response, one speaker at a conference held in Tetouan in the spring of 2004 proposed a number of concrete measures, including suing the German and French companies that participated in the manufacture of the toxic gases used by Spain and appealing to the Euro-pean Court of Human Rights.[15]

In Spain, as well, the subject was almost entirely kept out of the pub-lic eye, at least until recently. The growing ties of solidarity between the Amazigh movement and Catalan and Basque nationalists led the latter's representatives in early 2007 to introduce a bill in the Spanish Parliament which would recommend that the Spanish government apologize for its actions in the Rif war, compensate the victims and their families, and pro-vide proper equipment for oncology departments in the hospitals of Nador and al-Hoceima, where cancer rates were higher than average. An article in the Madrid daily *El Mundo* in Summer 2008, coinciding with the offi-cial visit to Morocco of Spanish Prime Minister José Luis Zapatero, was a rare, detailed treatment of the entire episode, and included mention of the use of napalm by Moroccan forces against Rifian rebels in 1958 as well.[16] As with the Rifian demands for indemnity for the victims of Spain's poison gas attacks, reopening the wounds of 1958 is not just a matter of concern to historians, or even identity-builders. In February 2004, the "Committee of Victims of the 1958 Walmas Events" was established, demanding not only the revelation of the truth, but also indemnity for the survivors of the re-pression against the mostly Berber Army of Liberation members, from the

Walmas tribal grouping, by the militia of the Istiqlal Party. As is usually the case, the royal family's role in the events was downplayed.[17]

BERBER MANIFESTO, AMAZIGH DAHIR

Meanwhile, the combination of a decade of Berber intellectual and cultural activism and the predilections and needs at the top of Morocco's political system was concretized during the first two years of Mohamed VI's reign by an alliance between the new king and his former tutor in secondary school, Mohamed Chafik, who represented what for want of a better term can be labeled the moderate Berberist current.[18] The process was marked by two seminal developments. The first was the issuing on March 1, 2000, of the "Berber Manifesto," following two years of intensive discussions. The second breakthrough event came eighteen months later on October 17, 2001, with the king's issuing of a Royal Dahir establishing the Institut Royal de la Culture Amazighe (IRCAM), to be headed by Chafik.

The lengthy Manifesto (nine thousand words in French) was composed mainly by Chafik and signed by 229 university professors, writers, poets, artists, industrialists, and civil servants, including Abdelhamid Zemmouri, a signatory of the 1944 Independence Manifesto, and Driss Benzekri. Like the Agadir Charter of 1991, the Manifesto is a core text for the modern Amazigh identity project, laying out a coherent historical narrative that stands in sharp contrast to the official Moroccan one, as well as a clear and specific program of remediation. One of the Manifesto's most striking aspects is its broadside attack on the ruling Moroccan establishment over the many centuries of Islamic history. Yet, Chafik was also very careful to avoid anything that might have hinted at a delegitimization of the monarchical institution, which of course is umbilically connected to Islam and the Prophet. Morocco, and its Amazigh population in particular, the Manifesto stated, had sunk into such a sorry state by 1912 that the colonial powers could almost just walk in and assume control. The reason for this dire situation was the triumph of the *makhzenian* political tradition of despotism and oppression, accompanied by "haughtiness, ostentation and pomp." This tradition was said to have been inherited from the Umayyad and Abbasid empires, "contrary to the spirit of political consultation prescribed by Islam" and practiced by the Prophet and the first four caliphs. Not coincidentally, the spirit of the Prophet and his companions was in line with Amazigh political traditions, which were "geared towards managing the affairs of the *jamaʿa* ("local community") . . . through dialogue and consultation." The *makhzen*, "pursuant to its heavy Heraclian-Khurasan heritage," was steered for centuries by "influential people," those who could "make or break," who preached contempt of the Amazigh, while reducing the historical roles played by "Berbers." Occasionally, the Manifesto said, enlightened sultans made commendable efforts toward the Amazigh population. However, the *makhzenian* circles "taught hatred towards anything Amazigh to generation after generation of their offspring." Their desire to preserve their privileges, declared the document, led them to blindly adhere to political traditions based upon dogmatic and tightly closed religious thinking. The resulting clash between these two worldviews resulted in violence and disorder, rendering the country easy prey for foreign invaders.

Moreover, claimed the Manifesto, *makhzenian* circles actually welcomed the French protectorate and were the main beneficiaries of its rule. Such a statement was a direct slap at the urban Arabic-speaking elites who had fashioned the Moroccan national narrative in their own image, stressing their patriotism and resistance, while belittling the Berbers. Together, said the Manifesto, the protectorate authorities and *makhzenian* circles were aligned against the "rebellious Berbers," who were militarily subjugated and then consigned to marginalization and nondevelopment. Still, when the time came for national rebellion against the French, it was the Imazighen who willingly provided it with the necessary manpower.

To be sure, the Manifesto studiously avoided any mention of the most powerful Berber leader during the protectorate years, the autocratic "Lord of the Atlas," Thami El Glaoui, an omission that can only be understood as a willful act. A positive reference to Glaoui, who was a staunch ally of the protectorate regime until the end, and who played a supportive role in France's attempt to replace the sultan in 1953 and whose power rivaled the sultan's, would have situated contemporary Berber discourse on the side of the French colonial power and in opposition to Moroccan nationalism and the ruling dynasty. Criticism of Glaoui, on the other hand, would run counter to the Manifesto's overall critique of the official national narrative. Given Glaoui's prominent role in Moroccan history during those tumultuous decades, one can perhaps expect that at some point, both dispassionate historians and Amazigh activists more militant than those affiliated with the Manifesto will take up the subject.

The independence era also came in for sharp critique in the Manifesto. The document hammered away at the denial of Morocco's "Amazighness," and the arrogation by professional politicians and most members of Morocco's elites of "monopolistic rights to 'patriotism' and 'political action.'" Even speaking of this monopolization, it said, has long been a taboo in Moroccan life.

Little by little, stated the Manifesto, it became clear after independence that none of the extant political forces, whether promonarchy or not, were going to give the Amazigh their due and include them in the definition of a modern Morocco. Instead, successive national governments pursued the policy of building an exclusively "Arab Maghrib," led by an Arabized Morocco. In presenting their demands for a reordering of national priorities, the signatories of the Manifesto were determined "to combat the *cultural hegemony* that has been programmed in order to *bury* a very important part of [Morocco's] civilizational heritage" (emphasis in original). Indeed, the "men of influence" were so strong that even King Hassan could not overcome them. Hassan's 1994 declaration of intent to launch the teaching of national "dialects" was effectively sabotaged, remaining nothing but a "sermon in the desert." "It is high time," the document declared, "that the recognition of our original national language—Tamazight—as an official language be *enshrined in the country's Constitution. .-. .* One of the most embittering things for an Amazigh, in the 'independence era,' is to hear some of his fellow citizens make a statement like the following: '*the official or national language is Arabic! . . . by virtue of the text of the Constitution!*' He is provoked by the uttering of these words, on every occasion, along with the explicit mockery and haughtiness which accompany it. Thus, he feels persecuted in the name of the supreme law of the country" (emphasis in original).

The Manifesto concluded with nine demands for the authorities:

(1) initiating a broad national debate on the nature of Moroccan collective identity and the place of Amazighité within it;

(2) ensuring constitutional recognition of Tamazight as an official language;

(3) undertaking serious planning for the economic development of the Amazigh-speaking areas in all fields, to make up for the cumulative damage suffered during the "long war" against colonialism and their subsequent economic marginalization, "the main cause lying behind their so-called 'cultural retardation' and the dwindling of their political role in the country";

(4) drafting laws aimed at enforcing the teaching of Tamazight in schools, institutes, and universities, and the creation of scientific institutions capable of codifying the Amazigh language and preparing the pedagogical instruments necessary for its

teaching; the demand was accompanied by a detailed rejection of the conflation of Islam and the Arabic language, while proclaiming Amazigh fidelity to Arabic as a cultural treasure;

(5) establishing a "National Scientific Commission" to devise history syllabi in the school system that would more accurately reflect the history of Morocco and its people, instead of the current emphasis on the "Arab race";

(6) making the use of Tamazight mandatory in public spheres that serve people who are not fluent in Arabic, e.g., courts, public administrations, the health services, and local and regional councils, as well as the mass media, and lifting the ban on registering newborn children with Amazigh names in the State Registry Services. In this way, it stated, millions of Tamazight speakers would be spared the feeling of alienation from their surroundings that is psychologically "more oppressive than the one experienced by our immigrants abroad";

(7) rehabilitating and modernizing Amazigh arts (dance, song, architecture, and decoration), removing them from the "folklore" category, and granting the same financial support to Amazigh artists as that given to Arab ones;

(8) ending the Arabization of Amazigh place and geographical names, and naming national institutions after Moroccan historical figures like Abdelkrim, not people unknown in the collective national memory; and

(9) providing sufficient state funding to Amazigh cultural associations and equalizing the funding of Amazigh publications with that of those in Arabic and foreign languages.

As a coda, "for the sake of eliminating any ambiguity and warding off any tendentious interpretation," the Manifesto insisted that its propagators had no anti-Arab agenda to promote, and that "We the Amazighs are brothers to the Arabs wherever they live," owing to their common belonging to the Islamic *umma,* strong ties, and common history.

The Manifesto's unstinting praise of Amazigh political and cultural traditions is familiar to students of ethnonational projects. At the same time, again like most other such projects, the Amazigh movement's demands were not just backward-looking, framed in terms of a return to an idealized "golden age." Rather, the Manifesto's vision was modern and forward-looking, one that was intended to allow Morocco to "enter the third millennium through its widest gate." Accepting the "Amazighité" of Morocco went hand in hand with the modern requirements of citizenship, it declared. Responding to charges that its demands for recognition of Tamazight as an official language constituted "separatism," the Manifesto retorted that the cause of separatism and fragmentation of societies was the

> *lack of civilizational maturity.* . . . We believe that diversity is an
> enrichment and that difference is a sharpener for the human
> designs . . . [and that] "uniformity" leads to the missing of op-
> portunities for opening up (to the outside world and to other
> ideas), for development and refinement. . . . We believe in the
> advent of a *universal civilization* which is capable of integrating
> all the contributions of mankind. [emphasis in the original][19]

For comparison's sake, Chafik's "universal civilization" possesses almost spiritual qualities, unlike Kemal Attatürk's explicit conflation of "civilization" with the "West." The distinction is a common one made over the last century by Muslim intellectuals, who often spoke (and still speak) of the "spiritual superiority" of the "East" over the "West." Chafik takes the notion a step further, in order to achieve a synthesis between "East" and "West." Nonetheless, for most Amazigh intellectuals, the Berberist project has important commonalities with "Attatürkism," in that it is explicitly both *laïque* and *ethnique,* opposing the use of religion as the basis for law, in line with the trends of contemporary Western political thought and practice. In addition, they do not define Morocco spatially in terms of the Muslim world only (al-Maghrib al-Aqsa). Rather, their image of Morocco is one of a crossroads, geographic, cultural, and ethnic. Here the comparison with Turkey's Attatürk reaches its limits, for Attatürkism stressed the centrality of a homogeneous "Turkish" nation and culture.

Chafik's erudition and prolific talents as a linguist and educator, and his status as a member of the Royal Academy, former director of the Royal College, where he tutored Mohamed VI, and former secretary of state in charge of secondary, technical, and higher education and management training, conferred upon him a special measure of gravitas, enabling him to bring the Berber question forward onto the Moroccan public agenda in an unprecedented fashion. But the Manifesto was, after all, not an academic treatise, but a highly political document coming out of a concrete and complex context, and with a specific agenda that built on the work of the 1991 Agadir Charter. Overall, the Manifesto presents a broad dichotomy between the "good" Berbers and the "bad" Istiqlal/*makhzen*/pan-Arabists, who exploited them "either to perform 'dirty jobs' for the circles monopolizing the means of government or to act as a 'spearhead' for fellow militants of the extremist opposition." Ironically, it replicates the French colonial vulgate, even while defining "good" Berbers as being the true resisters to colonialism. This view, denying any sort of agency for the Berbers as willing participants in other forms of political activity or social and religious praxis, is clearly a gross oversimplification of an enormously complex reality, in which Berbers were, and continue to be, for that matter, present all across the political and social spectrum of Morocco, and have hardly been only loyal and naïve servants either of the state and the king or of the left-wing opposition. But neither could this new counternarrative be summarily dismissed as simply a fabrication of history less valid than extant ones.

On May 12, 2000, the document was discussed at a conclave of 150 activists in the coastal town of Bouznika, which in turn designated a core group of 15 of the signatories, hailing variously from the country's three main Berberophone zones, to promote the document and mobilize the public behind it, even if the overall movement strategy remained amorphous. Over the next year, the committee held seven different meetings on the theme "Amazighité and politics," in six different Moroccan cities, from Nador in the north to Agadir in the south, as well as in Gouda, Holland.[20] The initial reaction of the authorities was one of considerable suspicion: in a familiar demonstration of *makhzen* concern with maintaining control over public life, they blocked public access to a second gathering in Bouznika scheduled for June 22–24, 2001, where an anticipated 500 participants were expected to discuss the wisdom of forming a political party and approve political and organizational platforms. Some of the advocates of forming a political party then tried to hold their own meeting at the end of the month, but were forbidden from doing so by Minister of the Interior Ahmed Midaoui.[21]

However, the Palace, once having asserted its authority, adopted flexibility as its watchword, and its representatives now met with people from the movement to work out the acceptable parameters regarding the Amazigh issue.[22] The outcome was not long in coming. On July 30, 2001, King Mohamed officially spread his royal patronage over the Moroccan Amazigh community, announcing his intent to establish the Institut Royal de la Culture Amazighe (IRCAM), which would be charged with protecting, researching, promoting, and disseminating the various manifestations of Amazigh culture. In his Discours du Trône marking the second anniversary of his ascension, Mohamed spoke of a number of interlocking needs underpinning the establishment of the IRCAM: democratization, regionalization (a "strategic choice, not simply an administrative construction"), social and economic development, and the "diversity of regional cultural particularisms," which constituted "a source of national enrichment." Citing his late father's 1994 commitments, the king adopted some of the Berber Manifesto's demands: teaching Tamazight in the schools, expanding the Amazigh presence in the audiovisual media, and confirming Amazigh culture as an important component of Moroccan national identity.[23] To be sure, Mohamed VI was careful to reassert the centrality of the Qur'an and its sacred language, Arabic, in Moroccan life. And his comments did not address the Manifesto's complaints of systematic discrimination against the Berbers over the course of Moroccan history, or the demand to amend the constitution to make Tamazight an official national language. But the king's move was significant, even historic. The monarchy had traditionally advocated political and social pluralism as part of its modus operandi of ruling. But now, the explicit embrace and support of the Amazigh component of Moroccan identity indicated that a new conflation of interests between those of the state and an emerging ethnocultural Amazigh movement was underway.

Any remaining doubts about Mohamed's intent to concretize those common interests were put to rest by his official *dahir* of October 17. Owing to their nature, royal *dahirs* had always been issued from one of the king's dozen palaces. However, for his new *dahir,* Mohamed chose for a setting the Middle Atlas Ajdir plateau overlooking Khenifra, the site of a historic meeting between Sultan Mohamed V and heads of Berber tribes in 1956.[24] In doing so, he was wrapping himself in the legacy of his revered grandfather. Nor could it have been lost on observers that Mohamed VI's mother, Lalla Latifa Hamou, was a native of the region, from the Zaiane tribe. To further emphasize his commitment to the Amazigh component of Moroccan identity and the conflation of his status as king with his Berber roots, Mohamed donned traditional Berber headgear, a round turban, for the ceremony.

The introductory clauses of the *dahir* reiterated nearly verbatim the main points of the king's July 30 Discours du Trône, emphasizing the pluralist nature of Moroccan national identity, the need to reinforce its cultural substratum and fabric, and the contribution that the Amazigh language and culture would make to the democratization of Moroccan life and expansion of opportunity for all citizens. The *dahir* itself, consisting of nineteen articles, constituted the basic governing statute for the IRCAM. It was to be established in Rabat, under the protection and tutelage of the "Sharifian Monarch," and guaranteed legal standing and financial autonomy, with its budget coming from the overall budget of the Royal Court. Special emphasis would be placed on introducing Tamazight into the educational curriculum. The institute's governing body would be an administrative council of up to forty members, including representatives of various government ministries and academic institutions, to be headed by a vice-rector. As befitting a royal institute, the king had formal standing as the ultimate decision-maker, similar to his place both within and above the political system. Under him was the vice-rector, who was none other than Mohamed Chafik.

The combination of the Berber Manifesto, Mohamed VI's Speech from the Throne, the *dahir* establishing IRCAM, and Chafik's assumption of leadership was a remarkable development, albeit hardly a simple matter. On one level, the mutual embrace of the Palace and the movement could be seen as the renewal, albeit under sharply different circumstances, of the historic post-independence alliance between the Palace and Berber rural notables in order to ensure continuity and stability in the Moroccan body politic. On a different, but not unrelated, level, it could be seen as yet another example of the tried-and-true *makhzenian* tactic of co-opting and taming potential opposition forces. From a different angle, though, one might view these developments as a profound historical departure from past patterns. The king himself had recognized the Amazigh as a collective entity central to Moroccan history and culture, and committed himself to ending the long-standing marginalization of the Berber communities in Moroccan life. In so doing, he had symbolically brought the Amazigh people directly into the center of the kingdom, whereas in the past, it had only been Berber individuals and specific tribal and group interests that had been "makhzenized." One cannot help but compare the infamous "Berber Dahir" of 1930, in which the protectorate authorities sought to legally separate the Berber rural world from Morocco's urban Arab-Islamic milieu, to this new "Amazigh Dahir," seventy-one years later, which legitimized the status of Morocco's Berber populations as never before.

This alliance was not without its critics, both within the Amazigh movement and the larger body politic of Morocco. The activities of the IRCAM, indeed its very existence as a Palace-supported institution, would be the subject of ongoing debate within the Amazigh movement, and even within the IRCAM itself. Was the king's patronage over the IRCAM just another typical example of *makhzen* tactics designed to co-opt and neutralize potential opposition? Did the costs, real and potential, of accepting the royal embrace outweigh the benefits of official support for Amazigh identity? Was the movement in danger of being defanged just as it was starting to spread its wings? Alternatively, was an effective division of labor emerging, in which the promotion of Amazigh identity could be advanced both within and outside of the establishment, making the Amazigh movement one of the main beneficiaries of the state's need for societal allies in the face of increased political and social challenges?

One practical manifestation of the authorities' commitment to the IRCAM was their generous budgetary allocations to the new institute, whose offices were situated within a brand-new complex of office buildings, pending the erection of a building of its own. But the intimate relationship between the authorities and the IRCAM was problematic for many activists. This was especially true for a number of people who had joined the IRCAM notwithstanding their suspicion of the authorities' motivations.

Concerns over policy sometimes overlapped with disagreements about appointments to the senior positions within the institute. Indeed, a number of Rifian Amazigh raised the issue of discrimination in recruitment, issuing a petition calling on the IRCAM to give equal representation to the "three great regions of Amazighité" (a substantial majority of the leadership was from the south).[25] It would be too simplistic to speak of a rigid moderate-radical dichotomy among Moroccan Amazigh activists: IRCAM's members include a number of people who would bristle at any attempt to diminish their militancy. Some, including the current vice-rector, Ahmed Boukous, who assumed the position upon Chafik's retirement in November 2003, even served time in prison and had their passports revoked for their past activities. Still, the Amazigh activist community continued to be confronted with the basic problem facing nearly all political bodies in Morocco: how far could one go in challenging the Palace, the ultimate seat of authority?

THE SCRIPT ISSUE

The question of Palace authority quickly became immediate, thanks to the controversy in 2002–2003 over the proper script to employ when introducing Tamazight into the educational curriculum, a central goal of the Amazigh Dahir. The choices were Latin, Arabic, or a modified version of Tifinagh. The battle demonstrated the Amazigh movement's double challenge: (1) the need to repel the efforts of Morocco's Islamist trend to contain Amazigh identity within traditional Arab-Islamic rubrics, and (2) the necessity of avoiding confrontation with the Palace, the main sponsor of the IRCAM, while simultaneously trying to advance the movement's agenda.

The differences with the Islamists were, of course, part of the larger battle being waged over Moroccan society's identity and orientation.[26] The legal Islamist Parti de la Justice et du Développement (PJD) garnered 42 seats in the September 2002 elections for the 325-member Chamber of Deputies, placing it in the leading tier of Moroccan political parties, along with the USFP and the Istiqlal, although unlike the latter two, the PJD did not subsequently become a member of the governing coalition. PJD officials campaigned hard for the adoption of Arabic script, particularly through their newspaper *Al-Tajdid*. The party even organized a declaration of allegedly Amazigh associations that endorsed the idea. In general, Moroccan Islamists ostensibly agreed with the need to recognize Amazigh culture as part of the Moroccan patrimony. However, they also viewed the struggle over the appropriate script as part of Francophone-Western civilization's efforts to undermine the primacy of Islam and promote secularization. Religious consciousness in the Maghrib, they noted, was expressed through the Arabic language. Indeed, they understood full well that the Amazigh movement's demands would place Tamazight on an equal footing with Arabic and thus posed a direct challenge to their own preferred vision of a Moroccan society imbued with Islamic values and guided by sacred Arabic-language texts. Not surprisingly, mosque sermons in a number of cities and *fatwas* by Islamic clerics were devoted to attacking the Berber associations and the Amazigh agenda, calling the Latin script option the "imperialist choice." One preacher even remonstrated his congregants for speaking Tamazight in the mosque, saying that it caused "confusion and anarchy" (*bilbala wa-fitna*) among the worshippers, particularly during the holy months of the year.[27]

The Berber Manifesto had sought to defuse the Islamists' criticism of the Amazigh movement and avoid confrontation. The Arabic language, said the text, was an inescapable part of Morocco's cultural heritage, crucial to "in-depth knowledge of religious matters" and the "strongest link with our Arab brothers in the Maghrib and the Middle East." But this could not come at the expense of Tamazight and Amazigh culture. Tamazight, the Manifesto noted, was the language of the Palace in Almohad times, and used for explaining the Qur'an and *hadiths* for many centuries. Most importantly, declared the Manifesto, "history has not ended," and the current need for Morocco, and for the Amazigh, was to interact creatively with other cultures and civilizations.[28]

To that end, a large majority of Amazigh activists believed that the "universal" (i.e., Latin) script was the most practical way to promote Tamazight as a living language, while some favored the adoption of Tifinagh, on the grounds of its identity-building value.[29] The Islamists' "sacralization of script," declared a communiqué issued by fourteen different Amazigh associations, "is nothing but a form of fetishism and animism which constitutes an insult to the principles of Islam."[30] The problem, wrote one Amazigh writer, was that the Moroccan Islamists' insistence on the Arabic script was underpinned by rejection and contempt for other peoples and languages, whether Western or Muslim.[31] One of the Manifesto's signatories declared that the advocates of Arabic transcription "want to maintain our language in the camp of the underdeveloped, stop our overture to the West and turn our language into a sub-dialect of Arabic."[32] Another commentator attacked the PJD on broader issues, calling it "anti-development" for rejecting a much-debated, controversial program to promote the status of women in order to alleviate poverty and illiteracy.[33] The Islamists' campaign against the Amazigh people, declared the fourteen Amazigh cultural associations' joint statement, was simply a diversion from their own inability to offer solutions to the real problems facing Morocco.[34]

At bottom, the script debate highlighted the dichotomy of views between the Amazigh and Islamist movements. The former's worldview, from its own perspective, was modern, open, progressive, and democratic, in harmony with an increasingly interdependent, globalized world. The Islamists' program, by contrast, in the Berberist view, was archaic, closed, regressive, and authoritarian. "In my part of the world," declared Chafik to a European audience,

> there is an urgent need to imbue culture with a humanism, modernism and universalism that rejects excess. This is because unitarianism and fundamentalism have demonstrated their destructive power throughout history to the extent that the threat of ethnic cleansing and religious conflict is still all too present.

In Chafik's view, making Muslim culture "more open to modern scientific knowledge and its positive aspects" could be done only gradually, through a "fruitful dialogue" with the West, which, for its part, needed to "get over its obsession with its dazzling material and organizational success." Chafik's universalist vision was dedicated to "achieving peace amongst different ethnic groups along with a real understanding between religious faiths," beginning with the Amazigh people, whose "vibrant culture" could, like all cultures, contribute something unique to the totality of human experience. Seeking to deflect criticism from the Islamists while placing the Amazigh movement firmly within the humanist fold, Chafik emphasized that

> because it [the Amazigh movement] does not claim to be the depository of the sacred, it is not opposed to evolution. In its way, it is humanist because it remembers a distant past when it was well represented in the concert of Mediterranean cultures by figures such as Terence (Afer) [Carthage-born Roman playwright, c. 190–160 BC], Juba (Juba II) [Roman client king of Mauretania, 25–23 BC], and Apuleius (Afulay) [second century AD philosopher and rhetorician in Roman North Africa]. In short, Amazigh culture can enter and benefit from the worlds of politics, economics, society and justice without the risk of any real prejudice to religious faith.[35]

The nearly unanimous rejection of the Arabic script was enough to block its adoption. But the large majority favoring the Latin script was not sufficient. After all, since this was a matter with ramifications for Moroccan society as a whole, the final decision was in the hands of the king. In February 2003, Mohamed VI resolved the matter: Tifinagh would be the official writing system for Tamazight. The move followed a recommendation to that effect by a bare majority of the IRCAM's administrative council, following considerable discussion on the relative merits of Tifinagh versus Latin scripts. According to one participant in the discussion, research showed that Tifinagh would be no more difficult for children learning Tamazight than any other script. The identity issue was also a factor in the decision, as younger people seemed especially keen on learning Tifinagh, and small children reportedly took special delight in the script. But at bottom, it seems that the decisive factor in the decision was political, namely, the pressure applied by the Moroccan authorities, who viewed Tifinagh as an appropriate compromise between the advocates of the Latin and Arabic scripts.[36]

The decision was controversial, to say the least, among many Amazigh activists, focusing their attention again on the formidable obstacles posed by the Moroccan state authorities to their movement. It also drew withering criticism from Salem Chaker in Paris. The decision, he said, was "hasty and badly founded," and "dangerous" for Tamazight's future development in Morocco. Its only purpose, he said, was to domesticate Tamazight by "driving this transitional period of Amazigh writing and teaching into a sure dead end." Moreover, he explained, the modern version of the ancient Tifinagh script was developed by Kabyle amateurs, albeit well-meaning ones, thus reflecting the Kabyle dialect and making it inappropriate for all-Amazigh usage. It would be up to the Moroccan Amazigh organizations, he said, to ensure that the progress made over the past twenty years in written expressions of the language in the Latin script did not grind to a halt. By contrast, Chaker emphasized, the development of a Latin script for Tamazight in Kabylie, and in Algeria in general, had evolved much farther, and over a longer period, and thus "one may not fear either an obstruction or regression."[37] However, the script issue would suddenly surface in Algeria in 2006, much to the chagrin of both Chaker and Kabyle activists (see Chapter 7). From a different direction, the head of an important Islamist group attacked the IRCAM's recommendation (but not the king's, of course) as "artificial, arbitrary and non-democratic," for it failed to involve the Moroccan public in the decision.[38]

It took nine years from the time that King Hassan II had first expressed his intention to have Moroccan "dialects" taught in the schools to the first actual lesson, in Fall 2003, to first-grade pupils in three hundred schools. Along the way, the 1999 "National Charter of Education and Training" had declared as a goal the introduction of Tamazight into the school system, albeit for the declared purpose of assisting young children in mastering Arabic, not as a language in which subjects would be taught. Moreover, the time had not been spent well. Teachers had only two weeks of training in the new materials, all written in the Tifinagh script mandated by the IRCAM; not all of the teachers possessed the ideological commitment that language experts deemed vital to the teaching of minority languages, but were merely doing it for extra remuneration; the initial instructional manuals were deemed by many to be of poor quality;[39] and the entire project had a pronounced improvised air to it.[40] IRCAM researchers, for their part, were often frustrated by the fact that theirs was an advisory capacity only, with the proper implementation depending on the activities of the Education Ministry, deemed by many to be hostile to the project. Meanwhile, many parents, and educators too, questioned the wisdom of demanding that young pupils learn three different alphabets, Arabic, Latin, and Tifinagh, in their first three years of studies, and non-Amazigh parents were often reluctant to have their children study Tamazight. Finally, the top-down planning of the program failed to take into account the very different needs of rural, poverty-stricken Tamazight-speaking regions, where real learning in the children's mother tongue might well contribute to a closing of the persistent and profound educational and social gaps between Morocco's urban and rural areas.[41] The gap between the Education Ministry's positive statements regarding the implementation of the program and the much less sanguine picture painted by IRCAM personnel and outside researchers and observers was stark. Still, the project went forward: the multiyear implementation plan intended to have all first- and second-graders in Morocco learning Tamazight by 2009–2010, and 20 percent of the sixth-grade classes. What level of proficiency would be attained, and what the effect of learning Tamazight would be on the self-identity of Amazigh children and on Moroccan collective identity, remained to be seen. In the meantime, surveys and interviews of a cross-section of Moroccan college students found prevailing attitudes regarding the Berber language, particularly regarding its usefulness, prestige, and connotations, to be quite negative, which hardly bode well for the movement's objectives.[42]

DISSENT

The difficulties experienced in the introduction of Tamazight into the educational curriculum, as well as the authorities' foot-dragging in other areas, such as the promotion of Amazigh language and culture in the audiovisual media,[43] music, and the arts, created great frustration within the IRCAM cadres, who were extremely sensitive to the notion that the IRCAM was serving the Palace's and the *makhzen*'s agenda more than that of the Amazigh community itself. Internal practices and appointments within the IRCAM also continued to be controversial. Hence, on February 21, 2005, seven members of the Advisory Council issued a public communiqué announcing their resignation. Four of them were Rifians and three were from the Middle Atlas region, reinforcing the perception held by some activists that IRCAM was largely the monopoly of the southern Ishelhin Berber bloc.[44] The resignation also sharpened the debate regarding IRCAM's effectiveness. Chafik and Boukous, naturally, stood on one side, while the resignees, including Chafik's classmate at the Collège d'Azrou, Dr. Abdelmalik Oussaden, stood on the other.

The resignation proclamation was a searing indictment of what they viewed as IRCAM's ineffectiveness in advancing the Amazigh cause, and as acquiescence of the leadership to the state's deliberate policies of co-option and containment. Notwithstanding the skepticism among Amazigh militants, they declared, they had accepted their appointment by the king to the IRCAM's board of directors in 2002, believing that the authorities had decided, once and for all, to turn the page on a painful past marked by "marginalization, contempt and cultural genocide," which had affected the whole of the Moroccan people since 1912. However, the hopes raised by the king's 2001 speech had not been fulfilled, and their actions on the IRCAM board had been without palpable effect. The empty promises of the national education and communications ministries, they said, were especially noticeable: notwithstanding the goal of universalizing the teaching of Tamazight at all levels of primary and secondary education, a reliable support system for improving the quality of teaching of Tamazight had not been established, while the officially assigned "humiliating" role of Tamazight as a support for Arabic-language studies in the first two years of school remained in place. On the university level, they said, educational reform had not taken place at all. As for the audiovisual media, the Amazigh language continued to be the "poor relation," without any change apart from occasional artistic evenings. The state's heavy hand was felt in other, often capricious ways: e.g., it interfered in the right of parents to name their children and withheld legal recognition of cultural associations; public life — the courts, governmental institutions, etc. — was conducted exclusively in Arabic, while Tamazight was limited to the IRCAM offices. Hence, they concluded, the anti-Amazigh forces within the state had gained the upper hand, effectively nullifying the intent of the king's 2001 *dahir*. The only way this could be reversed, they declared, would be a constitutional change explicitly stipulating that Tamazight was an official language, to be accompanied by laws designed to protect and develop its use in the public sphere, and by the abrogation of laws that relegated it to secondary status.

The public response from the more moderate wing of the Amazigh movement was low-key. Chafik, now retired from his position as IRCAM's vice-rector, declared that he personally would not have resigned, but he understood that those who did are in a hurry. It was his view, however, that working with the "renewed *makhzen*" offered the best chance to advance the Amazigh cause. Boukous echoed his predecessor, stating that before the IRCAM, there was no significant framework for action, and that many of the movement's intellectuals had paid a heavy price for their past activities, including jail terms and the revocation of their passports. The contemporary climate was incomparably better, he said, while those who placed themselves outside of the IRCAM framework were left with nothing.[45] As for the authorities, following the resignations and subsequent controversy, the communications and education ministries hastened to reiterate their commitment to promoting Amazigh culture.

Oussaden retorted that the IRCAM was an effort by the Palace to contain the Amazigh movement: activists felt that they were being "put to sleep." As a follow-up, the group of resignees, joined by others, met on a number of occasions and formulated a lengthy document, issued on January 14, 2007, and titled "Plate-forme: Option Amazighe/Ardiyya: al-Ikhtiyar al-Amazighi." It was, they declared, designed to analyze the "century of suffering" endured by the Amazigh community under the protectorate and independence regimes. Much of its content reiterated and elaborated on the themes articulated in the Berber Manifesto issued seven years earlier, which the Plate-forme praised as an important development in the struggle for recognition. However, its tone was sharper and less conciliatory. The frustration with the authorities' lack of commitment to the 2001 *dahir* and with IRCAM's inability to fulfill its mission of protecting and reviving Amazigh culture was palpable, as was the urgency. The 2004 Moroccan population census, noted the Plate-forme, indicated that, "with all the reservations that one has regarding the credibility of official figures," only 28 percent of Moroccans use the Amazigh language in their daily lives, against 34 percent ten years earlier. This wearing down of the Amazigh *identité*, it insisted, was not a "natural development," i.e., the outgrowth of a value-free, well-nigh-inevitable outcome of socioeconomic and political processes of modernization and national integration, but was the result of deliberate political action designed for that end. One may take issue with such a formulation, or at the very least with its exclusivity in ascribing Amazigh decline to hostile, anti-Amazigh policies. But what is important is the desire of the Plate-forme's framers to foreground the political sphere as the appropriate place for action to rescue Amazigh culture. The Amazigh movement, they declared, "has no alternative than to mobilize for a political struggle that would put the Amazigh question at the center of a national debate regarding a new social contract that would re-link the threads of history and enable the recovery of one's authentic roots."

One of the Plate-forme's most revealing points was its discussion of the bases of the Amazigh people's proprietary claim on Morocco. This had not been acquired by either blood or ethnicity, it declared, but by attachment to the land. The land, it stated, is the "cradle of Amazigh civilization" and the accompanying symbols of identity derived from the Amazigh language and history. Of course, most modern-day scholars would state that the bases of ethnonational identity are some combination of precisely all of the above factors—territory, language, history, blood ties, historical experiences and memory, and associated cultural attributes. But contemporary Moroccan Amazigh discourse adamantly rejects any effort to apply the ethnic label to the Amazigh population, for fear that it would place them on an "equal" basis with other groups in Morocco, whose identity had been fashioned by Arab, Andalusian, or African origins, and would open the door to others seeking to distinguish themselves on particular "biological, religious or mythical" grounds. Morocco, declared the Plate-forme, could not be categorized as a country composed of distinct communities, as is the case with Canada and Belgium. By contrast, France and Spain are deemed "interesting": anyone who chooses France as a homeland is welcome (the theory is more important than the reality for the Plate-forme's authors), while Spain is said to be proud of its "Iberian" identity, "notwithstanding the Arab and Amazigh blood which flows in its veins." The Amazigh movement discourse nearly always looks at Spain from a different angle: the success of the Catalan region in promoting its own linguistic, cultural, and political specificity is viewed with considerable envy and deemed a model worthy of emulation. In this case, the emphasis on geography, not blood ties, is what is important. The priority of geography over ethnicity in determining national identity is reiterated with reference to other cases as well (however problematic some may actually be): "the American identity, Chinese, Korean, German, Russian, etc."

Of course, the underlying culprits in this militant discourse rejecting Amazigh ethnicity are those who insist on Morocco's Arab identity and seek to Arabize the Amazigh population. The Arabs, unlike the native Amazigh rooted to their soil, are a defined "ethnic group," with a group consciousness deriving from linguistic, cultural, economic, and social commonalities and specific geographical roots, the Arabian Peninsula. The cardinal sin of Morocco's urban elites, backed by "foreign personalities, both French and Arab," was their desire to establish a new conception of national identity, based on a "new order" (*al-nizam al-jadid*) with an "Arabist tendency" (*al-nazʿa al-arabiyya*), on the ruins of the defeated Amazigh order. This "arrogance" and "hostility" toward "any presence of the Amazigh in his own country" resulted in their imposing a new kind of "cultural colonialism" on Morocco, based on a decision to "annex [it] to the Arab East after having ripped it from the French colonial empire."[46]

PROGRESS AND SETBACKS

Speaking in 2006, Ahmed Asid, one of the Amazigh movement's leading intellectuals, was optimistic that Tamazight would win official status through a change in the preamble of the Constitution, noting how different the current situation was from the early 1990s, when the very mention of the issue of Amazigh language status was unacceptable. At the same time, Asid was well aware of the need for additional measures. Linking the advancement of Amazigh status to the broader liberal discourse advocating the democratization of public life, Asid stressed that the democratization of local authorities and the expansion of their legal powers would be important in raising Amazigh status.[47]

A symposium held on the pages of the Moroccan Arabic-language daily *al-Ahdath al-Maghrabiyya* on November 15, 2006, provided further evidence that the subject of constitutional recognition of the Amazigh language and identity had made its way onto the public agenda and was no longer the exclusive province of the Amazigh movement. To be sure, sharp divisions on the issue persisted. Not surprisingly, the Istiqlal's Mohamed Larbi Messari, a former government minister, was unequivocal in declaring that there should be only one official language in the country, Arabic. To bolster his argument, he anachronistically declared that even the Almohad rulers had never insisted that Tamazight be made an official language.[48] Abdallah Baha of the Islamist PJD party spoke in moderate, albeit noncommittal, terms, advocating a national dialogue on the issue, while expressing concern over the potential divisiveness of the issue, as well as over the Amazigh movement's discourse linking Morocco's underdevelopment to anything Arab and Islamic. USFP Political Bureau member Muhammad Ali Hassani also warned against the political exploitation of the issue, while accepting that the Amazigh were a component of Morocco's multicultural society. It was left to Ouzzin Aherdane, activist and publisher/editor of the MP's daily newspaper *al-Haraka,* to wave the banner of Amazigh linguistic and cultural rights within a united, pluralist Morocco, while decrying what he termed a return to the atmosphere of the 1950s, when the Istiqlal-led political classes sought to marginalize and isolate the Amazigh from newly independent Morocco.[49]

One unmistakable sign of the Moroccan state's shift in the direction of the Amazigh movement's weltanschauung is to be found in a sixth-grade social studies textbook. Published in 2006, the book presents in a positive fashion important basic information regarding North Africa's pre-Islamic past, traditionally ignored by the educational system, and in a way that jibes with the Amazigh grand narrative.

Among the goals of lesson five, for example, is that the student become familiar with Amazigh (not "Berber"!) society and its forms of internal solidarity prior to the arrival of the Phoenicians/Carthaginians in North Africa. To that end, it provides succinct definitions of key terms, beginning with Amazigh itself: they are, the book says, the inhabitants of *bilad al-Amazigh* (parenthetically identified as al-Maghrib), a land stretching west of Egypt across North Africa to the Atlantic Ocean, who lived in the area for five thousand years before the birth of Christ. There is no mention of where they themselves came from: in other words, there is no reference to the traditional myth of the Eastern origin of the Berbers prevalent throughout Islamic history. Tribal society, says the text, was underpinned by the values of solidarity, consultation, and cooperation—although the word democracy isn't used, these are exactly the social practices claimed by Amazigh activists to prove the inherent "democratic" character of their society. Specific terms in the Amazigh language are introduced to reinforce the student's understanding of, and even identification with, Amazigh society: *amghar,* the head of a tribal unit and local council (*inflas,* or *ajma'a*); *iglid,* the head of a united tribal confederation, equivalent to *amir* or *malik;* and *taqbilt* (*kabila*/tribe). The Tifinagh script is, of course, also mentioned and presented as a combination of ancient Libyan and Phoenician script (students in the sixth grade at that time would presumably not yet have been exposed to the script in schools). Carthaginian influence is presented favorably in the context of the Maghrib being a civilizational crossroad. But the Roman conquests are not: here, the stress is on imperial conquest and exploitation of the population, especially the Amazigh people. In this context, notable Amazigh rulers, among them the Hellenistic-like Berber kings, are given their due: Massinissa, 202–148 BC; Yugurtha [Jugurtha], 118–105 BC; and Juba II, 25–23 BC (who, the text says, knew both Amazigh and Latin; whose son married Cleopatra; and who put his wife's picture on the back of the coins being minted, thus testifying to the important place that women had in Amazigh society). Noted also were Tacfarinas, a Numidian military leader who led a rebellion against Roman rule in AD 17–24, and Donatus, 391–411, leader of the Donatist rebellion, which nearly tore Christian North Africa apart. In mentioning these historical figures, and particularly their resistance (*muqawwama*) to brutal and exploitative Roman imperial rule, the textbook stresses that the goal of the lesson should be to make the students aware of Amazigh resistance, which serves as evidence of their unswerving dedication to freedom and independence. All of this seems to have been lifted right out of the pages of Berber memory workers.

To be sure, when it comes to describing the arrival of Islam to North Africa, the traditional Islamic narrative kicks in: the Islamic conquest by Arab armies is considered a *fath* (an "enlightenment," an "opening up"), and not another *ghazu* (invasion/raid) by foreign intruders—i.e., the conflict that did take place was primarily religious in nature, not ethnic. Still, some Amazigh resistance is given its due, even if only indirectly, as mention is made of the fabled Kahina, who unsuccessfully led Berber tribes in battle against the Arab conquerors, and whose sons adopted the Islamic faith and joined the leadership ranks of the victors.

In general, the coverage of the Islamic period avoids awkward episodes that might display not only religious schism, but the importance of the Amazigh element in them—e.g., the Kharijite revolt of 739–740 and the existence for three hundred years of the heretical Barghwata kingdom. But in a further bow to the place of the Amazigh in Moroccan and Islamic history, the book specifically refers to the great Almoravid and Almohad dynasties, which united North Africa and Andalusia as never before, as being of Amazigh origin.[50]

SUBALTERN HISTORY
AND GRASSROOTS ACTIVISM

Recovering and remembering rural and tribal history are very much part of the Amazigh Culture Movement's agenda. Here, and as noted in the discussion of the Plate-forme, the primary factor in determining identity is not language, per se, but land, around which society is organized. In Morocco, the authorities, whether French or Moroccan, are depicted as running roughshod over Amazigh communal land rights and traditions. For example, *Le Monde Amazigh* published a long article denouncing the administrative confiscation of the lands belonging to the Zaiane tribes in the Khenifra region, pointing to similarities between current policies and those used by the protectorate authorities, who had bought out one of the leading *caids,* Mouha U Hamou Zaiani. Previously, he had joined with Arab tribes in their fight against the French during their "pacification" campaign. However, in return for his agreement not to fight the French any further, Mouha U Hamou was granted the lands of neighboring tribes.

The confiscation of communal lands also had important negative effects on social and cultural life. For example, a traditional spring holiday gathering of the Zaiane tribes, which featured a theatrical performance by tribal notables involving pledges of mutual solidarity and a sharing of the lands, according to Berber customary law, vanished with the transfer of the lands to Mouha U Hamou. The administrative means for doing so were, and remain, Royal *dahirs,* which do not recognize customary law and view tribal lands as belonging to the state.[51]

The question of the relationship between customary law and Islamic law has been of continuing interest to scholars. The French protectorate authorities stepped into a minefield when they tried to formally institutionalize customary Berber practices, and thus officially place them on an equal footing with the Shari'a. It is generally held that Berber customary law (*izerf*) is not diametrically opposed to the Shari'a and takes it into account. However, Injaz Abdallah Habibi, in writing about the Zaiane tribes, openly questions whether this is the case, indicating a desire to diminish the religious aspects of Berber identity. His emphasis on the positive aspects of communal village customs is part of a broader theme of Amazigh memory work, namely, the essentially democratic nature of village society and, by extension, Berber culture as a whole. The upland village is idealistically and nostalgically presented as the repository of deep-rooted Berber traditions, with traditional art, handicrafts, and household management by women standing at the center of daily life.[52] Another writer even goes so far as to describe village society's organizing concept of *jama'a,* which is usually associated with a (negative) tribal mentality, as having the attributes of altruism and love of the land and the Other, and hence being not in contradiction to the requirements of modernity but rather in harmony with them.[53] However contrived this portrait, it serves as another example of Berber activists reinterpreting their history and society in a useful, instrumental fashion.

The rural world was understandably an important arena for Amazigh intellectuals seeking to fashion a new identity discourse. Even more important were the signs that their efforts were starting to have an impact among wider sectors of the rural world, especially in the south and southeast regions.[54] Over the course of the decade, and against the background of the creation of the IRCAM and the antiregime militancy being played out in Kabylie, Moroccan Amazigh activism began spreading beyond the confines of intellectual seminars and publications, particularly among an increasingly militant and politicized younger generation of students at the universities of Agadir, Errachidia, and Meknes, whose homes were in the villages and towns of the southeast and Souss regions, the core areas of the Berber rural world. In turn, they sought to mobilize their local home populations, their families, essentially, on both symbolic and concrete matters.[55]

Activism on campus, and in rural towns and villages involving students

home for vacation and post-university militants, employed a variety of
direct action tactics, including boycotts, sit-ins, and unauthorized meetings and marches. Specific student grievances included discrimination in
the face of privileged treatment accorded to Sahrawi students. Some of
this new activism had a more explicitly political bent. For example, villagers were encouraged to boycott the 2007 elections on the grounds that
the *makhzen* ignored their pressing material, developmental needs, and to
block access roads in protest against the authorities' neglect. Their militant
discourse also included reference to the past, such as the "heroic" battles
against the French conquerors, e.g., the 1933 battle of Bougafer; insistence
on proper compensation for the remaining elderly combatants; and demands for the rehabilitation and restoration of local kasbahs and palaces,
concrete symbols of Amazigh culture and history, most of which were
in an advanced state of decay. Some of these activities were organized by
a group called "La Coordination Ait Ghirouche," whose name explicitly
evoked an imaginary tribal confederation for the purpose of forging new
ties of solidarity among the Amazigh villagers and townsmen of the region. Others, from the Souss region, referred to themselves as "Ait Souss,"
giving their militancy a more specific regional cast.

STATE BACKLASH

Still, considerable limitations remained on the Amazigh
movement's ability to advance its aims. The increasingly public nature of
Amazigh activism and its desire to force issues, as well as the resistance of
the state authorities, were demonstrated in April 2003 in Nador, a port city
of approximately 180,000 persons in the Rif region. Following the official
decision to make Tifinagh the official script for Tamazight, the munici-
pality took the initiative of stamping all of its documents with the letter
"Z" in Tifinagh, and writing "Nador" in Tifinagh as well. On April 29, the
city's inhabitants awoke to discover street signs in Tifinagh, occasioning
considerable comment. However, the status quo ante was quickly restored,
as the Ministry of the Interior ordered their removal on the grounds that
only signs in the country's official language, Arabic, could be used to mark
streets (ignoring the widespread use of French), and ministry officials were
reportedly seen erasing "Z" graffiti on the walls of villages in the Nador
region. The following year, Amazigh students at Agadir University who
had organized commemorative activities on the twenty-fourth anniversary

of the now-mythical Tafsut Imazighen (Berber Spring) were arrested and badly beaten by the police.[56]

Newly formed Amazigh associations, which by 2009 numbered approximately four hundred, were repeatedly harassed by the authorities, who systematically delayed delivery of receipts acknowledging that they had paid the deposits required for legalization of their groups. No less disturbing were the continued difficulties experienced by parents intent on giving Amazigh names to their children, names that were not on the state's approved list. Interior Minister Chakib Benmoussa denied that there were any restrictions, or that such a list of banned names even existed. However, he also pointed to Law No. 37–99, which stated that "the name chosen by the person declaring the birth . . . must be Moroccan in nature and must not be either a family name nor a name composed of more than two forenames, nor the name of a town, village or tribe, similarly it must not be such that it would challenge morality or public order." Names considered unacceptable were shared with all of Morocco's registry offices and its embassies and consulates abroad. Obviously, the law left a great deal of room for interpretation, beginning with the requirement that the name be "Moroccan in nature." According to Amazigh activists, thirteen Amazigh names, including Illy, Tilili, Chaden, and Dihya, were added to the list in 2007 by the High Commission on Civil Status, the body charged with such matters, on the grounds that they were "un-Moroccan" names determined not to be in conformity with the law.[57] The issue was taken up by Human Rights Watch, which wrote a letter to Benmoussa on June 16, 2009, detailing five such cases and requesting an explanation.[58] Berber associations also repeatedly took umbrage at the ongoing Arabization of Amazigh toponyms: e.g., the towns Ifni being changed to Sidi Ifni, Askourene becoming Sekkoura, and Tazagourt becoming Zagoura.[59]

Three recent incidents seem to have again demonstrated that the Moroccan state, or at least portions thereof, were seeking to send "tough" messages to Amazigh activists. In May 2007, as part of a struggle over the control of campuses between Marxists and Amazigh movement groups, violent clashes broke out at Agadir University and elsewhere in which Amazigh activists were allegedly attacked by groups of Sahrawi origin, along with other leftists, all of them said to be promoting a pan-Arab ideology.[60] Among the Amazigh activists, suspicions were raised that a hidden hand was behind the incidents—namely, that government agents were seeking to manipulate the situation for some as yet undetermined purpose. In February 2008, ten activists, some of them high school students, were sentenced by a Ouarzazate court to a total of thirty-four years in prison.[61] In a spillover of these tensions to Meknes, the discovery of the body of a non-Amazigh student led to the arrest and extended imprisonment of ten Amazigh activists, which have drawn a number of solidarity protests, and even a sit-in in front of the Ministry of Justice in Rabat, during a hunger strike by the jailed activists. In October 2008, heavy sentences were handed down again: two persons were each sentenced to nine years in prison and fined eighty thousand dirhams, and the other eight received one-year prison terms.[62] The authorities' tough stance toward student activists was again displayed at the end of 2009: demonstrations in the village of Taghjijt, 200 kilometers south of Agadir, voicing demands for better housing, transport, and other social benefits, were met with a harsh response and prison sentences, not only for a number of protesters, but also for an Amazigh blogger reporting on the episode, who received a four-month sentence for "spreading false information about human rights that undermined the kingdom's image," and an Internet café owner who was sentenced to twelve months in prison for being in possession of publications that "incited racial hatred" (material from an Amazigh group was found on his flash drive).[63] Some months earlier, the authorities also demonstrated toughness toward the Amazigh intellectual cadre, blocking efforts by AMREC and Tamaynut to convene a conference in Casablanca entitled "The Falsification of Moroccan History."[64]

Seven

BOUTEFLIKA'S ALGERIA

AND KABYLE ALIENATION

$\mathbf{B}$acked by the military, which was badly in need of the legitimacy provided by civilian rule, Abdelaziz Bouteflika registered resounding success in consolidating his position in the decade following his ascent to the presidency in 1999. The Islamist insurgency was finally broken, although not entirely stamped out; Algeria's standing in the international community, which had been badly damaged during the civil war, improved substantially, particularly in the aftermath of the September 11, 2001, bombing of the World Trade Center in New York City by al-Qaʿida jihadists. The Algerian authorities now became a desired and cooperative partner in the U.S.-led "War on Terror." The increase in radical Islamist terrorism in Algeria in 2007–2008 under the rubric of a rebranded "al-Qaʿida of the Islamic Maghreb" and the specter of jihadists finding a haven in the Sahel region only further enhanced the Algerian regime's value in the eyes of Western governments.

Over the course of his first decade as president, Bouteflika was also able to gradually establish a degree of distance from, and authority over, the military establishment by pensioning off senior officials, including the chief of staff during most of the years of civil strife, Lieutenant-General Mohamed Lamari, and promoting younger officers and those more directly loyal to him. His decisive defeat of his former associate and now bitter rival, ex–Prime Minister Ali Benflis, in the 2004 general presidential elections further strengthened his power base. Eighteen months later, he registered another successful marker of his consolidation of power, with the overwhelming ratification of the "Charter for Peace and National Reconciliation" by 97 percent of participating voters. The Charter offered a broad amnesty for militants who had handed in their weapons, apart from those who were guilty of murder, rape, and bombings of public buildings, and freed the security services from any possible responsibility for the disappearance of more than six thousand Algerians during the civil strife of the 1990s. It also offered compensation to the families of the dead and disappeared. Finally, Bouteflika sufficiently weathered a bout with cancer to successfully amend the Algerian Constitution, which had mandated a two-term limit, paving the way for his overwhelming reelection to a third term in 2009.

One thing that Bouteflika did not do was fundamentally alter the nature of Algeria's authoritarian system. The military *nomenklatura,* often referred to by critics as "mafia clans," had come to control many of Algeria's economic enterprises, and although the Algerian economy required major overhaul in order to cope with high unemployment and poverty, the fundamental reforms required to make it competitive in the global market would have threatened to undermine the edifice on which the regime was built. So Bouteflika safeguarded the existing clientelist system—with its enormous income—and the military's (and his own) privileges in it. Limited economic liberalization measures were carried out in ways that did not result in the breaking up of unofficial monopolies held by various interest groups. Algeria remained a rentier state par excellence, deriving 95 percent of its revenues from the sale of natural gas and oil. Its destabilization in the late 1980s had been prompted by the precipitous drop in oil prices. To Bouteflika's, and the *nomenklatura's,* good fortune, the spike in petroleum revenues between 2000 and 2008 provided the state with unprecedented revenues. However, the world economic crisis of 2008–2009 adversely affected the cushion that had enabled the regime to avoid the necessity of adopting far-reaching measures to reform the economy.[1]

Although seriously deficient in the area of human rights and many other realms, Algeria's postrevolutionary authoritarian regime was also "soft," in the sense that the military-economic-political elites were large enough and diverse enough so as to preclude the accumulation of absolute power in the hands of one particular "clan." Internal divisions were thus often reflected in a lively press, which at times featured sharp criticism of public figures. Yet neither the pluralist press nor the other elements of secular civil society were sufficiently strong to challenge fundamentally the dominance of the existing *pouvoir.*

LE PRINTEMPS NOIR

Meanwhile, a broad swath of Algerian society remained profoundly alienated from its rulers. Unlike the bitter war of independence, which conferred legitimacy on the victorious FLN, thus enabling it to mobilize society behind its particular brand of nation-building and state-building, the triumph over the armed Islamist insurgency had left much of the population not only battered and weary, but empty of ideological and emotional affinity with the ruling elite. This was succinctly expressed in a phrase that became part of the political lexicon: *la hogra,* namely, contempt that the authorities show for the public, rendering it unable to hold them accountable for their actions, and thus profoundly angered. In the spring of 2001, this frustration and alienation burst out with great force. Not coincidentally, the primary focal point of this anger was Kabylie. On April 18, an eighteen-year-old secondary school student, Massinissa Guermah, was shot and mortally wounded by gendarmes after having been taken into custody in the village of Beni Douala, twelve miles from Tizi-Ouzou, following their intervention in fighting between rival youth gangs. His death on April 21 was announced in an official communiqué that cast aspersions on the victim. Together with the entry of security forces into a school the following day to arrest three students who had allegedly insulted them at a demonstration, the killing touched off what quickly became known as Le Printemps Noir (Black Spring; Tafsut Taberkant). The "most protracted rioting in Algerian history," which lasted until early July, and toward the end spread beyond Kabylie to the Aures Mountains, Annaba to the east and Biskra in the south, resulted in the death of between one and two hundred persons at the hands of the security forces, primarily the Gendarmerie National, who used indiscriminate force, including widespread beatings, torture, and extrajudicial killings.[2] As was the case in October 1988, there is considerable belief, and some supporting circumstantial evidence, to suggest that the violence was provoked by a faction within the Algerian official hierarchy to discredit President Bouteflika. The first genuinely independent investigative commission ever appointed by the Algerian state, headed by an eminent Kabyle jurist, Mohamed Issad, was guarded in its evaluation, suggesting that either senior commanders of the Gendarmerie had lost control of their subordinates or were being exploited by external forces. If the latter was true, they failed to undermine Bouteflika's hold on power, while wreaking havoc on Kabyle society and further sharpening the Kabyle population's confrontation with the state. Indeed, the Issad commission's report, which marked the first time ever that a government-sanctioned body had condemned part of the armed forces for excesses against the civilian population, expressed deep pessimism for Kabylie's future. Government policy, said the report, had been evolving for years from a "state of emergency" to a "state of siege," and the rapid and spontaneous emergence of new representatives outside the existing political channels, the *aarch* (see below), demonstrated the need for achieving a real representation of the population.[3]

Rioters, for their part, attacked symbols of state authority such as town halls, tax collection offices, state company buildings, and offices of the ruling political parties, as they had done in Spring 1980 and October 1988. Ironically, they taunted police with proclamations praising the insurgent Islamist leader Hassan Hattab.[4] Rioters also attacked the offices of the Kabyle political parties, the FFS and RCD, pointing to the degree of alienation toward their "own" political parties. Seeking to salvage the situation, the RCD withdrew from the governing coalition: "It is impossible for us to remain in a government that shoots at young people," declared Saïd Saadi.[5] The FFS, for its part, called for the withdrawal of the Gendarmerie from the region and organized a number of demonstrations, climaxed by the 300,000-strong "March of Democratic Hope" in Algiers, on May 31, as it sought to convert the regional unrest into a challenge to the regime's legitimacy.[6]

Still, the parties' base of support had been seriously compromised. One consequence, which was in fact perhaps the most striking development of the Black Spring, was the emergence of new, and previously unknown, local bodies, eventually organized under the rubric of the Coordination Interwilayas ["districts"] des aarchs [lit. "tribes"], daïras ["departments"] et communes (CIADC), also known as the Mouvement Citoyen Des Aarchs (Citizens Movement of the Tribes), a hybrid name if there ever was one. As was generally true of previous Berberist groups, the *aarch* sought to combine a modernist, national democratic agenda with a specific Kabyle orientation, befitting the fact that their social basis was rooted in Kabylie villages. Even the name by which they were commonly known, *aarch,* as well as their manner of conduct, derived from Kabyle political traditions. To be sure, the *aarch* were not actually relics of former extended kin groupings clustered in specific villages, but rather groupings that were the product of modern administrative decisions. Nonetheless, the term, and the style of consultations stemming from traditional village councils (*tajmaʿat*) and the harsh enforcement and punishment mechanisms employed against dissidents, were very familiar (all too much so, one might say). The entire structure would prove to be extremely unwieldy and ultimately unsustainable.[7]

At the outset, however, the mobilization and articulation capacities of these new bodies were extremely impressive, and the excitement generated by "The Citizens Movement" was considerable. On May 17, during the peak of the confrontation between Kabyle youth and the security forces, a series of demands focusing on the removal of those responsible for the killings were drawn up in the town of Illoula. Four days later, on May 21, up to a half-million persons gathered in Tizi-Ouzou in peaceful protest. Then, on June 11, a more comprehensive and sweeping set of demands, known as the El-Kseur (Leqsar) Platform, was issued at a meeting in the *wilaya* of Béjaïa. These included concrete demands related to the crisis: care for the victims of the state's repression and their families, the prosecution of those responsible, and the immediate withdrawal of the Gendarmerie from the region. There was attention to the Amazigh dimension, namely, "satisfaction of the Amazigh claim in all its (identity, civilisational, linguistic and cultural) dimensions, without a referendum or any conditions, and the consecration of Tamazight as the official national language," as well an emergency socioeconomic program for Kabylie and the rejection of "the policies of underdevelopment, impoverishment and reduction to vagrancy (*clochardisation*) of the Algerian people." Finally, the Platform called for a fundamental democratization of Algerian life, which would include "the placing of all executive functions of the state and the security corps under the authority of democratically elected bodies." One may argue, as Roberts does so cogently, that the language issue was not the root cause of the new crisis, nor the most important matter on the table.[8] Nonetheless, language and identity were clearly intertwined with concrete demands, and hardly marginal matters. Had that been the case, they would not have been given pride of place in the El-Kseur Platform's demands.[9]

On June 14, just three days after the issuing of the Platform, hundreds of thousands of persons, if not more, converged on Algiers from Kabylie in one of the biggest demonstrations in the country's history. The marchers' demands were both all-Algerian and particularist Kabyle: the establishment of a truly democratic regime in Algeria; and the recognition of Tamazight as an official language alongside Arabic, and of Amazigh identity as being an inseparable part of the Algerian collective. They were met by agents provocateurs shouting anti-Kabyle slogans, who incited violent confrontations in order to discredit the marchers in the eyes of the broader Algerian public. This view was reinforced by the state-run media. A reported four persons were killed and hundreds injured and arrested. The CIADC tried to organize another, smaller march on July 5, Algerian Independence Day, but were blocked at the outskirts of Algiers by police. As it happened, the mass march on Algiers of June 14 was never repeated, and the hopes that it would spearhead a broad movement for democratization, the rule of law, and respect for Algeria's pluralist character dissipated.

From this point on, the focus turned back to Kabylie. The region now entered into an extended state of quasi–civil revolt, manifested by repeated strikes and boycotts of parliamentary and municipal elections, as well as factional strife. Nationwide legislative elections in March 2002 were an unmitigated failure: the voter turnout in the Tizi-Ouzou region was 1.8 percent, and in Béjaïa, 2.6 percent; between 80 and 90 percent of the voting stations remained closed, and in some places where voting did take place, ballot boxes were burned by activists.[10] In the October 2002 municipal and provincial elections, voter turnout in Kabylie was only marginally higher, 7.6 percent in the Tizi-Ouzou province and 15.6 percent in the Béjaïa province. The increase was due to the FFS's decision to participate, a controversial move explained by Ait Ahmed as stemming from a desire "not to leave a vacuum in the municipalities of Kabylie and to block the way of all sorts of mafia which seek to bring turmoil to the Kabylie region and Algeria as a whole."[11] As a result, the FFS won a majority of the seats in the two provincial councils. However, its members were widely denounced as "traitors" by CIADC militants, and its offices were ransacked, as were polling stations that did not have police protection. Similarly, in the September 29, 2005, referendum on national reconciliation, official voter turnout was only 11.4 percent in Kabylie, where polling stations were again attacked and ballots destroyed, compared to the officially reported 79.76 percent nationwide. (Independent estimates placed the turnout in large cities as 20–30 percent lower.)[12]

AUTONOMY?

As a result of the 2002 election boycott, administrators appointed from the outside ran local assemblies. Development budgets for the region were cut during these years, and the population relied largely on the "informal" economy.[13] Manifestations of Kabyle-Berber ethnic identity continued to expand. Even the magic word "autonomy," the great bogeyman for the postcolonial state authorities in Morocco and Algeria, appeared in Kabyle public discourse, although it was widely viewed as an unrealistic notion. The concept had already been broached prior to the Black Spring by Berber intellectuals demanding recognition of the Amazigh language in Kabylie and other regions, within the framework of linguistic and cultural autonomy and as part of the construction of a genuine democratic alternative in Algeria.[14] Not only would Berber collective identity acquire the ability to engage in cultural reproduction and thus be preserved and developed, but the Berbers were also envisaged as playing a vital role as agents promoting the democratization of the Algerian state.[15]

Now, however, the demand for autonomy contained an overt political dimension.

Spearheading the notion was the veteran singer/poet/activist Ferhat Mehenni, whose involvement in Berberist activism and protest dated back decades, including being a founding member of the Berber Culture Movement (MCB), a member of the League of Human Rights, and subsequently part of the RCD. In June 2001, Mehenni resurfaced to found the Mouvement pour le Autonomie de la Kabylie (MAK). Unlike Morocco's Mohamed Chafik, Mehenni did not shy away from the specter of a Huntingtonian clash of civilizations by seeking to reconcile Western and Islamic cultures, but rather came down firmly in the secular Western camp, unequivocally adopting the French *laïcité* model. As articulated in the movement's platform, the core values of *la Kabylie autonome* are:

1. Respect for Human Rights, without distinction between sex, race, language or religion; consequently, the existing Family Code[16] would be abrogated, polygamy forbidden and personal status matters governed by civil laws.
2. Guaranteed freedom of worship, with religious matters being relegated to the private domain.
3. Democracy, which is a political system governed by elected institutions.[17]

Indeed, Mehenni was explicit that Kabyles should not wait for the reform of the Algerian state, which, from its outset in 1962, was on the other side of the civilizational divide. He also updated his message to fit the prevalent, post–September 11, 2001 Western discourse conflating fascism and radical Islamist terrorism. From the beginning, he said, Kabylie had stood in opposition to "arabo-muslim Algeria," which was "the antechamber of a fascist and arabo-islamist Algeria." Rather, Kabyles should take matters into their own hands. While advocating universal-Western values, Mehenni and his supporters were specifically Kabyle in orientation, putting little stock in larger pan-Amazigh notions and criticizing what they deemed to be a lack of real solidarity with the Kabyles during the Black Spring and afterwards by other Amazigh communities.[18]

Responding to charges that his movement was "separatist," Mehenni emphasized to an interviewer that "to build autonomy in Kabylie is also to build a modern, plural and democratic Algeria, where it will be good to live." As in "most of the regions of the EU," he said, where "regional flags cohabit harmoniously with the national and European flags[,] . . . a regional Kabyle flag will essentially occupy Kabylie's public space, next to the Algerian national emblem."[19] This view was echoed by RCD militants, who talked about "flexible regionalization," i.e., the application of the Catalan model of governance, first to Kabylie and then to other parts of the country.[20]

Notwithstanding its sophisticated use of the Internet to disseminate its message, MAK made no discernible headway in advancing its agenda. Roberts is even of the opinion that the radical Berberist agenda, as manifested by MAK and the RCD, was counterproductive, and adroitly manipulated by the regime in order to deflect the all-Algerian aspects of their demands, namely, the establishment of a genuine rule of law within a united national framework.[21] In any event, Mehenni persisted. Seven years after first putting forth the notion, MAK delivered a formal request to the Algerian authorities for autonomy:

> The chain of mistrust has led the two parties to a point of no return (dead-end). The Algerian authorities consider that the Kabyle requests can not be addressed at a State level. Kabyles who constitutes the native people of its land do not trust anymore the Algerian State whatever its declarations are, that are immediately refuted by its acts. One can not erase or mop up easily decades of suffering, discrimination and injustice against a People. A People has always a memory, even a formal request asking forgiveness for all it has gone through would not be enough to make up for the crimes committed against it. The healing process will only be possible the day Kabylie can proclaim its regional autonomy. It is vital to avoid the use of force and its violent byproducts in order to resolve, within the meaning of the rights recognized for every people, the Kabyle question.

Copies of the document were sent to a host of international organizations, including the UN, the EU, the Federation Internationale des ligues des Droits de l'Homme (FIDH), Human Rights Watch, and the July 2008 Mediterranean Union Summit in Paris, as well as to Nelson Mandela.[22] And in June 2010, Mehenni took the next logical, and even more provocative, step, proclaiming the establishment of a "Provisional Government of Kabylie," based in Paris, with himself as president and nine additional cabinet ministers, including two women.[23]

LANGUAGE AND IDENTITY —
TEACHING TAMAZIGHT?

Meanwhile, over the preceding seven years, the authorities had essentially sought to manage the crisis over Kabylie through the employment of a variety of tactics, on both the discursive and policy levels. Bouteflika's initial response to the Black Spring events, more than two weeks after they began, was halfhearted, although he did acknowledge Kabylie's identity issue and the demand for better treatment from the authorities. Subsequent remarks were more instructive. Seeking at once to downplay the severity of the events, demonstrate a measure of understanding, and maintain Algeria's Arabness, he declared:

> These things (the events) may happen in any country. Regarding the issue of identity, this takes us back to our Amazigh Berber origins. I must say that the Aures region is from a Berber origin. Also, Al-Tawariq [Touareg], in southern Algeria, is from a Berber origin. We have an Amazigh heritage, which I think has not been taken into consideration so far in our books. Perhaps we have focused more on our Arab and Islamic affiliation and have not taken this aspect into consideration, which is one of the aspects of the Algerian personality. This aspect must be taken into consideration in our basic texts, especially the constitution. I think the question is: Are we true Arabs or false Arabs?[24]

To have both an Amazigh heritage and be "true Arabs," for Bouteflika, could only mean one thing, namely, that the classic Arab-Islamic narrative lived on: the Berbers originated in Arabia in antiquity and were reunited with their long-lost relatives by Islam, creating an Arab-Berber synthesis in North Africa. The instrumental value of this narrative was later illustrated in a campaign poster from the 2004 presidential elections: a large smiling picture of Bouteflika accompanied by the slogan "We are Arab Amazigh" (Nihna Arab Amazigh).[25]

A recent study of Algerian language policy highlighted anew the linkage between language and national identity. Bouteflika, according to the study, had actually begun shifting the official discourse even before 2001, at least with regard to Western languages. Recognizing Algeria's need to link up more closely with the globalized economy and Western powers, he imparted new legitimacy to the importance of learning and employing Western languages, backing away from the state's long-standing discourse and policies of militant Arabization. For example, in this context, in 1999, Bouteflika declared that Algeria's identity needed to be modernized: "chauvinism and withdrawal," he said, were "sterile and destructive."[26] Such a shift, however subtle and partial, created the potential of increased space for Tamazight.

In October 2001, as part of the authorities' efforts to pacify and tame the situation in Kabylie, Bouteflika declared that he was planning to designate Tamazight as a "national language." Practical action came five months later, on March 12, 2002, with a speech announcing the imminent amending of Algeria's Constitution to that end. Moreover, said Bouteflika, the Algerian state would "work for the promotion and development of all [of Tamazight's] linguistic varieties in usage throughout the national territory." Despite previous talk of the need to have such an amendment approved in a national referendum, the approval was sealed and given the force of law, without debate, by the Algerian National Assembly on April 8th. The decision to go forward, and the amendment's summary approval, speak to the continuing weakness of Algerian political institutions, and suggest that the weight of the measure, and even its legitimacy, might easily be called into question. Still, the constitutional change marked a historic breakthrough, in which the Algerian state tendered official, legal acknowledgment of its Berber component.

To be sure, the amendment fell substantially short of the El-Kseur Platform's demand that Tamazight be made an official language, equal to Arabic, which was understood by both its proponents and detractors as something that would constitute a full embrace of Amazigh identity, requiring the state to commit substantial resources to the equalization project. However, the 2003 International Crisis Group Report on the two years of unrest in Kabylie, the most thorough and nuanced account of the events anywhere, suggested that this was as far as the government could go at that juncture. Official status could not be "meaningfully conceded," the report said, until either a modern standard version of Tamazight had been developed or until other dialects besides Taqbaylit had been developed into effective written languages. Either of these would take years, and until then, further constitutional change was not practical.[27] Nonetheless, the amendment established, in essence, a new norm. Berberists would seek to make the most of the concession in promoting the Berber language, while being fully aware that they were still fighting an uphill battle, as the authorities had not fundamentally transformed their worldview. Bouteflika, for example, declared in 2004 that "I don't know any country in the world where two official languages coexist" (ignoring the examples of Switzerland [actually with three official languages], Belgium, and Canada, at the very least) and that "Algeria will never have any other official language than Arabic."[28]

The language issue was, in fact, as contentious as ever.[29] The teaching of Tamazight had first been introduced in 1995, following the long school strike in Kabylie, in sixteen governates (out of a total of forty-eight), beginning in the fourth year of elementary school. But the process was haphazard: its optional status already relegated it to lower importance; the absence of qualified teachers among a total of 578 teachers was acutely felt; so was the absence of a uniform standard for the language. It was even initially decided that different dialects would be transcribed in different alphabets.

As of 2006, the language was being taught in only eleven governates, and 90 percent of the 100,000 students participating came from four Kabylie *wilayas*.[30] To be sure, the minister of national education, Boubekeur Benbouzid, stressed his willingness to promote Tamazight as a national language, announcing that it would be introduced in the BEM (Brevet de l'enseignement Moyen) exams in 2007 and baccalaureate exams in 2008.[31] But the overall picture was one of stagnation. As one activist put it in a withering attack on the government-sanctioned Haut Commissariat à l'Amazighité (HCA), "The reality is quite bitter: there are no students who can suitably read, write, recite or conjugate any Amazigh verb in the three principal tenses!"[32]

Moreover, Berberists had another reason to be distressed, for the Algerian authorities also sought to maintain the preeminence of Arabic by containing Tamazight within the Arab language and culture's symbolic universe through steps to standardize the writing of Tamazight in Arabic script. As noted earlier, the issue had been addressed in Morocco in 2003, with the state authorities intervening to impose a compromise neo-Tifinagh script for use in teaching Tamazight in primary school, much to the dismay of many of the Amazigh community's activists. Among Kabyles, the subject seemed to have been settled long ago in favor of the Latin script, thanks to the efforts of Kabyle Diaspora intellectuals who had taken the lead over many years in working to transform an essentially oral language into a modern, written one. However, the authorities apparently thought otherwise. In 2006, Abderrazak Douari, director of the National Teaching and Linguistic Center for Tamazight Education (CNPLET), an entity created by executive decree in November 2003, declared that the issue was very much on the table and needed to be addressed in order to move the teaching of Tamazight in Algerian schools beyond the "experimental" stage. In his view, using the Arabic script was more suitable for Tamazight, on national grounds, making it more appealing to all. In December 2006, he organized a colloquium on the subject. Arabic script was also reportedly going to be employed by the planned nationwide Amazigh-language state television channel. The website of the Kabyle-language TV channel already did so. According to one HCA official, those Berbers living in predominantly Arabic-speaking areas actually preferred the Arabic script. For example, in Batna, the fifth-largest city in Algeria and considered to be the capital of the Aures region, after a period of suspension of teaching Tamazight, more than four thousand pupils were said to have returned since 2005 on the condition that Arabic script would be employed. However, the official herself was opposed to the notion, pointing out that the 150-year-old process of forming a written basis for Tamazight was carried out with the Latin script. Thus, reverting to the Arabic script would be a waste of time. Turkey, she noted, used the Latin script without affecting its Muslim identity.[33]

Indeed, most Berberists reacted with anger and dismay over the state's encouragement of the Arabic script. Douari was sharply attacked by World Amazigh Congress president Belkacem Lounès on the issue. In Lounès's view, Douari's convening of a conference was yet another indication of the state's efforts to stall and contain the development of Tamazight.[34] Paris-based INALCO researcher Kamal Nait Zerrad scoffed at the idea that Arabophones would be more receptive to Tamazight if the Arabic script was employed.[35] INALCO had adopted a particular Latin character notation in 1996, based on an older one employed by Mouloud Mammeri. In Algeria, according to Zerrad, the notation in use was appropriate mainly for the Kabyle dialect; other Algerian Berber dialects had not progressed as far in developing their written forms. Each region, he said, needed to choose what was best for its particular form, after consulting with experts. In his view, only the Latin script could serve as an appropriate basis to meet their needs.

For Salem Chaker, the idea of adopting Arabic script for Tamazight constituted nothing less than a regression of at least a half-century in the coding and diffusing of a written language, done through the active social use of the Latin script, accompanied by serious linguistic research designed to adapt it to the needs of the Berber language in all of its varieties. Reopening the subject constituted the revival of an empty, decade-old "pseudo-debate" in both the academic and political spheres, in which one's preferred choice of script was predetermined by one's ideological predisposition, with the authorities weighing in heavily on the matter. In Morocco, the Palace had chosen neo-Tifinagh as a compromise option, for political reasons. In Algeria, the sudden emphasis on the Arabic script option clearly emanated from the authorities' desires. Nothing had changed since 1980, said Chaker, when President Benjedid, responding to the demands put forth during the Berber Spring, declared his willingness to have Tamazight taught in schools, provided the Arabic script was used. This strategy, said Chaker, was designed to channel the Berber language, indeed the Berber identity, into a cul-de-sac, rendering Berbers insignificant and thoroughly domesticated and newly subordinated to the Arab-Islamic womb and worldview—this after the Berbers had acquired from the West the tools necessary for linguistic and identity revival.[36] One militant Berberist responded by declaring his opposition to the adoption of the Arabic script of the "Qureishis." This reference to the rulers of Mecca whom the Prophet Mohamed battled and then won over to Islam presented the matter in stark terms, in line with the militant Berberist narrative: the Arabic language was a foreign import, brought from the Arabian Peninsula by perfidious conquerors. (Note the conflation between the initial opponents of the Prophet and the Arabic language; the fact that Mohamed himself was of the Qureish, and that it was Islam which the conquerors brought to North Africa, was not mentioned, presumably out of prudence.)[37]

BEYOND KABYLIE: THE SPREADING OF AMAZIGH IDENTITY

The Aures (Chaouia) region had long been more interlinked, materially and cognitively, with Algeria's "Arabness" than Kabylie. The mantra "I am a Shawi [Chaoui] Arab," according to Aicha Lemsine, a strident opponent of Berber particularism, was a familiar one during her youth.[38] But in recent years, the modern Berber identity discourse has surfaced there as well. According to one observer, "the growth in interest in Berber culture among many people" is obvious to all visitors to the Aures, including a small but growing movement to develop a Chaoui print culture.[39] Berber memory work in the Aures region, the site of the fabled Berber resistance to the invading Arab-Muslim forces at the end of the seventh century, has recently reached a new level. In February 2003, L'Association Aures El-Kahina erected a large statue of the fabled Berber queen in the center of the town of Baghaï, in the *wilaya* of Khenchela. The statue was designed by a graduate of the École Nationale des Beaux-Arts d'Alger.[40] Of course, such a public commemorative act could not be done in Algeria (except perhaps in Kabylie) without the consent of the authorities. In fact, the ceremony was attended by the President of the Republic himself. Bouteflika's presence was clearly intended as a gesture to the Amazigh community, with whom the state has been at loggerheads for so many years (albeit primarily in Kabylie, not in the Aures); it also indicated a desire to place greater emphasis on Algerian history, albeit a particular reading of it. Still, one shouldn't take this too far: his presence at the unveiling of the Kahina statue was ignored entirely by the national press, presumably acting according to its instructions. Eventually, however, the subject would be raised, albeit from a different, and overtly hostile, source. In August 2009, Othmane Saadi, the president of the Association for the Defense of the Arab Language, declared the erection of the statue an act of "blasphemy" ("*kufr*"), since the Kahina had fought to prevent the spread of Islam into the Aures.[41]

Of course, Amazigh activists contested the state's orientation to Berber heritage, whether it involved appropriation or neglect. One Aures-centered website, displaying the picture of the new Kahina statue, added superimposed images of the Amazigh flag on both sides of the statue's pedestal.[42] Activists bemoaned the degradation and official neglect of the archaeological site that is considered to have been the mountainous redoubt of the Kahina. Some academics have urged that UNESCO be approached to include it on its list of protected World Heritage sites, and that the Ministry of Culture take the lead in promoting its value, as it was inhabited since prehistoric times up until the eleventh-century Hilalian invasion.[43] Another site whose endangered status poses a threat to their collective memory, according to Chaouia activists, is the mausoleum of Imadghacen, an 18.5-meter-high, 59-meter-diameter cylindrical pedestal in the *wilaya* of Batna. The structure is among the oldest material evidence of the Massyle Amazigh dynasty, which under the subsequent rule of Massinissa is considered to have sought the political unification of North Africa.

Since the late 1990s, the Batna airport, whose terminal building was inspired, architecturally, by Imadghacen's tomb, has become a contested memory site, pitting some Chaoui Amazigh militants against the Bouteflika regime. At issue was the renaming of the airport: Chaoui militants demanded it be named after Imadghacen, while the Bouteflika regime, in line with its renewed symbolic embrace of the war of independence and efforts to include Amazigh figures within the national pantheon (and thus contain Amazigh identity as well), named it after Mostefa Ben Boulaïd, a founding member of the FLN leadership and native of the region, who was killed by the French in 1956.[44] The Amazigh militants were dismayed, and an image of the airport with the name "Madghacen" in Latin and Tifinagh script continues to appear on an Internet site devoted to the Amazigh movement in the Aures region.[45] The disagreement became intertwined with local political struggles as well: former governor of the region Med Chérif Djebari, who had been removed by Bouteflika allegedly following the pressure of the "local mafia," declared defiantly to the opponents of naming the airport for Imadghacen that "just as you have negated our origins at this moment, there will come a generation which will negate you."[46]

One additional piece of evidence regarding the iconic status of the Kahina for modern-day Berber culture activists and memory workers is provided by a contemporary illustrated book for children in French and Tamazight elaborating on the Kahina story, published in Algiers, Casablanca, and Paris. It added a new layer to the much-mined story by including a fabricated farewell speech, in which she exhorted her followers never to forget "our culture, our Tamazight language and our beliefs . . . otherwise our sacrifice will have been for nothing and it will be the end of our civilization.[47]

OUTLASTING THE *AARCH*

Meanwhile, on the political level, the authorities and the political forces in Kabylie remained locked in a standoff for nearly three years. Bouteflika's announcement of constitutional change had also included other gestures, including the withdrawal of some Gendarmerie units and promises of compensation for the victims of the previous year's violence, albeit without granting them the coveted "martyrs" status. Not only did these gestures and the upgrading of Tamazight's constitutional status fall short of the El-Kseur Platform's demands, they were also superseded in the public's mind by the arrests twelve days later of numerous members of the Coordinations, particularly radical ones.[48]

Government policy, led by Prime Ministers Ali Benflis (of Chaoui Berber origin from Batna), and then, as of May 2003, Ahmed Ouyahia (a Kabyle), sought to exploit the divisions within the CIADC by negotiating with the *dialogueiste* faction and thus water down and weaken the "nonnegotiability" of the El-Kseur demands. During the run-up to the April 2004 presidential elections, some progress was made. In an unprecedented

gesture, Ouyahia conducted a portion of his meetings with CIADC nego-
tiators in Taqbaylit.[49] In these discussions, the authorities tentatively agreed
to annul the results of the 2002 municipal elections in Kabylie, which had
been boycotted by 95 percent of the population, and to free prisoners incarcerated during the 2001 demonstrations, cancel the legal proceedings
against them, and more. The authorities' desire to calm the situation ahead
of the presidential election was clear, and the Kabyles' apprehensions regarding the regime's true intentions were understandable. However, two
crucial issues remained unresolved. The Gendarmerie, whose removal was
one of the prime demands of the Coordinations, were still ensconced in
the region, while Ouyahia reiterated that Tamazight could be made an
official language only through a national referendum. Thus, the deadlock
remained in force, and even Ouyahia'a interlocutors called for a boycott of
the upcoming elections.[50]

On a national level, the elections were a resounding triumph for Bouteflika, who officially received 85 percent of the vote from the 10.5 million
persons who participated (a 58 percent turnout). His bitter rival and former
prime minister, Benflis, received only 7 percent of the vote. Even when ac-
counting for a degree of fraud, Bouteflika's emphatic victory allowed him
to consolidate his hold on power. As usual, participation in Kabylie was far
lower than the national average, only 17 percent.[51] Remaining consistent
with their past actions, Saadi tendered his candidacy, and received less than
2 percent of the vote, while Ait Ahmed refused to do so.

Having successfully completed his first term in office (the first civilian
to do so since independence) and outmaneuvered both civilian and military opponents, Bouteflika could now address the still-unsettled Kabyle
issue from a position of strength, allowing him to make gestures and concessions that he could not previously. In his second inauguration speech,
Bouteflika called for the continuation of the dialogue with the CIADC,
since "Kabylie could not exist without Algeria and Algeria could not exist
without Kabylie."[52] On January 15, 2005, the stalemate was broken. After
two days of talks between Prime Minister Ouyahia and eighteen leading
members of the body, accompanied by six representatives of "martyrs'
families," the two sides announced the establishment of a "joint mecha-
nism" that would be "responsible for monitoring and implementing the
El-Kseur Platform according to the Constitution and accompanying
laws."[53] The Gendarmerie would be gradually replaced. Ouyahia visited
Kabylie in April, on the anniversary of the Black Spring. In July, the local
and regional assemblies that had been chosen in the almost universally

boycotted 2002 elections were dissolved by presidential decree, paving the way for new ones in November, in which the FFS and RCD together won over half of the seats. Voter turnout was up from past elections, but still only around 33 percent, pointing to the continued degree of alienation and malaise among the populace. CIADC *dialoguistes* characterized their actions as moving into a phase of partnership with the authorities. However, by the end of 2005, efforts to achieve full compensation for all of the Black Spring victims while bringing the perpetrators to justice floundered, and in May 2006, Prime Minister Abdelaziz Belkhadem declared that there was no more value to dialogue with CIADC representatives, as Kabylie had now elected its representatives. Overall, the state authorities had bent before Kabyle anger and mass action, but had regained the upper hand.

By 2007, the extraparliamentary "Citizens Movement" had clearly run out of steam. Its grassroots character, which had been so important in mobilizing the population in 2001, turned out to be a serious liability, as the movement failed to institutionalize and centralize itself behind a recognized leadership and coherent program. Moreover, the authorities had played the game they knew best: co-opting, manipulating, offering partial concessions, etc. Belaid Abrika, who had emerged seemingly out of nowhere as the recognizable face of the *aarch,* assisted by his Christlike image of one with long hair, beard, and flowing white robe, had spent many months incarcerated by the authorities. Despite, or perhaps because of, this, there was a great deal of suspicion within Kabylie that he was, in fact, playing a double game on behalf of the authorities. The motivation behind the attempt on his life on November 30, 2006, was, like so much else in Algeria, unclear. Hence, the mood among Kabyle activists in 2007–2008 was gloomy, a far cry from the excitement and hope generated in 2001. Algeria's parliamentary elections in spring 2007 reflected the changes that had occurred and the uncertainty regarding the future: Once again, the FFS boycotted the elections; unlike in 2002, the RCD did participate, garnering just under 200,000 votes (3.36 percent), good for nineteen seats. The FFS's boycott call resonated in Kabylie, where the voter turnout was again far lower (35 percent) than in the rest of the country. Abrika would resurface in 2008, attempting to push forward the claims for compensation of victims of the Black Spring and harshly criticizing the authorities for failing to bring the perpetrators to justice and address the root causes of the 2001 rage. Without real change, he said, there would be another such explosion. A few months later, the regime took Abrika and three of his associates back into custody.[54] In 2009, both the FFS and the RCD promoted a boycott of the stage-managed presidential election, which granted Boute-flika a third term in office; as usual, the turnout in Kabylie was far lower than the reported nationwide percentage of 74 percent. The RCD provoked a great deal of anger, and some criticism among its own followers, by removing the Algerian flag from its headquarters in Algiers and raising a black flag of mourning in its stead.[55]

Adding to the sense of malaise among Berber activists was their concern over an increasing state-directed Islamization of the region. Signs to that effect included the building of new mosques, state-directed sermons by mosque preachers, and the distribution by the Ministry of Religious Affairs and Endowments of print and audio copies of the Qur'an that had been translated into Tamazight by a Saudi institute.[56] There was a renewal of armed Islamist attacks in the region, which, as in the past, led Berberists to suspect the regime's hidden hand, including a fear that the attacks would be used as a convenient excuse to reintroduce the Gendarmerie. The regime also appeared to embrace the influential Qatar-based Islamist preacher, Shaikh Yusuf al-Qardawi, who visited Tizi-Ouzou in March 2006, just one week after the Algerian Parliament passed a law designed to limit the proliferation of Christian churches in the country, particularly in Kabylie. Qardawi forcefully addressed the issue, proclaiming that Kabylie had always been the "land of Islam," and hence could not be evangelized.[57] The issue would continue to be a live one, as Protestant evangelical churches undertook extensive proselytization efforts, resulting in thousands of converts (thirty to fifty thousand, according to one report), and the state redoubling its efforts to promote Islam and limit the ability of the churches to operate in Algeria.[58] For Islamists, in particular, the issue undoubtedly evoked old fears from the days of French colonialism.

Meanwhile, away from the attention of most observers, Berber-Arab ethnic tensions reared their head in the relatively remote Mzab valley on the fringes of the Algerian Sahara. The problems centered in the provincial town of Berriane (pop. 40,000), in Ghardaia province. Populated by a majority of Tamzabit-speaking Ibadi Berbers and a minority of the formerly nomadic Chambaa Sunni Arabs, the region had witnessed periodic bouts of tension over the last quarter-century, against a background of a competition for resources, state policies viewed as giving preferential treatment to newly settled Arabs, urban growth, and the national economic malaise. Politically, these differences were expressed in a number of violent incidents during the 1990–1991 elections, in which the Ibadi Berbers opposed the FIS, and FFS and RCD branches were established there. The 2008–2009 renewal of violent incidents, between gangs of young males, were clearly rooted more in local dynamics than any grand political schism. But the expression of these tensions through ethnosymbolic means, and the inability of either community leaders or state authorities to get a handle on them, illustrated that the modern Berberist mode was extending its reach into more traditionally remote regions, and spoke to the continued shortcomings of the Algerian national project.[59]

Conclusion   WHITHER THE STATE,
WHITHER THE BERBERS?

Over the course of recorded history, Berbers have straddled multiple worlds; they have been multilingual, multicultural, always part of the "other"; and always engaged in one form of accommodation or another with stronger, more advanced civilizations — from Roman to Byzantine, Islamic to modern times. Historical dynamics have ensured that Berber-Arab differences have been socially enduring but nonetheless muted: not since the initial Islamic conquests have there been significant episodes of interethnic violence in North Africa. Colonial policies had contrary effects, some intended, others not: while acting to reify Berber-Arab differences, with some success, they also initiated complex processes of territorial unification and national integration, processes further strengthened by the national movements that arose in opposition to colonial rule and the independent states that they established. However, the state-building and nation-building formulas of both Algeria and Morocco proved to be inadequate in addressing the specific Berber components of their societies in ways that would promote overall comity. To the surprise of many, an explicitly self-conscious Berber-Amazigh identity movement has emerged in recent decades, one that explicitly foregrounds the collective "self" while seeking to renegotiate the terms of the Berbers' accommodation with various "others" — the nation-state, Islam, and modernity. In Algeria, modern Berber community-building was centered in Kabylie and posed continual challenges to the authorities, resulting in political militancy, periodic spasms of confrontation, and bouts of civil revolt. In Morocco, Berber-Arab differences have been less politicized, but the Amazigh identity movement has now emerged onto the national stage in a meaningful fashion.

To be sure, neither country faces an imminent crisis along ethnic lines. In both, the state framework has struck deep roots, administratively and cognitively. There is no comparison between North Africa and the Turkish or Iraqi experiences: the violent confrontation between Turkish Kurdish groups and the state, and the emergence of an autonomous, nearly independent Iraqi Kurdistan after decades of struggle and hardship. Nonetheless, to borrow an image from, ironically, the Islamic East, the Berber "genie" is out of the proverbial bottle, and will not be returned to it for the foreseeable future—i.e., the efforts by North African nationalist movements and newly independent states to subsume Berber identity under state and Arab ethnic identity rubrics, and ultimately reduce it to insignificance, have proven a failure.

The Amazigh identity movement is both state-centered and transnational, drawing strength and sustenance from the Berber Diaspora in Western Europe and North America. Its overarching discourse is profoundly sympathetic to Western liberal-humanist values and strongly condemnatory of the predominant North African political and cultural order, which prioritizes Islam and Arab identity while coexisting uneasily and erratically with French linguistic and cultural influences. Accordingly, the Amazigh movement leaves little or no room for other, more Islam-centered aspects of Berber societal norms and praxis, which may well prove to be a serious shortcoming in its mobilization efforts.[1] Nor have deeply embedded political-cultural norms deriving from what were until recently tribal societies par excellence disappeared, by any means. One instructive example in this regard was the political culture reflected in the behavior of the Kabylie village councils underpinning the newly formed Coordinations movement during the 2001 Black Spring and afterwards, including "an insistence on consensual decision-making, the complete absence of women, a code of honor, and the resort to ostracism as a disciplinary sanction." Much of this modus operandi ultimately proved inadequate for the larger goal of transforming Algerian society.[2] From another angle, one young Amazigh activist in France complained to me that the myriad Berber associations which have sprung up all too often exhibit tribelike manners, working exclusively for the good of their particular village or clan, and not for the Amazigh community as a whole.[3] However, the fact that the Amazigh movement's discourse and praxis are not universally accepted among North African Berbers does not by itself indicate failure, for the task of ethnocultural movements in mobilizing their communities has hardly ever been a simple one. In this case, the Amazigh movement's intellectual, cultural, and political efforts have raised fundamental questions for North African states and societies, regarding both their past and their future, for the realities of state- and nation-formation and consolidation in North Africa place the Amazigh movement at odds with the dominant Arab-Islamic–centered national projects.

Apart from a few utopianists, the movement does not aspire to dissolve the existing state frameworks, but rather to refashion them by foregrounding the place of the Berbers within them. Moderate Berberists seek to redefine the meaning of the nation, equalizing, at the very least, the Amazigh component to the Arab one, and have states adopt appropriate policies to that end. More radical Berberists explicitly refer to territorial issues in their demands, varyingly employing the terminology of autonomy, federalism, and regional decentralization, with a focus on Kabylie in Algeria and, more recently, the Rif in Morocco.[4] This, of course, is anathema to the state authorities; for now, they have gained little traction among the Berber communities in any practical sense.

Nonetheless, the surfacing of a modern Amazigh agenda has gradually compelled ruling elites in North African states to sit up and take notice, against the background of their own acute needs for "re-contracting" with their societies and relegitimizing their rule, a half-century after achieving independence and in the face of myriad challenges, first and foremost those posed by vibrant Islamist movements offering their own solutions to the countries' all too apparent social, economic, and political shortcomings. The authorities in Morocco and Algeria, each in their own fashion and responding to the particular mix of factors shaping political and social life, have sought at varying junctures, and with varying degrees of success, to repress, manipulate, tame, co-opt, and incorporate Berber groups.

Each case is replete with paradoxes. Kabylie was the source of both considerable resistance to French colonialism and the focus of French desires to remake the country as a whole through the transformation of Kabyle Berbers into junior partners denuded of their Islamic coating. Kabylie has been, and remains, a reservoir of the Algerian elite, dating back to the days of the nationalist movement. Indeed, five of Algeria's twelve prime ministers since 1979 have been Kabyles (the prime minister as of April 2010, Ahmed Ouyahia, was serving in the post for the third time), two others have been Chaouis, and members of both communities have held key positions in the military and security services.[5] But Kabylie has also been the center of a well-defined force in opposition to Algeria's predominant Arab-Islamic self-definition. Kabyle Berberists have played a leading role in fashioning the grand pan-Berber narrative and in promulgating it in the Berber Diaspora and in the international arena, while also privileging their

"Kabyle-ness" and forging only minimal links with other Algerian Berber communities. The adoption of a secular outlook has been more widespread among Kabyles, both at home and in the Diaspora, than among any other Berber community, yet one also finds Kabyles among the most radical Algerian Islamist groups, and Kabylie mountain redoubts have become havens in recent years for Islamist insurgents still battling the Algerian regime.

On the level of state-Berber relations, the Kabylie-centered Berber Culture Movement played a vanguard role in challenging the hegemony of the Algerian *pouvoir* in the 1980s, breaking taboos and helping to set the stage for the sudden opening up of the system in 1989, which in turn enabled the flourishing of associational and political life that provided an alternative to both the regime and its Islamist current. During the brutal, violent strife of the 1990s, Kabyle Berberists reached a new level of activism, successfully implementing a lengthy school strike to force a degree of recognition of their demands from the state. The highest peak of Kabyle-state confrontation was reached in 2001, as blood was shed and Kabyle Berbers, organized under previously unknown, extrapolitical frameworks, marched on Algiers with demands that were both national and particularist: the democratization of Algerian political life and the recognition of Tamazight, along with the withdrawal of the hated Gendarmerie from the region. The authorities, for their part, pursued a variety of strategies and tactics during this turbulent decade: arming Berber village militias against Islamist bands, winning support for crushing the Islamist insurgency from the most militant secular wing of the Berber movement, and reluctantly and gradually conceding to a portion of the movement's demands while playing on its internal divisions and seeking to neutralize its thrust. The end result was that Algeria's ruling elites remained firmly in control while leaving underlying matters unresolved, both in Kabylie and the country as a whole. As for Algeria's collective identity, it remained problematic and contested. As the French-Algerian analyst Fanny Colonna has pointed out, even the leading intellectuals in the Arabic-, Tamazight-, and French-speaking communities were not successful in developing a common Algerian vision.[6]

Meanwhile, the current malaise among Kabyle activists is very real, and the state authorities, awash until recently in petrodollars and benefiting from the populace's exhaustion after the ordeals of the 1990s and Western governmental support in the "war against terror," proved to be more resilient than perhaps had been expected. Kabyle energies appear to have been contained, unlike in 2001, when there were signs that Kabyles had the potential of leading a civil movement for a more democratic and federal Algeria. Moreover, those who speak of actual autonomy for Kabylie remain marginalized. Still, from the perspective of the last three decades, the Kabyle-Amazigh identity project has made giant strides. For the moment, Salem Chaker's depiction of Kabyle culture as being one of "resistance"[7] has considerable merit, notwithstanding the variety of Kabyle positions toward the state, the meaning of "being Kabyle," and Islam. How the Kabyle culture of resistance will play out, and in what context, remains to be seen.

Just as the overall Moroccan experience differs radically from the Algerian one, so too do the history and profile of Moroccan Berbers differ from those of their Algerian cousins. Here too, though, paradoxes abound. The Arabization process was less encompassing in Morocco than in any other North African precolonial entity, leaving the large majority of Morocco's population Berberophone right up into the twentieth century. Yet, while the great medieval Berber Islamic empires originated in Morocco, the influx of Andalusian emigrants fleeing the Reconquista and the turn toward sharifian descent as a sine qua non to legitimate rule irretrievably marginalized a broad swath of the Berber population. As in Algeria, Berbers both resisted fiercely and served in the French military. French colonial policies both privileged the children of Middle Atlas tribal notables and sought to isolate rural Berbers from "pernicious" influences of urban Arabs. France's most famous "pro-Berber" act, the 1930 *dahir,* sparked a protest among urban Muslim Arabs that would, in retrospect, be the starting point for the Moroccan nationalist movement and impose a powerful stigma on the Berbers themselves. Ironically, it sparked no such comparable uproar among them. As for the two most prominent Berbers during the colonial era, neither figured in the nationalist movement's pantheon of stars, albeit for very different reasons: Mohamed bin Abdelkrim al-Khattabi, who led a five-year armed struggle in the Rif against Spanish and French forces, was viewed with a mixture of disdain and fear by the Fassi urban elite, while Thami El Glaoui, the unrivaled pasha of the south, came to personify the very meaning of collaborator (*glaouiste*) with colonialism.

Independence brought further paradoxes. Early revolts in the Rif were directed against Istiqlal hegemony, but were eventually put down brutally by the newly formed armed forces, commanded by Crown Prince Hassan. His right-hand man in the operation and during the first decade of his reign as king was Mohamed Oufkir, the most prominent member of the predominantly French-trained Berber officer corps. Like the military, rural Berber notables were made partners in the Palace's efforts to achieve hegemony over the Istiqlal Party and more radical left-wing groups, which also included a considerable number of young, educated Berbers. In other words, as in Algeria, Berbers could be found all across the Moroccan political spectrum, and apart from the first small stirrings of Berberist intellectual activity, Berber identity questions in Morocco were more muted and below the surface. Berbers would be heavily stigmatized by the failed military coups of the early 1970s, which shook the regime to its core and resulted in more than a decade of brutal repression of all suspected opponents. However, intellectual and political proponents of Arabization, as well as academic experts, had little cause at the time to doubt that Berber identity in Morocco was being reduced to the realm of national folklore.

The disappointment of educated Berber militants with leftist, Arab-oriented parties and the regime's crackdown on all autonomous political activity led some to reorient themselves toward rescuing the increasingly endangered Berber language, what they viewed as the pillar of their collective identity, beginning in the late 1970s. The state's initial response was one of bare, grudging tolerance. But in the early 1990s, matters began to change, inaugurating a dynamic between a cautiously liberalizing regime and an increasingly assertive Amazigh movement whose contours and content are still unfolding. Building on the initial steps of his late father, King Mohamed VI made a considerable leap forward in embracing the Amazigh movement as an integral part of Moroccan nationhood. Doing so was part of a concerted strategy to counterbalance a resurgent Islamist movement and maintain Palace hegemony over an increasingly liberalized political system.

As with other ethnonational/ethnocultural movements, modern-day Berberists have devoted much effort to fashioning a coherent and usable historical narrative, complete with commemorative rituals marking seminal events and cultural markers that transcend state boundaries, from the Yennayer New Year festival to the Berber Spring, accompanied by the appropriate trappings, including a calendar and flag (both designed by the Académie Berbère), an ancient script, and emblematic songs such as Idir's "A Vava Inouva" and Mohand Ait idir u Amrane's "Ekker a Mmis Umazigh" ("Rise Up, Son of Amazigh").[8] In recent years, Amrane's 1945 song has been translated into Tashelhit and sung by a Moroccan Amazigh band, with appropriate modifications in the text so as to universalize its message.[9] A different type of pan-Amazigh solidarity was expressed by an October

2005 meeting between the heads of the Chambers of Commerce of Nador and Tizi-Ouzou, bastions of Amazigh activism in Morocco and Algeria, respectively. A photograph of the meeting shows the Amazigh flag prominently displayed on the table, flanked by the Algerian and Moroccan flags.[10]

As in other ethnonational instances, language revival and development are central, indeed crucial, to the Amazigh project. To be sure, the Amazigh movement doesn't define itself exclusively in terms of a common language, but prioritizes the linguistic/cultural argument because of its urgency. Nor is it comfortable with being defined in Hrochsian terms as a "non-dominant ethnic group . . . [making] organized and deliberate efforts at achieving the status of a fully developed nation, in all its attributes."[11] Amazigh movement militants, particularly in Morocco, reject the notion that they are either an ethnic group or a minority, insisting with considerable justification that the large majority of North Africans are, in fact, of Berber origin, whether or not they acknowledge it or still speak Tamazight. Yet their supreme task, as has been true with so many other ethnonational movements, is to bring about a conceptual revolution among North Africans, to "reawaken" them to their Berber heritage and identity, to make it "matter" on a grand scale, even as it "matters" very much to individual Berbers in myriad ways and contexts.[12] The obstacles to success are daunting, to say the least.

Still, Berbers are hardly ready to be consigned to the museum. Being Berber today means many different things, to many different people, from second- and third-generation Diaspora-born non-native Tamazight speakers who nevertheless insist on identifying with their Berber roots, to monolingual illiterate women living in exclusively Amazigh milieus in pre-Saharan oases and poor Atlas Mountain villages; from avowedly secular scholars, urban intellectuals, and performing artists to prideful members of the formerly dominant Ait Atta tribal confederation in Morocco's southeast; from networks of Soussi traders and businessmen who compete with the Moroccan Fassi elite, to members of the Ibadi Muslim sect in Mzab and newly assertive Libyan Berbers in Jabal Nafusa; from avowedly Kabyle Berber patriots to self-defined Shawi "Berber-Arabs"; from those whose Berber roots are merely a historical fact without practical significance to those who seek to make "being Berber" the center of their personal and collective existence. Pierre Bourdieu once characterized the Kabyles as "une réalisation paradigmatique de la tradition méditerranéenne," having played a fundamental role in transmitting knowledge between the eastern and western ends of the Mediterranean.[13] One could take an even broader view: ethnically, culturally, and genetically, the Berbers as a whole may approximate a "Mediterranean" ideal type, in the sense of the Mediterranean being more of a "crossroads" of civilization than a "source."[14] Coincidentally, their historic collective weakness parallels the "thinness"-of-the-Mediterranean ideal that has been floated in various European and Mediterranean intellectual circles during the last decade.[15]

In the meantime, in an age of accelerated globalization and intensified identity politics, the West-centered Amazigh identity movement has risen to the surface and has taken its place within the North African firmament alongside of, and in partial alliance with, other "civil society" forces such as women's and human rights groups, liberal political voices, and blogging, text-messaging, and hip-hopping members of North Africa's overwhelmingly youthful population. The movement has also followed the path of other beleaguered minority groups by seeking inclusion in the growing global discourse on human rights, a discourse that governments ignore at their peril. With the Moroccan *makhzen* and the Algerian *pouvoir* each facing challenging and uncertain futures, Berber-state relations in each country are sure to evolve on a twisted path. No less significant will be the Amazigh movement's relations with other segments of Moroccan and Algerian societies, particularly the Islamists. The process of reshaping and redefining the meaning of Moroccan and Algerian collective identities has already begun and will surely be fraught with tension and difficulty. But veteran Amazigh movement activists, mindful of how far they have come, and not just how far they have to go, are not fazed. In their words, the movement is only at its very beginning: "We don't know where it's going, but we know it's going in the right direction."[16] Ideally, for the Berber Culture Movement, this will eventually result in the attainment of its agenda: the emergence of a polity that is at once more inclusive and more tolerant of diversity, allowing for cultural and linguistic flourishing within a framework of genuine democracy, adherence to the rule of law, and respect for human rights, thus enabling it to meet the challenges of the twenty-first century.[17]

Given the durability of authoritarianism and the centrality of religion-based collective identities in the Middle East and North Africa, the Amazigh movement's vision may well appear overly rosy, if not utopian, and the way forward is shrouded in uncertainty. Still, both the Moroccan and Algerian ruling elites have found it necessary and useful to partially accommodate their Amazigh currents in recent years, in recognition of the need for what Zartman termed "re-contracting" with their societies. Hence, the

Amazigh identity movement's efforts to return the Berbers to history as a self-defined, collective actor in possession of agency, i.e., with the ability to participate in the determination of their own future, may well have salutary value in the years ahead not only for North African Berbers themselves but for the Moroccan and Algerian states as a whole.

NOTES

INTRODUCTION

1. L. Carl Brown, "Maghrib Historiography: The Unit of Analysis Problem," in *The Maghrib in Question,* ed. Michel Le Gall and Kenneth Perkins (Austin: University of Texas Press, 1997), pp. 4–16, quotation from p. 9.

2. Fatima Mernissi, *Islam and Democracy: Fear of the Modern World* (Reading, Mass.: Addison-Wesley, 1992), pp. 13–14.

3. However, recent official Moroccan census figures put the number of those who use Tamazight in their daily lives as only 28 percent (see Chapter 6). Brett and Fentress suggest something similar, calling the accepted figures "decades out of date." Michael Brett and Elizabeth Fentress, *The Berbers* (Oxford: Blackwell, 1996), pp. 276–277.

4. For the Moroccan state's efforts in this regard, see Aomar Boum, "Dancing for the Moroccan State: Ethnic Folk Dances and the Production of National Hybridity," in *North African Mosaic: A Cultural Reappraisal of Ethnic and Religious Minorities,* ed. Nabil Boudraa and Joseph Krause (Newcastle: Cambridge Scholars Publishing, 2007), pp. 214–237.

5. David M. Hart, "Scratch a Moroccan, Find a Berber," *Journal of North African Studies* 4, no. 2 (Summer 1999): 26.

6. Mohamed Arkoun, quoted in Giampaolo Calchi Novati, "Post-Colonial State vs. Ethnicity: A Reassessment of Decolonization in Africa," *Latin American Perspectives* 23, no. 2 (April 1996): 134.

7. Gibbon elegantly discusses the term thus:

> The history of the word Barbar may be classed under four periods.
> 1. In the time of Homer, when the Greeks and Asiatics might probably use a common idiom, the imitative sound of Barbar was applied to the ruder tribes, whose pronunciation was most harsh, whose grammar was most defective.
> 2. From the time, at least, of Herodotus, it was extended to all

the nations who were strangers to the language and manners of the Greeks.

3. In the age, of Plautus, the Romans submitted to the insult (Pompeius Festus, l. ii. p. 48, edit. Dacier), and freely gave themselves the name of Barbarians. They insensibly claimed an exemption for Italy, and her subject provinces; and at length removed the disgraceful appellation to the savage or hostile nations beyond the pale of the empire.

4. In every sense, it was due to the Moors; the familiar word was borrowed from the Latin Provincials by the Arabian conquerors, and has justly settled as a local denomination (Barbary) along the northern coast of Africa. (Edward Gibbon, *The History of the Decline and Fall of the Roman Empire,* ed. the Reverend H. H. Milman [1782/1845], http://etext.library.adelaide.edu.au/g/gibbon/edward/g43d/chapter51.html#fn51.174/ [accessed May 26, 2010])

8. The numbers are taken from *Jeune Afrique,* nos. 2549 (November 15–21, 2009) and 2551 (November 29–December 5, 2009). Most mappings of Algeria's Berber dialects fail to mention the Chenoua and Touat-Gourara regions. See also Kossman and Stroomer.

9. Among the Ishelhin speakers of the Tashelhit dialect in southwestern Morocco (the Souss region), as well as in the southeast, "Amazigh" is both a literary archaism and a term denoting "white," or "true," Berbers, as distinguished from the black-skinned Berberophones of the region. Moroccans from the Rif Mountains of northern Morocco speak the Rifian dialect ("Tarrifit"). Sultan Moulay Hassan I's French doctor wrote in the 1890s that residents of Fez had displayed "Amazighophobie" in warning him of the dangers of travel in the countryside. In the Touareg world, covering large swaths of the Sahara Desert in Algeria, Mali, Niger, and Libya, as well as in parts of Tunisia and among other Libyan Berberophones, other variations of "Amazigh" and "Tamazight" are employed. By contrast, neither "Amazigh" nor "Tamazight" is known in the traditional culture of Algeria's main Berberophone regions outside of the Sahara—Kabylie, the Aures Mountains, and the Mzab oasis,. As general neologisms, they first came into use between 1945 and 1950 among Kabyles in the Algerian nationalist movement. Salem Chaker, "Amazigh," in *Encyclopédie Berbère,* ed. Gabriel Camps (Aix-en-Provence: Édisud, 1987), pp. 4:562–568; Fernand Linarès, "Voyages au Tafilalet avec S. M. le Sultan Moulay Hassan en 1893," *Bulletin de l'Institut d'Hygiène du Maroc* 1932, no. 3 (Julliet–Septembre): 100.

10. The AMU's five member states are Morocco, Algeria, Tunisia, Libya, and Mauritania. Established with great fanfare for the purpose of deepening economic, political, and societal cooperation among them, the AMU has been largely moribund since 1994, owing mainly to continuing Algerian-Moroccan differences over the fate of the Western Sahara. For its establishment, see Bruce Maddy-Weitzman,

"Inter-Arab Relations," in *Middle East Contemporary Survey (MECS)*, Vol. 13 (1989), ed. Ami Ayalon (Boulder, Colo.: Westview Press, 1991), pp. 144–147.

11. Robert Montagne, *The Berbers: Their Social and Political Organization*, trans. and with an Introduction by David Seddon (London: Frank Cass, 1973); Charles-André Julien, *History of North Africa* (New York: Praeger, 1970).

12. Miroslav Hroch, "The Social Interpretation of Linguistic Demands in European National Movements," in Hroch, *Social Preconditions of National Revival in Europe: A Comparative Analysis of the Social Composition of Patriotic Groups among the Smaller European Nations* (New York: Columbia University Press, 2000), p. 71; Susan Gal, "Migration, Minorities and Multilingualism: Language Ideologies in Europe," in *Language Ideologies, Policies and Practices*, ed. Clare Mar-Molinero and Patrick Stevenson (New York: Palgrave Macmillan, 2006), pp. 13–27.

13. Novati, "Post-Colonial State vs. Ethnicity," pp. 132–134.

14. Benjamin Stora, *Algerie Maroc, Histoires paralleles, destin croises* (Paris: Maisonneuve et Larose [Zellige], 2002).

15. Joseph Kostiner, ed., *Middle Eastern Monarchies* (Boulder, Colo.: Lynne Rienner, 2000).

16. The literature on the Arab state system's formation and evolution is lengthy. See, e.g., C. Ernest Dawn, *From Ottomanism to Arabism: Essays on the Origins of Arab Nationalism* (Urbana: University of Illinois Press, 1973); Rashid Khalidi, Lisa Anderson, Muhammad Muslih, and Reeva S. Simon, eds., *The Origins of Arab Nationalism* (New York: Columbia University Press, 1991); James Jankowski and Israel Gershoni, eds., *Rethinking Nationalism in the Arab Middle East* (New York: Columbia University Press, 1997); Michael Barnett, *Dialogues in Arab Politics: Negotiations in Regional Order* (New York: Columbia University Press, 1998); Adeed Dawisha, *Arab Nationalism in the 20th Century: From Triumph to Despair* (Princeton, N.J.: Princeton University Press, 2003); Patrick Seale, *The Struggle for Syria*, 2nd ed. (New Haven, Conn., and London: Yale University Press, 1986); Yehoshua Porath, *In Search of Arab Unity, 1930–1945* (London: Frank Cass, 1986); Bruce Maddy-Weitzman, *The Crystallization of the Arab State System, 1945–1954* (Syracuse, N.Y.: Syracuse University Press, 1993); Elie Podeh, "The Emergence of the Arab State System Reconsidered," *Diplomacy and Statecraft* 9, no. 3 (November 1998): 50–82.

17. Ernest Gellner, "Introduction," in *Arabs and Berbers: From Tribe to Nation in North Africa*, ed. Ernest Gellner and Charles Micaud (Lexington, Mass., and London: D. C. Heath/Duckworth, 1972/1973), p. 13.

18. Lawrence Rosen, "The Social and Conceptual Framework of Arab-Berber Relations in Central Morocco," in *Arabs and Berbers: From Tribe to Nation in North Africa*, ed. Ernest Gellner and Charles Micaud (Lexington, Mass., and London: D. C. Heath/Duckworth, 1972/1973), pp. 155–173.

19. Ch. Pellat et al., "Berbers," in *Encyclopaedia of Islam, Second Edition*, ed. P. Bearman, Th. Bianquis, C. E. Bosworth, E. van Donzel, and W. P. Heinrichs (Brill, 2010), *Brill Online*, http://www.brillonline.nl/subscriber/uid=1411/entry?entry=islam_COM-0114 (accessed June 27, 2010).

214 *Notes to pages 7–13*

20. William E. Hazen, "Minorities in Assimilation: The Berbers of North Africa," in *The Political Role of Minority Groups in the Middle East,* ed. R. D. McLaurin (New York: Praeger, 1979), p. 152.

21. I. William Zartman, ed., *The Political Economy of Morocco* (New York: Praeger, 1987); Rahma Bourqia and Susan Gilson Miller, eds., *In the Shadow of the Sultan: Culture, Power, and Politics in Morocco* (Cambridge, Mass.: Center for Middle Eastern Studies, Harvard University, 1999).

22. The nation, he says, is an "imagined political community." "Invention," however, does not connote "fabrication" or "falsity," as Ernest Gellner or Eric Hobsbawm would have it. Rather, it refers to a community whose members will never know one another, but will still have in their minds "the image of their communion"; is limited in space, beyond whose boundaries lie other nations; and is "conceived as a deep, horizontal comradeship . . . regardless of the actual inequality and exploitation that may prevail." Anderson also postulates the imagined community as sovereign, a barely extant component of modern Berber imagining. Benedict Anderson, *Imagined Communities,* 2nd ed. (London and New York: Verso, 1991), pp. 5–7.

23. Anthony D. Smith, *Nations and Nationalism in a Global Era* (Cambridge, UK: Polity Press, 1995), p. 59.

24. Hroch, "The Social Interpretation of Linguistic Demands in European National Movements," pp. 67–96; and Miroslav Hroch, *Comparative Studies in Modern European History: Nation, Nationalism, Social Change* (Aldershot, Hampshire, UK: Ashgate, Variorum, 2007).

25. For a discussion of some of the new thinking in social movement literature that focuses on the dynamic interaction among various factors in contentious political episodes, see Doug McAdam, Sidney Tarrow, and Charles Tilly, *Dynamics of Contention* (Cambridge: Cambridge University Press, 2001).

PART I

Chapter One

1. Anthony D. Smith, *The Ethnic Origins of Nations* (Oxford: Blackwell, 1996).

2. Miroslav Hroch, "The Social Interpretation of Linguistic Demands in European National Movements," in Hroch, *Social Preconditions of National Revival in Europe: A Comparative Analysis of the Social Composition of Patriotic Groups among the Smaller European Nations* (New York: Columbia University Press, 2000), p. 74.

3. Smith, *The Ethnic Origins of Nations,* Map 4.

4. Stephanie S. Saad, "Interpreting Ethnic Quiescence: A Brief History of the Berbers of Morocco," quoted by David Crawford, "Royal Interest in Local Culture: The Politics and Potential of Morocco's Imazighen," in *Nationalism and Minority Identities in Islamic Societies,* ed. Maya Shatzmiller (Montreal: McGill–Queen's University Press, 2005), p. 167.

5. By the tenth and eleventh centuries, they had been converted into descendants of eponymous ancestors, Abtar and Burnus, the sons of Barr, the grandson of Canaan and father of the race, in line with the concern shared by both Berber and Arab Muslims with conferring an appropriate origin upon the Berbers. Michael Brett and Elizabeth Fentress, *The Berbers* (Oxford: Blackwell, 1996), p. 131. Peter C. Scales, citing a Spanish historian, places the Butrs (constituting four subgroups) in a tribal confederation used by Arabs in their push westward and into Spain. Peter C. Scales, *The Fall of the Caliphate of Cordoba* (Leiden, New York, and Köln: E. J. Brill, 1994), p. 145.

6. Brett and Fentress, *The Berbers,* pp. 10–24.

7. http://whc.unesco.org/pg.cfm?cid=31&id_site=179 (accessed May 28, 2010); Malika Hachid, *Les Premiers Berbères, Entre Méditerranée, Tassili et Nil* (Alger and Aix-en-Provence: Ina-Yas, Édisud, 2000); Brett and Fentress, *The Berbers,* pp. 21–22.

8. Anthony D. Smith, *Nations and Nationalism in a Global Era* (Cambridge, UK: Polity Press, 1995), p. 146.

9. For a recent succinct discussion of the theoretical literature and its application to a particular case, see Meir Litvak, "Introduction: Collective Memory and the Palestinian Experience," in *Palestinian Collective Memory and National Identity,* ed. Litvak (New York: Palgrave Macmillan, 2009), pp. 1–26.

10. Brett and Fentress, *The Berbers,* pp. 22–23.

11. David Cherry, *Frontier and Society in Roman North Africa* (Oxford: Clarendon Press, 1998), p. 20.

12. Elisabeth W. B. Fentress, *Numidia and the Roman Army* (Oxford: B.A.R. International Series, 1979), p. 18. The term apparently has a Berber origin, and is not a derivation of the Greek word *nomades* (nomads). Gabriel Camps, *Les Berbères, Mémoire et Identité* (Arles: Babel, 2007), pp. 99–101.

13. Abdallah Laroui, *The History of the Maghrib: An Interpretive Essay* (Princeton, N.J.: Princeton University Press), pp. 29–32.

14. Henry Steele Commager, *The Search for a Usable Past, and Other Essays in Historiography* (New York: A. A. Knopf, 1967).

15. Laroui, *The History of the Maghrib,* p. 55. Earlier, he suggests, albeit indirectly, that Jugurtha was motivated by "Berber nationalism" (p. 30 n. 8).

16. Brett and Fentress, *The Berbers,* p. 47.

17. Ibid., pp. 48–49.

18. Miroslav Hroch, "From National Movement to the Fully-formed Nation: The Nation-building Process in Europe," in *Mapping the Nation,* ed. Balakrishnan Gopal (New York and London: Verso, 1996), pp. 78–97, quotation from p. 79.

19. Joshua A. Fishman, *Sociolinguistics* (Rowley, Mass.: Newbury House Publishers, 1972), p. 1.

20. Susan Gal and Kathryn A. Woolard, "Constructing Languages and Publics, Authority and Representation," in *Languages and Publics: The Making of Authority,* ed. Gal and Woolard (Manchester, UK: St. Jerome Publishing, 2001), pp. 10, 2.

21. Benedict Anderson, *Imagined Communities,* 2nd ed. (London and New York: Verso, 1991), p. 46.

22. Gal and Woolard, "Constructing Languages and Publics," pp. 8–9.

23. Joseph R. Applegate, "The Berber Languages," in *Current Trends in Linguistics,* ed. Thomas A. Seebok, Vol. 6, *Linguistics in South West Asia and North Africa* (The Hague: Mouton, 1970), pp. 586–661.

24. Brett and Fentress, *The Berbers,* pp. 14–15.

25. Helen Hagen, *The Shining Ones* (Philadelphia: Xlibris Corporation, 2000).

26. David J. Mattingly, "From One Colonialism to Another: Imperialism in the Maghreb," in *Roman Imperialism: Post-Colonial Perspectives,* ed. Jane Webster and Nick Cooper (Leicester: School of Archaeological Studies, University of Leicester, 1996), pp. 59–60.

27. In addition to Brett and Fentress, see, e.g., Susan Raven, who points to the relationship between the ancient Berber peoples' word for king, based on the consonants GLD, and the modern word *agellid* (*Rome in Africa,* 3rd ed. [London and New York: Routledge, 1993], p. 15). The word appears in all Berber dialects with the exception of that used by the Touareg, although even there one may discern traces of it. Salem Chaker, "Agellid," in *Encyclopédie Berbère,* ed. Gabriel Camps (Aix-en-Provence: Édisud, 1985), pp. 2:248–249.

28. Fergus Millar, "Local Cultures in the Roman Empire: Libyan, Punic and Latin in Roman Africa," *Journal of Roman Studies* 58, parts 1 and 2 (1968): 126–134, quotation from p. 128; Cherry, *Frontier and Society in Roman North Africa,* p. 10 n. 29.

29. Millar, "Local Cultures in the Roman Empire," pp. 132–133.

30. Cherry, *Frontier and Society in Roman North Africa,* p. 20.

31. Ibid., pp. 158–159.

32. Raven, *Rome in Africa,* p. 31.

33. Laroui, *The History of the Maghrib,* p. 64.

34. Mattingly, "From One Colonialism to Another," p. 58.

35. Fentress and Cherry disagree over the degree to which the Roman army served as an instrument of Romanization and an intermediary between imperial and indigenous cultures (Fentress believes it was significant; Cherry does not). Regarding the African population, see Mattingly, "From One Colonialism to Another," citing other studies, p. 59.

36. Raven, *Rome in Africa,* p. 147.

37. http://en.wikipedia.org/wiki/Apuleius (accessed May 29, 2010). "Gaetulia" refers to the area in Roman times south of the Aures Mountains stretching into the northern reaches of the Sahara Desert, and at times stretching westward to the Atlas Mountains and even as far as the Atlantic Ocean (http://en.wikipedia.org/wiki/Gaetulia [accessed May 29, 2010]).

38. Raven, *Rome in Africa,* pp. 122–123, 132–133.

39. Laroui, *The History of the Maghrib,* pp. 47, 49.

40. At its peak, there were between five hundred and six hundred "cities"

in Roman North Africa. Only one, Carthage, was likely to have had more than 100,000 inhabitants. Leptis Magna had perhaps 80,000. Most were small market towns, between a few and 10,000 inhabitants. Northern Tunisia, a rich agricultural area, had two hundred such towns. The overall population of the area, at its peak, may have reached 6–7 million persons, plus perhaps 100,000 tribesmen beyond the *limes*. Raven, *Rome in Africa,* pp. 100–103. For reference to the anti-chaos theory, see Maya Shatzmiller, *The Berbers and the Islamic State: The Marinid Experience in Pre-Protectorate Morocco* (Princeton, N.J.: Markus Wiener, 2000), p. xv.

41. Laroui, *The History of the Maghrib,* pp. 58–66, quotations from pp. 66, 59, 66, 63.

42. Brett and Fentress, *The Berbers,* pp. 120–121.

43. Recent scholarship deemphasizes the long-held notion that the *limes* functioned to demarcate and defend the "civilized world" from barbarism (Cherry, *Frontier and Society in Roman North Africa,* p. 24).

44. Ira M. Lapidus, *A History of Islamic Societies* (Cambridge: Cambridge University Press, 1988), pp. 365–378.

45. Charles-André Julien, *History of North Africa* (New York: Praeger, 1970), Chapters 2–4; Jamil Abun-Nasr, *A History of the Maghrib in the Islamic Period,* 2nd ed. (Cambridge: Cambridge University Press, 1987), Chapter 3; Phillip C. Naylor, *North Africa: A History from Antiquity to the Present* (Austin: University of Texas Press, 2009), Chapters 3–4. Marshall G. S. Hodgson characterizes the *"Murabit," "Muwahhid,"* Marinid, and Hafsid dynasties as examples of "reformist Berber political power," but avoids the term "empire" (*The Venture of Islam: Conscience and History in a World Civilization,* Vol. 2, *The Expansion of Islam in the Middle Periods* [Chicago and London: University of Chicago Press, 1974], pp. 268–270).

46. Lawrence Rosen, "The Social and Conceptual Framework of Arab-Berber Relations in Central Morocco," in *Arabs and Berbers: From Tribe to Nation in North Africa,* ed. Ernest Gellner and Charles Micaud (Lexington, Mass., and London: D. C. Heath/Duckworth, 1972/1973), pp. 155–173.

47. *Le Monde,* February 12, 2001.

48. Michael Brett, *The Islamisation of Egypt and North Africa* (Jerusalem: Nehemia Levtzion Center for Islamic Studies, 2006), p. 22.

49. Abun-Nasr, *A History of the Maghrib,* p. 16.

50. Abdelmajid Hannoum, *Post-Colonial Memories: The Legend of the Kahina, a North African Heroine* (Portsmouth, N.H.: Heinemann, 2001).

51. Brett, *The Islamisation of Egypt and North Africa,* pp. 18–19; Scales, *The Fall of the Caliphate of Cordoba,* p. 146; Abun-Nasr, *A History of the Maghrib,* pp. 33–39.

52. Brett, *The Islamisation of Egypt and North Africa,* p. 18.

53. "Kharijism," in Hsain Ilahiane, *Historical Dictionary of the Berbers (Imazighen)* (Lanham, Md.; Toronto; and Oxford: Scarecrow Press, 2006), pp. 78–80.

54. Abun-Nasr, *A History of the Maghrib,* pp. 50–52.

55. There are those who believe that the term stems from a phonetic defor-

mation of Barbati, denoting the Barbate region in Spain, from which the founder, Tarif, hailed. Fatima Moutaoukil, "Barghwata: Un royaume amazigh (berbère) méconnu," http://www.mondeberbere.com/civilisation/histoire/barghwata.htm (accessed May 20, 2010). See also "Barghwata," in Ilahiane, *Historical Dictionary of the Berbers (Imazighen),* p. 24.

56. Interview with Mohamed Chafik, Rabat, February 14, 2006.

57. Michael Peyron, "Barghawat et résistance," in *Le Resistance Marocaine a Travers L'Histoire ou le Maroc des Resistances,* Vol. 2, edited and coordinated by Mohammed Hammam et Abdellah Salih (Rabat: Rayume Du Maroc, Institut Royal de la Culture Amazighe, 2005), pp. 165–181; Mohamed al-Talibi and Ibrahim al-Abidi, *Al-Barghwatiyyun fil-Maghrib* (Casablanca: Matbaʿat al-Najah al-Jadida, 1999); interview with Mohamed Chafik; Mohamed Chafik, *A Brief Survey of Thirty-Three Centuries of Amazigh History,* rev. and ed. by Jilali Saib (Rabat: Institut Royal de la Culture Amazighe, 2005), pp. 43, 75; "Ha-Mim," http://en.wikipedia.org/wiki/Ha_Mim (accessed May 29, 2010).

58. "The Berbers Come Fighting Back," *The Economist,* February 13, 1999.

59. Maria Rosa Menocal, *The Ornament of the World* (Boston: Little, Brown, 2002), pp. 45, 96–100.

60. Neville Barbour, "The Berbers in al-Andalus," in *Proceedings of the First Congress on Mediterranean Studies of Arabo-Berber Influence,* ed. Micheline Galley, in collaboration with David R. Marshall (Algiers: Société Nationale D'Édition et De Diffusion, 1973), pp. 171–172; Helena De Felipe, "From the Maghreb to Al-Andalus: Berbers in a Medieval Islamic Society," in *North African Mosaic: A Cultural Reappraisal of Ethnic and Religious Minorities,* ed. Nabil Boudraa and Joseph Krause (Newcastle: Cambridge Scholars Publishing, 2007), p. 158.

61. Thomas F. Glick, *Islamic and Christian Spain in the Early Middle Ages* (Princeton, N.J.: Princeton University Press, 1979); David Wasserstein, *The Rise and Fall of the Party-Kings* (Princeton, N.J.: Princeton University Press, 1985); De Felipe, "From the Maghreb to Al-Andalus," pp. 150–162.

62. Otto Zwartjes, Geert Jan van Gelder, and Ed de Moor, eds., *Poetry, Politics and Polemics: Cultural Transfer between the Iberian Peninsula and North Africa* (Amsterdam and Atlanta, Ga.: Rodopi, 1996), p. 7.

63. David Wasserstein, "The Language Situation in al-Andalus," in *The Formation of al-Andalus,* Part 2: *Language, Religion, Culture and the Sciences,* ed. Maribel Fierro and Julio Samsó (Aldershot, UK: Ashgate, Variorum, 1998), pp. 12–13.

64. Wasserstein, *The Rise and Fall of the Party-Kings,* pp. 163–167; Scales, *The Fall of the Caliphate of Cordoba,* p. 143.

65. Pierre Guichard, *Structure Sociales "orientales" et "occidentales" dans l'Espagne musulmane* (Paris: Mouton & Co., 1977), cited by Scales, *The Fall of the Caliphate of Cordoba,* pp. 152–157.

66. Scales, *The Fall of the Caliphate of Cordoba,* pp. 157–159.

67. Thomas F. Glick, *From Muslim Fortress to Christian Castle: Social and Cultural*

Change in Medieval Spain (Manchester and New York: Manchester University Press, 1995), pp. 29–37.

68. Glick, *Islamic and Christian Spain in the Early Middle Ages,* pp. 180–182.

69. De Felipe, "From the Maghreb to Al-Andalus," pp. 155–156.

70. Abun-Nasr, *A History of the Maghrib,* p. 94.

71. Laroui, *The History of the Maghrib,* pp. 201–203; Abun-Nasr, *A History of the Maghrib,* p. 120.

72. Lapidus, *A History of Islamic Societies,* p. 375.

73. De Felipe, "From the Maghreb to Al-Andalus," p. 159; Shatzmiller, *The Berbers and the Islamic State,* p. xvi.

74. Shatzmiller, *The Berbers and the Islamic State,* pp. xiii–xv.

75. Michael Brett, "The Way of the Nomad," in Brett, *Ibn Khaldun and the Medieval Maghrib* (Aldershot, UK: Ashgate, Variorum, 1999), X, p. 267.

76. Brett and Fentress, *The Berbers,* p. 134.

77. Abun-Nasr, *A History of the Maghrib,* pp. 103–143.

78. Laroui, *The History of the Maghrib,* pp. 227–248.

79. Brett and Fentress, *The Berbers,* p. 130; Michael Brett, "Ibn Khaldun and the Arabisation of North Africa," *Maghreb Review* 4, no. 1 (January–February 1979): 9–16; David M. Hart, "The Role of Goliath in Moroccan Berber Genealogies," *Journal of North African Studies: A Special Issue on Tribe and Rural Society in Morocco* 4, no. 2 (Summer 1999): 37–47.

80. Shatzmiller, *The Berbers and the Islamic State,* pp. 21–22.

81. *Shuʿubiyya* refers to a movement in early Islam that sought to equalize the status of Persians and deny a privileged position to the Arabs. S. Enderwitz, "AL-S_H_uūbiyya," in Encyclopaedia of Islam, *Second Edition,* ed. by P. Bearman, Th. Bianquis, C. E. Bosworth, E. van Donzel, and W. P. Heinrichs (Brill, 2010), *Brill Online,* http://www.brillonline.nl/subscriber/uid=1411/entry?entry=islam_SIM-6997 (accessed June 27, 2010). The *shuʿubiyya* in al-Andalus was not limited to Berbers, but included converts of other origins. Its most well-known expression was an eleventh-century letter by Ibn Garcia al-Bahkunsi, who was apparently of Basque origin. Göran Larsson, *Ibn Garcia's Shuʿubiyya Letter: Ethnic and Theological Tensions in Medieval al-Andalus* (Leiden and Boston: Brill, 2003); James T. Monroe, *The Shuʿubiyya in Al-Andalus* (Berkeley: University of California Press, 1970).

82. Shatzmiller, *The Berbers and the Islamic State,* pp. xiv, 17–27, quotation from p. xiv.

83. Ibid., pp. 31–39.

84. Abun-Nasr, *A History of the Maghrib,* p. 150.

85. Naylor, *North Africa: A History,* pp. 120–121.

86. Tal Shuval, "The Ottoman Algerian Elite and Its Ideology," *International Journal of Middle East Studies* 32, no. 3 (August 2000): 323–344.

87. C. R. Pennell, *Morocco: From Empire to Independence* (Oxford: Oneworld, 2003), pp. 78–114.

88. Richard B. Parker, *Uncle Sam in Barbary* (Gainesville: University Press of Florida, 2004), p. xiv, note 1.

89. Mohamed El-Mansour, "Moroccan Islam Observed," *Maghreb Review* 29, nos. 1–4 (2004): 214.

90. Samir Benlayashi, "Secularism in the Moroccan-Amazigh Discourse," *Journal of North African Studies* 12, no. 7 (June 2007): 153–171.

91. Chafik, *A Brief Survey of Thirty-Three Centuries of Amazigh History,* pp. 73–74.

92. Ibid., pp. 70–71.

93. Ernest Gellner, *Muslim Society* (Cambridge: Cambridge University Press, 1981); Mohamed Chtatou, "Saints and Spirits and Their Significance in Moroccan Cultural Beliefs and Practices: An Analysis of Westermarck's Work," *Morocco,* n.s., no. 1 (1996): 62–84.

94. Pennell, *Morocco: From Empire to Independence,* p. 45. For a critique of the prevailing, colonialist-influenced maraboutic paradigm, see Vincent J. Cornell, *Realm of the Saint: Power and Authority in Moroccan Sufism* (Austin: University of Texas Press, 1998), pp. xxv–xxx. Cornell's brilliant and original analysis focuses on the interaction of Moroccan Sufism with the larger Islamic milieu, not on pre-Islamic Berber religious practices.

95. For a discussion of Ernest Renan's famous remark to this effect, see Benedict Anderson, *Imagined Communities,* pp. 199–201.

PART I

Chapter Two

1. Abdallah Laroui, *The History of the Maghrib: An Interpretive Essay* (Princeton, N.J.: Princeton University Press, 1977), pp. 295–306; Jamil Abun-Nasr, *A History of the Maghrib in the Islamic Period,* 2nd ed. (Cambridge: Cambridge University Press, 1987), pp. 251–258.

2. Benjamin Stora, *Algeria 1830–2000: A Short History* (Ithaca, N.Y., and London: Cornell University Press, 2001).

3. The Dey had unsuccessfully sought to correspond with the king of France in order to achieve repayment of a debt owed by France to two Jewish merchants, who in turn owed the Dey money. The consul had made it clear to the Dey that such a correspondence was beneath his king's dignity, hence the insult. John Ruedy, *Modern Algeria: The Origins and Development of a Nation,* 2nd ed. (Bloomington: Indiana University Press, 2005), pp. 45–51.

4. Ibid., pp. 42–43.

5. Andrea L. Smith, *Colonial Memory and Postcolonial Europe: Maltese Settlers in Algeria and France* (Bloomington: Indiana University Press, 2006), pp. 98–118.

6. There is some discrepancy regarding the exact numbers during the first decades of French rule. Detailed figures cited by Alain Mahé (*Histoire de la Grande*

Kabylie, XIXe-XXe siècles [Paris: Editions Bouchene, 2001], pp. 75–78) account for approximately 350,000 residents in Kabylie. Other French figures refer to Algeria circa 1860 as having 1 million Berberophones, 1.2 million Berber Arabophones, and 500,000 Arabs (Karina Direche-Slimani, *Chrétiens de Kabylie 1873-1954* [Paris: Editions Bouchene, 2004], p. 10). Assuming that Kabyles were two-thirds of all Berberophones, this would raise their numbers to 660,000.

7. Michael Brett and Elizabeth Fentress, *The Berbers* (Oxford: Blackwell, 1996), pp. 164–169.

8. Mahé, *Histoire de la Grande Kabylie,* pp. 73–77.

9. Hugh Roberts, "The Economics of Berberism: The Material Basis of the Kabyle Question in Contemporary Algeria," *Government and Opposition* 18, no. 2 (Spring 1983): 219–220; Abun-Nasr, *A History of the Maghrib,* pp. 266–268.

10. Jane Goodman, *Berber Culture on the World Stage* (Bloomington: Indiana University Press, 2005), pp. 99–103.

11. Abdelmajid Hannoum, *Post-Colonial Memories: The Legend of the Kahina, a North African Heroine* (Portsmouth, N.H.: Heinemann, 2001), pp. 29–69.

12. Patricia M. E. Lorcin, *Imperial Identities: Stereotyping, Prejudice and Race in Colonial Algeria* (London and New York: I. B. Tauris, 1995), pp. 146–195; Paul A. Silverstein, "The Kabyle Myth: Colonization and the Production of Ethnicity," in *From the Margins: Historical Anthropology and Its Futures,* ed. Brian Keith Axel (Durham, N.C.: Duke University Press, 2002), pp. 122–135.

13. Paul A. Silverstein, "France's *Mare Nostrum:* Colonial and Post-Colonial Constructions of the French Mediterranean," *Journal of North African Studies* 7, no. 4 (Winter 2002): 1–22.

14. Mohammed Harbi, "Nationalisme algérien et identité berbère," *Peuples Méditerranéens,* no. 11 (April–June 1980): 31.

15. Ruedy, *Modern Algeria,* pp. 76–79.

16. Abun-Nasr, *A History of the Maghrib,* p. 268.

17. Julia Clancy-Smith, *Rebel and Saint: Muslim Notables, Populist Protest, Colonial Encounters (Algeria and Tunisia, 1800-1904)* (Berkeley: University of California Press, 1994).

18. Ruedy, *Modern Algeria,* pp. 91–92; Charles-Robert Ageron, *Modern Algeria* (Trenton, N.J.: Africa World Press, 1991), pp. 69–73.

19. For a moving account of the life story of a Kabylian woman who went to school in one of the schools established by the Pères Blancs and did convert, see Fadhma Amrouche, *My Life Story: The Autobiography of a Berber Woman* (New Brunswick, N.J.: Rutgers University Press, 1989). She was the mother of the renowned France-based, French-language Kabyle writers Jean and Maurgerite-Taos Amrouche (the latter was also a renowned singer, in the Kabyle language).

20. Direche-Slimani, *Chrétiens de Kabylie 1873-1954,* pp. 73–112.

21. Roberts, "The Economics of Berberism," pp. 221–223; William Quandt, "The Berbers in the Algerian Political Elite," in *Arabs and Berbers: From Tribe to Nation*

in North Africa, ed. Ernest Gellner and Charles Micaud (Lexington, Mass., and London: D. C. Heath/Duckworth, 1972/1973), pp. 288–289; Jeane Favret, "Traditionalism through Ultra-Modernism," in ibid., p. 323.

22. Quoted in James McDougall, *History and the Culture of Nationalism in Algeria* (Cambridge: Cambridge University Press, 2006), pp. 84–85.

23. James McDougall, "Myth and Counter-Myth: 'The Berber' as National Signifier in Algerian Historiographies," *Radical History Review,* no. 86 (Spring 2003): 66–88; Hannoum, *Post-Colonial Memories,* pp. 112–116.

24. Gabi Kratochwil, *Die Berber in der historischen Entwicklung Algeriens von 1949 bis 1990. Zur Konstruktion einer ethnischen Identität* (Berlin: Klaus Schwarz, 1996), pp. 53–61; Omar Carlier, "La production sociale de l'image de soi/Note sur la 'crise berbèriste' de 1949," in *Annuaire de l'Afrique du Nord* 23 (1984): 347–371 (Paris: CNRS Editions, 1986).

25. Goodman, *Berber Culture on the World Stage,* pp. 103–106.

26. Kratochwil, *Die Berber in der historischen Entwicklung Algeriens,* p. 43; for more on the respective rival orientations of Messali and Imache during the 1930s, see Amar Ouerdane, "Genese De La 'Crise Berberiste' De 1949," *Tafsut,* no. 3 (June 1986): 109–120.

27. Rachid Chaker, "Journal Des Evenements De Kabylie (Mars–mai 1980)," *Les Temps Modernes,* nos. 432–433 (July–August 1982): 384; Kratochwil, *Die Berber in der historischen Entwicklung Algeriens,* pp. 48–49. See also note 7 in the Conclusion.

28. Harbi, "Nationalisme algérien et identité berbère," p. 33.

29. Mohand Tilmatine, "Religion and Morals of Imazighen According to Arab Writers of the Medieval Times," *Amazigh Voice* 9, nos. 2–3 (Spring/Summer 2000): 14–15.

30. Harbi, "Nationalisme algérien et identité berbère," p. 33.

31. Kratochwil, *Die Berber in der historischen Entwicklung Algeriens* (drawn from Benjamin Stora, *Dictionnaire Biographique de militants nationalistes Algériens 1926-1954* [Paris: L'Harmattan, 1985]), p. 257.

32. Pierre Monbeig, "Une Opposition Politique dans l'Impasse, Le FFS de Hocine Ait-Ahmed," in *L'Algérie Incertaine,* ed. Pierre Robert Baduel (Aix-en-Provence: Institute de Recherches et d'Études sur le Monde Arabe et Musulman [IREMAM], *Revue du Monde Musulman et de la Mediterranée* [REMMM], 1994), pp. 126–127.

33. Ibid., p. 131.

34. Alistair Horne, *A Savage War of Peace* (New York: Penguin Books, 1987), pp. 77–79.

35. Ruedy, *Modern Algeria,* pp. 166–167; Horne, *A Savage War of Peace,* pp. 141–146; Hugh Roberts, "The Unforeseen Development of the Kabyle Question in Contemporary Algeria," *Government and Opposition* 17, no. 3 (Summer 1982): 325–334.

36. Harbi, "Nationalisme algérien et identité berbère," pp. 33–34.

37. Horne, *A Savage War of Peace,* p. 78.

38. Mouloud Feraoun, *Journal, 1955–1962: Reflections on the French-Algerian War* (Lincoln: University of Nebraska Press, 2000), pp. 133, 261.

39. "Plateforme de la Soummam," http://www.el-mouradia.dz/francais/symbole/textes/soummam.htm (accessed July 28, 2010).

40. Roberts, "The Unforeseen Development of the Kabyle Question," p. 334; Harbi, "Nationalisme algérien et identité berbère," pp. 34–35; Amar Ouerdane, "Kabyles et Arabes Durant La Phase Decisive De La Guerre De Liberation Nationale: 1954–1957," *Tafsut,* no. 4 (October 1989): 87–113.

41. C. R. Pennell, *Morocco: From Empire to Independence* (Oxford: Oneworld, 2003).

42. For an elaboration on the concept of "stateness," see J. P. Nettl, "The State as a Conceptual Variable," *World Politics* 20, no. 4 (July 1968): 559–592.

43. Abun-Nasr, *A History of the Maghrib,* pp. 115, 236. Sultan Mawlay Isma'il rebuilt and enlarged it in 1719–1722.

44. John Waterbury, *Commander of the Faithful: The Moroccan Political Elite—A Study in Segmented Politics* (London: Weidenfeld and Nicholson, 1970), pp. 15–32.

45. Edmund Burke III, *Prelude to Protectorate in Morocco: Pre-colonial Protest and Resistance, 1860–1912* (Chicago: University of Chicago Press, 1976), pp. 13–40.

46. C. R. Pennell, *Morocco since 1830: A History* (New York: New York University Press, 2000), pp. 151–152; "Protectorate Treaty between France and Morocco," Supplement: Official Documents, *American Journal of International Law* 6, no. 3 (July 1912): 207–209.

47. Edmund Burke III, "The Image of the Moroccan State in French Ethnological Literature: A New Look at the Origin of Lyautey's Berber Policy," in *Arabs and Berbers: From Tribe to Nation in North Africa,* ed. Ernest Gellner and Charles Micaud (Lexington, Mass., and London: D. C. Heath/Duckworth, 1972/1973), pp. 175–199.

48. David M. Hart, "The Tribe in Modern Morocco: Two Case Studies," in *Arabs and Berbers: From Tribe to Nation in North Africa,* ed. Ernest Gellner and Charles Micaud (Lexington, Mass., and London: D. C. Heath/Duckworth, 1972/1973), pp. 27–28; Burke, *Prelude to Protectorate in Morocco,* pp. 12–13.

49. The term has a venerable heritage originating from the time of the Prophet Mohamed, and when applied to subsequent caliphs and by claimants to power, it carried the connotation of both spiritual and temporal authority. All Moroccan sultans since the Marinid Dynasty have claimed the title. H. A. R. Gibb, "Amīr al-Mu'minīn," in *Encyclopaedia of Islam, Second Edition,* ed. P. Bearman, Th. Bianquis, C. E. Bosworth, E. van Donzel, and W. P. Heinrichs (Brill, 2010), *Brill Online,* http://www.brillonline.nl/subscriber/entry?entry=islam_SIM-0617 (accessed June 27, 2010).

50. David M. Hart, "Tribalism: The Backbone of the Moroccan Nation," *Journal of North African Studies* 4, no. 2 (Summer 1999): 7–22.

51. Sebastian Balfour, *Deadly Embrace: Morocco and the Road to the Spanish Civil*

War (Oxford: Oxford University Press, 2002), pp. 61–75; Daniel Woolman, *Rebels in the Rif* (Stanford, Calif.: Stanford University Press, 1968), pp. 83–102.

52. Robert Montagne, *The Berbers: Their Social and Political Organisation,* trans. David Seddon (London: Frank Cass, 1973), pp. 79–83.

53. C. R. Pennell, *A Country with a Government and a Flag: The Rif War in Morocco, 1921–1926* (Wisbech, UK: Menas Press, 1986); Abun-Nasr, *A History of the Maghrib,* pp. 378–382.

54. Pessah Shinar, "ʿAbd al-Qadir and ʿAbd al-Krim, Religious Influences on Their Thought and Action," in Shinar, *Modern Islam in the Maghrib* (Jerusalem: Max Schloessinger Memorial Foundation, Hebrew University of Jerusalem, 2004), no. VI, p. 162.

55. Ibid., p. 165.

56. Ibid., p. 171.

57. Ibid., p. 174.

58. Abd al-Karim Ghallab, *Tarikh al-Haraka al-Wataniyya Bil-Maghrib,* Vol. 1 (Casablanca: Matbaʿat al-Najah al-Jadida, 2000), pp. 30–31, 453–464. Ghallab himself was a member of the Cairo-based Committee for Moroccan National Liberation, headed by Abdelkrim, in the late 1940s. Ghallab and the other committee members, he says, were more "realistic" in their views than Abdelkrim.

59. Ruedy, *Modern Algeria,* p. 139.

60. Abun-Nasr, *A History of the Maghrib,* p. 360.

61. Pennell, *Morocco since 1830,* pp. 286–287.

62. Kenneth Brown, "The Impact of the *Dahir Berbère* in Salé," in *Arabs and Berbers: From Tribe to Nation in North Africa,* ed. Ernest Gellner and Charles Micaud (Lexington, Mass., and London: D. C. Heath/Duckworth, 1972/1973), pp. 201–215.

63. Lawrence Rosen, "The Social and Conceptual Framework of Arab-Berber Relations in Central Morocco," in *Arabs and Berbers: From Tribe to Nation in North Africa,* ed. Ernest Gellner and Charles Micaud (Lexington, Mass., and London: D. C. Heath/Duckworth, 1972/1973), p. 173.

64. McDougall, "Myth and Counter-Myth."

65. For a new look at the Berber *dahir,* which includes an Amazigh activist's recent interpretation of the episode as having been manipulated by Moroccan nationalists to boost their credentials, when in fact it was the Berbers who had resisted the French more than the Arabs, see David M. Hart, "The Berber Dahir of 1930 in Colonial Morocco: Then and Now (1930–1960)," *Journal of North African Studies* 2, no. 4 (Autumn 1997): 11–33.

66. Pennell, *Morocco since 1830,* p. 216.

67. Hart, "The Berber Dahir of 1930," pp. 21–22.

68. Moshe Gershovich, *French Military Rule in Morocco* (London: Frank Cass, 1999), p. 216; Moshe Gershovich, "The Impact of French Colonialism in Contemporary Morocco" (paper delivered at the 7th International Association of Middle Eastern Studies [IAMES] conference, Free University of Berlin, October 4–8, 2000).

69. Mohamed Benhlal, *Le collège d'Azrou: Une élite berbère civile et militaire au maroc (1927-1959)* (Paris and Aix-en-Provence: Éditions Karthala, IREMAN, 2005), pp. 277–279.

70. Ibid., in Preface by Daniel Rivet, p. 7.

71. Ibid., p. 317.

72. Gabi Kratochwil, *Die Berberbewegung in Marokko: Zur Geschichte der Konstruktion einer ethnischen Identität (1912-1997)* (Berlin: Klaus Schwarz Verlag, 2002), pp. 114–115.

73. Ibid., p. 351.

74. Jacques Berque, *French North Africa: The Maghrib between Two World Wars* (New York: Praeger, 1967), pp. 217–220.

75. Pennell, *Morocco since 1830,* p. 278.

76. Abdessadeq El Glaoui, *Le ralliement: Le Glaoui, mon père* (Rabat: Editions Marsam, 2004).

77. Louis-Jean Duclos, "The Berbers and the Rise of Moroccan Nationalism," in *Arabs and Berbers: From Tribe to Nation in North Africa,* ed. Ernest Gellner and Charles Micaud (Lexington, Mass., and London: D. C. Heath/Duckworth, 1972/1973), pp. 217–229.

PART II

Chapter Three

1. Benjamin Stora, *Algerie Maroc, Histoires paralleles, destin croises* (Paris: Maisonneuve et Larose [Zellige], 2002).

2. I. William Zartman, *Ripe for Resolution: Conflict and Intervention in Africa* (New York: Oxford, 1989), pp. 30–31; Tony Hodges, *Western Sahara: The Roots of a Desert War* (Westport, Conn.: Lawrence Hill and Company, 1983), pp. 91–95.

3. John Damis, *Conflict in Northwest Africa* (Stanford, Calif.: Hoover Institution Press, 1983); Hodges, *Western Sahara;* Erik Jensen, *Western Sahara: Anatomy of a Stalemate* (Boulder, Colo.: Lynne Rienner, 2005).

4. For the AMU's founding in 1989 during a momentary Algerian-Moroccan thaw, see Bruce Maddy-Weitzman, "Inter-Arab Relations," in *Middle East Contemporary Survey (MECS),* Vol. 13 (1989), ed. Ami Ayalon (Boulder, Colo.: Westview Press, 1991), pp. 144–147.

5. Benjamin Stora, *Algeria 1830-2000: A Short History* (Ithaca, N.Y., and London: Cornell University Press, 2001), p. xi.

6. Charles Micaud, "Conclusion," in *Arabs and Berbers: From Tribe to Nation in North Africa,* ed. Ernest Gellner and Charles Micaud (Lexington, Mass., and London: D. C. Heath/Duckworth, 1972/1973), p. 436.

7. Jeane Favret, "Traditionalism through Ultra-Modernism," in *Arabs and Berbers: From Tribe to Nation in North Africa,* ed. Ernest Gellner and Charles Micaud (Lexington, Mass., and London: D. C. Heath/Duckworth, 1972/1973), pp. 307–324.

8. Malika Matoub, *Matoub Lounès, Mon Frère* (Paris: Albin Michel, 1999), p. 52 (she also quotes directly from Matoub Lounès's own book, *Rebelle*).

9. William Quandt, "The Berbers in the Algerian Political Elite," in *Arabs and Berbers: From Tribe to Nation in North Africa,* ed. Ernest Gellner and Charles Micaud (Lexington, Mass., and London: D. C. Heath/Duckworth, 1972/1973), pp. 285–303.

10. Salem Chaker, *Berbères Aujourd'hui,* 2nd ed. (Paris: L'Harmattan, 1998), pp. 123–124.

11. Martin Evans and John Phillips, *Algeria: Anger of the Dispossessed* (New Haven, Conn.: Yale University Press, 2008), p. 87.

12. Hafid Gafaïti, "The Monotheism of the Other: Language and De/Construction of National Identity in Postcolonial Algeria," in *Algeria in Others' Languages,* ed. Anne-Emmanuelle Berger (Ithaca, N.Y.: Cornell University Press, 2002), pp. 31–32. In making this point, the author cites Michael Willis, *The Islamist Challenge in Algeria: A Political History* (New York: New York University Press, 1999), pp. 51–52.

13. Information conveyed to me by Algerian students of that generation.

14. Djamila Saadi-Mokrane, "The Algerian Linguicide," in *Algeria in Others' Languages,* ed. Anne-Emmanuelle Berger (Ithaca, N.Y.: Cornell University Press, 2002), p. 54; Anne-Emmanuelle Berger, "The Impossible Wedding: Nationalism, Language and Mother Tongue in Post-Colonial Algeria," in ibid., pp. 69–71.

15. Djaafar Messaoudi, "The Strategies of the Algerian Regime to Subdue Kabylia," October 5, 2007, http://www.north-of-africa.com/article.php3?id_article=442 (accessed June 23, 2010).

16. Hugh Roberts, summarizing articles from the early 1980s, in "Co-opting Identity: The Manipulation of Berberism, the Frustration of Democratisation, and the Generation of Violence in Algeria," Crisis States Programme Working Papers, no. 7 (December 2001) (http://www.crisisstates.com/download/wp/WP7HR.pdf [accessed May 20, 2010]), p. 13.

17. Salem Chaker, "Les bases sociales du berbérisme: critique d'un mythe," in *Berbères Aujourd'hui,* 2nd ed. (Paris and Montreal: L'Harmattan, 1998), pp. 97–110 (appears without the annex at http://www.tamazgha.fr/Les-bases-sociales-du-berberisme-critique-d-un-mythe,209.html [accessed May 19, 2010]).

18. Anthony D. Smith, *Nations and Nationalism in a Global Era* (Cambridge, UK: Polity Press, 1995).

19. Franklin Foer, *How Soccer Explains the World: An Unlikely Theory of Globalization* (New York: HarperCollins, 2004).

20. Maxime Ait Kaki, *De la question berbère au dilemma kabyle à l'aube du XXIème siècle* (Paris: L'Harmattan, 2004), p. 85. Founded in 1946 as l'Olympique de Tizi-Ouzou (OTO), the name would be changed in 1962 to JSK. The team's official website states that the "Swift Stars" appellation was affixed in 1977. According to another source, however, it was first applied in 1972 by the state's director of sports as part of the Arabization and antiregionalization policies. Youssef Fatès, "Le Jeun-

esse sportive de Kabylie, Entre Sport et Politique," *AWAL: Cahiers d'études berbères,* no. 25 (2002): 49–57, esp. pp. 53, 55.

21. Salem Chaker, "La Question Berbère Dans L'Algerie Indépendante: La Fracture Inévitable?," in *L'Algérie Incertaine,* ed. Pierre Robert Baduel, *Revue du Monde Musulman et de la Méditerranée,* no. 65 (1992): 98.

22. According to Evans and Phillips, frustration among younger members eventually led them to engage in "terrorism," pointing to an attack on the headquarters of the FLN daily newspaper *El Moudjahid* and subsequent protests over efforts to restrict the airtime of Kabyle Radio (p. 87). To be sure, Berberist protests would at times result in property damage and clashes with security forces. But this hardly qualifies as "terrorism," the deliberate effort to violently target noncombatants as part of a political struggle. Indeed, the movement's nonviolent nature and modus operandi have been a consistent feature of its raison d'être from the outset.

23. Jane Goodman, *Berber Culture on the World Stage* (Bloomington: Indiana University Press, 2005), passim, and esp. pp. 49–68.

24. Paul A. Silverstein, *Algeria in France: Transpolitics, Race and Nation* (Bloomington: Indiana University Press, 2004), p. 71.

25. Ibid., pp. 10–11, 238.

26. Karina Direche-Slimani, *Histoire de l'émigration Kabyle en France au XX° siècle* (Paris: L'Harmattan, 1997), p. 2.

27. Mohamed Tilmatine and Yasir Suleiman, "Language and Identity: The Case of the Berbers," in *Language and Identity in the Middle East and North Africa,* ed. Yasir Suleiman (Richmond, Surrey, UK: Curzon Press, 1996), p. 168; Paul A. Silverstein, "Realizing Myth: Berbers in France and Algeria," *Middle East Report,* July–September 1998, p. 12.

28. Direche-Slimani, *Histoire de l'émigration Kabyle en France,* pp. 92–93; Silverstein, *Algeria in France,* p. 71; Goodman, *Berber Culture on the World Stage,* pp. 37–40.

29. Alistair Horne, *A Savage War of Peace* (New York: Penguin Books, 1987), pp. 227–229, 322–324, 326.

30. "Communiqué Hommage du CMA à Mohand Arav Bessaoud," http://www.afrique-du-nord.com/article.php3?id_article=560 (accessed June 4, 2010).

31. Abdenour Kilou, "Obituary: Mohand Aarav Bessaoud," *The Guardian,* January 30, 2002, http://www.guardian.co.uk/news/2002/jan/30/guardianobituaries .books (accessed May 20, 2010); "Communiqué Hommage du CMA à Mohand Arav Bessaoud."

32. Mohand Loukad, "Bessaoud Mohand Aarav: Le triomphe de la conviction," *Izuran-Racines,* January 8–21, 2007.

33. One Amazigh movement member told me that he had first heard of Bessaoud and the Academy while attending a boarding technical high school in Dellys in the mid-1970s. One day, in 1975, the local gendarmerie entered the high school premises and checked the notebooks of several students. Many students, who had written things in Tifinagh, were taken to the station for questioning.

One never returned to finish his studies. Communicated to me by Rabah Seffal, June 27, 2010.

34. Direche-Slimani, *Histoire de l'émigration Kabyle en France,* pp. 94–96; interview with former Académie Berbère activist Ould Slimane Salem, *Izuran-Racines,* January 8–21, 2007.

35. Goodman, *Berber Culture on the World Stage,* p. 40.

36. Ibid., pp. 99–101, 116; Tarik Mira, "Ait Ahmed et le FFS," *Tafsut,* no. 3 (June 1986): 104–105.

37. As of 2000, twenty-three volumes, encompassing more than three thousand pages of French-language entries up through "Icosum," had been published. Following Camps's death in 2002, Salem Chaker, professor at INALCO, assumed responsibility for the project. Volume 28–29, "De K á L," was published in 2008.

38. Bessaoud Mohand Arav often reproached Mammeri for his "coldness" and lack of involvement at the grassroots level. Interview with Ould Slimane Salem, *Izuran-Racines,* January 8–21, 2007.

39. Salem Chaker, "Mammeri Mouloud (1917–1989): le berberisant," in *Hommes et Femmes de Kabylie,* Vol. 1, ed. Salem Chaker (Paris and Aix-en-Provence: INALCO, Centre de Recherche Berbère, and Édisud, 2001), pp. 162–166, esp. p. 163.

40. Mohand Tilmatine, "Pouvoir, violence et revendications berbères," *AWAL: Cahiers d'études berbères,* no. 17 (1998): 25; Rachid Chaker, "Journal Des Evenements De Kabylie (Mars–mai 1980)," *Les Temps Modernes,* nos. 432–433 (July–August 1982): 384–385.

41. S. Chaker, "Mammeri Mouloud (1917–1989)," pp. 163–164.

42. Rachid Bellil and Salem Chaker, "Mammeri Mouloud, directeur du Crape," in *Hommes et Femmes de Kabylie,* Vol. 1, ed. Salem Chaker (Paris and Aix-en-Provence: INALCO, Centre de Recherche Berbère, and Édisud, 2001), pp. 167–169.

43. Mohammed Harbi, "Nationalisme algérien et identité berbère," *Peuples Méditerranéens,* no. 11 (April–June 1980): 36.

44. Goodman, *Berber Culture on the World Stage,* p. 33, citing Amar Ouerdane, *Le question berbère dans le mouvement national algérien, 1926–1980* (Quebec: Septentrion, 1990), p. 185.

45. Team supporters responded by declaring that JET stood for *Jugurtha existe toujours,* conflating Jugurtha's resistance to Rome with current Kabyle opposition to the Algerian state. Fatès, "Le Jeunesse sportive de Kabylie," p. 53.

46. Gabi Kratochwil, *Die Berber in der historischen Entwicklung Algeriens von 1949 bis 1990* (Berlin: Klaus Schwarz, 1996), p. 146; S. Chaker, *Berbères Aujourd'hui,* pp. 128, 147; Tilmatine, "Pouvoir, violence et revendications berbères," pp. 24–26; Fatès, "Le Jeunesse sportive de Kabylie," p. 52 n. 5.

47. R. Chaker, "Journal Des Evenements De Kabylie," pp. 389–390. Yacine came from a family of scholars, of Arabized Chaoui Berber origin. Considered among the most important of Maghribian writers in French, the trilingual Yacine became a strong advocate of Berber culture in his later years, advocating the elevation of Tamazight (and dialectal Arabic, as well) to the status of national lan-

guage (Charles Bonn and Richard Bjornson, "Kateb Yacine," in *Research in African Literatures* 23, no. 2 [Summer 1992]: 61–70; Marina Da Silva, "Kateb Yacine, l'éternel perturbateur," *Le Monde Diplomatique,* November 2009, http://www.monde-diplomatique.fr/2009/11/DA_SILVA/18424 [accessed June 28, 2010]).

48. S. Chaker, *Berbères Aujourd'hui,* p. 129.

49. Salem Mezhoud, "Glasnost the Algerian Way: The Role of Berber Nationalists in Political Reform," in *North Africa: Nation, State and Region,* ed. George Joffé (London: Routledge, 1993), p. 153.

50. Direche-Slimani, *Histoire de l'émigration Kabyle en France,* pp. 116–117. To be sure, the tone of the FFS's discourse was in tune with the revolutionary socialist idiom that dominated Algerian political life at that time, and is absent from the subsequent Berberist lexicon. Nonetheless, the reference to both "national" (Algerian) and "particularist" (Berber) matters became from that time on a permanent feature of the Berberist movement.

51. Goodman, *Berber Culture on the World Stage,* pp. 29–30.

52. Roberts, "Co-Opting Identity," p. 39 n. 94.

53. Evans and Phillips repeat the number of thirty fatalities in their recent book. Goodman appears to set the record straight (*Berber Culture on the World Stage,* pp. 33, 202 n. 7).

54. Pierre Nora, ed., *Les Lieux de memoire* (Paris: Gallimard, 1997).

55. Eventually, Mammeri would transfer his physical and intellectual base to France, founding the Centre d'l'Étude et Recherche Amazigh (CERAM) and the high-level scholarly journal *Awal* (word), and teaching at the École des Hautes Études en Sciences Sociales (EHESS). He would die in a car accident on February 26, 1989. Two hundred thousand persons attended his funeral the next day in Algiers, some of whom shouted antigovernment slogans (no government representatives attended). Mammeri's iconization after his death includes the naming of two public institutions in Tizi-Ouzou after him (the university where his canceled lecture in 1980 had triggered the Berber Spring, and the Maison de Culture) and the establishment of the Mouloud Mammeri Prize for outstanding literary works in Tamazight.

56. Roberts, "Co-opting Identity," pp. 38–39.

57. Goodman, *Berber Culture on the World Stage,* pp. 29–48, quotations from p. 32.

58. For a sampling of official and state media reactions, see Arezki Metref, "La question berbère: quand le politique capture l'identitaire," *Monde arabe Maghreb Machrek,* no. 154 (October–December 1996): 26–28.

59. Evans and Phillips, *Algeria: Anger of the Dispossessed,* p. 122; S. Chaker, *Berbères Aujourd'hui,* p. 124.

60. S. Chaker, *Berbères Aujourd'hui,* pp. 132–136.

61. Mezhoud, "Glasnost the Algerian Way," p. 143.

62. Stora, *Algeria 1830–2000: A Short History,* p. 182.

63. S. Chaker, *Berbères Aujourd'hui,* p. 60.

64. Mohamed Arkoun, "Algeria," in *The Politics of Islamic Revivalism: Diversity and Unity*, ed. Shireen T. Hunter (Bloomington: Indiana University Press, 1987), pp. 173–174.

65. Evans and Phillips, *Algeria: Anger of the Dispossessed*, pp. 124–134.

66. Roberts, "Co-opting Identity," p. 15.

67. Ibid., p. 16.

68. Jane Goodman, "Imazighen on Trial: Human Rights and Berber Identity in Algeria, 1985," in *Berbers and Others: Shifting Parameters of Ethnicity in the Contemporary Maghrib*, ed. Susan Gilson Miller and Katherine E. Hoffman (Bloomington: Indiana University Press, 2010), pp. 103–126.

69. Hugh Roberts, "Towards an Understanding of the Kabyle Question in Contemporary Algeria," *Maghreb Review* 5, nos. 5–6 (September–December 1980): 120.

70. http://www.populstat.info/Africa/moroccoc.htm (accessed June 4, 2010).

71. C. R. Pennell, *Morocco since 1830: A History* (New York: New York University Press, 2000), p. 305.

72. I. William Zartman, *Morocco: Problems of New Power* (New York: Atherton Press, 1964), p. 13. Powerful and disturbing accounts of life in these poverty-stricken areas are provided by Brick Oussaid (*Mountains Forgotten by God* [Boulder, Colo.: Three Continents Press, 1989]) and Muhammad Shukri (*For Bread Alone,* trans. Paul Bowles [London: Peter Owen Books, 1973]).

73. Louis-Jean Duclos, "The Berbers and the Rise of Moroccan Nationalism," in *Arabs and Berbers: From Tribe to Nation in North Africa,* ed. Ernest Gellner and Charles Micaud (Lexington, Mass., and London: D. C. Heath/Duckworth, 1972/1973), pp. 217–229.

74. For the confrontation regarding the transfer of his body from Fez to Agadir, see John Waterbury, *Commander of the Faithful: The Moroccan Political Elite—A Study in Segmented Politics* (London: Weidenfeld and Nicholson, 1970), p. 39.

75. *Le Monde Amazigh,* February 15, 2002.

76. David M. Hart, "Tribalism: The Backbone of the Moroccan Nation," *Journal of North African Studies* 4, no. 2 (Summer 1999): 18–19.

77. Maati Monib, "Le Rif, Mohammed V et l'Istiqlal," *Le Journal Hebdomadaire,* no. 368 (October 25–31, 2008): 28–29.

78. David M. Hart, "Rural and Tribal Uprisings in Post-Colonial Morocco, 1957–1960: An Overview and a Reappraisal," *Journal of North African Studies, A Special Issue on Tribe and Rural Society in Morocco* 4, no. 2 (Summer 1999): 93.

79. Waterbury, *Commander of the Faithful,* pp. 241–243.

80. For example, at the end of his questioning of a Rifian *fqih,* Oufkir reportedly ran a red-hot iron up and down his arms. Omar Brousky, "Quand Moulay Hassan matait les Rifains," *Le Journal Hebdomadaire,* no. 368 (October 25–31, 2008).

81. Adel Darwish, "Mohammed's First 100 Days," *The Middle East,* December 1999, pp. 16–18.

82. Maghreb Arab Press Agency, in English, January 23, 1984 — Foreign Broadcast Information Service, Daily Report, "The Middle East and Africa," January 24, 1984.

83. Adballah Hammoudi, *Master and Disciple: The Cultural Foundations of Moroccan Authoritarianism* (Chicago: University of Chicago Press, 1997); John P. Entelis, *Culture and Counterculture in Moroccan Politics* (Boulder, Colo.: Westview, 1989).

84. Waterbury, *Commander of the Faithful*, pp. 267–298; Remy Leveau, *Le Fellah Marocain, Defenseur Du Trone* (Paris: Presses De La Fondation Nationale Des Sciences Politiques, 1985).

85. Waterbury, *Commander of the Faithful*, p. 235.

86. Michael Brett and Elizabeth Fentress, *The Berbers* (Oxford: Blackwell, 1996), p. 195.

87. Waterbury, *Commander of the Faithful*, p. 244.

88. Gabi Kratochwil, *Die Berberbewegung in Marokko: Zur Geschichte der Konstruktion einer ethnischen Identität (1912-1997)* (Berlin: Klaus Schwarz Verlag, 2002), pp. 180–182.

89. Zartman, *Morocco: Problems of New Power*, pp. 63–116; Waterbury, *Commander of the Faithful*, pp. 287–289.

90. El Khatir Aboulkacem, "Etre berbère ou amazigh dans le Maroc modern: histoire d'une connotation négative," in *Berbères ou Arab? Le tango des specialists,* ed. Hélène Claudot-Hawad (Aix-en-Provence: Non Lieu/IREMAMM, 2006), p. 123.

91. Gilbert Grandguillaume, *Arabisation et politique linguistique au Maghreb* (Paris: Maisonneuve, 1983).

92. Ibid., p. 127.

93. Kratochwil, *Die Berberbewegung in Marokko*, pp. 212–215; Aboulkacem, "Etre berbère ou amazigh dans le Maroc modern," pp. 128–129.

94. Jean and Simonne Lacouture, *Le Maroc, a l'epreuve* (Paris: Editions du Seuil, 1958), p. 83, quoted by Aboulkacem, "Etre berbère ou amazigh dans le Maroc modern," p. 127.

95. Grandguillaume, *Arabisation et politique linguistique au Maghreb,* pp. 73–74, 90–91.

96. Kratochwil, *Die Berberbewegung in Marokko,* p. 274. John Waterbury suggested that the Swasa (Soussi)-Fassi economic rivalry was not, at bottom, ethnically based; however, he also noted that the Swasa's initial entry into politics in the early years of the state was at the ethnic group level and in reference to other ethnic groups, and without affinity to the UNFP's socialist ideology ("Tribalism, Trade and Politics: The Transformation of the Swasa of Morocco," in *Arabs and Berbers: From Tribe to Nation in North Africa,* ed. Ernest Gellner and Charles Micaud [Lexington, Mass., and London: D. C. Heath/Duckworth, 1972/1973], p. 232). For a recent journalistic account of the Fassi-Soussi divide in a Moroccan newsweekly, see Souleiman Bencheikh and Hassan Hamdam, "Fassis vs. Soussis: Histoire d'une Rivalité," *TelQuel,* April 5–11, 2008.

97. John Waterbury, "The Coup Manqué," in *Arabs and Berbers: From Tribe to Nation in North Africa,* ed. Ernest Gellner and Charles Micaud (Lexington, Mass., and London: D. C. Heath/Duckworth, 1972/1973), p. 404.

98. Frank H. Braun, "Morocco: Anatomy of a Palace Revolution That Failed," *International Journal of Middle East Studies* 9 (1978): 63–72; John Waterbury, "The Coup Manqué," pp. 397–423; A. Coram, "The Berbers and the Coup," in *Arabs and Berbers: From Tribe to Nation in North Africa,* ed. Ernest Gellner and Charles Micaud (Lexington, Mass., and London: D. C. Heath/Duckworth, 1972/1973), pp. 425–430.

99. Waterbury, "The Coup Manqué," p. 406.

100. Ibid., p. 405.

101. The announcement came on the morrow of Israel's shooting down of a Libyan passenger aircraft over the Israeli-controlled Sinai peninsula, killing 113 persons. A total of three brigades, totaling 2,500 "volunteers," would be dispatched, and would see action in the October 1973 Arab-Israeli war.

102. U.S. National Archives, RG59, Confidential Tel 0831, Rabat to Secretary of State (Priority 8263), February 23, 1973; "Le Discours Royal," *Maroc Soir,* February 23, 1973.

103. Quote reported to me by John Damis.

104. Waterbury, "The Coup Manqué," p. 397.

105. Coram, "The Berbers and the Coup," p. 430.

106. Malik Oufkir and Michele Fitoussi, *Stolen Lives* (New York: Hyperion, 1999), p. 15.

107. Michael Laskier, *Israel and the Maghreb: From Statehood to Oslo* (Gainesville: University Press of Florida, 2004), pp. 144–156.

108. Longtime Reuters correspondent Stephen O. Hughes is the one person who suggests that Oufkir may not have actually been involved (*Morocco under King Hassan* [Reading, UK: Ithaca Press, 2001], pp. 180–185).

109. Oufkir and Fitoussi, *Stolen Lives;* Raouf Oufkir, *Les Invités, vingt ans dans les prisons du Roi* (Paris: Flammarion, 2003); Fatéma Oufkir, *Les Jardins du roi* (Paris: Éditions Michel Lafon, 2000).

110. Bernard Lewis, *History—Remembered, Recovered, Invented* (Princeton, N.J.: Princeton University Press, 1976).

111. Interviews with Amazigh activists, Rabat, February 2006; U.S. National Archives, RG59, Rockwell to DOS, Tel A-236, November 27, 1971. In Oufkir's conversation with U.S. ambassador to Morocco Stuart Rockwell four months after the Skhirat events, he lamented the king's failure to launch a full-scale anticorruption campaign, including against his brother. Even doing nothing, he said, would be better than the existing policy of pursuing half-measures. He also expressed his confidence that the basic political structure of the kingdom would continue even if the king were to be assassinated. We do not know whether he would have stuck to this view had the coup succeeded; Hassan, for his part, dismissed the possibility

that Oufkir and his followers would have been able to govern without the monarchy, agreeing, in essence, with Oufkir's earlier statement.

112. *FRUS, 1969–76,* Vol. E, Part 2, Documents on Africa, 1969–1972, Rockwell to Secretary of State, Rabat, Tel. #4204, August 19, 1971, http://history.state.gov/historicaldocuments/frus1969-76ve05p2/d121 (accessed August 3, 2010).

113. Oufkir and Fitoussi, *Stolen Lives,* p. 239.

114. Hroch's class analysis refers to a portion of the "intelligentsia" ("Social and Territorial Characteristics in the Composition of the Leading Groups of National Movements," in Hroch, *Social Preconditions of National Revival in Europe: A Comparative Analysis of the Social Composition of Patriotic Groups among the Smaller European Nations* [New York: Columbia University Press, 2000], pp. 257–275). For a brief discussion on the broader theme of intellectuals in politics, see Bruce Maddy-Weitzman, *Palestinian and Israeli Intellectuals in the Shadow of Oslo and Initifadat al-Aqsa* (Tel Aviv: Tami Steinmetz Center for Peace Research, 2002), pp. 13–16, http://www.dayan.org/PalestinianandIsraeliIntellectuals-bruce.pdf (accessed May 20, 2010).

115. Aziz Chahir, "Leadership politique amazigh," in *Usages de l'identité Amazighe au Maroc,* ed. Hassan Rachik (Casablanca: Imprimerie Najah El Jadida, 2006), pp. 196, 226.

116. Personal communiqué.

117. Kratochwil, *Die Berberbewegung in Marokko,* p. 301.

118. Waterbury, "The Coup Manqué," pp. 295–300.

119. Interview with Hassan Idbelkassem, Rabat, October 2003.

120. *Jeune Afrique,* February 19, 1968, cited in Grandguillaume, *Arabisation et politique linguistique au Maghreb,* p. 92.

121. Lahsine Waʿzi, *Nashʾat al-Haraka al-Thaqafiya al-Amazighiyya bil-Maghrib, 1967–1991* (Rabat: Matbaʿat al-Maʿarif al-Jadida, 2000), p. 61.

122. Mustapha Elqadery, "L'état national et les berberes, le cas du maroc, mythe colonial et negation nationale" (Ph.D. thesis, Universite Paul Valery, Montpellier III, 1995), p. 78, quoted in ibid., p. 193 n. 61.

123. Chahir, "Leadership politique amazigh," p. 212 n. 291.

124. Kratochwil, *Die Berberbewegung in Marokko,* p. 182. Among his nonofficial activities, Chafik, with Abdelhamid Zemmouri, founded the first explicitly titled Berberist society in 1979, the Association Culturelle Amazighe (ibid., p. 217; Chahir, "Leadership politique amazigh," p. 199).

125. Brahim Akhiat, the first head of AMREC, was also instrumental in its founding, along with Brahim Aqdim and Ahmed El-Hariri (Chahir, "Leadership politique amazigh," p. 207).

126. Kratochwil, *Die Berberbewegung in Marokko,* p. 325.

127. Chahir, "Leadership politique amazigh," p. 217 n. 308.

128. Ibid., p. 218.

129. Ali Sidqi Azaykou, "Fi Sabil Mafhum Haqiqi Li-Thaqafatna al-Wataniyya," *Amazigh,* no. 1 (1982): 62–76, quotation from p. 72.

130. Kratochwil, *Die Berberbewegung in Marokko,* pp. 320–331.

131. Mbarek Boulkayid, "Ali Sidqi Azaykou—and the Arab Media in Our Country," *Le Monde Amazigh,* no. 50 (October 2004): 6. The issue also contained a number of other tributes to the man who "exposed the falsifications of our history," a reprint of the article that landed him in prison, and reference to the source of the ailments that eventually did him in, according to Mohamed Chafik's commentary in the same issue.

132. Kratochwil, *Die Berberbewegung in Marokko,* pp. 332–337. One of the trenchant responses, emphasizing that a wholesale Arabization and the concomitant destruction of the Berber language and culture ran explicitly counter to the author's declared goal of promoting a democratic and progressive Morocco, was that of Abdallah Bounfour, "L'Etat unitaire et le statut de la langue berbère: les positions de la gauche marocaine," *Annuaire de l'Afrique du Nord* 23 (1984): 509–521.

PART II

Chapter Four

1. Daniel Dishon and Bruce Maddy-Weitzman, "Inter-Arab Relations," in *Middle East Contemporary Survey (MECS),* Vol. 4 (1979–1980) and Vol. 5 (1980–1981), ed. Colin Legum, Haim Shaked, and Daniel Dishon, pp. 4:176–177, 5:234 (New York: Holmes and Meier, 1981, 1982).

2. This counting excludes the politically volatile but peripheral Arab states of North and South Yemen (which united under one roof in 1990), Mauritania (admitted to the League in 1973), the League's single nonstate member, the Palestine Liberation Organization (admitted in 1976, and now participating as "Palestine"), and the not even nominally Arab Somalia and Djibouti (League members since 1974 and 1977, respectively, as is the Comoros Islands, since 1993).

3. E.g., Hamied Ansari, *Egypt, the Stalled Society* (Albany, N.Y.: SUNY Press, 1986).

4. Nazih N. Ayubi, *Overstating the Arab State: Politics and Society in the Middle East* (London: I. B. Tauris, 1995).

5. Samuel P. Huntington, *The Third Wave: Democratization in the Late Twentieth Century* (Norman: University of Oklahoma Press, 1993).

6. Emmanuel Sivan, "Arab Nationalism in the Age of Islamic Resurgence," in *Rethinking Nationalism in the Arab Middle East,* ed. James Jankowski and Israel Gershoni (New York: Columbia University Press, 1997), pp. 207–228.

7. See Chapter 7, note 16.

8. Martin Evans and John Phillips, *Algeria: Anger of the Dispossessed* (New Haven, Conn.: Yale University Press, 2008), pp. 140–141.

9. Ouali Ilikoud, "Le Printemps berbère et Octobere 88," in *Émutes et Mouvement Sociaux au Maghreb,* ed. Didier Le Saout and Marguerite Rollande (Paris: Karthala/Institut Maghreb-Europe, 1999), p. 140; Benjamin Stora, *Algeria 1830–*

2000: A Short History (Ithaca, N.Y., and London: Cornell University Press, 2001), pp. 195–197.

10. Hugh Roberts, *The Battlefield: Algeria 1988-2002, Studies in a Broken Polity* (London: Verso, 2003), pp. 84–94. See also Boutheina Cheriet, "The Resilience of Algerian Populism," *Middle East Report,* January/February 1992, pp. 12–13; and Stora, *Algeria 1830-2000,* pp. 197–198.

11. Salem Mezhoud, "Glasnost the Algerian Way: The Role of Berber Nationalists in Political Reform," in *North Africa: Nation, State and Region,* ed. George Joffé (London: Routledge, 1993), pp. 159–161.

12. Ilikoud, "Le Printemps berbère," pp. 144–146; Stora, *Algeria 1830-2000,* p. 198; Hugh Roberts, "Co-opting Identity: The Manipulation of Berberism, the Frustration of Democratisation, and the Generation of Violence in Algeria," Crisis States Programme Working Papers, no. 7 (December 2001) (http://www.crisisstates.com/download/wp/WP7HR.pdf [accessed May 20, 2010]), pp. 14–21.

13. Roberts, "Co-opting Identity," pp. 34–35.

14. Salem Chaker, "La langue berbère dans le champ politique maghrébin. La cas algérien: rupture ou continuité?," in *Langues et Pouvoir, De l'afrique du Nord à l'Extrême-Orient,* ed. S. Chaker (Aix-en-Provence: Édisud, 1998), pp. 27–28.

15. Private communiqué, 1995.

16. Pierre Monbeig, "Une Opposition Politique dans l'Impasse, Le FFS de Hocine Ait-Ahmed," in *L'Algérie Incertaine,* ed. Pierre Robert Baduel (Aix-en-Provence: Institute de Recherches et d'Études sur le Monde Arabe et Musulman [IREMAM], *Revue du Monde Musulman et de la Méditerranée* [REMMM], 1994), p. 134.

17. Interview with Ahmad Fettani, *al-Watan al-Arabi,* November 20, 1992, translated version appears in Joint Publication Research Service, Near East and South Asia, February 1, 1993.

18. Roberts, *The Battlefield,* p. 144.

19. Ibid., p. 17.

20. Paul A. Silverstein, *Algeria in France: Transpolitics, Race and Nation* (Bloomington: Indiana University Press, 2004), p. 221.

21. Radio Algiers, April 3, 1990—Foreign Broadcast Information Service, The Middle East and North Africa, Daily Report (DR), April 4, 1990. Ait Ahmed was blamed by opponents for wanting to create an "Algerian Kurdistan" (Reporters Sans Frontières, *Le Drame Algérien, Un peuple en otage* [Paris: Le Découverte, 1996], p. 128).

22. Patrick Bishop in the *Daily Telegraph,* reprinted in the *Jerusalem Post,* March 14, 1990.

23. Francis Ghiles, in the *Financial Times,* June 11, 1990; Algerian Press Service, Daily Report (DR), May 31–June 1, 1990.

24. Salem Chaker, "'Question berbère,' 'Problème kabyle,' où en est-on?," *Annuaire de l'Afrique du Nord* 40 (2002) (Paris: CNRS Editions, 2004), p. 289.

25. Youssef Fatès, "Le Jeunesse sportive de Kabylie, Entre Sport et Politique," *AWAL: Cahiers d'études berbères,* no. 25 (2002): 54.

26. Michael Willis, *The Islamist Challenge in Algeria: A Political History* (New York: New York University Press, 1999), pp. 208–209.

27. *Le Figaro*, June 7, 1991, quoted in Monbeig, "Une Opposition Politique," p. 134.

28. *Financial Times*, June 19, 1991.

29. FIS candidates received 1.2 million fewer votes than in the 1990 municipal elections. The turnout for the two elections was approximately the same. But over 900,000 ballots, nearly 12 percent of the total, were invalidated. Whether these votes would have strengthened or weakened the FIS cannot be known. Similarly, the FLN suffered a drop of approximately 630,000 votes. Fawzi Rouzeik, "Algérie 1990–1993: La Démocratie Confisquée?," in *L'Algérie Incertaine*, ed. Pierre Robert Baduel (Aix-en-Provence: Institute de Recherches et d'Études sur le Monde Arabe et Musulman [IREMAM], *Revue du Monde Musulman et de la Mediterranée* [REMMM], 1994), p. 44.

30. *Financial Times*, January 2, 6, 1992; *Libération*, January 1, 1992.

31. Cited by Yahia H. Zoubir, "The Painful Transition from Authoritarianism in Algeria," *Arab Studies Quarterly* 15, no. 3 (Summer 1993): 84.

32. For an analytical account of Algerian developments during the civil war years, see Maddy-Weitzman, "Maghrib Affairs" (in *Middle East Contemporary Survey [MECS]*, Vol. 17 [1993], ed. Ami Ayalon [Boulder, Colo.: Westview Press, 1995], pp. 83–108), and annual "Algeria" chapters by Gideon Gera (in *Middle East Contemporary Survey [MECS]*, Vol. 18 [1994], ed. Ami Ayalon and Bruce Maddy-Weitzman [Boulder, Colo.: Westview, 1996], pp. 233–252) and Meir Litvak (in *Middle East Contemporary Survey [MECS]*, Vols. 19–24 [1995–2000], ed. Bruce Maddy-Weitzman [Boulder, Colo., and Tel Aviv: Westview/Dayan Center, 1997–2002]).

33. Maxime Ait Kaki, *De la question berbère au dilemma kabyle à l'aube du XXIeme siècle* (Paris: L'Harmattan, 2004), p. 157.

34. *Le Figaro*, March 30, 1994; Saïd Saadi, "No Longer Can We Spend Our Time Burying Our Dead," *Middle East Quarterly* 1, no. 2 (June 1994): 92–94.

35. Ait Kaki, *De la question berbère*, pp. 156–157.

36. Willis, *The Islamist Challenge in Algeria*, pp. 340–346. Ali Yahia Abdenour, head of the Ligue Algerienne de Defense des Droits de l'Homme (LADDH), and prominent figure in the trials of MCB activists in the mid-1980s (see Chapter 3), acted as a spokesman for the meeting's outcome. Saadi, on the other hand, attacked the meeting for "reinforcing the FIS's power" (p. 343 nn. 93, 94).

37. *Al-Sharq al-Awsat*, January 14, 1995—Foreign Broadcast Information Service, Daily Report, January 18, 1995.

38. Ait Ahmed's interview in *al-Sharq al-Awsat*, February 9—FBIS-DR, February 11, 1993.

39. *El Pais*, May 10–16, 1995.

40. See interview with Salem Chaker in *L'Express*, November 24, 2005, http://www.tamazgha.fr/article.php3?id_article=1529 (accessed June 15, 2010).

41. "Amazighité—Communiqué De La Presidence," issued by the Embassy of

Algeria, Washington, D.C., April 23, 1995; for an analysis, see Dahbia Abrous, "Le Haut Commissariat À L'Amazighté, ou le méandres d'une phagocytose," *Annuaire de l'Afrique du Nord* 34 (1995) (Paris: CNRS Editions, 1997), pp. 583–590.

42. Meir Litvak, "Algeria," *MECS,* Vol. 19 (1995), pp. 220–221, and Vol. 20 (1996), pp. 225–234.

43. Ibid., Vol. 20 (1996), p. 232.

44. Zighen Aym, "Tamazight Lost Its Popular Singer and Activist," *Amazigh Voice* 7, no. 3 (Fall 1998): 5–6. The text of the letter/song is on p. 7.

45. Evans and Phillips, *Algeria: Anger of the Dispossessed,* pp. 248–250; Litvak, "Algeria," *MECS,* Vol. 22 (1998), pp. 196–197.

46. *Le Monde,* July 11, 1999; Salem Chaker, "Quelques Évidences sur la Question Berbère en Algèrie?," *Confluences Méditerannées,* no. 11, *Comprendre l'Algérie* (Summer 1994): 103–111; *Imazighen ASS-A,* October 1998, pp. 8–9.

47. Statement by the Federal Council of the World Amazigh Congress, meeting in Paris on November 25–26, 2000 (www.kabyle.com).

48. Litvak, "Algeria," in *MECS,* Vol. 23 (1999), p. 178.

49. Ait Kaki, *De la question berbère,* pp. 148–149; Litvak, "Algeria," in *MECS,* Vol. 23 (1999), pp. 169, 173, 178.

50. Maddy-Weitzman, "Morocco," in *MECS,* Vol. 22 (1998) (Boulder, Colo.: Westview, 2001), pp. 451–460.

51. Aziz Chahir, "Leadership politique amazigh," in *Usages de l'identité Amazighe au Maroc,* ed. Hassan Rachik (Casablanca: Imprimerie Najah el Jadida, 2006), p. 208.

52. The text of the charter is in Hassan Rachik, ed., *Usages de l'identité Amazighe au Maroc* (Casablanca: Imprimerie Najah el Jadida, 2006), Annexe 2, pp. 237–241.

53. Chahir, "Leadership politique amazigh," p. 218 n. 309.

54. *Amazigh Voice* 3, no. 2 (November 1994); U.S. Department of State, "Morocco Human Rights Practices 1994," February 1995, http://dosfan.lib.uic.edu/ERC/democracy/1994_hrp_report/94hrp_report_nea/Morocco.html (accessed May 21, 2010).

55. Katherine E. Hoffman, *We Share Walls: Language, Land, and Gender in Berber Morocco* (Malden, Mass.: Blackwell, 2008), pp. 196–198.

56. Chahir, "Leadership politique amazigh," p. 212 n. 291.

57. Six hundred soldiers and thirty-three officers were killed, and the victorious Zaiane tribesmen acquired considerable amounts of abandoned weaponry. The defeat was the worst ever inflicted on the French army in Morocco. Moshe Gershovich, *French Military Rule in Morocco* (London: Frank Cass, 1999), pp. 103–104.

58. The full text of the speech is contained in *al-Alam,* August 22, 1994. A partial version in English can be found in Moroccan RTM-TV, August 20, 1994—BBC Monitoring, Summary of World Broadcasts, Part 4, The Middle East, August 23, 1994, pp. 19–20.

59. Abdesselam Cheddadi, "Pour Une Politique de la Langue," *Prologues,* no. 17, *Langues Et Culture Au Maghreb* (1999): 34; for a practical manifestation of this common identity, see Mohamed Chtatou, "The Influence of the Berber Language

on Moroccan Arabic," *International Journal of the Sociology of Language,* no. 123, *Berber Sociolinguistics,* ed. Moha Ennaji (1997): 101–118.

60. The letter was signed by Akhiat, Oussaden, Ahmad Adghirni, Idbelkassem, and Mohamed Chami, professor of Arabic literature at Oujda University and USFP and AMREC member from Nador, in northeast Morocco. *Pour Le Reconnaissance Constitutionnelle de l'Amazighite* (Rabat: AMREC, 2002), pp. 16–17.

61. *Amazigh Voice* 7, no. 2 (Spring 1998): 4.

62. From proceedings of a conference marking the thirtieth anniversary of the establishment of the Moroccan Association for Research and Cultural Exchange (AMREC). *Al-Amazighiyya al-An* (Kenitra, Morocco: Al-Bukeili Publishing, 1998), p. 7.

63. Bruce Maddy-Weitzman and Meir Litvak, "Islamism and the State in North Africa," in *Revolutionaries and Reformers: Contemporary Islamist Movements in the Middle East,* ed. Barry Rubin (Albany, N.Y.: SUNY Press, 2003), pp. 74–76.

64. Malika Zeghal, *Islamism in Morocco* (Princeton, N.J.: Markus Wiener Publishers, 2008); Michael Willis, "Justice and Development or Justice and Spirituality? The Challenge of Morocco's Nonviolent Islamist Movements," in *The Maghrib in the New Century: Identity, Religion and Politics,* ed. Bruce Maddy-Weitzman and Daniel Zisenwine (Gainesville: University Press of Florida, 2007), pp. 150–174.

65. The *jahiliyya* ("Age of Ignorance") refers to the state of affairs in the Arabian peninsula prior to the advent of Islam. William E. Shepard, "Age of Ignorance," in *Encyclopaedia of the Qurʾān,* ed. Jane Dammen McAuliffe, Georgetown University (Washington, D.C.: Brill, 2010), *Brill Online,* http://www.brillonline.nl/subscriber/entry?entry=q3_SIM-00013 (accessed June 27, 2010).

66. Abdeslam Yassine, *Hiwar maʿa Sadiq Amazighi* (Beirut: Dar Lubnan Liltabaʿa Wal-Nashr, 2003). His remarks concerning Abdelkrim and another Rifian *mujahid,* the sharif Mohamed Amziyan, appear on pp. 221–222. For his remarks regarding the Amazigh Congress and the Western-led agenda to fragment the Maghrib and remove religion from the world, see pp. 239–245. The entire book is posted on Yassine's website (http://yassine.net/mishkate/pages/YOChapterDetailPage.aspx?BookID=10&ChapterID=1&Lang=1256&CategoryID=2).

67. For Chafik's view of Islam and reason, see ibid., pp. 13–14. For his comment regarding *laïcisme,* see pp. 143–144. His citation regarding Arabs, foreigners, and piety appears on p. 152; on *shuʿubiyya,* see p. 149.

68. *Le Monde Amazigh,* no. 60, May 2005.

69. Gabi Kratochwil, *Die Berberbewegung in Marokko: Zur Geschichte der Konstruktion einer ethnischen Identität (1912–1997)* (Berlin: Klaus Schwarz Verlag, 2002), p. 389 n. 938.

70. Ahmed Asid, *al-Amazighiyya fi khitab al-Islam al-siyasi* (Rabat: Imprimerie Najah Aljadida, 2000), pp. 117–118, 122–124.

71. Ibid., p. 124.

72. *Al-Amazighiyya al-An,* p. 24.

73. *The Economist,* February 13, 1999.

74. Daniel Byman, "Explaining Ethnic Peace in Morocco," *Harvard Middle Eastern and Islamic Review* 4, nos. 1–2 (1997–1998): 1–29.

75. *Al-Amazighiyya al-An,* p. 159.

76. Mohamed Chafik, in ibid., p. 28.

77. Moha Ennaji, "The Sociology of Berber, Change and Continuity," *Berber Sociolinguistics,* ed. Ennaji, special issue of *International Journal of the Sociology of Language,* no. 123 (1997): 32.

PART III (OPENER)

1. I. William Zartman, "Introduction: Rewriting the Future in the Maghrib," in *Economic Crisis and Political Change in North Africa,* ed. Azzedine Layachi (Westport, Conn., and London: Praeger, 1998), pp. 1–5; Clement M. Henry, "North Africa's Desperate Regimes" (review article), *Middle East Journal* 59, no. 4 (Summer 2005): 475–484, and "Crises of Money and Power: Transitions to Democracy," in *Islam, Democracy, and the State in North Africa,* ed. John P. Entelis (Bloomington: Indiana University Press, 1997), pp. 177–204; Benjamin Stora, "The Maghrib at the Dawn of the 21st Century," in *The Maghrib in the New Century: Identity, Religion and Politics,* ed. Bruce Maddy-Weitzman and Daniel Zisenwine (Gainesville: University Press of Florida, 2007), pp. 1–9; for a recent interview with Laroui, "Tradition, modernité: le mariage impossible," see *TelQuel,* November 22–28, 2008.

PART III

Chapter Five

1. Daniela Merolla, "Digital Imagination and the 'Landscapes of Group Identities': The Flourishing of Theatre, Video and 'Amazigh Net' in the Maghrib and Berber Diaspora," *Journal of North African Studies* 7, no. 4 (Winter 2002): 122–131.

2. Second World Amazigh Congress, General Assembly, Université libére de Bruxelles, August 7–9, 2000 (an additional expression of the danger that globalization poses to the Amazigh language and culture is at http://www.ipacc.org.za/eng/regional_northafrica.asp [accessed July 31, 2010]).

3. Interview with Hassan Idbelkassem, Rabat, October 2003.

4. Aicha Belhabib, "Mobilisation collective et internationalisation de la question amazighe," in *Usages de l'identité Amazighe au Maroc,* ed. Hassan Rachik (Casablanca: Imprimerie Najah El Jadida, 2006), pp. 167–171.

5. For further context, see Minorities at Risk Project, "Assessment for Tuareg in Niger," December 31, 2003, available at http://www.unhcr.org/refworld/country,,MARP,,NER,456d621e2,469f3ab81e,0.html (accessed June 10, 2010); Kalifa Keita, "Conflict and Conflict Resolution in the Sahel: The Tuareg Insurgency in Mali," *Small Wars & Insurgencies* 9, no. 3 (Winter 1998): 102–128.

6. Adghirni, Idbelkassem, and the London-based Kabyle Salem Mezhoud, according to Belhabib, played central roles in developing the idea of a Congress and drew inspiration from the contact with other groups at the Vienna meeting in June (Belhabib, "Mobilisation collective," pp. 171–172). It is the view of at least one analyst that the concept drew inspiration from the establishment in 1936 of the World Jewish Congress, in Geneva, which would become an important body among the plethora of international Jewish organizations (Maxime Ait Kaki, *De la question berbère au dilemma kabyle à l'aube du XXIeme siècle* [Paris: L'Harmattan, 2004], p. 269).

7. Belhabib, "Mobilisation collective," pp. 174–175.

8. Hsen Larbi, "The Amazigh World Congress," *The Amazigh Voice,* December 1995–March 1996, http://www.ece.umd.edu/~sellami/DEC95/congress.html (accessed July 31, 2010); Belhabib, "Mobilisation collective," p. 176.

9. For a website devoted to promoting awareness and knowledge of the Touareg, see http://www.temoust.org (accessed July 2, 2010).

10. Ait Kaki, *De la question berbère,* pp. 270–276.

11. Ibid., p. 272.

12. Gabi Kratochwil, "Some Observations on the First Amazigh World Congress (27–30 August, Tafira, Canary Islands)," *Die Welt Des Islams* 39, no. 2 (July 1999): 149–158.

13. Ait Kaki, *De la question berbère,* pp. 277–279.

14. "Le CMA poursuit en justice la wilaya de Tizi Ouzou," http://www.presse-dz.com/revue-de-presse/6832-le-cma-poursuit-en-justice-la-wilaya-de-tizi-ouzou.html (accessed June 10, 2010); Omar Berbiche, *El Watan,* July 16, 2008, as appears on http://www.amazighworld.org/human_rights/cma_reports/index.php (accessed July 17, 2008).

15. "5 octobre 2008 Conference de presse de Belkacem Lounes a Tizi-Wezzu," http://www.bladi.net/forum/168540-president-cma-reclame-ouverture-frontiere-algero/ (accessed June 10, 2010).

16. Moh Si Belkacem, "Congrès Mondial Amazigh: A qui profite la déchirure?," n.d., http://www.amazighnews.net/20081027264/A-qui-profite-la-dechirure.html (accessed June 10, 2010).

17. "Lettre du CMA au Parlement Européen," March 9, 2009, http://www.cmamazigh.com/index.php?option=com_content&view=article&id=67:parl&catid=35:tawuri&Itemid=56; http://www.cmamazigh.com/documents/rapport.swf (accessed July 5, 2010).

18. Statement by the Federal Council of the World Amazigh Congress, meeting in Paris November 25–26, 2000 (www.kabyle.com).

19. Ait Kaki, *De la question berbère,* pp. 279–294.

20. "Les Amazighs en visite auprès des instances européennes," http://www.amazighworld.org/human_rights/cma_reports/index_show.php?Id=1547 (accessed June 10, 2010).

21. Jane Goodman, "Imazighen on Trial: Human Rights and Berber Identity in Algeria, 1985," in *Berbers and Others: Shifting Parameters of Ethnicity in the Contemporary*

Maghrib, ed. Susan Gilson Miller and Katherine E. Hoffman (Bloomington: Indiana University Press, 2010), pp. 103–126.

22. According to Aisha al-Rumi, most Libyan Ibadis consider themselves Sunnis and don't have their own separate mosques. Others have sought to forge ties with Oman and its Ibadi heritage and teachings ("Libyan Berbers Struggle to Assert Their Identity Online," *Arab Media and Society,* no. 8 [Summer 2009]: 3–4, http://www.arabmediasociety.com/?article=713 [accessed June 28, 2010]).

23. For various demarches on the subject, see http://www.amazighworld.org/human_rights/libya/index.php (accessed June 10, 2010); "Imazighen en Libye: rapport de Tamazgha au CERD," http://www.tamazgha.fr/article.php3?id_article=541 (accessed May 21, 2010).

24. al-Rumi, "Libyan Berbers Struggle to Assert Their Identity Online," p. 1. Umadi apparently bowed to official pressure and closed down the site in 2009, but it reopened in 2010.

25. "Imazighen en Libye: rapport de Tamazgha au CERD"; United Nations Press Release, Committee on Economic, Social and Cultural Rights Reviews Second Periodic Report of Libya, November 17, 2005, http://tamazgha.fr/The-CESCR-reviews-second-report-of-Libya,1491.html (accessed May 21, 2010).

26. "Libya's Berbers Come In from the Cold," AFP, posted on August 27, 2007, at http://www.alarabiya.net/articles/2007/08/27/38384.html (accessed June 10, 2010).

27. For a thorough analysis of Qaddafi's foreign policies and the motivations behind them, see Yehudit Ronen, *Qaddafi's Libya in World Politics* (Boulder, Colo.: Lynne Rienner, 2008).

28. These tribes, he declared, may themselves have been of Semitic or Eastern origin.

29. See Chapter 1, note 81.

30. Excerpt of March 1, 2007, speech contained in MEMRI Special Dispatch— No. 1535, April 6, 2007, http://memri.org/bin/articles.cgi?Page=archives&Area=sd&ID=SP153507#_edn6 (accessed June 10, 2010).

31. Ibid.

32. Excerpts of the open letter can be found in http://memri.org/bin/articles.cgi?Page=archives&Area=sd&ID=SP156907 (accessed June 10, 2010); the full text can be read at http://www.north-of-africa.com/article.php3?id_article=397 (accessed June 10, 2010).

33. "Libya's Berbers Come In from the Cold."

34. CMA Bureau statement, "Libye: Halte aux appels à la haine anti-amazighe," December 28, 2008, http://www.amazighworld.org/human_rights/cma_reports/index_show.php?Id=1707 (accessed June 10, 2010).

35. "Intense activité de la délégation du Congrès Mondial Amazigh à Genève," April 25, 2009, http://www.drzz.info/article-30671064-6.html (accessed July 31, 2010).

36. This number is probably inflated, even if one uses a broad definition of

what constitutes Amazigh origin. A recent detailed survey in France of language transmission by North African immigrants to their children indicated that approximately 80 percent of them were Arabophones (Alexandra Filhon, *Langues d'ici et d'ailleurs: Transmettre l'arabe et le berbere en France* [Paris: Ined, 2009], pp. 48–49).

37. The fact that fifteen minority languages could be studied only added insult to injury. See "France: Discriminations à l'égard des Amazighs," February 22, 2005, http://forum-francophone.bbactif.com/immigration-et-integration-f65/la-france-rejette-ses-mauvais-immigres-t292.htm (accessed July 1, 2010).

38. Ibid.

39. Paul A. Silverstein, *Algeria in France: Transpolitics, Race and Nation* (Bloomington: Indiana University Press, 2004), p. 7.

40. For a discussion of the Kabyle house (*akham;* alt. *axxam*), in the context of special uprooting and migration engendered by the encounter with colonialism, migration, and modernity, see ibid., Chapter 3.

41. Interview, Paris, October 2003.

42. Filhon, *Langues d'ici et d'ailleurs,* p. 103.

43. Interview with Maxime Ait Kaki, Paris, October 2003.

44. "Plate-forme: Option Amazighe," January 13, 2007, http://www.amazigh world.org/auteur.php?auteur=Groupe%20Option%20Amazighe (accessed May 20, 2010). The point was driven home to me personally in the following manner: in a conversation with a Moroccan Berber activist, I referred to David M. Hart's article, "Scratch a Moroccan, Find a Berber." My interlocutor quickly suggested that the author should have added an addendum: "Scratch a Berber, Find a Jew!"

45. In a discussion of religious festivals in Kabylie, Youcef Allioui wonders whether the Kabyles borrowed the holiday of Nnisan from North African Jews, and relates that his grandfather told him that the inhabitants of a number of Kabylie villages, and Algerians inhabiting other regions as well, were of Jewish origin, while cautioning him not to repeat the information to anyone (Youcef Allioui, *Les archs, tribus berbères de kabylie* [Paris: L'Harmattan, 2006], p. 309). In a January 2010 discussion of the Amazigh question in North Africa on al-Jazeera's English-language television channel, the sociologist Marnia Lazreg noted with astonishment that some young Kabyles were declaring that they were of Jewish origin (http://en glish.aljazeera.net/programmes/insidestory/2010/01/2010121125817226470.html [accessed June 10, 2010]).

46. H. Z. Hirschberg, Norman Stillman, and Daniel Schroeter all reject the older view, promoted by French colonial scholars and the early-twentieth-century traveler and scholar Nahum Slouschz and picked up by other Jewish writers, who assert definitively that the Berber-Jewish synthesis ran very deep in North Africa. Paul Wexler presents an even more controversial thesis, asserting linguistic evidence points to the Berber origin of most Sephardic Jews. H. Z. Hirschberg, "The Problem of the Judaized Berbers," *Journal of African History* 4, no. 3 (1963): 313–339; Norman A. Stillman, *The Jews of Arab Lands: A History and Source Book* (Philadelphia: Jewish Publication Society of America, 1979), pp. 78–80; Daniel Schroeter,

"On the Origins and Identity of Indigenous North African Jews," in *North African Mosaic: A Cultural Reappraisal of Ethnic and Religious Minorities,* ed. Nabil Boudraa and Joseph Krause (Newcastle: Cambridge Scholars Publishing, 2007), pp. 164–177; André N. Chouraqui, *Between East and West: A History of the Jews of North Africa* (Philadelphia: Jewish Publication Society of America, 1968); Haim Zaafrani, "Judaeo-Berber," *Encyclopedia of Islam, New Edition* (Leiden: Brill, 1986), pp. 5:307–308; Paul Wexler, *The Non-Jewish Origins of the Sephardic Jews* (Albany, N.Y.: SUNY Press, 1996); Nahum Slouschz, *Archives Marocaines,* Vol. 14, *Hebreo-Phéniciens et Judéo-Berbères* (Paris: Ernest Leroux, 1908), pp. 365–454; David Corcos, *Studies in the History of the Jews of Morocco* (Jerusalem: Ruben Mass, 1976).

47. Samir Benlayashi and Bruce Maddy-Weitzman, "Myth, History and *Realpolitik:* Morocco's Jewish Community," *Journal of Modern Jewish Studies* 9, no. 1 (March 2010): 89–106.

48. Harvey E. Goldberg, "The Mellahs of Southern Morocco: Report of a Survey," *The Maghreb Review* 8, nos. 3–4 (1983): 61–69, http://www.mondeberbere.com/juifs/mellahs.htm (accessed May 19, 2010).

49. Malika Hachid, *Les Premiers Berbères, Entre Méditerranée, Tassili et Nil* (Alger and Aix-en-Provence: Ina-Yas, Édisud, 2000), p. 311.

50. Paul A. Silverstein, "Islam, *Laïcité,* and Amazigh Activism in France and North Africa," in *North African Mosaic: A Cultural Reappraisal of Ethnic and Religious Minorities,* ed. Nabil Boudraa and Joseph Krause (Newcastle: Cambridge Scholars Publishing, 2007), pp. 104–118.

51. Communicated to me by Paul Silverstein.

52. "An Israeli and Amazigh Friendship Association Project/Projet d'une association d'amitie entre le peuple Amazigh et le peuple Hebreu" (document outlining main objectives, communicated to me by one of the founders).

53. MEMRI, Special Dispatch—No. 1695, August 24, 2007, Debate about New Berber-Jewish Friendship Association in Morocco on Iranian Al-Alam TV, http://www.memri.org/bin/articles.cgi?Page=archives&Area=sd&ID=SP169507 (accessed June 10, 2010).

54. Robin Stoller, "Die vergangenen zwei Monate waren die Hölle" (interview with Mohamed Mouha), http://jungle-world.com/artikel/2008/14/21486.html (accessed June 10, 2010).

55. "Second Berber-Jewish Friendship Association in Morocco," http://www.alarabiya.net/, cited by "The MEMRI Blog," February 5, 2008, http://www.thememriblog.org/blog_personal/en/5125.htm (accessed June 29, 2010).

56. *Al-Sabah* (Casablanca), March 22–23, 2008.

57. Abdallah Saaf, "For Gaza, Moroccan Civil Society Reveals Itself as a Political Society," *Arab Reform Initiative* e-letter, February 1, 2009, http://arab-reform.net/spip.php?article1793 (accessed May 20, 2010).

58. *Al-Tajdid,* January 14, 2009, quoted in MEMRI, Special Dispatch—No. 2262, February 26, 2009, "Berbers, Where Do You Stand on Palestine?," http://www.memri.org/report/en/0/0/0/0/0/0/3171.htm (accessed June 10, 2010).

59. www.hespress.com, January 23, 2009, quoted in ibid.

60. Ahmed Asid, "Aynkum, Ya Arab?," January 24, 2009, http://www.maghress .com/dalilrif/1824 (accessed July 31, 2010).

61. Moha Moukhlis, "Intégrisme, Gaza et Tamazight. Pour L'Amour De La Vie," January 23, 2009, http://www.amazighworld.org/news/index_show.php?id=1734 (accessed May 20, 2010); Kabyle writers cited in MEMRI, Special Dispatch No. 2262, "Berbers, Where Do You Stand on Palestine?"

62. *Al-Jarida al-Awla,* November 18, 2009; *al-Masa'a,* November 18, 30, 2009; *Maghrib al-Yawm,* December 3, 2009; *al-Arab,* December 4, 2009; *al-Sharq al-Awsat,* January 6, 2010.

PART III

Chapter Six

1. Samuel Huntington, *Political Order in Changing Societies* (New Haven, Conn.: Yale University Press, 1968), pp. 177–191.

2. Abdelsalam Maghraoui, "Depoliticization in Morocco," *Journal of Democracy* 13, no. 4 (October 2002): 24–32; Daniel Zisenwine, "From Hassan II to Muhammad VI: Plus Ça Change?," in *The Maghrib in the New Century: Identity, Religion and Politics,* ed. Bruce Maddy-Weitzman and Daniel Zisenwine (Gainesville: University Press of Florida, 2007), pp. 132–149.

3. For the richest treatment of the entire subject in North Africa, see Mounira M. Charrad, *States and Women's Rights: The Making of Postcolonial Tunisia, Algeria, and Morocco* (Berkeley and Los Angeles: University of California Press, 2001); for an account of the reform efforts in Morocco, see Bruce Maddy-Weitzman, "Women, Islam and the Moroccan State: The Struggle over the Personal Status Law," *Middle East Journal* 59, no. 3 (Summer 2005): 393–410; see also Maddy-Weitzman, "Population Growth and Family Planning in Morocco," *Asian and African Studies* 26, no. 1 (March 1992): 63–79, http://www.dayan.org/articles/POPULATION_GROWTH .pdf (accessed June 13, 2010).

4. *L'Economiste,* October 13, 2003.

5. For a critical, in-depth review of this process, see Susan Slymovics, *The Performance of Human Rights in Morocco* (Philadelphia: University of Pennsylvania Press, 2005). For an update on the human rights situation in Morocco, see Younes Alami and Ali Amar, "The Security and Intelligence Dossier—Morocco: To Tell the Truth," *Le Monde Diplomatique,* April 2005, http://mondediplo.com/2005/04/06morocco (accessed April 14, 2005).

6. According to *Le Monde Amazigh,* the commission's session in al-Hoceima, in the Rif, was delayed a number of times owing to the fear of the Istiqlal Party that it would be implicated in the 1956–1959 violence there (see Chapter 3) (*Le Monde Amazigh,* no. 61 [June 2005]: 6).

7. Aziz Chahir, "Leadership politique amazigh," in *Usages de l'identité Ama-*

zighe au Maroc, ed. Hassan Rachik (Casablanca: Imprimerie Najah El Jadida, 2006), p. 209 n. 281.

8. James Ketterer, "Networks of Discontent in Northern Morocco: Drugs, Opposition and Urban Unrest," *Middle East Report,* no. 218 (Spring 2001), http://www.merip.org/mer/mer218/218_ketterer.html (accessed May 20, 2010).

9. Tony Allen-Mills and Nick Pelham, "King Unlocks Father's Skeleton Closet," *The Sunday Times,* October 18, 1999.

10. Adel Darwish, "Mohammed's First 100 Days," *The Middle East,* December 1999, pp. 16–18.

11. Ibid., p. 18. This was not, however, the flag used by Abdelkrim.

12. *TelQuel,* July 26–August 1, 2008.

13. Sebastian Balfour, *Deadly Embrace: Morocco and the Road to the Spanish Civil War* (Oxford: Oxford University Press, 2002).

14. "Gaz Toxique Contre Le Rif," *Le Monde Amazigh,* no. 43 (March 2004): 13 (article originally published in *Nador,* February 18, 2004); "Before the Hiroshima and Nagasaki Bombs, the Rif Resistance Was Confronted with the Use of Weapons of Mass Destruction" (in Arabic), *Le Monde Amazigh,* no. 44 (April 2004): 4–6 (report on a conference addressing Spain's use of poison gas in the Rif war).

15. Resumé de l'intervention de Mimoun Charki, "Pour Des Revendications, Aux Fins De Reparations, Pour Les Prejudices Subis Suite a L'Utilisation D'Armes Chimiques De Destructions Massives Dans Le Rif," *Le Monde Amazigh,* no. 44 (April 2004): 4; *Maroc Hebdo International,* December 10–16, 2004.

16. Salma Salsa, "L'Espagne et ses bombes toxiques sur le Rif. Nous ne pouvons pas oublier ce crime contre l'humanité," *El Mundo,* July 5, 2008, translated from the Spanish by Mohamed Sihaddou, http://www.emarrakech.info/L-Espagne-et-ses-bombes-toxiques-sur-le-Rif_a15270.html (accessed May 20, 2010).

17. *Le Monde Amazigh,* no. 46 (June 2004): 4–5.

18. Samir Benlayashi, "Secularism in the Moroccan-Amazigh Discourse," *Journal of North African Studies* 12, no. 7 (June 2007): 153–171.

19. The text of the Manifesto in English and French can be found at http://www.mondeberbere.com/societe/manifest-index-en.htm (accessed June 11, 2010).

20. Le Document, "Que Veulent Les Berbères," *Jeune Afrique/L'Intelligent,* April 24–May 7, 2001, pp. 100–111.

21. Chahir, "Leadership politique amazigh," p. 209.

22. Moha Arehal, "Histoire du Mouvement Amazigh au Maroc, Amazighes apres l'instauration de l'Etat Nation, 4 et fin," *Le Monde Amazigh,* no. 70 (March 2006).

23. http://www.maroc.ma/NR/exeres/B7C145A9-1B87-48EC-AB9C-61B52169A592 (accessed June 13, 2010).

24. Mohamed Benhlal, *Le collège d'Azrou: Une élite berbère civile et militaire au maroc (1927-1959)* (Paris and Aix-en-Provence: Éditions Karthala, IREMAM, 2005), pp. 315–316.

25. Arehal, "Histoire du Mouvement Amazigh au Maroc"; interviews with various activists conducted in Morocco in February 2006.

26. Mickael Bensadoun, "The (Re-)Fashioning of Moroccan National Identity," in *The Maghrib in the New Century: Identity, Religion and Politics,* ed. Bruce Maddy-Weitzman and Daniel Zisenwine (Gainesville: University Press of Florida, 2007), pp. 13–35.

27. *Le Monde Amazigh,* nos. 29, 31, 32, 33, 34, 39 (November 2002, February, March, April, May, November 2003), the last containing the report of the imam's remonstration of his congregants for using Tamazight.

28. http://www.mondeberbere.com/societe/manifest-index-en.htm (accessed June 11, 2010).

29. Interviews with Amazigh activists, Rabat, October 2003.

30. *Le Monde Amazigh,* no. 29 (November 2002): 17.

31. L. Walnaʿam, "Al-Khitab al-Islamawi wal-Khat al-Ansab Likitabat al-Amazighiyya," *Le Monde Amazigh,* no. 29 (November 2002): 4.

32. Meryam Demnati, "Royal Amazigh Institute: Worries for Imazighen," *Amazigh Voice* 10, nos. 3–4 (Winter/Spring 2002): 14.

33. B. Anghir, "Dawr Hizb al-Adala wal-Tanmiyya fi Taʾtil al-Tanmiyya wa Munahadat al-Adala," *Le Monde Amazigh,* no. 32 (March 2003): 27. For background on the issue, see Bruce Maddy-Weitzman, "Morocco," in *Middle East Contemporary Survey (MECS),* Vol. 24 (2000) (Boulder, Colo.: Westview, 2002), pp. 427–429.

34. *Le Monde Amazigh,* no. 29 (November 2002): 17.

35. Remarks delivered upon receiving Prince Claus Award, 2002.

36. H. Larbi, "Which Script for Tamazight, Whose Choice Is It?," *Amazigh Voice* 12, no. 2 (Summer/Fall 2003): 3–8. Also based on interviews with Amazigh scholars and activists, Rabat, October 2003.

37. "La monarchie marocaine impose une transcription pour Tamazight," interview with Salem Chaker, February 2003, http://www.tamazgha.fr/La-monarchie-marocaine-impose-une-transcription-pour-tamazight,051.html (accessed June 13, 2010).

38. *Al-Tajdid,* February 3, 2003, cited in Press Review, Ambassade De France Au Maroc, http://www.ambafrance-ma.org/presse/index.html (accessed March 25, 2003).

39. Mohamed Chtatou, a leading educator specializing in the Rifian dialect, told me that they are worthless (interview, February 2006, Rabat).

40. Mohammed Errihani, "Language Policy in Morocco: Problems and Prospects of Teaching Tamazight," *Journal of North African Studies* 11, no. 2 (June 2006): 143–154; Elizabeth Buckner, "Language Drama in Morocco: Another Perspective on the Problems and Prospects of Teaching Tamazight," *Journal of North African Studies* 11, no. 4 (December 2006): 421–433; Arehal, "Histoire du Mouvement Amazigh au Maroc."

41. Buckner, "Language Drama in Morocco."

42. Mohammed Errihani, "Language Attitudes and Language Use in Morocco:

Effects of Attitudes on 'Berber Language Policy,'" *Journal of North African Studies* 13, no. 4 (December 2008): 411–428.

43. After repeated delays, an Amazigh television channel was officially launched in January 2010, broadcasting initially for six hours daily (18:00–24:00) and ten hours on the weekends. Seventy percent of the content was to be in one or another of Morocco's three main Amazigh dialects, and the other 30 percent in Arabic (http://www.magharebia.com/cocoon/awi/xhtml1/en_GB/features/awi/features/2010/01/11/feature-02; http://www.itnsource.com/shot list//RTV/2010/01/11/RTV72210/ [accessed June 13, 2010]).

44. Interviews with Amazigh activists, Rabat, February 2006.

45. Interviews with Boukous and Chafik, February 2006.

46. http://www.amazighworld.org/countries/morocco/documents/option_amazighe.php (accessed June 29, 2010).

47. Interview with Asid, http://www.magharebia.com/cocoon/awi/xhtml1/en_GB/features/awi/articles/2006/04/25/feature-02 (accessed June 29, 2010).

48. Of course, the question of a constitutionally determined "official language" did not exist at that time.

49. *Al-Ahdath al-Maghrabiyya,* November 15, 2006.

50. *Al-Najah fi al-Ijtimaʿiyyat: al-Sana al-Sadisa min al-Taʿlim al-Ibtidaʾi* (Casablanca: Imprimerie Najah El Jadida, 2006), pp. 24–36, 41, 46.

51. Injaz Abdallah Habibi, "Collective Lands from Joint Tribal Ownership to State Administrative Control: An Example from the Zayan [Zaiane] Tribes in the Khenifra Region" (in Arabic), *Le Monde Amazigh,* no. 52 (November 2004): 4–5.

52. For a sensitive and loving account of one educated Kabyle's return to his native village and the aesthetics of his mother's housekeeping, see Rabah Seffal, "Remember Me?," *The World & I,* September 1992, pp. 612–623.

53. Muhammad Aswayq, "Manthuma al-Qiyam al-Amazighiyya: Mafahim lil-fikr wal-tarikh wal-hadatha," *Le Monde Amazigh,* no. 52 (November 2004): 12.

54. This section is based on Didier Le Saout, "La radicalization de la revendication amazighe au Maroc. Le sud-est comme imaginaire militant," in *L'Année du Maghreb,* Vol. 5 (2009) (Paris: CNRS Éditions, 2009), pp. 75–93.

55. The appeal of the Amazigh discourse was explained by one interviewee: "[It] is real. It talks about my mother, it talks about my father, it speaks of the culture of Tinghir, my region, of my neighborhood. This is something that is real, which is close to me. This is not about Islam or Islamists. . . . I know nothing of Iraq and Palestine." In ibid., p. 91.

56. "L'État marocain et la question amazighe," Rapport alternative de Tamazgha au Comité des droits économiques, sociaux et culturels, Nations Unies, Conseil Économique e Social, 36eme session du Comité des droits économiques sociaux et culturels, Genève, 1er au 19 mai 2006.

57. Hassan Benmehdi, "Moroccan Authorities Refuse to Register Amazigh Names," June 10, 2008, http://www.magharebia.com/cocoon/awi/xhtml1/en_GB/features/awi/features/2008/06/10/feature-01 (accessed May 18, 2010). For a

recent court judgment against a family's efforts to compel the authorities to register their daughter with an Amazigh first name, and the angry response of the "Azetta" association, see http://www.forumalternatives.org/rac/article266.html (accessed June 13, 2010).

58. "Letter to Morocco Interior Minister Benmoussa on the Refusal of Amazigh Names," June 16, 2009, http://www.hrw.org/en/news/2009/09/02/letter-morocco-interior-minister-benmoussa-refusal-amazigh-names (accessed July 5, 2010); "Morocco: Lift Restrictions on Amazigh (Berber) Names," September 3, 2009, http://www.hrw.org/en/news/2009/09/03/morocco-lift-restrictions-amazigh-berber-names (accessed July 5, 2010).

59. "L'État marocain et la question amazighe."

60. Tension between Sahrawis and Berbers is rooted in another, more concrete dimension as well. Many Berbers in the south and southeast are resentful of the Sahrawis in Morocco for having benefited from state largesse, including pensions, housing allowances, and school subsidies. Their acquiring of grazing rights across Berber tribal lands has also come into play (communicated to me by Paul Silverstein). Of course, the *makhzen*'s generosity is a calculated policy to ensure the successful incorporation of the disputed Western Sahara territory into the Moroccan kingdom.

61. http://www.tamazgha.org/1/post/2008/02/warzazat-morocco-10-amazigh-activists-get-heavy-sentences.html (accessed June 13, 2010).

62. http://www.north-of-africa.com/article.php3?id_article=537 (accessed June 13, 2010).

63. http://en.rsf.org/morocco-jail-sentences-for-blogger-and-16-12-2009,35349.html (accessed June 13, 2010).

64. http://www.moroccoboard.com/news/409-amazigh-conference-banned-in-casablanca (accessed March 29, 2009).

PART III

Chapter Seven

1. For a fuller account of Bouteflika's consolidation of power during this decade, see Gideon Gera, "Reflections on the Aftermath of Civil Strife: Algeria, 2006," in *The Maghrib in the New Century: Identity, Religion and Politics,* ed. Bruce Maddy-Weitzman and Daniel Zisenwine (Gainesville: University Press of Florida, 2007), pp. 75–102. For discussions regarding the Algerian economy, see Ahmed Aghrout and Michael Hodd, "Algeria's Economy: Mutations, Performance, and Challenges," in ibid., pp. 217–233; and Ahmed Aghrout, "Policy Reforms in Algeria: Genuine Change or Adjustments?," in *North Africa: Politics, Region, and the Limits of Transformation,* ed. Yahia H. Zoubir and Haizam Amirah-Fernández (London and New York: Routledge, 2008), pp. 31–52.

2. The International Crisis Group report on the events, the most thorough and nuanced account made, speaks of 123 dead and many more injured, with some maimed for life (International Crisis Group, "Algeria: Unrest and Impasse in Kabylia," Middle East/North Africa Report N° 15, June 10, 2003, http://www.crisisgroup.org/~/media/Files/Middle%20East%20North%20Africa/North%20Africa/Algeria/Algeria%20Unrest%20and%20Impasse%20in%20Kabylia.ashx [accessed May 21, 2010]); Martin Evans and John Phillips report around 200 fatalities (*Algeria: Anger of the Dispossessed* [New Haven, Conn.: Yale University Press, 2008], pp. 275–277); Lucy Dean, ed., *The Middle East and North Africa, 2009* (London: Routledge, 2008), p. 199.

3. International Crisis Group, "Algeria: Unrest and Impasse in Kabylia," pp. 9–10; Evans and Phillips, *Algeria: Anger of the Dispossessed*, p. 277; Dean, *The Middle East and North Africa, 2009*, p. 200; "Dernier rapport de la Commission nationale d'enquête sur les événéments de Kabylie," Décembre 2001, published in *La Jeune Indépendant*, December 30, 2001, http://www.algeria-watch.org/farticle/revolte/issad_complement.htm (accessed May 21, 2010).

4. Evans and Phillips, *Algeria: Anger of the Dispossessed*, p. 275.

5. *Le Monde*, May 2, 2001, cited by Robert Mortimer, "Algeria," in *Africa Contemporary Record (ACR)*, Vol. 28 (2001–2002) (Teaneck, N.J.: Africana Publishing, 2006), p. B599.

6. Mortimer, "Algeria," p. B600.

7. For a rich discussion of the phenomenon, see International Crisis Group, "Algeria: Unrest and Impasse in Kabylia."

8. Hugh Roberts, "Co-opting Identity: The Manipulation of Berberism, the Frustration of Democratisation, and the Generation of Violence in Algeria," Crisis States Programme Working Papers, no. 7 (December 2001) (http://www.crisisstates.com/download/wp/WP7HR.pdf [accessed May 20, 2010]), passim.

9. The text of the El-Kseur Platform is contained in International Crisis Group, "Algeria: Unrest and Impasse in Kabylia," Appendix C, p. 38.

10. Dean, *The Middle East and North Africa, 2009*, p. 200.

11. "Le Occidental Doron: Hussein Ayat Ahmad Accuses Mafia of Destabilizing Berber Area," Arabicnews.com, August 20, 2002 (http://www.arabicnews.com/ansub/Daily/Day/020820/2002082004.html [accessed June 14, 2010]).

12. Dean, *The Middle East and North Africa, 2009*, p. 201; http://www.magharebia.com/cocoon/awi/xhtml1/en_GB/features/awi/features/2005/09/30/feature-01 (accessed June 14, 2010); Evans and Phillips, *Algeria: Anger of the Dispossessed*, p. 290.

13. Gera, "Reflections on the Aftermath of Civil Strife," p. 86.

14. For two texts addressing the matter, see "Interview accordée a Arzeki Aït-Larbi," *Liberté*, February 21–22, 1995, pp. 4, 11, and Salem Chaker's article in *Le Monde*, July 11, 1998, contained in Salem Chaker, *Berbères Aujourd'hui*, 2nd ed. (Paris and Montreal: L'Harmattan, 1998), pp. 196–206.

15. For a discussion on the continuous interactions among civil society, the

state, and ethnicity as essential underpinnings of democratic nationhood, see George Schöpflin, *Nations, Identity, Power* (New York: New York University Press, 2000), Chapter 3.

16. The framework for the Code is the Shariʿa (Marnia Lazreg, *The Eloquence of Silence: Algerian Women in Question* [New York: Routledge, 1994], pp. 150–157; Mounira M. Charrad, *States and Women's Rights: The Making of Postcolonial Tunisia, Algeria, and Morocco* [Berkeley and Los Angeles: University of California Press, 2001], pp. 183–200). Some modifications were made in 2005. The entire issue of women's status, in law and in society, remains highly contested (Doris Gray, "Women in Algeria Today and the Debate over Family Law," *MERIA Journal* 13, no. 1 [March 2005], http://www.gloria-center.org/meria/2009/03/gray.html [accessed May 19, 2010]).

17. Ferhat Mehenni, *Algérie: la question kabyle* (Paris: Éditions Michalon, 2004), p. 184.

18. Interview with Ferhat Mehenni, Paris, October 2003.

19. Ferhat Mehenni, "The Autonomy of Kabylia in Questions," first published in French by Stéphane Arrami (Kabyle.com), May 25, 2002, translated by Michelle Duvall, http://waac.info/amazigh/politics/algeria/autonomy/ferhat_autonomy_in_questions.html (accessed January 27, 2004).

20. International Crisis Group, "Algeria: Unrest and Impasse in Kabylia," p. 28.

21. Roberts, "Co-opting Identity," pp. 33–38; International Crisis Group, "Algeria: Unrest and Impasse in Kabylia," pp. 24–26.

22. "Official request for an autonomy status for Kabylia," Tuesday, June 24, 2008, http://www.kabylia.info/official-request-autonomy-status-kabylia (posted October 29, 2008); the original French text can be found at http://mak.makabylie .info/Demande-officielle-d-une-autonomie?lang=fr (accessed June 14, 2010).

23. "Ferhat Mehenni Proposes Kabylie 'Provisional Government,'" http://www .magharebia.com/cocoon/awi/xhtml1/en/features/awi/features/2010/06/09/ feature-02 (accessed July 5, 2010); Provisional Government of Kabylia, http:// www.kabylia-gov.org/?lang=en (accessed July 5, 2010).

24. *Al-Sharq al-Awsat,* July 16, 2001 (Foreign Broadcast Information Service, Near East and Asia, Daily Report).

25. Evans and Phillips, *Algeria: Anger of the Dispossessed,* photo insert between pp. 176 and 177.

26. Mohamed Benrabah, "The Language Planning Situation in Algeria," *Current Issues in Linguistic Planning* 6, no. 4 (2005): 379–502, quotation from p. 383, citing *El Watan,* August 3, 1999.

27. International Crisis Group, "Algeria: Unrest and Impasse in Kabylia," p. 33.

28. http://www.search.com/reference/Abdelaziz_Bouteflika (accessed July 1, 2010).

29. Hafid Gafaïti, "The Monotheism of the Other: Language and De/Construction of National Identity in Postcolonial Algeria" (pp. 19–43), and Lucette Valensi,

"The Scheherazade Syndrome" (pp. 139–153), in *Algeria in Others' Languages,* ed. Anne-Emmanuelle Berger (Ithaca, N.Y.: Cornell University Press, 2002).

30. Lyes Aflou, "Amazigh Language Teaching in Algeria Lacks Standardisation, Qualified Teachers," December 10, 2006, http://www.magharebia.com/cocoon/awi/xhtml1/en_GB/features/awi/features/2006/12/10/feature-01 (accessed May 18, 2010); "L'enseignement du Tamazight en Algérie piétine," December 6, 2006, http://www.algerie-dz.com/article7301.html (accessed June 14, 2010); "Algérie, stagnation de l'enseignement de la langue amazighe," interview reported on www.LeMonde.fr, http://www.bladi.net/forum/83062-algerie-stagnation-lenseignement-langue-amazighe/ (accessed June 14, 2010).

31. Aflou, "Amazigh Language Teaching in Algeria."

32. Bahbouh Lehsene, "Haut Commissariat à l'Amazighité, 13 ans après," http://www.kabyle.com/haut-commissariat-%C3%A0-lamazighit%C3%A9-13-ans-apr%C3%A8s-470-090908.html (accessed May 20, 2010).

33. "L'enseignement du Tamazight en Algérie piétine."

34. Letter from Belkacem Lounès, October 14, 2006, "Le CMA écrit au Professeur Dourari," published in *Racines-Izuran,* no. 10 (October 23–November 5, 2006): 10.

35. *Racines-Izuran,* no. 12 (November 6–19, 2006).

36. "La monarchie marocaine impose une transcription pour Tamazight," interview with Salem Chaker, February 2003, http://www.tamazgha.fr/La-monarchie-marocaine-impose-une-transcription-pour-tamazight,051.html (accessed June 13, 2010).

37. L'Hocine Ukerdis, "Kabylie: Plus rien à attendre du pouvoir central," August 24, 2006, http://www.kabyle.com/archives/Kabylie-plus-rien-a-attendre-du.html (accessed August 2, 2010).

38. Aicha Lemsine, "Berberism: An Historical Travesty in Algeria's Time of Travail," *Washington Report on Middle East Affairs,* January/February 1995, pp. 31, 89–90.

39. "Berriane, Hogra and the Spread of Berberism," February 24, 2009, http://themoornextdoor.wordpress.com/2009/02/24/berriane-hogra-and-the-growth-of-berberism/ (accessed June 14, 2010).

40. For details on the statue, see A. Maachi, "Khenchela/Baghaï aura sa reine El-Kahina," *El Watan,* August 16, 2001 (appears on http://www.aureschaouia.free.fr).

41. Amar Naït Messaoud, "L'impasse intellectuelle des 'mandarins,'" http://www.depechedekabylie.com/national/75072-limpasse-intellectuelle-des-mandarins.html (accessed July 5, 2010).

42. The superimposed image of the Amazigh flag, viewed on March 4, 2005, was later removed from the site (http://aureschaouia.free.fr), and I have not been able to find it anywhere else. A picture of the statue, including the Arabic-language inscription on its pedestal, can be found at "Histoire d'une grande reine Amazighe:

Dihia (Kahina)," http://aokas-aitsmail.forumactif.info/histoire-f15/histoire-d-une-grande-reine-amazighe-dihia-kahina-t896.htm (accessed July 1, 2010).

43. "Khenchela: Kasr El-Kahina en peril," *Le Journal des locales,* December 5, 2004, http://aureschaouia.free.fr (accessed March 4, 2005).

44. According to one source, Bouteflika's predecessor, Liamine Zeroual, had agreed to name the airport after Imadghacen, but Bouteflika then altered the decision (http://archbis.one-forum.net/cours-et-recherches-f3/medghassen-medra cen-t54.htm [accessed July 1, 2010]). An approving report on a high-budget film dramatizing Boulaïd's life appeared on another website devoted to the Aures region, highlighting the difficulty of prioritizing one's icons (Samira Hadj Amar, "Mustapha Ben Boulaid: Une légende vivante!," *Le Soir d'Algérie,* September 15, 2008, http://membres.multimania.fr/auresnews/article00.htm [accessed July 4, 2010]).

45. http://aureschaouia.free.fr (accessed July 1, 2010).

46. "BATNA: Menaces sur le mausolée amazigh d'Imadghacen," September 5, 2003, http://www.kabyle.com/archives/BATNA-Menaces-sur-le-mausolee.html (accessed July 4, 2010).

47. Moh Cherbi and Thierry Deslot, *La Kahena, Reine des Berbères* (Algiers: EDIF, 2000/Paris: Éditions-Mediterranée, 2002/Casablanca: La Croisée des Chemins, 2002), p. 41.

48. International Crisis Group, "Algeria: Unrest and Impasse in Kabylia," pp. 29–30.

49. *La Dépêche De Kabylie,* January 7, 2004 (http://www.depechedekabylie .com/).

50. Dean, *The Middle East and North Africa, 2009,* p. 201.

51. Gera, "Reflections on the Aftermath of Civil Strife," pp. 86–87, 90.

52. *Le Monde,* April 10, 19, 2004.

53. The text of the declaration can be found at http://www.google.com/gwt/ n?u=http://www.aarach.com/dialogue/protocole_d.htm&hl=en&source=m (accessed June 14, 2010).

54. *Le Dépêche de Kabylie,* June 17, September 25, 2008, http://www.depeche dekabylie.com/national/56864-nous-nous-diregeons-tout-droit-vers-une-autre-implosion.html and http://www.depechedekabylie.com/evenement/60988-ab rika-trois-ses-compagnons-arretes.html (accessed July 1, 2010).

55. Hugh Roberts, "Algeria: The Subterranean Logics of a Non-election," Real Instituto Elcano, ARI 68/2009, April 22, 2009.

56. Bualem Ghomarasa, "Amazigh al-Jaza'ir Yahsulun Li-Awal Mara ala al-Mushaf Mutarjaman," *Al-Sharq al-Awsat,* August 20, 2009, http://aawsat.com/ print.asp?did=532572&issueno=11233 (accessed August 20, 2009).

57. Nouri Lumendifi, "Qaradawi à Tizi-Ouzou," October 20, 2008, http:// www.afrique-du-nord.com/article.php3?id_article=1424 (accessed May 20, 2010).

58. Karina Direche, "Évangelisation en Algérie: débats sur la liberté de culte," in *L'Année du Maghreb,* Vol. 5 (2009) (Paris: CNRS Éditions, 2009), pp. 275–284.

59. For a degree of nuance and detail not found elsewhere, see "Berriane in Context," on the blog "The Moor Next Door," February 6, 2009, and subsequent posts, http://themoornextdoor.wordpress.com/2009/02/06/berriane-in-context/ (accessed June 14, 2010); and Michael Collins Dunn, "Backgrounder: Ibadi-Sunni Violence in Algeria," February 1, 2009, http://mideasti.blogspot .com/2009/02/backgrounder-sunni-ibadi-violence-in.html (accessed June 14, 2010).

CONCLUSION

1. For insightful looks at various expressions of religious sensibilities among Berber communities, see Judith Scheele, "Recycling Baraka: Knowledge, Politics, and Religion in Contemporary Algeria," *Comparative Studies in Society and History* 49, no. 2 (April 2007): 304–328; Jillali El-Adani, "Regionalism, Islamism and Amazigh Identity: Translocality in the Sus Region of Morocco According to Muhammed Mukhtar Soussi," *Comparative Studies of South Asia, Africa and the Middle East* 27, no. 1 (2007): 41–51; for a trenchant criticism of the radical secular Berberist adoption of the French *laïcité* model, at the expense of other, deeply rooted features in Kabyle political culture and society, see Hugh Roberts, "Co-opting Identity: The Manipulation of Berberism, the Frustration of Democratisation, and the Generation of Violence in Algeria," Crisis States Programme Working Papers, no. 7 (December 2001) (http://www.crisisstates.com/download/wp/WP7HR.pdf [accessed May 20, 2010]).

2. International Crisis Group, "Algeria: Unrest and Impasse in Kabylia," Middle East/North Africa Report N° 15, June 10, 2003, http://www.crisisgroup .org/~/media/Files/Middle%20East%20North%20Africa/North%20Africa/ Algeria/Algeria%20Unrest%20and%20Impasse%20in%20Kabylia.ashx (accessed May 21, 2010), pp. 17–19.

3. Personal communiqué, December 6, 2008.

4. See the cover story, the interview with Dr. Mohamed Chami, and accompanying articles trumpeting self-rule in the Rif as a "democratic demand" in *Le Monde Amazigh,* December 2006, pp. 4–6. For a lengthy petition putting forth the demand for autonomy, signed by scores of Rifian Amazigh activists, see "For a greater autonomy in the Rif," March 3, 2008, http://www.north-of-africa.com/ article.php3?id_article=475 (accessed July 6, 2010).

5. In addition, General Liamine Zeroual, president from 1996 to 1999, is a Chaoui. The Kabyle Kasdi Merbah was the powerful head of the intelligence services from 1962 to 1979 and Benjedid's prime minister during the crucial years of 1988–1989. For details, including the names of key Kabyle and Chaoui officials, see International Crisis Group, "Algeria: Unrest and Impasse in Kabylia," p. 5, and especially nn. 14–16.

6. Fanny Colonna, "The Nation's 'Unknowing Other': Three Intellectuals

and the Culture(s) of Being Algerian, or the Impossibility of Subaltern Studies in Algeria," *Journal of North African Studies* 8, no. 1 (Spring 2003): 155–170.

7. Interview with *L'Express,* November 24, 2005, http://www.tamazgha.fr/ article.php3?id_article=1529 (accessed June 15, 2010).

8. Amrane, a Kabyle Algerian nationalist activist then in secondary school in Algiers, composed "Ekker a Mmis Umazigh" in 1945. Its lyrics express both a pan-Amazigh identity, geographically and historically, and a strong identification with an Algeria struggling to break free of colonialism. In 1995, Amrane would be appointed the head of the Algerian state-sponsored Amazigh High Commission (HCA). One year after his death in 2004, the Algerian Cultural Center in Paris would hold a special commemorative event in honor of his life and work. For the text of the anthem in Taqbaylit and French, a report on the event, and online responses that deem him not sufficiently militant, see http://www.kabyle.com/ archives/Hommage-a-Mohand-u-idir-Ait-Amrane.html (accessed June 15, 2010).

9. Communicated to me by Khalid Hajjiou.

10. http://www.amazighworld.org/news/index_show.php?id=298 (accessed June 15, 2010).

11. Miroslav Hroch, "Social and Territorial Characteristics in the Composition of the Leading Groups of National Movements," in Hroch, *Social Preconditions of National Revival in Europe: A Comparative Analysis of the Social Composition of Patriotic Groups among the Smaller European Nations* (New York: Columbia University Press, 2000), p. 67.

12. David Crawford, "How 'Berber' Matters in the Middle of Nowhere," *Middle East Report,* no. 219 (Summer 2001): 20–25.

13. Quoted in *Kabylie, L'autonome en Débat* (Paris: Seminaire D'Ecancourt, 2002), p. 72.

14. Paul A. Silverstein, "France's *Mare Nostrum:* Colonial and Post-Colonial Constructions of the French Mediterranean," *Journal of North African Studies* 7, no. 4 (Winter 2002): 1–22.

15. Paul Balta, ed., *La Méditerranée réinventée: Réalités et espoirs de la coopération* (Paris: Éditions La Découverte/Fondation René Seydoux, 1992); Wolfgang Freund, ed., *L'emergence d'une nouvelle culture méditerranéene— The Emergence of a New Mediterranean Culture* (Frankfurt am Main: Peter Lang, Europaischer Verlag der Wissenchaften, 2000).

16. Interviews conducted in Rabat, February 2006.

17. *Al-Amazighiyya al-An* (Kenitra, Morocco: Al-Bukeili Publishing, 1998), pp. 11, 23.

SOURCES

BOOKS AND ARTICLES

Aboulkacem, El Khatir. "Etre berbère ou amazigh dans le Maroc modern: histoire d'une connotation négative." In *Berbères ou Arab? Le tango des specialists,* ed. Hélène Claudot-Hawad, pp. 115–135. Aix-en-Provence: Non Lieu/IREMAMM, 2006.

Abrous, Dahbia. "Le Haut Commissariat à L'Amazighité, ou le méandres d'une phagocytose." *Annuaire de l'Afrique du Nord* 34 (1995): 583–590. Paris: CNRS Editions, 1997.

Abun-Nasr, Jamil. *A History of the Maghrib in the Islamic Period.* 2nd ed. Cambridge: Cambridge University Press, 1987.

Aflou, Lyes. "Amazigh Language Teaching in Algeria Lacks Standardisation, Qualified Teachers." December 10, 2006. http://www.magharebia.com/cocoon/awi/xhtml1/en_GB/features/awi/features/2006/12/10/feature-01 (accessed May 18, 2010).

Ageron, Charles-Robert. *Modern Algeria.* Trenton, N.J.: Africa World Press, 1991.

Aghrout, Ahmed. "Policy Reforms in Algeria: Genuine Change or Adjustments?" In *North Africa: Politics, Region, and the Limits of Transformation,* ed. Yahia H. Zoubir and Haizam Amirah-Fernández, pp. 31–52. London and New York: Routledge, 2008.

Aghrout, Ahmed, and Michael Hodd. "Algeria's Economy: Mutations, Performance, and Challenges." In *The Maghrib in the New Century: Identity, Religion and Politics,* ed. Bruce Maddy-Weitzman and Daniel Zisenwine, pp. 217–233. Gainesville: University Press of Florida, 2007.

Ait Kaki, Maxime. *De la question berbère au dilemma kabyle à l'aube du XXIème siècle.* Paris: L'Harmattan, 2004.

Alami, Younes, and Ali Amar. "The Security and Intelligence Dossier—Morocco: To Tell the Truth." *Le Monde Diplomatique,* April 2005. http://mondediplo .com/2005/04/06morocco (accessed April 14, 2005).

Allioui, Youcef. *Les archs, tribus berbères de kabylie.* Paris: L'Harmattan, 2006.

Al-Amazighiyya al-An. Kenitra, Morocco: Al-Bukeili Publishing, 1998.

Amrouche, Fadhma. *My Life Story: The Autobiography of a Berber Woman.* New Brunswick, N.J.: Rutgers University Press, 1989.

Anderson, Benedict. *Imagined Communities.* 2nd ed. London and New York: Verso, 1991.

Anghir, B. "Dawr Hizb al-Adala wal-Tanmiyya fi Ta'til al-Tanmiyya wa Munahadat al-'Adala." *Le Monde Amazigh,* no. 32 (March 2003): 17.

Ansari, Hamied. *Egypt, the Stalled Society.* Albany, N.Y.: SUNY Press, 1986.

Applegate, Joseph R. "The Berber Languages." In *Current Trends in Linguistics,* ed. Thomas A. Seebok. Vol. 6, *Linguistics in South West Asia and North Africa,* pp. 586–661. The Hague: Mouton, 1970.

Arehal, Moha. "Histoire du Mouvement Amazigh au Maroc, Amazighes apres l'instauration de l'Etat Nation, 4 et fin." *Le Monde Amazigh,* no. 70 (March 2006).

Arkoun, Mohamed. "Algeria." In *The Politics of Islamic Revivalism: Diversity and Unity,* ed. Shireen T. Hunter, pp. 171–186. Bloomington: Indiana University Press, 1987.

Asid, Ahmed. *Al-Amazighiyya fi khitab al-Islam al-siyasi.* Rabat: Imprimerie Najah El Jadida, 2000.

———. "Aynkum, Ya Arab?" January 24, 2009. http://www.maghress.com/dalilrif/1824 (accessed July 31, 2010).

Aswayq, Muhammad. "Manthuma al-Qiyam al-Amazighiyya: Mafahim lil-fikr wal-tarikh wal-hadatha." *Le Monde Amazigh,* no. 52 (November 2004): 12.

Aym, Zighen. "Tamazight Lost Its Popular Singer and Activist." *Amazigh Voice* 7, no. 3 (Fall 1998): 5–6.

Ayubi, Nazih N. *Overstating the Arab State: Politics and Society in the Middle East.* London: I. B. Tauris, 1995.

Azaykou, Ali Sidqi. "Fi Sabil Mafhum Haqiqi Li-Thaqafatna al-Wataniyya." *Amazigh,* no. 1 (1982): 62–76. Also contained in *Ma'arik Fikriyya Hawla al-Amazighiyya* (Rabat: Centro Tarik Ibn Zyad, 2002), pp. 35–41, and in *Le Monde Amazigh,* no. 50, (October 2004): 9–10.

Balfour, Sebastian. *Deadly Embrace: Morocco and the Road to the Spanish Civil War.* Oxford: Oxford University Press, 2002.

Balta, Paul, ed. *La Méditerranée réinventée: Réalités et espoirs de la coopération.* Paris: Éditions La Découverte/Fondation René Seydoux, 1992.

Barbour, Neville. "The Berbers in al-Andalus." In *Proceedings of the First Congress on Mediterranean Studies of Arabo-Berber Influence,* ed. Micheline Galley, in collaboration with David R. Marshall, pp. 171–174. Algiers: Société Nationale D'Édition et De Diffusion, 1973.

Barnett, Michael. *Dialogues in Arab Politics: Negotiations in Regional Order.* New York: Columbia University Press, 1998.

Becker, Cynthia. *Amazigh Arts in Morocco: Women Shaping Berber Identity.* Austin: University of Texas Press, 2006.

Belhabib, Aicha. "Mobilisation collective et internationalisation de la question amazighe." In *Usages de l'identité Amazighe au Maroc,* ed. Hassan Rachik, pp. 165–192. Casablanca: Imprimerie Najah El Jadida, 2006.

Belkacem, Moh Si. "Congrès Mondial Amazigh: A qui profite la déchirure?" n.d. http://www.amazighnews.net/20081027264/A-qui-profite-la-dechirure.html (accessed June 10, 2010).

Bellil, Rachid, and Salem Chaker. "Mammeri Mouloud, directeur du Crape." In *Hommes et Femmes de Kabylie,* Vol. 1, ed. Salem Chaker, pp. 167–169. Paris and Aix-en-Provence: INALCO, Centre de Recherche Berbère, and Édisud, 2001.

Bencheikh, Souleiman, and Hassan Hamdam. "Fassis vs. Soussis: Histoire d'une Rivalité." *TelQuel,* April 5–11, 2008.

Benhlal, Mohamed. *Le collège d'Azrou: Une élite berbère civile et militaire au maroc (1927–1959).* Paris and Aix-en-Provence: Éditions Karthala, IREMAN, 2005.

Benlayashi, Samir. "Secularism in the Moroccan-Amazigh Discourse." *Journal of North African Studies* 12, no. 7 (June 2007): 153–171.

Benlayashi, Samir, and Bruce Maddy-Weitzman. "Myth, History and *Realpolitik:* Morocco's Jewish Community." *Journal of Modern Jewish Studies* 9, no. 1 (March 2010): 89–106.

Benmehdi, Hassan. "Moroccan Authorities Refuse to Register Amazigh Names." June 10, 2008. http://www.magharebia.com/cocoon/awi/xhtml1/en_GB/features/awi/features/2008/06/10/feature-01 (accessed May 18, 2010).

Benrabah, Mohamed. "The Language Planning Situation in Algeria." *Current Issues in Linguistic Planning* 6, no. 4 (2005): 379–502.

Bensadoun, Mickael. "The (Re-)Fashioning of Moroccan National Identity." In *The Maghrib in the New Century: Identity, Religion and Politics,* ed. Bruce Maddy-Weitzman and Daniel Zisenwine, pp. 13–35. Gainesville: University Press of Florida, 2007.

Berger, Anne-Emmanuelle. "The Impossible Wedding: Nationalism, Language and Mother Tongue in Post-Colonial Algeria." In *Algeria in Others' Languages,* ed. Anne-Emmanuelle Berger, pp. 60–78. Ithaca, N.Y.: Cornell University Press, 2002.

Berque, Jacques. *French North Africa: The Maghrib between Two World Wars.* New York: Praeger, 1967.

Bonn, Charles, and Richard Bjornson. "Kateb Yacine." *Research in African Literatures* 23, no. 2 (Summer 1992): 61–70.

Boudraa, Nabil, and Joseph Krause, eds. *North African Mosaic: A Cultural Reappraisal of Ethnic and Religious Minorities.* Newcastle: Cambridge Scholars Publishing, 2007.

Boukous, Ahmed. *Societé, Langues et Cultures au Maroc.* Casablanca: Imprimerie Najah El Jadida, 1995.

Boulkayid, Mbarek. "Ali Sidqi Azaykou—and the Arab Media in Our Country." *Le Monde Amazigh,* no. 50 (October 2004): 6.

Boum, Aomar. "Dancing for the Moroccan State: Ethnic Folk Dances and the Production of National Hybridity." In *North African Mosaic: A Cultural Reappraisal of Ethnic and Religious Minorities,* ed. Nabil Boudraa and Joseph Krause, pp. 214–237. Newcastle: Cambridge Scholars Publishing, 2007.

Bounfour, Abdallah. "L'État unitaire et le statut de la langue berbère: les positions de la gauche marocaine." *Annuaire de l'Afrique du Nord* 23 (1984): 509–521.

Bourdieu, Pierre. *Algeria 1960/Essays.* Cambridge: Cambridge University Press, 1979.

Bourqia, Rahma, and Susan Gilson Miller, eds. *In the Shadow of the Sultan: Culture, Power, and Politics in Morocco.* Cambridge, Mass.: Center for Middle Eastern Studies, Harvard University, 1999.

Braun, Frank H. "Morocco: Anatomy of a Palace Revolution That Failed." *International Journal of Middle East Studies* 9 (1978): 63–72.

Brett, Michael. "Ibn Khaldun and the Arabisation of North Africa." *Maghreb Review* 4, no. 1 (January–February 1979): 9–16.

———. *The Islamisation of Egypt and North Africa.* Jerusalem: Nehemia Levtzion Center for Islamic Studies, 2006.

———. "The Way of the Nomad." *Bulletin of the School of Oriental and African Studies* 58 (1995). Reprinted in Brett, *Ibn Khaldun and the Medieval Maghrib,* X, pp. 251–269. Aldershot, UK: Ashgate, Variorum, 1999.

Brett, Michael, and Elizabeth Fentress. *The Berbers.* Oxford: Blackwell, 1996.

Brousky, Omar. "Quand Moulay Hassan matait les Rifains." *Le Journal Hebdomadaire,* no. 368 (October 25–31, 2008): 22–28.

Brown, Kenneth. "The Impact of the *Dahir Berbère* in Salé." In *Arabs and Berbers: From Tribe to Nation in North Africa,* ed. Ernest Gellner and Charles Micaud, pp. 201–215. Lexington, Mass., and London: D. C. Heath/Duckworth, 1972/1973.

Brown, L. Carl. "Maghrib Historiography: The Unit of Analysis Problem." In *The Maghrib in Question,* ed. Michel Le Gall and Kenneth Perkins, pp. 4–16. Austin: University of Texas Press, 1997.

Buckner, Elizabeth. "Language Drama in Morocco: Another Perspective on the Problems and Prospects of Teaching Tamazight." *Journal of North African Studies* 11, no. 4 (December 2006): 421–433.

Burke, Edmund, III. "The Image of the Moroccan State in French Ethnological Literature: A New Look at the Origin of Lyautey's Berber Policy." In *Arabs and Berbers: From Tribe to Nation in North Africa,* ed. Ernest Gellner and Charles Micaud, pp. 175–199. Lexington, Mass., and London: D. C. Heath/Duckworth, 1972/1973.

———. *Prelude to Protectorate in Morocco: Pre-colonial Protest and Resistance, 1860–1912.* Chicago: University of Chicago Press, 1976.

Byman, Daniel. "Explaining Ethnic Peace in Morocco." *Harvard Middle Eastern and Islamic Review* 4, nos. 1–2 (1997–1998): pp. 1–29.

Camps, Gabriel. *Les Berbères, Mémoire et Identité.* Arles: Babel, 2007.

Carlier, Omar. "La production sociale de l'image de soi/Note sur la 'crise berbèriste' de 1949." In *Annuaire de l'Afrique du Nord* 23 (1984): 347–371. Paris: CNRS Editions, 1986.

Chafik, Mohamed. *A Brief Survey of Thirty-Three Centuries of Amazigh History.* Revised and edited by Jilali Saib. Rabat: Institut Royal de la Culture Amazighe, 2005.

————. *Pour un Maghreb d'abord Maghrébin*. Rabat: Centre Tarik Ibn Zyad, 2000.

Chahir, Aziz. "Leadership politique amazigh." In *Usages de l'identité Amazighe au Maroc*, ed. Hassan Rachik, pp. 193–233. Casablanca: Imprimerie Najah El Jadida, 2006.

Chaker, Rachid. "Journal Des Evenements De Kabylie (Mars–mai 1980)." *Les Temps Modernes*, nos. 432–433 (July–August 1982): 385–436.

Chaker, Salem. "Agellid." In *Encyclopédie Berbère*, ed. Gabriel Camps, pp. 2:248–249. Aix-en-Provence: Édisud, 1985.

————. "Amazigh." In *Encyclopédie Berbère*, ed. Gabriel Camps, pp. 4:562–568. Aix-en-Provence: Édisud, 1987.

————. *Berbères Aujourd'hui*. 2nd ed. Paris and Montreal: L'Harmattan, 1998.

————. *Berbères, une identité en construction, numéro special de la ROMM*. Aix-en-Provence: Édisud, 1987.

————. "La langue berbère dans le champ politique maghrébin. La cas algérien: rupture ou continuité?" In *Langues et Pouvoir, De l'Afrique du Nord à l'Extrême-Orient*, ed. S. Chaker, pp. 25–40. Aix-en-Provence: Édisud, 1998.

————. "La Question Berbère Dans L'Algérie Indépendante: La Fracture Inévitable?" In *L'Algérie Incertaine*, ed. Pierre Robert Baduel, *Revue du Monde Musulman et de la Méditerranée*, no. 65 (1992): 97–105.

————. "Les bases sociales du berbérisme: critique d'un mythe." In Chaker, *Berbères Aujoud'hui*, pp. 97–110. Appears without the annex at http://www.tamazgha.fr/Les-bases-sociales-du-berberisme-critique-d-un-mythe,209.html (accessed May 19, 2010).

————. "Mammeri Mouloud (1917–1989): le berberisant." In *Hommes et Femmes de Kabylie*, Vol. 1, ed. S. Chaker, pp. 162–166. Paris and Aix-en-Provence: INALCO, Centre de Recherche Berbère, and Édisud, 2001.

————. "Quelques Évidences sur la Question Berbère en Algèrie?" *Confluences Méditerannées*, no. 11, *Comprendre l'Algérie* (Summer 1994): 103–111.

————. " 'Question berbère,' 'Problème kabyle,' où en est-on?" *Annuaire de l'Afrique du Nord* 40 (2002): 285–294. Paris: CNRS Editions, 2004.

Charrad, Mounira M. *States and Women's Rights: The Making of Postcolonial Tunisia, Algeria, and Morocco*. Berkeley and Los Angeles: University of California Press, 2001.

Cheddadi, Abdesselam. "Pour Une Politique de la Langue." *Prologues*, no. 17, *Langues Et Culture Au Maghreb* (1999): 30–36.

Chemakh, Said, and Masin Ferkal. "Professor Chaker Speaks Out on the Tifinagh Script Issue." January 18, 2004. http://www.tamazgha.fr/Professor-Chaker-Speaks-Out-on-the-Tifinagh-Script-Issue,427.html (accessed May 19, 2010).

Cherbi, Moh, and Thierry Deslot. *La Kahena, Reine des Berbères*. Algiers: EDIF, 2000; Paris: Éditions-Mediterranée, 2002; Casablanca: La Croisée des Chemins, 2002.

Cheriet, Boutheina. "The Resilience of Algerian Populism." *Middle East Report*, January/February 1992, pp. 9–14, 34.

Cherry, David. *Frontier and Society in Roman North Africa.* Oxford: Clarendon Press, 1998.

Chouraqui, André N. *Between East and West: A History of the Jews of North Africa.* Philadelphia: Jewish Publication Society of America, 1968.

Chtatou, Mohamed. "The Influence of the Berber Language on Moroccan Arabic." *International Journal of the Sociology of Language,* no. 123, *Berber Sociolinguistics,* ed. Moha Ennaji (1997): 101–118.

———. "Saints and Spirits and Their Significance in Moroccan Cultural Beliefs and Practices: An Analysis of Westermarck's Work." *Morocco,* n.s., no. 1 (1996): 62–84.

Clancy-Smith, Julia. *Rebel and Saint: Muslim Notables, Populist Protest, Colonial Encounters (Algeria and Tunisia, 1800–1904).* Berkeley: University of California Press, 1994.

Colonna, Fanny. "The Nation's 'Unknowing Other': Three Intellectuals and the Culture(s) of Being Algerian, or the Impossibility of Subaltern Studies in Algeria." *Journal of North African Studies* 8, no. 1 (Spring 2003): 155–170.

Commager, Henry Steele. *The Search for a Usable Past, and Other Essays in Historiography.* New York: A. A. Knopf, 1967.

Coram, A. "The Berbers and the Coup." In *Arabs and Berbers: From Tribe to Nation in North Africa,* ed. Ernest Gellner and Charles Micaud, pp. 425–430. Lexington, Mass., and London: D. C. Heath/Duckworth, 1972/1973.

Corcos, David. *Studies in the History of the Jews of Morocco.* Jerusalem: Ruben Mass, 1976.

Cornell, Vincent J. *Realm of the Saint: Power and Authority in Moroccan Sufism.* Austin: University of Texas Press, 1998.

Crawford, David. "How 'Berber' Matters in the Middle of Nowhere." *Middle East Report,* no. 219 (Summer 2001): 20–25.

———. "Morocco's Forgotten Imazighen." *Journal of North African Studies* 7, no. 1 (Spring 2002): 53–70.

———. "Royal Interest in Local Culture: The Politics and Potential of Morocco's Imazighen." In *Nationalism and Minority Identities in Islamic Societies,* ed. Maya Shatzmiller, pp. 164–194. Montreal: McGill–Queen's University Press, 2005.

Damis, John. *Conflict in Northwest Africa.* Stanford, Calif.: Hoover Institution Press, 1983.

Darwish, Adel. "Mohammed's First 100 Days." *The Middle East,* December 1999, pp. 16–18.

Da Silva, Marina. "Kateb Yacine, l'éternel perturbateur." *Le Monde Diplomatique,* November 2009. http://www.monde-diplomatique.fr/2009/11/DA_SILVA/18424 (accessed June 28, 2010).

Dawisha, Adeed. *Arab Nationalism in the 20th Century: From Triumph to Despair.* Princeton, N.J.: Princeton University Press, 2003.

Dawn, C. Ernest. *From Ottomanism to Arabism: Essays on the Origins of Arab Nationalism.* Urbana: University of Illinois Press, 1973.

Dean, Lucy, ed. *The Middle East and North Africa, 2009*. London: Routledge, 2008.

De Felipe, Helena. "From the Maghreb to Al-Andalus: Berbers in a Medieval Islamic Society." In *North African Mosaic: A Cultural Reappraisal of Ethnic and Religious Minorities*, ed. Nabil Boudraa and Joseph Krause, pp. 150–162. Newcastle: Cambridge Scholars Publishing, 2007.

Demnati, Meryam. "Royal Amazigh Institute: Worries for Imazighen." *Amazigh Voice* 10, nos. 3–4 (Winter/Spring 2002): 14.

Direche, Karina. "Évangelisation en Algérie: débats sur la liberté de culte." In *L'Année du Maghreb*, Vol. 5 (2009), pp. 275–284. Paris: CNRS Éditions, 2009.

Direche-Slimani, Karina. *Chrétiens de Kabylie 1873-1954*. Paris: Editions Bouchene, 2004.

———. *Histoire de l'émigration Kabyle en France au XX° siècle*. Paris: L'Harmattan, 1997.

Dishon, Daniel, and Bruce Maddy-Weitzman. "Inter-Arab Relations." In *Middle East Contemporary Survey (MECS)*, Vol. 4 (1979–1980) and Vol. 5 (1980–1981), ed. Colin Legum, Haim Shaked, and Daniel Dishon, pp. 4:169–230, 5:227–290. New York: Holmes and Meier, 1981, 1982.

Duclos, Louis-Jean. "The Berbers and the Rise of Moroccan Nationalism." In *Arabs and Berbers: From Tribe to Nation in North Africa*, ed. Ernest Gellner and Charles Micaud, pp. 217–229. Lexington, Mass., and London: D. C. Heath/Duckworth, 1972/1973.

Eickelman, Dale. *Moroccan Islam: Tradition and Society in a Pilgrimage Center*. Austin: University of Texas Press, 1976.

El-Adani, Jillali. "Regionalism, Islamism and Amazigh Identity: Translocality in the Sus Region of Morocco According to Muhammed Mukhtar Soussi." *Comparative Studies of South Asia, Africa and the Middle East* 27, no. 1 (2007): 41–51.

El Glaoui, Abdessadeq. *Le ralliement: Le Glaoui, mon père*. Rabat: Editions Marsam, 2004.

El Kirat, Yamina. "Some Causes of the Beni Iznassen Berber Language Loss." *Langues et Stigmatisation Sociale au Maghreb*, special issue of *Peuples Méditerranéens* 79 (April–June 1997): 35–54.

El-Mansour, Mohamed. "Moroccan Islam Observed." *The Maghreb Review* 29, nos. 1–4 (2004): 208–218.

Elmedlaoui, Mohamed. "Le berbère et l'histoire du plurilinguisme au Maghreb (le Cas du Maroc)." *Prologues*, nos. 27/28 (Ete/Automne 2003): 83–103.

Elqadery, Mustapha. "L'état national et les berbères, le cas du maroc, mythe colonial et negation nationale." Ph.D. thesis, Universite Paul Valery, Montpellier III, 1995.

Enderwitz, S. "AL-S_H_uūbiyya." In *Encyclopaedia of Islam, Second Edition*, ed. P. Bearman, Th. Bianquis, C. E. Bosworth, E. van Donzel, and W. P. Heinrichs. Brill, 2010. *Brill Online*. http://www.brillonline.nl/subscriber/entry?entry=islam_SIM-6907 (accessed June 27, 2010).

Ennaji, Moha. "The Sociology of Berber, Change and Continuity." *Berber Sociolin-*

guistics, ed. Ennaji, special issue of *International Journal of the Sociology of Language,* no. 123 (1997): 23–40.

———, ed. *Sociolinguistics in Morocco,* special issue of *International Journal of the Sociology of Language,* no. 112 (1995).

Entelis, John P. *Culture and Counterculture in Moroccan Politics.* Boulder, Colo.: Westview, 1989.

Errihani, Mohammed. "Language Attitudes and Language Use in Morocco: Effects of Attitudes on 'Berber Language Policy.'" *Journal of North African Studies* 13, no. 4 (December 2008): 411–428.

———. "Language Policy in Morocco: Problems and Prospects of Teaching Tamazight." *Journal of North African Studies* 11, no. 2 (June 2006): 143–154.

Evans, Martin, and John Phillips. *Algeria: Anger of the Dispossessed.* New Haven, Conn.: Yale University Press, 2008.

Fatès, Youssef. "Le Jeunesse sportive de Kabylie, Entre Sport et Politique." *AWAL: Cahiers d'études berbères,* no. 25 (2002): 49–57.

Favret, Jeane. "Traditionalism through Ultra-Modernism." In *Arabs and Berbers: From Tribe to Nation in North Africa,* ed. Ernest Gellner and Charles Micaud, pp. 307–324. Lexington, Mass., and London: D. C. Heath/Duckworth, 1972/1973.

Fentress, Elisabeth W. B. *Numidia and the Roman Army.* Oxford: B.A.R. International Series, 1979.

Feraoun, Mouloud. *Journal, 1955–1962: Reflections on the French-Algerian War.* Lincoln: University of Nebraska Press, 2000.

Filhon, Alexandra. *Langues d'ici et d'ailleurs: Transmettre l'arabe et le berbère en France.* Paris: Ined, 2009.

Fishman, Joshua A. *Sociolinguistics.* Rowley, Mass.: Newbury House Publishers, 1972.

Foer, Franklin. *How Soccer Explains the World: An Unlikely Theory of Globalization.* New York: HarperCollins, 2004.

Freund, Wolfgang F., ed. *L'émergence d'une nouvelle culture méditerranéene— The Emergence of a New Mediterranean Culture.* Frankfurt am Main: Peter Lang, Europaischer Verlag der Wissenchaften, 2000.

Gafaïti, Hafid. "The Monotheism of the Other: Language and De/Construction of National Identity in Postcolonial Algeria." In *Algeria in Others' Languages,* ed. Anne-Emmanuelle Berger, pp. 19–43. Ithaca, N.Y.: Cornell University Press, 2002.

Gal, Susan. "Migration, Minorities and Multilingualism: Language Ideologies in Europe." In *Language Ideologies, Policies and Practices,* ed. Clare Mar-Molinero and Patrick Stevenson, pp. 13–27. New York: Palgrave Macmillan, 2006.

Gal, Susan, and Kathryn A. Woolard. "Constructing Languages and Publics, Authority and Representation." In *Languages and Publics: The Making of Authority,* ed. Gal and Woolard, pp. 1–12. Manchester, UK: St. Jerome Publishing, 2001.

Gellner, Ernest. "Introduction." In *Arabs and Berbers: From Tribe to Nation in North Africa,* ed. Ernest Gellner and Charles Micaud, pp. 11–21. Lexington, Mass., and London: D. C. Heath/Duckworth, 1972/1973.

————. *Muslim Society.* Cambridge: Cambridge University Press, 1981.

Gellner, Ernest, and Charles Micaud, eds. *Arabs and Berbers: From Tribe to Nation in North Africa.* Lexington, Mass., and London: D. C. Heath/Duckworth, 1972/1973.

Gera, Gideon. "Algeria." In *Middle East Contemporary Survey (MECS),* Vol. 18 (1994), ed. Ami Ayalon and Bruce Maddy-Weitzman, pp. 233–252. Boulder, Colo.: Westview, 1996.

————. "Reflections on the Aftermath of Civil Strife: Algeria, 2006." In *The Maghrib in the New Century: Identity, Religion and Politics,* ed. Bruce Maddy-Weitzman and Daniel Zisenwine, pp. 75–102. Gainesville: University Press of Florida, 2007.

Gershovich, Moshe. "The Impact of French Colonialism in Contemporary Morocco." Paper delivered at the 7th International Association of Middle Eastern Studies (IAMES) conference, Free University of Berlin, October 4–8, 2000.

————. *French Military Rule in Morocco.* London: Frank Cass, 1999.

Ghallab, Abd al-Karim. *Tarikh al-Haraka al-Wataniyya Bil-Maghrib,* Vol. 1. Casablanca: Matbaʿat al-Najah al-Jadida, 2000.

Gibb, H. A. R. "Amīr al-Muʾminīn." In *Encyclopaedia of Islam, Second Edition,* ed. P. Bearman, Th. Bianquis, C. E. Bosworth, E. van Donzel, and W. P. Heinrichs. Brill, 2010. *Brill Online.* http://www.brillonline.nl/subscriber/entry?entry=islam_SIM-0617 (accessed June 27, 2010).

Gibbon, Edward. *The History of the Decline and Fall of the Roman Empire,* ed. the Reverend H. H. Milman (1782/1845). http://ebooks.adelaide.edu.au/g/gibbon/edward/g43d/index.html (accessed May 19, 2010).

Glick, Thomas F. *From Muslim Fortress to Christian Castle: Social and Cultural Change in Medieval Spain.* Manchester and New York: Manchester University Press, 1995.

————. *Islamic and Christian Spain in the Early Middle Ages.* Princeton, N.J.: Princeton University Press, 1979.

Goldberg, Harvey E. "The Mellahs of Southern Morocco: Report of a Survey." *The Maghreb Review* 8, nos. 3–4 (1983): 61–69. http://www.mondeberbere.com/juifs/mellahs.htm (accessed May 19, 2010).

Goodman, Jane. *Berber Culture on the World Stage.* Bloomington: Indiana University Press, 2005.

————. "Imazighen on Trial: Human Rights and Berber Identity in Algeria, 1985." In *Berbers and Others: Shifting Parameters of Ethnicity in the Contemporary Maghrib,* ed. Susan Gilson Miller and Katherine E. Hoffman, pp. 103–126. Bloomington: Indiana University Press, 2010.

Grandguillaume, Gilbert. *Arabisation et politique linguistique au Maghreb.* Paris: Maisonneuve, 1983.

Gray, Doris. "Women in Algeria Today and the Debate over Family Law." *MERIA Journal* 13, no. 1 (March 2005). http://www.gloria-center.org/meria/2009/03/gray.html (accessed May 19, 2010).

Habibi, Injaz Abdallah. "Collective Lands from Joint Tribal Ownership to State

Administrative Control: An Example from the Zayan [Zaiane] Tribes in the Khenifra Region." *Le Monde Amazigh,* no. 52 (November 2004): 4–5.

Hachid, Malika. *Les Premiers Berbères, Entre Méditerranée, Tassili et Nil.* Alger and Aix-en-Provence: Ina-Yas, Édisud, 2000.

Hagen, Helen. *The Shining Ones.* Philadelphia: Xlibris Corporation, 2000.

Hammoudi, Abdallah. *Master and Disciple: The Cultural Foundations of Moroccan Authoritarianism.* Chicago: University of Chicago Press, 1997.

Hannoum, Abdelmajid. *Post-Colonial Memories: The Legend of the Kahina, a North African Heroine.* Portsmouth, N.H.: Heinemann, 2001.

Harbi, Mohammed. "Nationalisme algérien et identité berbère." *Peuples Méditerranéens,* no. 11 (April–June 1980): 31–37.

Hart, David M. "The Berber Dahir of 1930 in Colonial Morocco: Then and Now (1930–1960)." *Journal of North African Studies* 2, no. 4 (Autumn 1997): 11–33.

———. "The Role of Goliath in Moroccan Berber Genealogies." *Journal of North African Studies: A Special Issue on Tribe and Rural Society in Morocco* 4, no. 2 (Summer 1999). Also published in Hart, *Tribe and Society in Rural Morocco.* Portland, Ore.: Frank Cass, 2000, pp. 37–47.

———. "Rural and Tribal Uprisings in Post-Colonial Morocco, 1957–1960: An Overview and a Reappraisal." *Journal of North African Studies, A Special Issue on Tribe and Rural Society in Morocco* 4, no. 2 (Summer 1999). Also published in Hart, *Tribe and Society in Rural Morocco.* Portland, Ore.: Frank Cass, 2000, pp. 84–102.

———. "Scratch a Moroccan, Find a Berber." *Journal of North African Studies* 4, no. 2 (Summer 1999). Also published in Hart, *Tribe and Society in Rural Morocco.* Portland, Ore.: Frank Cass, 2000, pp. 23–26.

———. "Tribalism: The Backbone of the Moroccan Nation." *Journal of North African Studies* 4, no. 2 (Summer 1999). Also published in Hart, *Tribe and Society in Rural Morocco.* Portland, Ore.: Frank Cass, 2000, pp. 7–22.

———. "The Tribe in Modern Morocco: Two Case Studies." In *Arabs and Berbers: From Tribe to Nation in North Africa,* ed. Ernest Gellner and Charles Micaud, pp. 25–58. Lexington, Mass., and London: D. C. Heath/Duckworth, 1972/1973.

Hazen, William E. "Minorities in Assimilation: The Berbers of North Africa." In *The Political Role of Minority Groups in the Middle East,* ed. R. D. McLaurin, pp. 135–155. New York: Praeger, 1979.

Henry, Clement M. "Crises of Money and Power: Transitions to Democracy." In *Islam, Democracy, and the State in North Africa,* ed. John P. Entelis, pp. 177–204. Bloomington: Indiana University Press, 1997.

———. "North Africa's Desperate Regimes" (review article). *Middle East Journal* 59, no. 4 (Summer 2005): 475–484.

Hirschberg, H. Z. "The Problem of the Judaized Berbers." *Journal of African History* 4, no. 3 (1963): 313–339.

Hodges, Tony. *Western Sahara: The Roots of a Desert War.* Westport, Conn.: Lawrence Hill and Company, 1983.

Hodgson, Marshall G. S. *The Venture of Islam: Conscience and History in a World Civilization*. Vol. 2, *The Expansion of Islam in the Middle Periods*. Chicago and London: University of Chicago Press, 1974.

Hoffman, Katherine E. *We Share Walls: Language, Land, and Gender in Berber Morocco*. Malden, Mass.: Blackwell, 2008.

Horne, Alistair. *A Savage War of Peace*. New York: Penguin Books, 1987.

Hroch, Miroslav. *Comparative Studies in Modern European History: Nation, Nationalism, Social Change*. Aldershot, Hampshire, UK: Ashgate, Variorum, 2007.

———. "From National Movement to the Fully-formed Nation: The Nation-building Process in Europe." In *Mapping the Nation*, ed. Balakrishnan Gopal, pp. 78–97. New York and London: Verso, 1996. http://www.nationalismproject.org/what/hroch.htm (accessed May 20, 2010).

———. "Social and Territorial Characteristics in the Composition of the Leading Groups of National Movements." In Hroch, *Social Preconditions of National Revival in Europe: A Comparative Analysis of the Social Composition of Patriotic Groups among the Smaller European Nations*, pp. 257–275. New York: Columbia University Press, 2000.

———. "The Social Interpretation of Linguistic Demands in European National Movements." In Hroch, *Social Preconditions of National Revival in Europe: A Comparative Analysis of the Social Composition of Patriotic Groups among the Smaller European Nations*, pp. 67–96. New York: Columbia University Press, 2000.

Hughes, Stephen O. *Morocco under King Hassan*. Reading, UK: Ithaca Press, 2001.

Huntington, Samuel P. *The Clash of Civilizations and the Remaking of World Order*. New York: Simon & Schuster, 1996.

———. *Political Order in Changing Societies*. New Haven, Conn.: Yale University Press, 1968.

———. *The Third Wave: Democratization in the Late Twentieth Century*. Norman: University of Oklahoma Press, 1993.

Ilahiane, Hsain. *Historical Dictionary of the Berbers (Imazighen)*. Lanham, Md.; Toronto; and Oxford: Scarecrow Press, 2006.

Ilikoud, Ouali. "Le Printemps berbère et Octobere 88." In *Émutes et Mouvement Sociaux au Maghreb*, ed. Didier Le Saout and Marguerite Rollande, pp. 137–146. Paris: Karthala/Institut Maghreb–Europe, 1999.

Jankowski, James, and Israel Gershoni, eds. *Rethinking Nationalism in the Arab Middle East*. New York: Columbia University Press, 1997.

Jensen, Erik. *Western Sahara: Anatomy of a Stalemate*. Boulder, Colo.: Lynne Rienner Publishers, 2005.

Julien, Charles-André. *History of North Africa*. New York: Praeger, 1970. Translation of the second edition of *Histoire de l'Afrique du Nord* (Paris: Payot, 1951–1952).

Kabylie, L'autonome en Débat. Paris: Seminaire D'Ecancourt, 2002.

Keenan, Jeremy. *The Tuareg, People of Ahaggar*. London: Sickle Moon Books, 2002.

Keita, Kalifa. "Conflict and Conflict Resolution in the Sahel: The Tuareg Insurgency in Mali." *Small Wars & Insurgencies* 9, no. 3 (Winter 1998): 102–128. http://www.informaworld.com/smpp/content~db=all~content=a787270637~frm=titlelink (accessed May 20, 2010).

Ketterer, James. "Networks of Discontent in Northern Morocco: Drugs, Opposition and Urban Unrest." *Middle East Report,* no. 218 (Spring 2001). http://www.merip.org/mer/mer218/218_ketterer.html (accessed May 20, 2010).

Khalidi, Rashid, Lisa Anderson, Muhammad Muslih, and Reeva S. Simon, eds. *The Origins of Arab Nationalism.* New York: Columbia University Press, 1991.

Kilou, Abdenour. "Obituary: Mohand Aarav Bessaoud." *The Guardian,* January 30, 2002. http://www.guardian.co.uk/news/2002/jan/30/guardianobituaries.books (accessed May 20, 2010).

Kossman, Maarten G., and Harry J. Stroomer. "Berber Phonology." In *Phonologies of Asia and Africa,* ed. Alan S. Kaye (Winona Lake, IN: Eisenbrauns, 1997).

Kostiner, Joseph, ed. *Middle Eastern Monarchies.* Boulder, Colo.: Lynne Rienner, 2000.

Kratochwil, Gabi. *Die Berberbewegung in Marokko: Zur Geschichte der Konstruktion einer ethnischen Identität (1912-1997).* Berlin: Klaus Schwarz Verlag, 2002.

———. *Die Berber in der historischen Entwicklung Algeriens von 1949 bis 1990. Zur Konstruktion einer ethnischen Identität.* Berlin: Klaus Schwarz, 1996.

———. "Some Observations on the First Amazigh World Congress (27–30 August, Tafira, Canary Islands)." *Die Welt Des Islams* 39, no. 2 (July 1999): 149–158.

Lapidus, Ira M. *A History of Islamic Societies.* Cambridge: Cambridge University Press, 1988.

Larbi, H. "Which Script for Tamazight, Whose Choice Is It?" *Amazigh Voice* 12, no. 2 (Summer/Fall 2003): 3–8.

Larbi, Hsen. "The Amazigh World Congress." *The Amazigh Voice,* December 1995–March 1996, http://www.ece.umd.edu/~sellami/DEC95/congress.html (accessed July 31, 2010).

Laroui, Abdallah. *The History of the Maghrib: An Interpretive Essay.* Princeton, N.J.: Princeton University Press, 1977.

Larsson, Göran. *Ibn Garcia's shu'ubiyya Letter: Ethnic and Theological Tensions in Medieval al-Andalus.* Leiden and Boston: Brill, 2003.

Laskier, Michael. *Israel and the Maghreb: From Statehood to Oslo.* Gainesville: University Press of Florida, 2004.

Lazreg, Marnia. *The Eloquence of Silence: Algerian Women in Question.* New York: Routledge, 1994.

Lehsene, Bahbouh. "Haut Commissariat à l'Amazighité, 13 ans après." http://www.kabyle.com/haut-commissariat-%C3%A0-lamazighit%C3%A9-13-ans-apr%C3%A8s-470-090908.html (accessed May 20, 2010).

Lemsine, Aicha. "Berberism: An Historical Travesty in Algeria's Time of Travail." *Washington Report on Middle East Affairs,* January/February 1995, pp. 31, 89–90.

Le Saout, Didier. "La radicalization de la revendication amazighe au Maroc. Le sud-est comme imaginaire militant." In *L'Année du Maghreb*, Vol. 5 (2009), pp. 75–93. Paris: CNRS Éditions, 2009.

Leveau, Remy. *Le Fellah Marocain, Defenseur Du Trone*. Paris: Presses De La Fondation Nationale Des Sciences Politiques, 1985.

Lewis, Bernard. *History — Remembered, Recovered, Invented*. Princeton, N.J.: Princeton University Press, 1976.

Linarès, Fernand. "Voyages au Tafilalet avec S. M. le Sultan Moulay Hassan en 1893." *Bulletin de l'Institut d'Hygiène du Maroc* 1932, no. 3 (Julliet–Septembre): 93–116.

Litvak, Meir. "Algeria." In *Middle East Contemporary Survey (MECS)*, Vols. 19–24 (1995–2000), ed. Bruce Maddy-Weitzman. Boulder, Colo., and Tel Aviv: Westview/Dayan Center, 1997–2002.

———. "Introduction: Collective Memory and the Palestinian Experience." In *Palestinian Collective Memory and National Identity*, ed. Litvak, pp. 1–26. New York: Palgrave Macmillan, 2009.

Lorcin, Patricia M. E. *Imperial Identities: Stereotyping, Prejudice and Race in Colonial Algeria*. London and New York: I. B. Tauris, 1995.

Loukad, Mohand. "Bessaoud Mohand Aarav: Le triomphe de la conviction." *Izuran-Racines*, January 8–21, 2007.

Lumendifi, Nouri. "Qaradawi à Tizi-Ouzou." October 20, 2008. http://www.afrique-du-nord.com/article.php3?id_article=1424 (accessed May 20, 2010).

Ma'arik Fikriyya Hawla al-Amazighiyya/Amazighité, Debát Intellectuel. Rabat: Centre Tarik Ibn Zyad, 2002.

McAdam, Doug, Sidney Tarrow, and Charles Tilly. *Dynamics of Contention*. Cambridge: Cambridge University Press, 2001.

McDougall, James. *History and the Culture of Nationalism in Algeria*. Cambridge: Cambridge University Press, 2006.

———. "Myth and Counter-Myth: 'The Berber' as National Signifier in Algerian Historiographies." *Radical History Review*, no. 86 (Spring 2003): 66–88.

Maddy-Weitzman, Bruce. "Berber/Amazigh Memory Work." In *The Maghrib in the New Century: Identity, Religion and Politics*, ed. Bruce Maddy-Weitzman and Daniel Zisenwine, pp. 50–71. Gainesville: University Press of Florida, 2007.

———. "The Berber Question in Algeria: Nationalism in the Making?" In *Minorities and the State in the Arab World*, ed. Ofra Bengio and Gabriel Ben-Dor, pp. 31–52. Boulder, Colo.: Lynne Rienner, 1998.

———. "Contested Identities: Berbers, 'Berberism,' and the State in North Africa." *Journal of North African Studies* 6, no. 3 (Autumn 2001): 23–47.

———. *The Crystallization of the Arab State System, 1945-1954*. Syracuse, N.Y.: Syracuse University Press, 1993.

———. "Ethno-Politics and Globalization in North Africa: The Berber Culture Movement." *Journal of North African Studies* 11, no. 1 (March 2006): 71–83.

———. "Inter-Arab Relations." In *Middle East Contemporary Survey (MECS)*, Vol. 13 (1989), ed. Ami Ayalon, pp. 119-171. Boulder, Colo.: Westview Press, 1991.

————. "Maghrib Affairs." In *Middle East Contemporary Survey (MECS),* Vol. 17 (1993), ed. Ami Ayalon, pp. 83–108. Boulder, Colo.: Westview Press, 1995.

————. "Morocco." In *Middle East Contemporary Survey (MECS),* Vol. 24 (2000), ed. Maddy-Weitzman, pp. 413–439. Boulder, Colo.: Westview, 2002.

————. *Palestinian and Israeli Intellectuals in the Shadow of Oslo and Initifadat al-Aqsa.* Tel Aviv: Tami Steinmetz Center for Peace Research, 2002. http://www.dayan .org/PalestinianandIsraeliIntellectuals-bruce.pdf (accessed May 20, 2010).

————. "Population Growth and Family Planning in Morocco." *Asian and African Studies* 26, no. 1 (March 1992): 63–79, http://www.dayan.org/articles/POPU LATION_GROWTH.pdf (accessed June 13, 2010).

————. "Women, Islam and the Moroccan State: The Struggle over the Personal Status Law." *Middle East Journal* 59, no. 3 (Summer 2005): 393–410.

Maddy-Weitzman, Bruce, and Meir Litvak. "Islamism and the State in North Africa." In *Revolutionaries and Reformers: Contemporary Islamist Movements in the Middle East,* ed. Barry Rubin, pp. 69–89. Albany, N.Y.: SUNY Press, 2003.

Maddy-Weitzman, Bruce, and Daniel Zisenwine, eds. *The Maghrib in the New Century: Identity, Religion and Politics.* Gainesville: University Press of Florida, 2007.

Maghraoui, Abdelsalam. "Depoliticization in Morocco." *Journal of Democracy* 13, no. 4 (October 2002): 24–32.

Mahé, Alain. *Histoire de la Grande Kabylie, XIXe-XXe siècles.* Paris: Editions Bouchenes, 2001.

Matoub, Malika. *Matoub Lounès, Mon Frère.* Paris: Albin Michel, 1999.

Mattingly, David J. "From One Colonialism to Another: Imperialism in the Maghreb." In *Roman Imperialism: Post-Colonial Perspectives,* ed. Jane Webster and Nick Cooper, pp. 49–69. Leicester: School of Archaeological Studies, University of Leicester, 1996.

Mehenni, Ferhat. *Algérie: la question kabyle.* Paris: Éditions Michalon, 2004.

————. "The Autonomy of Kabylia in Questions." First published in French by Stéphane Arrami (Kabyle.com), May 25, 2002. Translated by Michelle Duvall. http://waac.info/amazigh/politics/algeria/autonomy/ferhat_autonomy_in_ questions.html (accessed January 27, 2004).

Menocal, Maria Rosa. *The Ornament of the World.* Boston: Little, Brown, 2002.

Mernissi, Fatima. *Islam and Democracy: Fear of the Modern World.* Reading, Mass.: Addison-Wesley, 1992.

Merolla, Daniela. "Digital Imagination and the 'Landscapes of Group Identities': The Flourishing of Theatre, Video and 'Amazigh Net' in the Maghrib and Berber Diaspora." *Journal of North African Studies* 7, no. 4 (Winter 2002): 122–131.

Messaoudi, Djaafar. "The Strategies of the Algerian Regime to Subdue Kabylia." October 5, 2007. http://www.north-of-africa.com/article.php3?id_article=442 (accessed June 23, 2010).

Metref, Arezki. "La question berbère: quand le politique capture l'identitaire." *Monde arabe Maghreb Machrek,* no. 154 (October–December 1996): 26–28.

Mezhoud, Salem. "Glasnost the Algerian Way: The Role of Berber Nationalists in

Political Reform." In *North Africa: Nation, State and Region,* ed. George Joffé, pp. 142–169. London: Routledge, 1993.

Micaud, Charles. "Conclusion." In *Arabs and Berbers: From Tribe to Nation in North Africa,* ed. Ernest Gellner and Charles Micaud, pp. 432–438. Lexington, Mass., and London: D. C. Heath/Duckworth, 1972/1973.

Millar, Fergus. "Local Cultures in the Roman Empire: Libyan, Punic and Latin in Roman Africa." *Journal of Roman Studies* 58, parts 1 and 2 (1968): 126–134.

Mira, Tarik. "Ait Ahmed et le FFS." *Tafsut,* no. 3 (June 1986): 99–108.

Monbeig, Pierre. "Une Opposition Politique dans l'Impasse, Le FFS de Hocine Ait-Ahmed." In *L'Algérie Incertaine,* ed. Pierre Robert Baduel, pp. 125–140. Aix-en-Provence: Institute de Recherches et d'Études sur le Monde Arabe et Musulman (IREMAM), *Revue du Monde Musulman et de la Méditerranée* (REMMM), 1994.

Monib, Maati. "Le Rif, Mohammed V et l'Istiqlal." *Le Journal Hebdomadaire,* no. 368 (October 25–31, 2008): 28–29.

Monroe, James T. *The Shu'ubiyya in Al-Andalus.* Berkeley: University of California Press, 1970.

Montagne, Robert. *La Vie Sociale et la Vie Politique des Berbères.* Paris: la Société de l'Afrique Française, 1931. English version: *The Berbers: Their Social and Political Organisation.* Translated by, and with an Introduction by, David Seddon. London: Frank Cass, 1973.

Mortimer, Robert. "Algeria." In *Africa Contemporary Record (ACR),* Vol. 28 (2001–2002), pp. B599–B610. Teaneck, N.J.: Africana Publishing, 2006.

Moukhlis, Moha. "Intégrisme, Gaza et Tamazight. Pour L'Amour De La Vie." January 23, 2009. http://www.amazighworld.org/news/index_show.php?id=1734 (accessed May 20, 2010).

Moutaoukil, Fatima. "Barghwata: Un royaume amazigh (berbère) méconnu." http://www.mondeberbere.com/civilisation/histoire/barghwata.htm (accessed May 20, 2010).

Al-Najah fi al-Ijtima'iyyat: al-Sana al-Sadisa min al-Ta'lim al-Ibtida'i. Casablanca: Imprimerie Najah El Jadida, 2006.

Naylor, Phillip C. *North Africa: A History from Antiquity to the Present.* Austin: University of Texas Press, 2009.

Nettl, J. P. "The State as a Conceptual Variable." *World Politics* 20, no. 4 (July 1968): 559–592.

Nora, Pierre, ed. *Les Lieux de memoire.* Paris: Gallimard, 1997.

Novati, Giampaolo Calchi. "Post-Colonial State vs. Ethnicity: A Reassessment of Decolonization in Africa." *Latin American Perspectives* 23, no. 2 (April 1996): 130–138.

Ouerdane, Amar. "Genese De La 'Crise Berberiste' De 1949." *Tafsut,* no. 3 (June 1986): 109–120.

———. "Kabyles et Arabes Durant La Phase Decisive De La Guerre De Liberation Nationale: 1954–1957." *Tafsut,* no. 4 (October 1989): 87–113.

————. *Le question berbère dans le mouvement national algérien, 1926-1980.* Quebec: Septentrion, 1990.

Oufkir, Fatéma. *Les Jardins du roi.* Paris: Éditions Michel Lafon, 2000.

Oufkir, Malika, and Michele Fitoussi. *Stolen Lives.* New York: Hyperion, 1999.

Oufkir, Raouf. *Les Invités, vingt ans dans les prisons du Roi.* Paris: Flammarion, 2003.

Oussaid, Brick. *Mountains Forgotten by God.* Boulder, Colo.: Three Continents Press, 1989.

Parker, Richard B. *Uncle Sam in Barbary.* Gainesville: University Press of Florida, 2004.

Pellat, Ch., et al. "Berbers." In *Encyclopaedia of Islam, Second Edition,* ed. P. Bearman, Th. Bianquis, C. E. Bosworth, E. van Donzel, and W. P. Heinrichs. Brill, 2010. *Brill Online.* http://www.brillonline.nl/subscriber/uid=1411/entry?entry=is lam_COM-0114 (accessed June 27, 2010).

Pennell, C. R. *A Country with a Government and a Flag: The Rif War in Morocco, 1921-1926.* Wisbech, UK: Menas Press, 1986.

————. *Morocco: From Empire to Independence.* Oxford: Oneworld, 2003.

————. *Morocco since 1830: A History.* New York: New York University Press, 2000.

Peyron, Michael. "Barghawat et résistance." In *Le Resistance Marocaine a Travers L'Histoire ou le Maroc des Resistances,* Vol. 2, edited and coordinated by Mohammed Hammam et Abdellah Salih, pp. 165–181. Rabat: Rayume Du Maroc, Institut Royal de la Culture Amazighe, 2005.

Podeh, Elie. "The Emergence of the Arab State System Reconsidered." *Diplomacy and Statecraft* 9, no. 3 (November 1998): 50–82.

Porath, Yehoshua. *In Search of Arab Unity, 1930-1945.* London: Frank Cass, 1986.

Pour Le Reconnaissance Constitutionnelle de l'Amazighite. Rabat: AMREC, 2002.

Quandt, William. "The Berbers in the Algerian Political Elite." In *Arabs and Berbers: From Tribe to Nation in North Africa,* ed. Ernest Gellner and Charles Micaud, pp. 285–303. Lexington, Mass., and London: D. C. Heath/Duckworth, 1972/1973.

Rachik, Hassan, ed. *Usages de l'identité Amazighe au Maroc.* Casablanca: Imprimerie Najah El Jadida, 2006.

Raven, Susan. *Rome in Africa.* 3rd ed. London and New York: Routledge, 1993.

Reporters Sans Frontières. *Le Drame Algérien, Un peuple en otage.* Paris: Le Découverte, 1996.

Roberts, Hugh. "Algeria: The Subterranean Logics of a Non-election." Real Instituto Elcano, ARI 68/2009, April 22, 2009.

————. *The Battlefield: Algeria 1988-2002, Studies in a Broken Polity.* London: Verso, 2003.

————. "Co-opting Identity: The Manipulation of Berberism, the Frustration of Democratisation, and the Generation of Violence in Algeria." Crisis States Programme Working Papers, no. 7 (December 2001). http://www.crisisstates.com/download/wp/WP7HR.pdf (accessed May 20, 2010).

————. "The Economics of Berberism: The Material Basis of the Kabyle Question in Contemporary Algeria." *Government and Opposition* 18, no. 2 (Spring 1983): 218–235.

———. "Towards an Understanding of the Kabyle Question in Contemporary Algeria." *The Maghreb Review* 5, nos. 5–6 (September–December 1980): 115–124.

———. "The Unforeseen Development of the Kabyle Question in Contemporary Algeria." *Government and Opposition* 17, no. 3 (Summer 1982): 312–334.

Ronen, Yehudit. *Qaddafi's Libya in World Politics.* Boulder, Colo.: Lynne Rienner, 2008.

Rosen, Lawrence. "The Social and Conceptual Framework of Arab-Berber Relations in Central Morocco." In *Arabs and Berbers: From Tribe to Nation in North Africa,* ed. Ernest Gellner and Charles Micaud, pp. 155–173. Lexington, Mass., and London: D. C. Heath/Duckworth, 1972/1973.

Rouzeik, Fawzi. "Algérie 1990–1993: La Démocratie Confisquée?" In *L'Algérie Incertaine,* ed. Pierre Robert Baduel, pp. 29–60. Aix-en-Provence: Institute de Recherches et d'Études sur le Monde Arabe et Musulman (IREMAM), *Revue du Monde Musulman et de la Méditerranée* (REMMM), 1994.

Ruedy, John. *Modern Algeria: The Origins and Development of a Nation.* 2nd ed. Bloomington: Indiana University Press, 2005.

al-Rumi, Aisha. "Libyan Berbers Struggle to Assert Their Identity Online." *Arab Media and Society,* no. 8 (Summer 2009): 1–8. http://www.arabmediasociety.com/?article=713 (accessed June 28, 2010).

Saad, Stephanie S. "Interpreting Ethnic Quiescence: A Brief History of the Berbers of Morocco." In *The Arab-African and Islamic Worlds,* ed. R. M. Coury and R. K. Lacey, pp. 167–181. New York: Peter Lang, 2000.

Saadi, Saïd. "No Longer Can We Spend Our Time Burying Our Dead." *Middle East Quarterly* 1, no. 2 (June 1994): 92–94.

Saadi-Mokrane, Djamila. "The Algerian Linguicide." In *Algeria in Others' Languages,* ed. Anne-Emmanuelle Berger, pp. 44–58. Ithaca, N.Y.: Cornell University Press, 2002.

Saaf, Abdallah. "For Gaza, Moroccan Civil Society Reveals Itself as a Political Society." *Arab Reform Initiative* e-letter, February 1, 2009. http://arab-reform.net/spip.php?article1793 (accessed May 20, 2010).

Salsa, Salma. "L'Espagne et ses bombes toxiques sur le Rif. Nous ne pouvons pas oublier ce crime contre l'humanité." *El Mundo,* July 5, 2008. Translated from the Spanish by Mohamed Sihaddou. http://www.emarrakech.info/L-Espagne-et-ses-bombes-toxiques-sur-le-Rif_a15270.html (accessed May 20, 2010).

Scales, Peter C. *The Fall of the Caliphate of Cordoba.* Leiden, New York, and Köln: E. J. Brill, 1994.

Scheele, Judith. "Recycling *Baraka:* Knowledge, Politics, and Religion in Contemporary Algeria." *Comparative Studies in Society and History* 49, no. 2 (April 2007): 304–328.

Schöpflin, George. *Nations, Identity, Power.* New York: New York University Press, 2000.

Schroeter, Daniel. "On the Origins and Identity of Indigenous North African Jews." In *North African Mosaic: A Cultural Reappraisal of Ethnic and Religious Minorities*, ed. Nabil Boudraa and Joseph Krause, pp. 164–177. Newcastle: Cambridge Scholars Publishing, 2007.

Seale, Patrick. *The Struggle for Syria.* 2nd ed. New Haven, Conn., and London: Yale University Press, 1986.

Seffal, Rabah. "Remember Me?" *The World & I,* September 1992, pp. 612–623.

Shatzmiller, Maya. *The Berbers and the Islamic State: The Marinid Experience in Pre-Protectorate Morocco.* Princeton, N.J.: Markus Wiener, 2000.

———, ed. *Nationalism and Minority Identities in Islamic Societies.* Montreal/Kingston: McGill–Queen's University Press, 2005.

Shepard, William E. "Age of Ignorance." In *Encyclopaedia of the Qur'ān,* ed. Jane Dammen McAuliffe, Georgetown University. Washington, D.C.: Brill, 2010. *Brill Online.* http://www.brillonline.nl/subscriber/entry?entry=q3_SIM-00013 (accessed June 27, 2010).

Shinar, Pessah. "'Abd al-Qadir and 'Abd al-Krim, Religious Influences on Their Thought and Action." In Shinar, *Modern Islam in the Maghrib,* VI, pp. 139–174. Jerusalem: Max Schloessinger Memorial Foundation, Hebrew University of Jerusalem, 2004.

Shukri, Muhammad. *For Bread Alone.* Translated by Paul Bowles. London: Peter Owen Books, 1973.

Shuval, Tal. "The Ottoman Algerian Elite and Its Ideology." *International Journal of Middle East Studies* 32, no. 3 (August 2000): 323–344.

Silverstein, Paul A. *Algeria in France: Transpolitics, Race and Nation.* Bloomington: Indiana University Press, 2004.

———. "Amazigh Activism and the Racial Politics of Space in Southeastern Morocco." Paper delivered at the Middle East Studies Association annual conference, Montreal, Quebec, November 17–20, 2007.

———. "France's *Mare Nostrum:* Colonial and Post-Colonial Constructions of the French Mediterranean." *Journal of North African Studies* 7, no. 4 (Winter 2002): 1–22.

———. "Islam, *Laïcité,* and Amazigh Activism in France and North Africa." In *North African Mosaic: A Cultural Reappraisal of Ethnic and Religious Minorities,* ed. Nabil Boudraa and Joseph Krause, pp. 104–118. Newcastle: Cambridge Scholars Publishing, 2007.

———. "The Kabyle Myth: Colonization and the Production of Ethnicity." In *From the Margins: Historical Anthropology and Its Futures,* ed. Brian Keith Axel, pp. 122–135. Durham, N.C.: Duke University Press, 2002.

———. "Martyrs and Patriots: Ethnic, National and Transnational Dimensions of Kabyle Politics." *Journal of North African Studies* 8, no. 1 (Spring 2003): 87–111.

———. "Realizing Myth: Berbers in France and Algeria." *Middle East Report,* no. 200 (Summer 1996): 111–115.

Sivan, Emmanuel. "Arab Nationalism in the Age of Islamic Resurgence." In *Rethinking Nationalism in the Arab Middle East,* ed. James Jankowski and Israel Gershoni, pp. 207–228. New York: Columbia University Press, 1997.

Slouschz, Nahum. *Archives Marocaines.* Vol. 14, *Hebreo-Phéniciens et Judéo-Berbères.* Paris: Ernest Leroux, 1908.

Slymovics, Susan. *The Performance of Human Rights in Morocco.* Philadelphia: University of Pennsylvania Press, 2005.

Smith, Andrea L. *Colonial Memory and Postcolonial Europe: Maltese Settlers in Algeria and France.* Bloomington: Indiana University Press, 2006.

Smith, Anthony D. *The Ethnic Origins of Nations.* Oxford: Blackwell, 1996.

———. *Nations and Nationalism in a Global Era.* Cambridge, UK: Polity Press, 1995.

Stillman, Norman A. *The Jews of Arab Lands: A History and Source Book.* Philadelphia: Jewish Publication Society of America, 1979.

Stora, Benjamin. *Algeria 1830-2000: A Short History.* Ithaca, N.Y., and London: Cornell University Press, 2001.

———. *Algerie Maroc, Histoires paralleles, destin croises.* Paris: Maisonneuve et Larose (Zellige), 2002.

———. "The Maghrib at the Dawn of the 21st Century." In *The Maghrib in the New Century: Identity, Religion and Politics,* ed. Bruce Maddy-Weitzman and Daniel Zisenwine, pp. 1–9. Gainesville: University Press of Florida, 2007.

al-Talibi, Mohamed, and Ibrahim al-Abidi. *Al-Barghwatiyyun fil-Maghrib.* Casablanca: Matba'at al-Najah al-Jadida, 1999.

Tilmatine, Mohamed, and Yasir Suleiman. "Language and Identity: The Case of the Berbers." In *Language and Identity in the Middle East and North Africa,* ed. Yasir Suleiman, pp. 165–179. Richmond, Surrey, UK: Curzon Press, 1996.

Tilmatine, Mohand. "Pouvoir, violence et revendications berbères." *AWAL: Cahiers d'études berbères,* no. 17 (1998): 21–38.

———. "Religion and Morals of Imazighen According to Arab Writers of the Medieval Times." *Amazigh Voice* 9, nos. 2–3 (Spring/Summer 2000): 14–15.

Valensi, Lucette. "The Scheherazade Syndrome." In *Algeria in Others' Languages,* ed. Anne-Emmanuelle Berger, pp. 139–153. Ithaca, N.Y.: Cornell University Press, 2002.

Walna'am, Lahcen. "Al-Khitab al-Islamawi wal-Khat al-Ansab Likitabat al-Amazighiyya." *Le Monde Amazigh,* no. 29 (November 2002): 4.

Wasserstein, David. "The Language Situation in al-Andalus." In *The Formation of al-Andalus,* Part 2: *Language, Religion, Culture and the Sciences,* ed. Maribel Fierro and Julio Samsó, pp. 3–17. Aldershot, UK: Ashgate, Variorum, 1998.

———. *The Rise and Fall of the Party-Kings.* Princeton, N.J.: Princeton University Press, 1985.

Waterbury, John. *Commander of the Faithful: The Moroccan Political Elite—A Study in Segmented Politics.* London: Weidenfeld and Nicholson, 1970.

———. "The Coup Manqué." In *Arabs and Berbers: From Tribe to Nation in North*

Africa, ed. Ernest Gellner and Charles Micaud, pp. 397–423. Lexington, Mass., and London: D. C. Heath/Duckworth, 1972/1973.

———. "Tribalism, Trade and Politics: The Transformation of the Swasa of Morocco." In *Arabs and Berbers: From Tribe to Nation in North Africa*, ed. Ernest Gellner and Charles Micaud, pp. 231–257. Lexington, Mass., and London: D. C. Heath/Duckworth, 1972/1973.

Waʿzi, Lahsine. *Nashʾat al-haraka al-Thaqafiya al-Amazighiyya bil-Maghrib, 1967–1991*. Rabat: Matbaʿat al-Maʿarif al-Jadida, 2000.

Wexler, Paul. *The Non-Jewish Origins of the Sephardic Jews*. Albany, N.Y.: SUNY Press, 1996.

Willis, Michael. *The Islamist Challenge in Algeria: A Political History*. New York: New York University Press, 1999.

———. "Justice and Development or Justice and Spirituality? The Challenge of Morocco's Nonviolent Islamist Movements." In *The Maghrib in the New Century: Identity, Religion and Politics*, ed. Bruce Maddy-Weitzman and Daniel Zisenwine, pp. 150–174. Gainesville: University Press of Florida, 2007.

Woolman, Daniel. *Rebels in the Rif*. Stanford, Calif.: Stanford University Press, 1968.

Yassine, Abdeslam. *Hiwar maʿa Sadiq Amazighi*. Beirut: Dar Lubnan Liltabaʿa Wal-Nashr, 2003.

Zaafrani, Haim. "Judaeo-Berber." In *Encyclopaedia of Islam, New Edition*, pp. 5:307–308. Leiden: Brill, 1986.

Zartman, I. William. "Introduction: Rewriting the Future in the Maghrib." In *Economic Crisis and Political Change in North Africa*, ed. Azzedine Layachi, pp. 1–5. Westport, Conn., and London: Praeger, 1998.

———. *Morocco: Problems of New Power*. New York: Atherton Press, 1964.

———. *Ripe for Resolution: Conflict and Intervention in Africa*. New York: Oxford University Press, 1989.

———, ed. *The Political Economy of Morocco*. New York: Praeger, 1987.

Zeghal, Malika. *Islamism in Morocco*. Princeton, N.J.: Markus Wiener Publishers, 2008.

Zisenwine, Daniel. "From Hassan II to Muhammad VI: Plus Ça Change?" In *The Maghrib in the New Century: Identity, Religion and Politics*, ed. Bruce Maddy-Weitzman and Daniel Zisenwine, pp. 132–149. Gainesville: University Press of Florida, 2007.

Zoubir, Yahia H. "The Painful Transition from Authoritarianism in Algeria." *Arab Studies Quarterly* 15, no. 3 (Summer 1993): 83–110.

Zoubir, Yahia H., and Haizam Amirah-Fernández, eds. *North Africa: Politics, Region, and the Limits of Transformation*. London and New York: Routledge, 2008.

Zwartjes, Otto, Geert Jan van Gelder, and Ed de Moor, eds. *Poetry, Politics and Polemics: Cultural Transfer between the Iberian Peninsula and North Africa*. Amsterdam and Atlanta, Ga.: Rodopi, 1996.

WEBSITES

www.aarach.com
www.afrique-du-nord.com
www.alarabiya.net
www.algeria-watch.org
www.algerie-dz.com
www.amazighworld.org
www.ambafrance-ma.org
www.Arabicnews.com
www.archbis.one-forum.net
aureschaouia.free.fr
www.bladi.net
www.cmamazigh.com
www.congres-mondial-amazigh.org
www.depechedekabylie.com
www.emarrakech.info
en.wikipedia.org
english.aljazeera.net
www.forumalternatives.org
www.hrw.org
www.ipacc.org.za/eng
www.itnsource.com
jungle-world.com
www.kabyle.com
www.kabylia.info
www.magharebia.com
www.maroc.ma
www.memri.org
mideasti.blogspot.com
www.mondeberbere.com
www.monde-diplomatique.fr
www.north-of-africa.com
www.populstat.info
www.presse-dz.com
www.rsf.org
www.tamazgha.fr
www.tamazgha.org
www.tamurt-imazighen.com
www.tawiza.nl
www.temoust.org
themoornextdoor.wordpress.com
waac.info

whc.unesco.org
www.unhcr.org
yassine.net

NEWSPAPERS, MAGAZINES, NEWS AGENCIES, AND RADIO AND TELEVISION STATIONS

al-Alam
Algerian Press Service
Amazigh
Amazigh Voice
Al-Arab
Daily Telegraph
Le Dépêche de Kabylie
The Economist
L'Economiste
L'Express
Le Figaro
Financial Times
Imazighen ASS-A
Izuran-Racines. See also *Racines-Izuran*
Al-Jamaa Review, no. 4
Al-Jarida al-Awla
Jerusalem Post
Jeune Afrique
Le Journal des locales
Le Journal Hebdomadaire
Libération
Maghreb Arab Press Agency
Maghrib al-Yawm
Maroc Soir
Al-Masa'a
Le Monde
Le Monde Amazigh
Moroccan RTM TV
El Pais
Racines-Izuran. See also *Izuran-Racines*
Radio Algiers
Al-Sabah
Al-Sharq al-Awsat
Le Soir d'Algérie

Al-Tajdid
TelQuel
Times (London)
El Watan
Al-Watan al-Arabi

MONITORING SERVICES

BBC Monitoring, Summary of World Broadcasts, The Middle East and Africa.
Foreign Broadcast Information Service (FBIS), The Middle East and North Africa, Daily Report (DR).
Joint Publication Research Service, Near East and South Asia.

ARCHIVES

FRUS, 1969-76, Vol. E-5, Part 2, Documents on North Africa, 1969–1972. http://history.state.gov/historicaldocuments/frus1969-76ve05p2/ (accessed August 3, 2010).
U.S. National Archives, RG59.

DOCUMENTS AND REPORTS

"Agadir Charter."
"Amazighité—Communiqué De La Presidence." Issued by the Embassy of Algeria, Washington, D.C., April 23, 1995.
"Assessment for Tuareg in Niger." Minorities at Risk Project. December 31 2003.
"The Berber Manifesto."
"Dernier rapport de la Commission nationale d'enquête sur les évenéments de Kabylie," Décembre 2001. Published in *La Jeune Indépendant,* December 30, 2001. http://www.algeria-watch.org/farticle/revolte/issad_complement.htm (accessed May 21, 2010).
El-Kseur Platform.
"France: Discriminations à l'égard des Amazighs." February 22, 2005. http://forum-francophone.bbactif.com/immigration-et-integration-f65/la-france-rejette-ses-mauvais-immigres-t292.htm (accessed July 1, 2010).
"Imazighen en Libye: rapport de Tamazgha au CERD." http://www.tamazgha.fr/article.php3?id_article=541 (accessed May 21, 2010).
International Crisis Group. "Algeria: Unrest and Impasse in Kabylia." Middle East/North Africa Report N° 15, June 10, 2003. http://www.crisisgroup.org/~/

media/Files/Middle%20East%20North%20Africa/North%20Africa/Alge ria/Algeria%20Unrest%20and%20Impasse%20in%20Kabylia.ashx   (accessed May 21, 2010).

"L'Etat marocain et la question amazighe." Rapport alternative de Tamazgha au Comité des droits économiques, sociaux et culturels, Nations Unies, Conseil Économique et Social, 36eme session du Comité des droits économiques sociaux et culturels, Genève, 1er au 19 mai 2006.

"Platforme de la Soummam." July 28, 2010. http://www.el-mouradia.dz/francais/ symbole/textes/soummam.htm.

"Plate-forme: Option Amazighe." January 13, 2007. http://www.amazighworld .org/auteur.php?auteur=Groupe%20Option%20Amazighe (accessed May 20, 2010).

"Protectorate Treaty between France and Morocco." Supplement: Official Documents. *American Journal of International Law* 6, no. 3 (July 1912): 207–209.

Le Document. "Que Veulent Les Berbères." *Jeune Afrique/L'Intelligent,* April 24– May 7, 2001.

United Nations Press Release. Committee on Economic, Social and Cultural Rights Reviews Second Periodic Report of Libya, November 17, 2005. http:// tamazgha.fr/The-CESCR-reviews-second-report-of-Libya,1491.html   (accessed May 21, 2010).

U.S. Department of State. "Morocco Human Rights Practices 1994." February 1995. http://dosfan.lib.uic.edu/ERC/democracy/1994_hrp_report/94hrp_report_ nea/Morocco.html (accessed May 21, 2010).

INDEX

Family Law (Morocco), 154
Fasi, Allal al-, 59
Fassi (Moroccan elite), 60, 91, 206, 208,
    231n96
Fatima, Lalla, 88
Fatimid dynasty, 26
Fentress, Elizabeth, 16, 17–18, 31, 216n35
Feraoun, Mouloud, 49
Ferkal, Mabrouk, 134, 135–136
FFS. *See* Front des Forces Socialistes
Filali, Abdellatif, 119, 120
FIS. *See* Islamist Front Islamique de Salut
FLN. *See* Front de Libération Nationale
Forces Armées Royales (FAR), 86, 88, 157
France, 73, 81, 133–134, 135, 143–146, 175,
    220n3, 229n55. *See also* French colo-
    nialism
Francophones, 70, 114, 125. *See also*
    French language
French colonialism, 21, 22, 37–38, 164,
    200, 202; in Algeria, 38–49, 51, 55,
    204, 220–221n6; and focus on Ber-
    ber origins and distinction between
    Arabs and Berbers, 2, 4–5, 14, 66; in
    Morocco, 37, 38, 49–62, 86, 100, 121,
    160, 206, 237n57; in West Africa, 133
French language, 79, 93, 96, 228n37, 228–
    229n47; in Algeria, 39, 46, 69, 70, 77,
    109, 114, 205; fault line between Ara-
    bic and, 65–66; in Morocco, 57–58,
    86, 89, 90, 95, 97, 99, 120, 122, 180.
    See also Francophones
Front de Libération Nationale (FLN),
    6, 47, 48, 49, 74, 81, 104, 106, 197,
    227n22; poor performance of, in
    1990s elections, 108, 109–110, 236n29;
    post-independence dominance of, 66,
    67, 107, 184–185
Front des Forces Socialistes (FFS), 112,
    113, 116, 188, 199, 200, 229n50; anti-
    government demonstrations orga-
    nized by, 109, 186; boycott of 1990
    election by, 107–108; electoral per-

formance of, 110, 188, 199; establish-
    ment of, 67–68; platform of, in 1979,
    75–76, 79; rivalry of, with the RCD,
    105, 106, 107, 115

Gaetulians, 14
Gal, Susan, 17
Garamantes, 14, 15
Garrot, Henri, 45
Geertz, Clifford, 8
Gellner, Ernest, 7, 75, 214n22
Gendarmerie National, 185, 186, 187, 197,
    198, 200, 205
Germany, 51
Ghallab, Abd al-Karim, 224n58
Ghomara, 29
Ghozali, Ahmad Sid, 109
Gibbon, Edward, 211–212n7
Glaoui, Abdessadeq, 61
Glaoui, Thami El, 59, 60, 61, 94, 160,
    206
Glick, Thomas, 29
Goodman, Jane, 46, 72, 80–81, 229n53
Great Britain, 51, 74
Greeks, 2, 14, 32
Groupe d'Études Berbères (GEB), 73, 75
Group Islamique Armé (GIA), 111, 115
Guermah, Massinissa, 185
Guessous, Mohammed, 103
Guichard, Pierre, 28–29
Guillaume, August-Leon, 60

Habermas, Jürgen, 17
Habibi, Injaz Abdallah, 179
Hadj, Mohand Ou el, 67
Hafsid dynasty, 30, 31, 33, 34, 217n45
Hajj, Messali al-, 44, 45, 46, 48
Hamas, 150, 151
Hamim al-Ghomari al-Motanabbi, 27
Hammoudi, Abdallah, 22
Hamou, Lalla Latifa, 88, 165
Hanoteau, Adolphe, 40, 46
Harbi, Mohammed, 41

59, 206, 224n65; Berberism in, first
stirrings of, 94–101; Berber language/
dialects in, 2, 5–6, 52, 89, 90, 95, 96,
118, 127, 161, 195, 207, 211n3, 234n132;
Berber Manifesto in, 155, 159–167,
168, 169, 174; culture of, Berber contributions to, 35; current status of
Amazigh movement in, 202, 204,
206, 208, 210; failed military coups
in, 91–94; French colonial era in,
37, 38, 49–62, 86, 100, 121, 160, 206,
237n57; international focus on plight
of Berbers in, 131, 133, 134, 138, 142–
143, 151; Islamist opposition movements in, 6, 103, 123–127, 150, 151, 152,
154, 168, 169, 207; last decade of King
Hassan's rule in, 117–123; nationalist
movement in, 22, 50, 55, 56, 58–62,
121, 122, 160, 206; Ottoman period in,
34; post-independence era in, 65–66,
84–101; during the reign of Mohamed VI, 153–182; Sahrawis in, 154,
180, 181, 248n60; sultans/sultanate of,
34, 50, 52–53, 55, 60, 61, 65, 223n49.
See also under specific rulers
El Moudjahid, 78, 227n22
Mouha U Hamou Zaiani, 178
Moukhlis, Moha, 151
Mouloudji, Marcel, 144
Mouloud Mammeri Prize, 229n55
Mouti', Abdelkrim, 124
Mouvement Citoyen Des Aarchs (Citi-
zens Movement of the Tribes). *See*
Coordination Interwilayas des aarchs,
daïras, et communes
Mouvement Culturel Amazigh
(Morocco), 95
Mouvement Culturel Berbère (MCB),
(Algeria), 72, 83, 105, 107, 113, 116, 189,
236n36
Mouvement Populaire (MP), 58, 85, 88,
91, 96, 97

Mouvement Populaire Démocratique et
Constitutionnel (MPDC), 124
Mouvement pour le Autonomie de la
Kabylie (MAK), 139, 189, 190
"Murabit" dynasty, 217n45
murabit revolution, 35
Muslims. *See* Ibadi Berber Muslims;
Islam; Islamist opposition move-
ments; Islamization
Mustansir, Mohamed al-, 30
"Muwahhid" dynasty, 217n45
Mzab valley, 2, 25, 106, 139, 200, 208,
212n9

Napoleon III, 41
Nasir, Abd al-, 69
Nasrallah, Hassan, 151
National Coordination Council, 119
National Institute for Tamazight Studies
and Research, 119
National Teaching and Linguistic Center
for Tamazight Education (CNPLET),
193–194
National Union of Moroccan Students
(UNEM), 95
Naylor, Phillip, 34
Nekli, A., 46
Niger, 3, 9, 131, 133, 134, 135, 139, 151,
212n9
North Africa: arrival of Islam in, 21–32,
177–178; Donatist rebellion in, 177;
early (pre-Islamic) history of, 13–21,
216–217n40; interethnic conflict
in, 202–203; Jewish communities
in, 147; as the object of rival European powers, 51; Ottoman Empire in,
33–36; political unification of, 196. *See*
also specific North African countries
Nouvelle Association de la Culture et des
Arts Amazighs. *See* Tamaynut
Nu'man al-Ghassani, Hassan bin al-, 23, 45
Numidia/Numidians, 13, 16